*No Place
for a Woman*

Rutgers Series on Women and Politics

No Place
for a Woman

A Life of Senator
Margaret Chase Smith

JANANN SHERMAN

RUTGERS UNIVERSITY PRESS
New Brunswick, New Jersey, and London

First paperback printing, 2001

Library of Congress Cataloging-in-Publication Data

Sherman, Janann.
    No place for a woman : a life of Senator Margaret Chase Smith /
Janann Sherman.
        p.   cm.
    Includes bibliographical references (p.   ) and index.
    ISBN 0–8135–2722–8 (alk. paper) — ISBN 0–8135–2967–0 (pbk.)
        1. Smith, Margaret Chase, 1897–   . 2. Women legislators—United
States—Biography.   3. Legislators—United States—Biography.
4. United States.   Congress.   Senate—Biography.   I. Title.
E748.S667S54   2000
328.73'092—dc21
    [b]   99–12901
                                                                                                        CIP

British Cataloging-in-Publication data for this book is available from the
British Library

Manufactured in the United States of America

To
Charles
whose love never wavered

Contents

Illustrations appear between pages 126 and 127.

Acknowledgments

I wish to thank all the scholars and friends who cared about me and about this project. To avoid implicit hierarchies they are listed alphabetically, and to satisfy a childish whim of someone who has spent her life as an "S," I am reversing the order. Virginia Yans-McLaughlin, Genora Woodruff, Larry Williams, Jeanette Stephenson, Karen Shea, Evelyn Shaw, Debra Schultz, Carol Petillo, Kathleen Paparchontis, David Oshinsky, Lisa Norling, Kimberly Nichols, Lynn Mirassou, Georgia McKearley, Ruth Mandel, Marilyn Locke, Sharon Legge, Suzanne Lebsock, Mert Henry, Stephanie Gilmore, Gregory Gallant, Gretchen Galbraith, Richard and Linda Gagnon, Sara Evans, Muriel and Carl Clawans, Paula Casey, Susan Carroll, Margaret Caffrey, Beverly Bond, John Bernier, Julia Bear, Paula Barnes. Thank you one and all. A special thanks to my research assistant, Angela Stockwell, and to Marlie Wasserman who said the right things when I needed to hear them.

I also gratefully acknowledge financial assistance from the Center for the American Woman and Politics, the Ada Leeke Foundation, the Everett McKinley Dirksen Congressional Leadership Research Center, the Margaret Chase Smith Foundation, the Lyndon Baines Johnson Foundation, and the University of Memphis Professional Development Assignment.

No Place
for a Woman

Introduction:
Double Vision

I first went to see Margaret Chase Smith on a crisp
fall day in 1986, turning north from the urban den-
sity and studied quaintness of lower New England toward the farmlands
and scattered hamlets of interior Maine. Then in her eighty-eighth year,
Senator Smith still lived and worked within a mile of her birthplace,
the small mill town of Skowhegan. Hours from the fabled Maine of
rockbound coasts and solitary lighthouses, Skowhegan flanks the
Kennebec River, a major tributary bisecting pine forest and gently rolling hills, at the crossroads of two major highways—one leading from
Portland to Quebec City, the other from New Hampshire to Bangor and
Bar Harbor. Tourists stop for food and gas as they pass through on their
way elsewhere.

I crossed the Kennebec where it divides around a small island and
drove over the two "Margaret Chase Smith" bridges into downtown. Most
of the buildings on the short main street had been constructed in the
early 1900s, during the zenith of town prosperity, changing only own-
ers and awnings since then. I paused for a sandwich, served on a pink
placemat embossed with a single red rose and the proud words: "Welcome to Skowhegan, the home of Senator Margaret Chase Smith," then
headed up the hill beside the river to the Margaret Chase Smith Library
Center.

A mixture of museum and archive, the Library is housed in an annex wrapped around Smith's home, filled with the artifacts of a public
life. Colorful hoods from each of her ninety-five honorary degrees hang
from pegs near the ceiling; glass cases display photographs, speech notes,

awards and citations, campaign miscellany, and collected mementos. Smith awaited me in her atrium, an area between her private home and public archive. Visitors, including myself, were often surprised to meet this tiny, fragile-looking woman; those of us who knew her career had always thought her tall. But she only appeared frail. Though age had shrunken her frame and dimmed her eyesight, her energy and enthusiasm remained undiminished.

Out of the political mainstream since her defeat in 1972, Smith remained active in her role as elder stateswoman. Maine's print and broadcast media frequently sought her opinions, and she made herself available to nearly anyone who came to see her. Smith's mail continued to be substantial, and she answered, as she always had, every piece the day it arrived. When her schedule ran short of commencements and dedications, she filled many of her days greeting the dozens of visitors who found their way to her home, shaking hands, posing for snapshots and videotapes, and submitting to interviews such as mine.

I was a graduate student of history, I told her, interested in women and American politics. You must understand, she told me that first afternoon, that "I never was a woman. I never was a woman politician. I never was a woman senator." And "I'm not a feminist, either." Her words sounded like a challenge determined to dissuade me at the outset from any notions to the contrary. Smith dutifully answered my questions about major events in her career, as I carefully avoided asking too much about being a woman. When I expressed interest in writing her biography, she put me off, saying she might write her own one day soon. She always thought Mr. Lewis, her administrative aide, would write it, she said, her eyes glistening. Only he really knew her and her career. But he had died suddenly, and she could not think about working with anyone else. Not now.[1]

I returned for more interviews and began my research into her papers, first working on small projects, then my Ph.D. dissertation, and finally this biography.[2] Over the years, we built a relationship of mutual respect and trust as I labored to assemble the chronology of her career and she reviewed her life with me.

Each of us creates an ideal narrative, a story not only to tell to each other but also to ourselves. Smith's retrospective was composed of layers of self-understanding and responses to social expectations. Her recollections were further entangled within her efforts in the final years of her life to impose a pattern of meaning upon her experiences. All of this was filtered through an astute politician's heightened sense of self and concern for her historical legacy. In a very real sense, we were engaged in a parallel enterprise, attempting to apply order to the confusion of details, to impose a logical process on the randomness of life.

Having suffered her share of the slings and arrows a public life invites, Smith sometimes welcomed, sometimes resisted, my inquiries into her past. Moreover, she had designed her life to do, not to savor. "Sometimes I pinch myself," she said, "to see if I am I. I keep wondering if it is possible I—Margaret—did all those things."[3] Unable or unwilling to articulate her feelings about her own history, she responded, when pressed about her inner self, by describing her actions. Look at my record, she would say, look at what I have done. That will tell you who I am.

Her record is long and voluminous. My exploration of her thirty-three-year congressional career required engagement with numerous thick volumes of published materials, mountains of government documents, and the considerable holdings in her collection. Smith's archives contain more than eighty-eight file drawers, some 300,000 primary source documents, letters, bills, office notes, and hearing transcripts, forty bound volumes of statements and speeches, more than three thousand photographs, dozens of audio and video tapes, and nearly five hundred scrapbooks of clippings, personal items, and memorabilia.[4] Still, there are significant gaps in the record. Much important legislative work is conducted face-to-face. Personal relationships and personality quirks, understandings and agreements, cloakroom conversations and private phone calls, are seldom recorded. Neither are many political maneuvers. Office correspondence is routine and purposefully impersonal; speeches and statements are couched in general terms to minimize political consequences. While traditional sources could usually reveal what happened, only Smith could tell me how, and what it meant to her.

We spent long afternoons together exploring her memories. When comparing my interview notes with her records and papers, I realized that many of the stories she told me had been related countless times over her long career, often in almost identical words. She did, in fact, tell many of them to me numerous times. These well-worn stories revealed a limited variety of characteristics and attitudes, as well as stylized patterns of recall. In the process of assimilating the past into the present, her lived events had become portents of the future, moralizing lessons, and simple explanations for complex phenomena.[5] I struggled to find the right questions to move beyond these limited replies. From those first interviews, which ranged widely across time and circumstances, I gradually narrowed my focus to pinpoints of information, soliciting her memory to fill in the blanks and answer specific questions that arose as I researched her papers. Try as I might to avoid them, though, the same stories kept surfacing, with certain themes thrown into relief by the telling.

Smith's self-descriptions reflected a woman carried along by circumstance, responding to external forces as they occurred, without plan or forethought. She saw herself as simply cooperating with the wishes of others or the imperatives of "destiny." Yet, her experiences disclosed, to me, a coherent pattern of achievement, a clear path toward public acclaim and personal fulfillment. Frustrated in my attempts to get behind her constructed self, I was forced to confront why it was there, why she created herself in this way, and further, why it was necessary for her to believe it. Smith's rehearsed memories, however repetitive and seemingly unproductive, contain clues to her personality, the private entity that defined the public one. The manner in which she described the contents of her memories conveyed the meanings they held for her.

For example, Smith campaigned for and won four separate political contests in the five months immediately following her husband's death. Congressional widows are often thought of as passively completing unexpired terms awarded to them as sentimental gestures of respect. Contrary to popular belief, however, no one, not even a widow, can be "appointed" to fill a House seat. The pervasiveness of this perception reflects society's reluctance to accept the image of a newly widowed woman launching a campaign for a position of public power.[6] Smith shared that aversion. While her vigorous drive for a place of her own in Congress suggests ambition, self-interest, and assertiveness, she remembered herself as "just pushed along." She became a candidate at her husband's insistence, she said, and when he died, she saw no alternatives. "Sometimes I think these things were my destiny and in a sense I didn't have anything to do with it. A life of public service was just thrust on me."[7] She had neither sought nor contemplated political office, but had been inadvertently groomed for the job because "destiny" was guiding her life: "It was just to be and I had little to do about it."[8]

One of the most persistent themes in Smith's narrative is her simultaneous affirmation and denial of gender, her celebration of femininity while denying its relevance. While she surely recognized fundamental differences between men and women, she saw the acknowledgment of such differences used to restrict individual action. Invoking a generic, sexless "person," Smith affirmed the American creed of individualistic freedom and meritorious success. Yet, at the same time, this self-interested pursuit of power, status, and achievement ran counter to her assumption of feminine self-deprecation. She danced between a kind of pure individualism and an implicit understanding that women's positions were socially constructed and politically demanded. On the one hand, she exhorted women to be competent and seize opportunity, on the other, she denied any agency in her own success. Because she had defined herself in opposition to prescribed gender roles, Smith bent over backward to accommodate herself to them. She understood that while power enhances a male image, it threatens a female one. For her, success required a special combination of hard work, masked ambition, and proper womanly behavior. Unlike her male counterparts, she needed excuses for her self-centered behavior; her self-definition rested on her conviction that her life had been dedicated to serving others. "I was never ambitious," she told me. "I know that doesn't sound honest. I wanted to win. Anyone wants to win. But . . . I missed a great deal by not enjoying it more. . . . I am only now beginning to realize what it meant to be powerful or to have influence. I didn't recognize it then. I worked so hard."[9] Here then, she minimizes her "selfish" need to be significant by ascribing her motivation to chance and duty, by working very hard and not allowing herself to enjoy it.[10]

Unlike her gender identity, Smith wore her regional identity comfortably. The values that guided her life read like a Yankee litany: loyalty, order, regularity, directness, self-reliance, moderation, balance, frugality, hard work, self-discipline, conscience, and integrity. Concurrent with those qualities was her sense of propriety, a patrician respect for order and reasoned discourse, and an abhorrence of rebelliousness, intemperate language, and extremism in any form, whether that of Joseph McCarthy, radical feminists, black power advocates, or political ideologues like Barry Goldwater. If leadership is problematic for women, one form remains appropriate, that of moral authority. It was a venue through which Smith strode with self-conscious courage and pride. She seldom made important speeches or thrust herself out front on an issue, unless she felt justified by a higher moral imperative. When Smith acted as a moral speaker, she created a role for herself outside politics, above politics, a strategy to obtain power by criticizing power. Smith became well known for her propensity to chastise others for breaches of ethics or morality. In cartoons and commentary, she was often characterized as a pursed-lipped schoolmarm, reducing her colleagues to little boys who had forgotten their manners. This gendered trope, this symbol of female authority, was one with which both she and her contemporaries were comfortable. Convinced that there was a right way and a wrong way to do things, Smith's political orientation was based upon her trust in her own conscience and her intention, right from the beginning, to keep her agenda her own. She was a simple, rural, New England conservative—just like her constituents—tempered by her woman's sensibilities and the courage of her convictions.

Smith's occupational identity was, to her, foremost: "I didn't have anything else. My job was my love. My job was my life. And I devoted my entire time and thoughts to it."[11] And despite appearances to the contrary, she denied ever being left out of the circles of power and influence. Smith contended that gender was never a consideration in her ability to be a successful legislator and emphatically rejected the adjective woman. "My whole history of pubic service," she said, "was determination to show that I was a woman who could do what a man could do without apologizing."[12] Earning her legitimacy through large election pluralities, experience, and seniority, she made a virtue out of an independence born of rejection yet connoting honesty and courage. Smith's artful and often unwitting blend of self-effacement and modesty, combined with toughness and competence, was central to her longevity in office. Her challenge, throughout her long career, was to prove again and again that she was both a lady and a sexless legislator, that she was strong enough to wield power while remaining womanly. And always she confronted patronizing, dominating male figures who insisted that politics, that law making, that public life, was no place for a woman.

The sharp dissonance between Smith's self-descriptions and what I deduced from documentary evidence was a key to help me decipher how she experienced the historical reality of her life, especially in terms of her cultural context and the ways in which she was circumscribed by gender expectations, by the ways a woman is supposed to think and feel and act.[13] The themes of Smith's narrative—self-deprecation and disavowal of personal agency, rejection of the relevance of gender affiliation, the importance of success and achievement, the assumption of moral leadership—are interrelated. They all refer to the entangling conundrum of an ambitious woman. The authorization of her career by chance and her commitment to public service were ways to simultaneously achieve and deny personal ambitions, to resolve the conflict between social expectations and her desire for autonomy and personal fulfillment.

A double vision, her narrative and my understanding of that narrative, forms the basis upon which this biography rests.[14] Her world is filtered and sorted through my perceptions, her experiences translated through my interpretations of the intersections of documentary evidence with her recollections. The conclusions herein are strictly my own.

Central to the entire enterprise that was Margaret Chase Smith was the single most important person in her life, William Chesley Lewis, Jr. They met during the war; he was counsel to the House Naval Affairs Committee and she a junior representative. Their friendship blossomed during the 1940s, and she hired him as her administrative assistant after she had won election to the Senate. In all, he devoted forty years to her, insulating her from what he perceived, sometimes accurately, as jealous challengers, a mean-spirited press, and ungrateful constituents with short memories. At the same time, Lewis also isolated her, leaving no room for a network of advisers or a coterie of contending voices. After 1948, if not before, there was only Bill. I regret never having met this complex man, but traces of him survive throughout documentary and anecdotal evidence. Senator Smith talked often and plaintively about him. Though he was frequently prickly and tendentious, I have resisted the temptation to assign all the negatives to him. I resist as well allowing him to dominate her story. That very resistance speaks to gendered assumptions in American culture. Bill was always there; his role was important but supportive. Through the years, as a friend put it, Lewis was "the voice off-stage, coaching, prompting, leading the applause, and handing her the roses when the performance was over."[15]

A note about conventions: In order to give Smith a voice without confusing the reader more than necessary, I have chosen to use "MCS" to designate her recollections used herein. In my story, I call her "Margaret" when she is a child or when her identity is subsumed into her husband's during her marriage, "Chase" for the brief period when as a young woman she established and cultivated her own identity, and "Smith" after Clyde Smith died and she assumed public office.

1 | A Sense of Place

Although she resided for thirty-six years in the environs of Washington, D.C., Margaret Chase Smith never considered any place but Skowhegan, Maine, home. The eldest of six, she was born Margaret Madeline Chase, to a barber, George Emery Chase, and his wife, Carrie Murray, on December 14, 1897, three years before the turn of the twentieth century. Growing up in the ideological and cultural homogeneity of this small town, she acquired a strong regional identity and a keen sense of her own capacities. Skowhegan was central to her understanding of the world.

Legend has it that settlement began at the place where Abnaki Indians speared salmon jumping the granite falls of the Kennebec River. They called the spot Skowhegan, "the place to watch." [1] Long an agricultural town, after the Civil War Skowhegan harnessed the Kennebec for manufacturing. Massive mill buildings sprang up beside the river, producing oilcloth, shoes, lumber and wood pulp, pulled-wool and textiles. Soon woolen mills took a commanding lead, employing more than thirteen hundred of Skowhegan's five thousand people at the turn of the century. [2] Logging and pulp mills were close behind, fed by pine from the forests of northern Maine, delivered by the convenient conveyer belt—the river. The height of town prosperity spanned the first two decades of the twentieth century. Skowhegan boasted the greatest number of manufacturing enterprises of any incorporated town in Maine in 1910, but by the late 1920s, its star began to fade, further dimmed by the Great Depression from which its manufacturing base never recovered. [3]

During Margaret's childhood, Skowhegan rang with the sounds of a self-important town rushing headlong into industry. Piercing factory whistles punctuated the screams of silver saws, the clop of horses' hooves, and the rumbling of four trains a day through town. From the river came the thump and crash of logs striking one another as they thundered and tumbled on the current to the shouts of "river rats" goading them along.[4]

In summer, the tangy smell of the river mixed with the strong clean fragrance of freshly sawn boards and the acrid odor of dyes and acids from the textile mills. Warm summer evenings would find the streets as busy as day, until the nine o'clock bell called "children to come off the streets and . . . callers to begin to make their adieus."[5] The Fourth of July was the centerpiece of summer. The day began with an eight o'clock salute to the flag, announced exactly on the hour by six steam whistles—four town fire alarms and two Maine Central locomotives—and the bells in every church and school steeple. "The din was simply glorious." Band concerts, fire drills, logrolling exhibitions, kids games, feats of daring, and a giant parade crowded the day.[6]

Fall slipped by in riotous color, a gay gift before the long monochromic repose. When the sharp winds of winter arrived, the river skimmed over with gray glass and thick blankets of snow muffled village sounds. The thermometer dropped to zero and stayed there; the river snapped and boomed as it froze. The Kennebec transformed into a glistening skating rink splashed with brightly colored snowsuits and trailing mufflers. Upriver, teams of horses and men, their breath changing to icicles, mined "Kennebec diamonds," clear blocks of ice packed in insulating sawdust to cool next summer's lemonade.[7] Springtime brought ice-out and freshets, when the river ran unrestrained and wild through the north country. Eager to move the winter's accumulation of fallen trees, woodsmen pushed thousands of them into the churning water where "they reared their ends sleek and wicked, looking for trouble." They came "roaring down the Kennebec, going over the falls and filling the valley with thunder and white flowers."[8]

New buildings with turn-of-the-century facades decorated Skowhegan's short main street. Prosperous years built impressive white stone banks and brick office blocks, broad boulevards of turreted Victorian homes. Quiet elm-shaded streets with more modest dwellings extended north and east, harboring a largely working-class population, most of whom claimed English or French-Canadian ancestry.[9] Skowhegan prided itself on having "a class of people who work in the factories and yet are permanent residents of the town," about three-fourths of them owning their own homes.[10] At the same time, the village retained its agricultural connections. The 1911 town inventory found 798 horses and mules, 84 colts, 681 cows, 35 oxen, 254 cattle, 867 sheep, and 300 swine.[11]

This provincial hamlet was home to the familiar time-honored Mainer: laconic, shrewd, frugal, contrary, pragmatic, and often brutally honest, with a stern morality that comes from hard times in hard climates.[12] Skowhegan was a town where common sense was valued over intellect, simplicity over ostentation, the familiar over the novel, the insider over the outsider—where aphorisms embroidered on parlor pillows admonished idle children to work hard, play fair, stand on their own, tell the truth, cherish God and country, and obey the Golden Rule.[13]

Margaret's maternal grandfather, born Lambert Morin in 1843 at St. Georges, Quebec, Canada, came to Skowhegan as a child, probably as part of the massive emigration following a dramatic drop in Canadian wheat production.[14] French Canadians fled south along the Canada road from Quebec to Skowhegan, dragging wagons, carts, and "slides" (a sort of buckboard called "slague" in French). Many arrived "in extreme destitution . . . [with] their numerous children and scanty household goods." Most settled in a farmer's unused pasture north of town that came to be derisively called "Little Canada."[15]

At some point, Lambert Morin changed his name to John L. Murray.[16] For much of his life, it was difficult to be a French-Canadian Catholic in Maine. Reluctant to assimilate, linguistically and religiously separate from their neighbors, French Canadians were objects of prejudice, hostility, and sometimes, violence. The mid-1850s were years of extreme nativist agitation throughout the Northeast. In Maine, xenophobia found expression in a series of ugly incidents involving the burning of Catholic homes and churches, and in one case at least, the stripping, tarring and feathering of a Catholic priest.[17]

Murray, a carpenter and cabinetmaker, and his wife, Marie Boulette, reared three children. He built a small six-room clapboard house and barn at 81 North Avenue on a quarter acre in "Little Canada," where his daughter Carrie and all of her children, including Margaret, were born.[18]

Margaret's paternal ancestors, Aquila and Thomas Chase, settled in Fairfield, Maine, in 1771, homesteading along the Kennebec River about six miles from Skowhegan.[19] Her father's father, John Wesley Chase, was a fairly prosperous civil engineer living on the family claim, a large farm house and 125 acres, when he was called to service in the Civil War. Upon his return, Chase became a Methodist minister and apparently his resources deteriorated as a result. He died of pneumonia just a few months past his fortieth birthday, leaving his wife, Margaret Nolan Chase, with four children and a mortgaged farm that she soon lost to the Fairfield

Savings Bank.[20] Her youngest son, George Emery Chase, barely three years old when his father died, left school early to seek his fortune in the West. Finding none, he returned to central Maine.[21] While working as a head-waiter at the Hotel Coburn in Skowhegan, George married Caroline Morin (Murray) in Our Lady of Lourdes Catholic Church, October 25, 1896, and the couple moved into her father's house.[22] Margaret Madeline, named for her paternal grandmother, was born one year later.[23] Shortly there-after, George moved his wife and daughter into the Hotel North in Augusta, where he again worked as headwaiter. When that job ended, the family returned to 81 North Avenue, where their son Wilbur was born in 1899 and another son, Roland, in 1901. Venturing on their own again, the Chases lived briefly in Shawmut, a nearby community where George tried his hand at barbering. Roland, barely a year and a half, died of pneu-monia, and eight months later, Carrie bore her fourth child, another son, Lawrence. The business failed and the family came back to Skowhegan. More tragedy followed. Lawrence perished of childhood dysentery in 1906—never to celebrate his third birthday. After that, George and Carrie lived out their lives on North Avenue, and until John Murray died in 1922, he lived there with them.[24] Built for a smaller family, the house at 81 North bulged with three adults and four children. After two more daughters, Evelyn and Laura, arrived in 1909 and 1912, the doors banged constantly as children ran in and out. Privacy was nearly impossible.

MCS fondly remembers her grandfather, the owner and patriarch of the house, as a man of principle and frugality. Family legend celebrates these traits, including the cautionary tale of how Carrie, despite his strong opposition, quit high school to work in the shoe factory. Since she was employed, her father required her to pay $5 a week in board. He depos-ited the money in the bank and, on Carrie's wedding day two years later, presented her with the $500 she had paid him. Another story has Mar-garet, as a child, unable to pronounce the word "grandpa," calling him "banker" instead. "Banker" deposited fifty cents of his salary every Fri-day of his life. He died leaving a remarkable estate of more than $10,000, including the North Avenue property.[25]

George resumed barbering in a three-man shop downtown, but within a short time went into business for himself, adding a single-chair bar-bershop to the house. Income from this small enterprise was sporadic, sometimes not enough to cover the Chase budget, because George was frequently incapacitated with migraine headaches and the alcohol he used to deaden the pain. The close quarters and money troubles caused con-siderable tension between the two men. While the older man was sel-dom confrontational, preferring a place on the periphery of the family circle, George could not forget that he lived in John's house. Religious discord may have also been at least a minor undercurrent. Carrie and her father were Roman Catholic; George was the son of a Methodist minister.[26] Particularly when he was in pain, or when he had too much to drink, George's temper flared and he lashed out at his father-in-law. Liquor, Margaret noted in her diary, made her father "ugly and hot-tempered."[27]

Often called upon to mediate between her husband and father, Carrie Chase was the strength of the family. While rearing six children, Carrie frequently worked at menial, physically demanding jobs: waiting tables at the Hotel Coburn, clerking at the Green Brothers' 5-and-10-cent store, and sewing shoes as a "fancy stitcher" at the Skowhegan shoe factory.[28]

When her two young sons died, Mrs. Chase earned the money to pay for their headstones by taking in washing and ironing and selling milk from the family cow, delivered by Margaret every morning to a neighbor. Everyone in the household helped, but Carrie depended most on her oldest daughter—her only daughter for twelve years until Evelyn was born. Largely because of the differences in their ages and their mother's other occupations, Margaret acted as an "assistant mother," caring for her younger siblings and arbitrating their disputes.[29]

When old enough, Margaret took jobs to help out. Some eighty years later, MCS still vividly recalled her experience as a temporary domestic for a large local dinner party. For seven hours work, serving and washing dishes for one of the more "prominent" families in Skowhegan, she earned the miserly sum of thirty-five cents.[30] After that, she looked for other ways to earn money, sometimes helping her mother wait tables at the Hotel Coburn, sometimes working for local merchants during the Christmas rush. "We were poor, I guess," MCS allowed. "We always had warm clothes and enough to eat, but we had none of the frills that a lot of families had."[31] Hard work, thrift, and self-sacrifice were the primary lessons Margaret learned at home. Among the very few books she could remember having read, her grandfather's set of Horatio Alger stories were her favorites, she said, for they "had a good philosophy all through them." Margaret absorbed the lessons and believed in the possibilities. She did not know yet what she wanted to be, only that it should be other than her mother's life of self-sacrifice.[32]

Desiring independence and money of her own, twelve-year-old Margaret applied for her first "real" job at the Green Brothers' 5-and-10-cent store; she was, however, too short to reach the highest shelves. In a story that has become part of the Margaret Chase Smith legend, Margaret returned a few months later, demonstrated her increased height as well as her persistence and determination, and won the position. She immediately purchased a life insurance policy so her parents would be compensated if anything happened to her.[33] Unlike her father, who "never gave a darn for his opportunities," MCS believed that she was most like her mother and grandfather, supposing it was "in the genes. They had more drive."[34] Neither of her sisters nor any of her peers worked for wages beyond occasional babysitting jobs. "They didn't have ambition like I did," she recalled.[35] Her siblings chose conventional lives, leaving them in roughly the same social class in which they began. Margaret's energy and drive would lead her in a very different direction.

As much as anything else, her mother's example kept her in school. Along with nearly half the girls in her class, Margaret took the commercial course through high school, acquiring a girl's best assortment of marketable skills: shorthand, typing and office etiquette.[36] The feminization of office work in the 1910s and 1920s provided an avenue of social mobility for working-class daughters like her. Pink-collar work had more pleasant surroundings, if not higher salaries, than industrial jobs, and allowed young women to associate with people of a higher social stratum. The pinnacle of such a career was to be a successful man's secretary, or better yet, his wife.[37]

Although school and her job kept her quite busy, Margaret did find time for her passion: basketball. Sports provided a safe outlet for her competitive impulse. During her freshman year in 1912, Margaret became a member of the first Skowhegan High School girls' basketball team. Decked out in their billowy knee-length black serge bloomers, pleated white middy blouses, and black silk kerchief ties, the team played all across central Maine. In her senior year, when the Skowhegan girl's team won the state championship, Margaret was their captain. After graduation, she hung on to her association with the team, becoming the coach for the 1918–19 season and sometimes, in later years, refereeing.[38] Recalling her participation, MCS applauded sports for developing "good-looking girls," not just pretty faces, but girls who were "healthy, well-proportioned and well-poised, with good personality and good sportsmanship attitude." Sports, then, enhanced a girl's social and moral, as well as physical, development. Success in basketball boosted Margaret's self-esteem, taught her poise and self-reliance, and two other important lessons: "that one receives about what they [sic] give and that one side only can win."[39]

Individual dating was rare in her band of friends. Usually they would gather at someone's home for card parties, recitations, home musicales, jigsaw puzzles, or fudge-making parties. Margaret's circle included her best friend, Pauline Bragg, and two fellows she favored: Bob Merrow, who frequently walked her home and visited with her on her front porch on summer evenings, and Harry St. Ledger, then captain of the football team, who usually took her to the movies—his father managed the Bijou Theater.[40]

During her graduation year, Margaret fervently wanted to join her friends on their senior class trip to Washington, D.C., but she needed to raise the enormous sum of $60. When she gingerly approached her grandfather, the "banker," for the money, he treated the matter as a business deal, requiring her to sign a note to repay him at 6 percent interest.[41] Money in hand, and refusing to think about her financial obligation, she excitedly embarked on her first trip away from home. The young people and their chaperones took the train to Fall River, Massachusetts, then a boat to New York City, where they caught another train to Philadelphia, then still another to Washington. After seeing the monuments they had read about in school, the students had a chance to mingle with the rich and important, visiting with a variety of Washington dignitaries and joining their congressman, John Peters, at the White House to shake hands with President Woodrow Wilson.[42]

MCS's memories of that trip illustrate her assumptions about status and her eagerness to improve her own. While in Washington, the group visited with the Coburn-Smiths, one of the most prestigious Skowhegan families. Dr. George Otis Smith, then head of the U.S. Geological Service, and his wife, Grace Coburn Smith, niece of Skowhegan's only Maine governor, were parents of Charles, one of her classmates.[43] The rich trappings of their home and their formal social etiquette impressed young Margaret: "This was an experience for most of us who did little socially." Perhaps more telling is her account of a shopping trip during which she bought a piece of heavy wool plaid fabric. She later learned this same fabric had been purchased by two other girls, "the two most attractive in the class. . . . They were such fine dressers that I was sure I was right in my shopping." She took such delight in learning that her taste matched theirs that she wrote about it in some detail many years later. Wealth, prominence, and in the case of women, attractiveness, defined quality and the good life.[44]

During Margaret's last year in high school, distressing news of war began to intrude. The front pages of the weekly *Independent-Reporter* carried stories about the recruitment of local boys into the Skowhegan Light Infantry, Company E, Second Maine National Guard, and Margaret's commencement shared the front page with President Wilson's call-up of all state militia to fight Pancho Villa, who was terrorizing Americans on both sides of the border. Company E was on its way to Laredo, Texas. That morning, amid great excitement in town, one hundred more young men volunteered. They were gone four months; the front page of every issue was devoted to their exploits fighting the "greasers" on the border.[45]

Their homecoming was muted. The shadow of war hung heavy. Company E was home barely half a year when President Wilson asked Congress to declare war on Germany. On the morning of April 18, 1917, the "militia call was sounded by the fire alarm," and ninety young men hastened to the armory.[46] The newspaper captured the scene as the boys departed:

> To the tune of martial airs and patriotic songs and between rows of hundreds of people who thronged the station platform to see them off, Company E left Skowhegan . . . amidst cheers and tears. . . . It was all over in a very few minutes and as the people slowly turned from the station to go back to their homes, some of which will seem very empty. . . . [M]any a silent prayer was offered for the welfare and safety of the boys who were going forth through unknown ordeals and hazards to fight under the Stars and Stripes.[47]

Skowhegan was at war.

Wars touch small towns more intensely; everyone knows those who participate. In the first selective draft of Somerset County, three hundred men were called up from Skowhegan; a week later, three hundred more.[48] Margaret and her girlfriends donned white uniforms and did what they could to help at the Red Cross.[49] When war was officially declared, the headlines screamed: "WE ARE AT WAR—AT WAR! . . . We must arm! We must prepare! The call has come! Awake! Take part—and put your *back* into it! Arise!"[50] War news took over the pages: lists of draft calls, exemption board news, Red Cross activities, and patriotic demonstrations. Anxious mothers shared their precious letters with the whole community. They were printed in their entirety on the front page, along with lists of the missing and the dead.[51]

The community closely followed the exploits of a group of eight local boys, dubbed the "High School Squad," who signed up while still students. One of them was Margaret's friend, Harry St. Ledger.[52] Five of the boys came home in uniform to graduate with their peers before returning to the war. "'Twas a sight Skowhegan friends will never forget," wrote a reporter, "these five young patriots in khaki, standing in line to receive their diplomas."[53] Two of the five never came home again; Corporals Alvan W. Bucknam and Harry St. Ledger were killed at Belleau Wood. Skowhegan lost seventeen young men in the Great War.[54] For her part, Margaret's adolescent experience with the pain and sacrifices of war had a profound effect on her attitudes toward peace and national security throughout her life.[55]

Finishing her last year in high school, Margaret dreamed of attending

Sargents' College in Boston to become a physical education teacher. But college seemed a distant and very expensive dream. For the past two years, she had been working nights and weekends as a relief operator for the Maine Telephone Company, for ten cents an hour or one dollar a night. Late one evening, the fabled first contact between Margaret and Clyde Smith took place. He called to inquire about the time and, as the story goes, she was intrigued by his mellifluous voice. Flirtatious calls lengthened into conversations.[56]

Clyde Harold Smith was recently divorced, an influential business-man in the community, and first selectman of the town of Skowhegan, a position comparable to mayor. He soon offered Margaret a job record-ing the town inventory in the Tax Assessor's books, a three-month as-signment for the lavish sum of $12 a week. When Margaret explained that she still had several weeks of school left and could not abandon her studies even for the higher salary, Clyde simply called his friend, the high school principal, smoothing the way for her to work during school days and make up her classwork on her own time.[57]

Although his overtures were discreet, Smith began to see a good deal of Miss Chase and her family. He gave her rides home in his "low, shiny El Car which would impress any young lady," although she lived only a couple of blocks from the office. Mindful of appearances, he invited her parents along for Sunday drives and lakeside picnics.[58] Carrie Chase regarded her daughter's suitor warily. Mr. Smith was her own age and a libertine.[59] Margaret knew he "had a reputation for liking the girls, es-pecially younger girls," but, despite her mother's warning, or perhaps because of it, she found him charming. He was so different from the younger boys she knew. "Clyde was older, sophisticated. I was fascinated with him."[60] And, apparently, he with her. It was the beginning of a very long courtship.

Margaret's city job soon ran out, and she needed permanent employ-ment to earn money for college. Smith encouraged her to go on to busi-ness school; "he didn't think much of my interest in Sargent's." When she persisted, he suggested she try teaching school. It paid a good deal less than her temporary job. Figuring $8.50 a week, less $5 room and board and $1.50 to her mother for weekends at home, it left little to be-gin her school fund, but she would gain experience. He called the su-perintendent. Margaret would "become a teacher for a time at least," as the newspaper put it, accepting the position at the one-room Pitts School, five miles from town.[61]

She boarded with a farm couple, the Jewitts, a mile from the school. They had no indoor toilet facilities and no central heat. Neither did the school. In the pale light of early morning, she climbed the steep hill to the schoolhouse and built a fire in the stove before the children arrived. In her sailor-suit dress and flat shoes, her hair pulled into a no-nonsense knot on the back of her neck, Margaret "was as plain as was the living." On her own for the first time, she felt overwhelmed by her responsibilities. Although she had done well in school herself, she was ill-prepared to teach her nine pupils, ages four to fourteen. They were mostly poor, often underfed, and tired from early mornings of chores before school. She spent a long, cold winter huddled with the children around the wood stove in the middle of the drafty building. Trying to learn to teach as she went along, Margaret hurried from student to student, subject to subject, frustrated by her inability to teach and their apparent inability to learn.[62]

She continued to see Mr. Smith. Most weekends he drove her back and forth between home and the Jewitts's, sometimes with a horse and sleigh when the snow was deep. Winter evenings she sat in front of the fire, listening to Mr. Jewitts's poetic recitations while she crocheted pieces for her "Hope Chest," longing for the weekends and home. After twenty-eight weeks, she had had enough. She was cold; she was lonely. Teaching was not for her; it was too difficult and unrewarding. Margaret went home.[63]

2 | Political Education

Margaret returned from her brief exile at the Pitts School determined to make a niche for herself in Skowhegan. She was looking for a job with a future; surely her training qualified her for a dignified office position. All she could find at first was her old job at Maine Telephone. She stayed there two years, at $12 a week, until she switched to the newspaper business. Roland Patten, editor and owner (in partnership with Clyde Smith) of the *Independent-Reporter*, lured her with a $16 salary and chance for advancement.[1] Patten, though a bit eccentric and fond of practical jokes, trusted Margaret's intelligence and judgment and encouraged her to tackle a variety of tasks.[2] In her eight years at the paper, she did nearly every job short of setting type—reporting, advertising, editorials, circulation and, finally, business and office manager.[3] During her tenure as circulation manager, the *Independent-Reporter* had the largest circulation—5,148—of any New England weekly, earning Miss Chase recognition as a "hustler" in her profession.[4]

The 1920s were a period of growth and maturity for Margaret Chase as an adult, as a productive member of the community, and as a woman. She never made it to Sargent's College, MCS remarked, because "every time I thought I could see a way of doing it, someone would give me a raise, or somebody would ask me to take a bigger position with more money."[5] Her jobs progressively earned her more salary, more responsibility, and higher status. At the same time, she became deeply involved in women's clubs where she found a community who believed in the things she did. What she learned on the job and in these affinity groups helped her build an ideological framework for understanding society and her place in it.

A variety of women's voluntary associations emerged around the turn of the century, offering the pleasures of collegiality, opportunities to improve one's cultural education, and vehicles for charitable work and civic change. There were at least seven women's clubs active in Skowhegan, most of them benevolent organizations founded by elites for the betterment of their community and the less fortunate.[6] Her first club affiliation was with the Daughters of the American Revolution (DAR), the pinnacle of small town social climbing. Membership was restricted by invitation and the requisite pedigree. With the help of Patten's wife, Margaret traced her family tree on her father's side to a Revolutionary soldier, content to omit the French Canadians on her mother's. The respectable genealogy enhanced her self-esteem, but the club's patriotic pageantry and historic preservation was a bit too staid for such a dynamic young woman.[7]

Before long, Chase was invited to join Skowhegan Sorosis, part of a federation of national clubs specifically designed for achieving women. The genesis of Sorosis was the celebrated visit of Charles Dickens to the United States in 1868. He was scheduled to be guest of honor at a glittering dinner hosted by the New York Press Club. Two popular women journalists, "Jennie June" (Jane Cunningham) Croly and "Fanny Fern" (Sara Payson Willis Parton) were excluded from the "men only" affair. They organized the "women only" Sorosis, taking their name from a botanical term for a kind of fruit in which many flowers are united (as in a pineapple). The association quickly grew into a broad network of local clubs, with the Skowhegan chapter beginning in 1886.[8]

By the time Chase joined in 1920, the club was involved in civic and community projects echoing the trend of "Municipal Housekeeping" prevalent in the period.[9] Sorosis made contributions to the poor and raised scholarships for local girls. They inaugurated and, for a time, single-handedly supported the Skowhegan Community Nursing Service. They established and maintained "Rest Rooms" for women. Comparable to men's clubs, this downtown suite of rooms provided a place for women to meet, rest, and have lunch, and a haven for mothers and children during a busy day in town.[10] In Sorosis, Chase learned leadership and cooperative skills. By 1922, she was president.

That same year she began to invest her time and energy in a new organization that focused more closely on the needs and goals of business and professional women, a cohort with which she hoped to become identified. With her friend, Elizabeth Dyer, she traveled to Portland for the opening of the permanent clubrooms of the newly organized Maine

Federation of Business and Professional Women's Clubs (BPW). Captivated by their message of self-help and women's solidarity, they hurried home to form their own branch in Skowhegan.[11] It was a pivotal moment for Chase, the beginning of an association that would last seventy years.

Though avowedly nonpartisan and nonfeminist, the BPW was at the vanguard of organizing and mobilizing women for political participation. The National Federation of Business and Professional Women's Clubs grew out of the efforts of the War Work Council to activate "woman power" for the Great War. Business and professional women, until then unorganized and without community, had responded in great numbers. Although the armistice was signed before the association began, the momentum was not to be stopped. More than one hundred women met at the first meeting and committed themselves to assessing the needs and improving the conditions of self-supporting women.[12]

Composed of career women keenly aware of sexism (although they did not use that term) in their work experiences, the BPW set as its "ultimate goal: the absolute elimination of consideration of the sex of the person in occupation, opportunity, or remuneration."[13] That objective required members to become politically astute and masters of the art of pressure group politics. *Independent Woman*, the aptly named official voice of the BPW, functioned as a training manual for active female citizenship. Expressly committed to improving and mobilizing federation women, it kept its readership informed of federal legislation, offered tips on how to succeed in the male world of business and the professions, and urged women to meet the challenge of civic duty, including the paramount task of political office.[14] Dismissing the notion that pursuit of a business or political career was unfeminine, the BPW endorsed ambition, validated strength, and celebrated achievement. For the young Chase, it was an empowering message.

Every other Tuesday night, the Skowhegan BPW met to "promote good fellowship and the spirit of unity" among women.[15] Under President Chase the club grew to an incredible 125 paying members, whom she urged to develop the "clarity of vision" that marks "all true progress." She encouraged risk taking and self-reliance; members practiced public speaking and polished office skills.[16] Margaret highly valued her affiliation with other young women who shared her problems and concerns, which she found were "lightened by friendship" and smoothed by the combined helpfulness of the members.[17]

In 1923, while still president of both Skowhegan Sorosis and BPW, Chase became involved in the BPW's Maine State Federation, as chair of the education committee that devised the first state scholarship plan for young women. She also chaired the Maine delegation to her first national convention in West Baden, Indiana, her second excursion out of Maine. The convention opened a whole new world for her as she mingled with hundreds of other accomplished women. After Maine's successful bid to host the next national convention, Chase chaired the publicity and program committees and took over the state federation's sporadically mimeographed newsletter, turning it into a multipage printed magazine, *The Pine Cone*. Two years later, Margaret Chase was elected president of the Maine State Federation.[18]

Despite efforts to sustain a nonpartisan organization, the Maine BPW was divided along party lines. Looking back, it is ironic to note that one of the major appeals of Chase's candidacy for state federation president was her appearance of political neutrality. Outgoing president Flora Weed, a Democrat, backed Chase in a successful effort to prevent vice-president Jennie Flood Kreger, a Republican, from winning the post. Chase's political affiliation only became apparent when her home club sponsored the state convention the following year. Then she chose two prominent Republican office holders to give the keynote speeches: Governor Ralph Owen Brewster and State Senator/Skowhegan Selectman Clyde H. Smith.[19]

In the BPW, Chase began her political education. She learned to negotiate, mediate, supervise, and compromise.[20] Speaking to the federation later in her career, MCS credited it with giving her "basic training" in political leadership, teaching her "the very touchstones of political success."[21] Her travels and responsibilities within the BPW broadened her horizons and helped forge a sense of identity and a new realization of her own abilities and possibilities. Chase's speeches and press clippings reveal a young woman emerging as the ideal of the 1920s "New Woman." This archetype, arising from a restricted past, throwing off the cult of true womanhood and impatient with feminist fuss, strode into the public world with aplomb, determination, and self-confidence, demanding recognition of her individuality.[22] Looking back, MCS does not recall her past self in this way. She sees an ingenue, unsophisticated and unsure, doing the best she could in uncertain situations.[23] It is possible, indeed likely, given the complexity of human nature, that she was both.

Clyde Smith hovered in the background, and sometimes in the foreground, as Margaret moved through the 1920s, pursuing her career and women's club projects. Smith took her to train stations and picked her up. He made numerous appearances at her BPW meetings in his capacities as first selectman of Skowhegan and Maine state senator, addressing the group about local and state issues.[24] He sent anxious telegrams to her and messages through her sister, Evelyn, when she did not write or wire him as often as she promised.[25] But he did not reveal his intentions.

Smith had been elected to his first public office a few months before Margaret Chase was born. In 1898, he became the youngest representative, at age twenty-one, to serve in the Maine House. After two terms (1898–1902), Smith returned to his hometown of Hartland, opened a clothing store, and served as superintendent of schools and town selectman. Two years later, Ed P. Page, a Skowhegan banker with whom he had served in the Maine House, persuaded Smith to run on the Republican slate for High Sheriff of Somerset County.[26] Following his election, "the boy sheriff" moved to Skowhegan, the shiretown of Somerset County where Page's friendship smoothed his entry into society and politics but fueled the resentment of Page's son, Blin. For a time, the two young men were frequent companions, but following the older man's death, they fell into a bitter mutual enmity that eventually doomed the aspirations of both for Maine's highest office.[27]

Smith made a name for himself prosecuting largely liquor-related crimes. Temperance was a critical issue in Maine, where the national movement had its origins. The "Maine Law," a complete ban on the manufacture and sale of liquor, passed in 1851, remained in effect in one form or another until the repeal of national prohibition in 1934.[28] Liquor control was therefore a central feature of Maine politics. "Dry" Republicans, mostly Protestant Yankees, were challenged by "Wet" Democrats, a large portion of whom were Franco-American Catholics. Despite accusations of inconsistent and hypocritical enforcement, the more numerous Republicans consistently controlled Maine elections. Smith, a lifelong teetotaler, attracted considerable attention for his zealous pursuit of alcoholic miscreants, and his flights of oratory in berating those responsible for "destitute widows with the canopy of heaven as her [sic] only shelter . . . for the homeless children with their aching pangs of hunger, for the mothers that are trudging their way over the hills to the poorhouse, and, yes, for the young men, the life blood, youth and vigor of our land that are marching into the bottomless pit and filling a drunkard's grave."[29]

After about a year in office, Smith enhanced his local visibility and, he asserted, his ability to do his job, when he bought a new 1905 Cadillac. Automobiles were novel and rare in Maine. Roads were poor. It took Smith eight hours to drive his new car the 100 miles home from Portland. Nonetheless, he said the machine would "enable him to economize his time and to reach any point in the county practically with the speed of a railway train."[30] His automobile became an important tool and a symbol for Smith's successful law enforcement in his large district (3,633 square miles). His experiences on rural Maine roads no doubt fostered a commitment to expanding and improving them. By 1927, when Smith was named to chair the State Highway Commission, Skowhegan, largely through his efforts, had more miles of paved road per capita than any other town in Maine.[31]

In 1908, just after his mentor died, and following four years as a very popular and successful sheriff, Smith chose not to run for reelection and suddenly married Page's daughter, Edna. The marriage came as a great surprise in the small town. While Edna's activities had apparently been faithfully described in the society pages, there was no mention of her keeping company with the local sheriff, much less planning a wedding. The *Somerset Reporter* noted the startling event, cribbed from the pages of the *Boston Globe*, in a piece entitled "Quietly Wedded," adding with classic understatement that "the prominence the contracting parties occupy in our town renders the nuptials of more than passing interest."[32]

The newlyweds bought a large home on Water Street and began extensive renovations. Clyde Smith launched a number of business ventures, including joining a partnership to buy a large factory to manufacture starch from potatoes, overseeing a lumbering operation upstate, operating a motion picture theater and, together with his wife, setting up a corporation to acquire three small weekly newspapers that they consolidated into the *Independent-Reporter* in 1909. Smith also continued his automobile business (started up in 1907 when he was sheriff) and joined a group of stockholders engineering the reorganization of the Second National Bank into the Skowhegan Trust Company, in direct competition with the other two banks in town, both of them headed by Blin Page.[33]

Then, about 1912, Smith began to pull back. He sold the Smith Publishing Company to a New York firm and the *Independent-Reporter*, except for one share and the title of president, to Roland Patten.[34] In January 1914, the Clyde Smiths divorced.[35] Though she met him nearly two years after the event, MCS had an economic explanation for the split. Edna and Clyde, she said, were "a bad match—she was wealth and society, he was rural with no money."[36] That being the case, his fortunes changed. Just three months later, Smith purchased a large chunk of property in the heart of the Skowhegan business district and went back into politics.[37]

Easily elected first selectman of Skowhegan in 1915, Smith held that post until 1932, except for one year, his first in the Maine Senate, when he chose not to run.[38] Known for his elegant oratory and reasoned judgment, Smith rapidly gained respect and power in his community, which he eagerly pushed toward progress. During his long tenure in town office, his accomplishments included miles of paved roads, downtown lighting, a motorized fire department, a new high school building, and numerous new industries. "Long before I knew him," MCS said, "I knew him. He was the town; he was Skowhegan."[39] Smith, others said, was a "natural politician—one of those men who couldn't keep out of politics if he wanted to, and he didn't want to."[40] A small-town face-to-face selectman, he was personable, friendly, and always had a dollar or two to help a constituent out of a jam. "He had a way of making poor people feel important."[41]

After his fourth year as selectman, Smith ran for the Maine House. He was challenged in the primary by his former brother-in-law, Blin Page, in the first of many increasingly acrimonious encounters. Page ran a lackluster campaign, and Smith soundly defeated him. He went on to serve two terms in the Maine House, and three in the Maine Senate, concurrent with his post as first selectman.[42] Although nominally a Republican, Smith built a reputation as a compassionate progressive, a champion of the working man. During his years in the Maine legislature, he wrote and supported a series of state measures increasing the scope of workman's compensation, mandating protection for working women, and limiting child labor. Smith introduced the first old-age pension bill in Maine in 1923.[43] With all his political activities, Smith still found time to earn a living for himself, often managing several businesses at once.[44] During the 1920s, he was part owner of a shoe company, sold automobiles, culverts, and tractors. His real estate ventures led him to acquire a series of large Victorian houses. But Smith's ultimate goal was the governor's mansion.

Since their first meeting in 1916, Clyde and Margaret had fallen into a pattern of "keeping company." Her photograph album provides a peek into their moments together in the 1920s. Scattered among family snapshots are pictures of Smith, wearing a top hat and riding in open cars in numerous small-town parades, and photos of the two of them together. They are often beside a large automobile in a rural setting, she shyly smiling, appearing girlish and fetching in bobbed hair and long waistless dresses, he inevitably in a three-piece suit with watch chain, looking secure and self-possessed. With a thick shock of white hair, strong features, and a steady gaze, he looked the stereotypical politician.[45]

Through the decade, the trajectory of their relationship remained indefinite. No longer a girl, not yet married, Margaret grappled with questions of marriage and career. A fragment of her diary from 1920 is filled with longing and uncertainty. Clyde's friendship, his daily telephone calls, the weekend picnics—did they, she wondered, constitute a courtship? Every night she recorded whether he called her, what he said he was doing, and whether she believed him. She feared he was avoiding her, was seeing other women: "Guess he has other ladies to attend to, but how am I going to find out."[46] Suspecting that something "was up" with Clyde, but not knowing what it was, she agonized over every word or missed telephone call. When he called to say he was tired and was not coming over, she wrote, "Imagine he is, but you never can tell when he is telling you the truth. Oh, I am so lonesome for someone to like me. . . . Mother says I hate myself and everyone around me. Guess she is right."[47] Throughout the diary, Margaret reports feeling poorly. The doctor gave her pills and a tonic and told her "my heart wasn't right."[48] She recognized that her heart trouble was a metaphor for her pain with a romance going nowhere. "How I'd like to know what it is . . . would like to know what ails him. I think that is what makes me feel so [sick] all the time."[49]

In early February, Clyde invited her to dine at his new home. "He is getting the house to looking pretty well, asked what I thot [sic] about several things. Wonder what his intentions are."[50] When Margaret was mistakenly introduced to strangers as Mrs. Clyde Smith, she remarked to her diary, "Some joke. Not so much for me tho [sic]. . . . People can hardly tell what we are to each other."[51] She had not figured that out either, vowing, "Am going to ask him soon what he means, what he is to me."[52]

Others wondered as well, and the speculation about the couple irked Clyde. He wrote an angry and sarcastic retort to a woman he referred to as a gossip: "I have never stated to you or any other human being that I did not care for Miss Chase or that I would or was not going to marry her and neither do I consider this any of your affairs [sic] or do either of us need your advice in the matter, although as I understand it you have freely offered the same."[53]

Margaret knew what she wanted—a comfortable home and a loving family, security and respect. She watched her high school friends marrying and starting families and confessed she would like to be doing the same. "My, but I would just like to be married and be able to live at ease with children, etc.," she wrote.[54] She had pinned her hopes on an older man whose future seemed assured, who could give her the stability and status for which she was willing to surrender her independence, but she harbored serious doubts about his attachment to her.

MCS recalled little contact with Smith throughout the 1920s, believing they hardly saw one another between their first encounters when she was a girl and a short time of reacquaintance just prior to their marriage. Newspaper clippings, however, reveal that in 1925 the couple had a brief aborted engagement for which MCS could not later account.

Announcements of the approaching marriage of "one of Skowhegan's most popular young women" to State Senator Clyde Smith ran in a number of newspapers around the state.[55] Then somehow it ended. They did not marry for another five years.

Throughout the decade, newspaper stories find Smith and Chase attending a number of political gatherings at the same time, although not necessarily together. They both went to governor's balls and Republican meetings, luncheons at the capital, and dinners at the governor's mansion. Though there was no public indication that they were considered a couple in these reports, they were moving in the same circles.[56] In 1927, Margaret Chase was twice invited to dine with the Governor and Mrs. Brewster at Blaine House, the governor's mansion. The first time, she was the principal speaker at a BPW-sponsored banquet honoring the six Maine women state legislators.[57] Her second visit to the Blaine House was for a more intimate dinner. Knowing little about formal entertaining and unsure of protocol, she asked the housekeeper who showed her to her room for advice on dressing for dinner and whether she should wait until summoned. Another question Chase had, which she did not feel free to ask anyone, was whether she should acknowledge her acquaintance with State Senator Clyde H. Smith, who would also be attending.[58]

Despite her apparent uneasiness with acknowledging Senator Smith at the governor's table, the relationship was common knowledge to many who knew them. Even so distant an acquaintance as Emma Dot Partridge, the Executive Secretary of the National BPW, could not resist publicly teasing the couple. At the Maine State Federation Convention in Skowhegan, at which Chase presided and Smith spoke, Partridge told the audience: "Not long ago, one of the neighbors of the place where he [Clyde] frequents heard this conversation. 'Well, Senator,' as the window was thrown up with a bang, 'I don't object to your sitting up half the night with Margaret—I don't object to your talking for two hours on the front doorsteps, but for the sake of the household, take your elbow off the bell-push.'"[59]

The convention was her last as BPW president. During her tenure she had earned a statewide reputation as a smart and competent young woman. She also began cultivating her interest in party politics with membership in, then secretary to, the Skowhegan Republican Committee in 1926. Two years later, she became recording secretary for the Somerset County Republican Committee and, in 1930, was elected Maine State Republican Committeewoman.[60]

Part of the stimulus for partisan activities seems to have come from Chase's new boss, which may have been just about enough to balance the discouragement she was getting from Clyde. After eight years at the newspaper, Margaret became Willard H. Cummings's office manager, overseeing a staff of three, at the Cummings Shoddy Mill.[61] Cummings was deeply involved in Republican politics, chairing both the town and county committees. In 1930, as campaign manager for Wallace White's U.S. Senate race, he was eager to install a state committee favorable to White. Smith did not approve of her getting involved in politics, MCS said, "but Mr. Cummings had made it part of my job to run."[62]

At first unopposed, Margaret Chase was challenged at the convention by Jennie Flood Kreger, whom she had defeated for state BPW president four years earlier. This last minute move animated some of the most intense lobbying the convention had seen in years.[63] Chase won. Her election, however, put her in an awkward personal and political position. Politics in Maine meant the Republican Party. As is often the case in single-party states, the Party contained conservative and liberal wings that mimicked a two-party system and heightened the importance of the primary. The "Old Guard" conservatives were challenged by the progressive "Young Turks." As a result, primaries became vicious battles where the real political contests were settled.[64] In Somerset County, those groups were represented primarily by the Page-Cummings coalition and the Smith forces.[65] The 1930 primary contest for U.S. Senator was between former Governor Brewster, a longtime associate of Clyde Smith's, and Wallace White, whose campaign manager was Margaret's boss. "And that was hard," she said, "because I was about to marry Clyde."[66]

Smith, a divorced man, longing to be governor of Maine to cap his political career, needed a wife. Waiting in the wings for more than ten years was a dynamic, politically astute, well-spoken young woman with a positive state reputation of her own, the perfect partner for a potential governor. In the spring of 1930, Miss Chase, "socially prominent throughout the state, a popular and much beloved young lady," and Mr. Smith, the esteemed "statesman of rare ability," announced their intention to marry.[67] Following a flurry of showers and parties and publicity, the couple wed on May 14, 1930, at the home of the bride on North Avenue. Only the immediate families crowded into the tiny Chase family parlor for the private ceremony. The bride wore a handmade royal blue lace dress from Berthe's of Paris with dyed-to-match shoes and crystal beads.[68] Following a light buffet lunch, the wedding party moved to the "palatial" home of the groom where the newlywed couple welcomed some three hundred friends, "some of whom came long distances from various parts of the state for this delightful function."[69]

The Smith home on Fairview Avenue was most impressive. Built about 1882 by Governor Coburn, the mansion had thirty-two rooms arranged in three stories, a full dozen bedrooms on the second floor, each plumbed with running water from a spring on the estate. Eight carved and tiled fireplaces, a vestibule frieze featuring Grecian dancing girls, and chandeliers of heavy copper with etched glass globes and crystal baubles graced the home. Every room contained hand-carved archways and wainscoting with matching furniture—the dining room in quartered oak, the master bedroom in bird's-eye maple.[70] "We are unusually well off," the new bride recorded in her "Wedding Memories" album, "as we have one of the finest places in this part of the state." She blissfully added: "We are still enjoying ourselves attempting to make our entire life together one long honeymoon."[71]

3 | Mrs. Clyde Smith

He called her "Sis" and his "little girl." She still called him "Mr. Smith."[1] These terms of endearment eloquently reflected their asymmetrical relationship. Given the differences in their ages and status in the community, and traditional notions of marital harmony, she knew she was expected to channel her energies to furthering his career. But Margaret surrendered her independence reluctantly. She kept her job at the woolen mill following her marriage, but not for long. After a difficult six months, she yielded to her husband's disapproval and the increasing demands of her new role, and quit her salaried job to work full time for Smith.[2]

Looking after their grand home required considerable labor, especially in light of Smith's tendency to bring home large groups of friends for dinner and frequently overnight, without notice. Margaret refused to allow Smith to hire servants to help her. She was determined to do everything herself. Painfully aware of her comparative youth, she saw disapproval in the eyes of others. His relatives "didn't think much of me," MCS remembered. His political cronies wondered, she thought, "what's he gonna do with her? Here he is going higher and higher politically. Why does he want her?" She reacted to this presumed disfavor by resolving to prove herself worthy of her new position. "I was just determined to show them I could do it all by myself." He insisted on punctuality and a well-managed household. "Mr. Smith valued promptness," MCS said. He wanted his meals precisely on time and "his soup on the table when he came in . . . he would rather have his soup wait for him than he wait for his soup."[3]

Fueled by her resolve, Margaret's management skills translated well, and she gradually learned the finer points of cooking and entertaining under the tutelage of her elderly stepmother-in-law, who lived with the Smiths for a few months after they married.[4] Margaret adopted a couple of classic recipes and a few easy-to-prepare but elegant dishes to impress her guests with her flair in the kitchen while expending as little time and energy as possible. Large Saturday night suppers of maple-sweetened baked beans and steamed brown bread became a tradition for the Smiths. Guests sang around the piano in the parlor and debated politics in the library.[5]

Having mastered the domestic arts, Margaret soon discovered a way to use them to make money. Her sister-in-law was doing a considerable business opening her home to tourists in the summer for a dollar a night. Pressed for space, she began to send her overflow to Margaret and Clyde. Eventually as many as twenty guests filled their spare bedrooms. Both Smiths enjoyed meeting and talking with new people; they played cards and served refreshments. Even with the extra work, it seemed like a pleasant series of "house parties" to Margaret. What's more, after six weeks she had earned almost $300. But when she began excitedly making plans to expand her business for the next season by finishing additional rooms and posting "neon Smith signs on the main highway," she was halted by her husband, who reminded her that she had "enough to do."[6]

Like most marriages, this one left little documentary evidence revealing its nature. Traces are scattered and tantalizing—a few fading photographs, a small packet of letters, a handful of telegrams. All that remains to reveal Clyde's perception of the relationship are five letters he sent his wife while on a two-week business trip during their second married year. Addressed to "Dearest Little Girl," the letters express loneliness and regret that she is not with him. "So much wish you were here. Never again will go away without you if I can have my way," he wrote. "It seems so strange and unnecessary to be separated." In each daily missive, he tenderly assures her that "hardly a minute goes by without thinking of my dear girl."[7]

Besides sweet sentiments, these letters also carry a message of distress and a plea for forgiveness. From Massachusetts, he wrote: "Many times today I have shed tears when thinking of being impatient yesterday morning. I am so sorry. You are the best living girl and at this distance I can hear you saying 'I am not worried.' The noblest thoughts that a woman can express. . . . I can not get back to the house you so nobly enrich soon enough." A few days later, he again pledged his devotion and predicted happier times: "Now then, little girl, don't worry anymore. If you could look into my heart tonight you would plainly see you need not worry. God alone knows how much I would like to be with you tonight. . . . Be brave little girl. The sun will shine again and we will appreciate its rays more than ever before."[8]

From this distance it is impossible to know the specific circumstances prompting these messages. Her "worry" might have been that he did not love her, or perhaps she had expressed concern for his safety. It may also be a reference to an undercurrent that surfaces repeatedly whenever MCS talked about her marriage. Her husband, she often said flatly, "loved the ladies and they loved him, and I took it after a fashion."[9] Her references to Smith's extramarital interests and her efforts to cope with them make it clear that the marriage was not, to her, idyllic. She once hastened to correct a writer whose portrayal of her marriage was at odds with her estimation by saying, "as great a man as Clyde was, he was not as devoted to me as you seem to think. Let me limit my observations to saying that he gave me many heartaches."[10] When asked directly about the union, MCS said simply, "It was not a great love, not that kind. It was more a business arrangement."[11]

Their business was politics, and Smith's political fortunes had come to a crossroads. He had recently lost his position as chair of the State Highway Commission, a political plum of some importance, in the midst of a federal fraud investigation. He would ultimately be exonerated, but not without considerable political and personal damage.[12] Skowhegan politics had also taken a particularly nasty turn under the leadership of his old nemesis, Blin Page. In addition to a hefty lawsuit filed on the eve of Smith's reelection as selectman, the Page coalition kept up a steady barrage of political assaults throughout what would become Smith's last term.[13] And not least, Smith struggled to bolster several business enterprises staggered by the national Depression.[14] By the summer of 1930, the accumulated pressures precipitated a "nervous breakdown," along with a reevaluation of his political career.[15] In the spring of 1932, for the first time in many years, Clyde Smith held no local nor state post. He continued, though, to enjoy high visibility, thanks in large part to the activities of his wife.

Mrs. Margaret Chase Smith appeared in the news as frequently as her statesman husband. Her choice to continue to use her maiden as well as married name ensured that she did not surrender her individual identity. While press references always included her marital status, they never failed to note her own achievements as a businesswoman and women's club activist. Margaret maintained her close association with the BPW, acting as hostess, speaker, and officer in the town and district groups. Smith often accompanied his wife to meetings, addressing them on legislative matters. Sometimes, the two of them would host BPW and other women's club meetings in their home, both giving talks.[16] As Republican State committeewoman, a post to which she was reelected twice (serving six years), Mrs. Smith's principal task was to build and maintain a local organization to do the basic work of the party. She appointed women at the county level who in turn appointed district and town campaign workers.[17] Margaret's connections with women's groups gave Smith access to women voters that other politicians envied. They recognized her endeavors and high visibility as an "augmentive factor" in his political fortunes.[18] At the same time, her committee work yielded a cadre of loyal women, many of whom remained her active supporters when she launched her own political career.

Margaret was methodical and well organized, capacities she had developed through years of office and club management. In 1932, she deftly arranged an exhausting tour, a series of Republican rallies across the district, in which she, along with a handful of candidates, addressed groups of voters in several towns every day between August 25 and September 10. She earned high marks "for the careful and efficient arrangement of the countless details necessary for the proper carrying out of the tour."[19] That fall, the Republican National Committee appointed Margaret Smith to organize Maine women for Herbert Hoover.[20] Across town, the former Mrs. Smith was also stumping for Herbert Hoover. Edna Page Smith Bunker, whose second husband had died in 1925, chaired the Women's Division of Engineers' National Committee for Hoover. Throughout the campaign, the two women often shared the front page; both were active in the Women's Republican Club and recruited from state and local women's clubs, but apparently managed to avoid one another's functions.[21]

Though Hoover won in Maine—he carried only Maine and Vermont in 1932—a Democratic executive captured the statehouse. Governor Louis J. Brann was carried into office by the widening cleavage between the conservatives and the progressives within the Maine Republican Party and "the FDR tidal wave." The Smiths' party loyalty notwithstanding, they were glad to see the Republican governor defeated. Besides their lingering bitterness over the highway commission controversy, the previous administration had been astonishingly inept, increasing expenditures and rejecting federal aid as the Depression deepened.[22]

Smith was close to Brann personally and philosophically. They had become friends while serving together in the state legislature. During the campaign, Smith had done little to hide his support for Brann, whose views on reform legislation and fiscal responsibility he endorsed, regardless of party labels. Mr. and Mrs. Smith attended Brann's campaign speeches and entertained him at their home in Skowhegan. Just before the election, anticipating Brann's success, Smith persuaded his friends in the legislature to elect him to the governor's Executive Council. The council of seven men, similar to a board of directors, shared the power of administering state government.[23]

For Margaret, the new post meant relocation to the Augusta House, a large residential hotel, for most of the year. At first, she spent her days at needlepoint, waiting for her husband to come home.[24] The Smiths participated in the formal social functions of the capital as little as possible. Smith disliked them and usually found an excuse to regret, though he was quite fond of entertaining a limited circle of friends. They continued their Saturday night suppers and several times a month Clyde and the boys took over the Smith suite for extended poker games. Margaret did needlework in the lobby or retired to the bathroom with a book until the men left. "I was not happy with the situation," she recalled, "but . . . I was the heroine among those men . . . because I did not interrupt their game or make a scene." Praised for being unobtrusive, Margaret sought other ways to keep out of the way. She found a ready companion in Mrs. Louis Brann, who also often felt extraneous.[25]

On the final day of the session his first year on the Governor's Council, Smith was rushed to Augusta General Hospital where he spent five days. The press said it was acute indigestion caused, in part, by "the severe strain of the many and varied duties that fall to the lot of an executive councillor."[26] It was an attack of angina. Smith soon resumed his normal routine, but his wife now helped him read and interpret documents, write position papers, and accompanied him to council meetings for the rest of the term.[27] He sat out the 1934 campaign. Brann appeared unbeatable. In a show of political virtuosity, the governor had capitalized on more than $100 million in federal relief funds while dissociating himself and his administration from the increasingly unpopular New Deal.[28] The Republican Party, still wrangling among themselves, divided their vote among four candidates in 1934, including Blin Page. In the end, Alfred K. Ames, "a colorless and rather helpless candidate," carried the party standard.[29] Business and industry leaders, even segments of the Republican press, openly advocated Brann's reelection. He won easily.[30]

Two days later, Clyde Smith and Blin Page announced their candidacies for governor in 1936.[31] Republican leaders, determined to avert another free-for-all in the next election, looked with particular dismay upon the Page-Smith confrontation. Press commentators never mentioned their candidacies without remarking on the prolonged hostility between the two gentlemen from Skowhegan, who were "not only opposed politically but bitter personal enemies."[32] "For more than twenty years," said one, "there has been a chasm wider than the grand canyon between these two men."[33] Smith positioned himself as Brann's heir apparent, a champion of the working man.[34] Page stood foursquare against New Deal "socialism,"and just for good measure, launched a whispering campaign about Smith's "womanizing," an effort Margaret found particularly painful.[35]

The Smiths campaigned together. Margaret drove the car and kept track of the details. In a campaign diary, she carefully recorded on hand-drawn maps the routes in the district, names of key people with their addresses and businesses, meeting places, lists of contacts in each town, radio stations and reporters, vote tallies, clippings on general state information, campaign expenses, and willing workers.[36] While Clyde Smith met with potential constituents in post offices, grange halls, town squares, private homes, and on the street, his wife would sit in the back seat typing correspondence on a portable typewriter propped on an empty suitcase.[37] It was not unusual for Smith to be tied up for hours with political business while his wife patiently waited. On one occasion, Smith dined with a group of local politicians in a seaside town, attended a program at the local Opera House, then returned to the home of one of the participants for coffee and more political conversation. All the while, Mrs. Smith waited in the car.[38] Other times she joined him, especially when there were women in the group. Smith was actively courting the woman's vote, one reporter observed, ably assisted by his wife, "one of the cleverest women political workers in Maine."[39]

After nearly a year of statewide campaigning, Smith withdrew his gubernatorial candidacy and announced instead for his party's nomination for U.S. Representative from the Second District. Because there were "two antagonistic candidates from Skowhegan" in the race, and "the selection of either man would mean losses to the party," he said, "I made the sacrifice in the interest of party harmony."[40] That was part of it, although Page's poor showing in the 1934 primaries (he finished a distant third) amply demonstrated he would be little threat to Smith's candidacy. More significant was the entry of Lewis Barrows into the race. Then secretary of state, Barrows had the backing of what was left of the party machine and that of business and manufacturing interests against the "Raw Deal." Party leaders, wishing to back a more viable candidate, and distrustful of Smith's "tinge of radicalism" and advocacy of "social panaceas," apparently offered him machine support only if he would switch his candidacy to Congress.[41] His chances looked good. National Democrats assessed him as a "clever politician, a man who makes a good appearance, and who has a charming wife who is of help to him. . . . There is great danger that Smith may be elected."[42]

Increasing dissatisfaction with New Deal policies animated the 1936 campaign. While generally distrustful of relief measures, Mainers were, at the same time, concerned about not receiving their fair share.[43] With such an ambivalent attitude, Smith was betting that they were unlikely to back an unrestricted New Dealer but would vote for a Republican who cared. He made his record of compassionate legislation the centerpiece of his campaign, reminding voters of his past efforts in the Maine legislature on behalf of child labor protection, workmen's compensation insurance, and old age pensions. Additionally, he proposed to lead the way out of the New Deal, "one of the most gigantic political blunders of all ages," by withdrawing government interference between capital and labor, and by erecting "a protective tariff so high that not a dollar's worth of foreign goods will reach our shores that can be produced by American labor."[44]

Smith was being pushed hard in the primary by an endorsed Townsendite J. Clarence Leckenby. Dr. Francis Townsend's panacea for ending the Depression while alleviating the financial burdens of the elderly spawned at least 150 Townsend Clubs in Maine (over 3,200 nationwide) by 1936.[45] Townsend's plan to disburse a pension of $200 a month to all citizens more than sixty years old provided they spend the entire amount within thirty days would, according to its originator, support the aged, open up employment opportunities by withdrawing older workers from the labor pool, speed the circulation of money to "prime the pump" of the Depression economy and pay for itself. Critics assailed its administrative provisions and economists demolished its pecuniary assumptions. But just because Townsend's plan was fiscally impossible did not discourage its countless adherents, nor weaken it as a political cause.[46] Smith could, and did, point to his lengthy record of advocacy for elderly pensions, having pushed the issue in the state legislature nearly every session since he first proposed it in 1923. He was skeptical of Townsend, though, urging pensions "be independent of and free from any scheme or combination."[47] It almost cost him the primary; he won by fewer than 2,000 votes. Once past that hurdle, and with the help of the Republican machine, Smith soundly defeated his Democratic opponent.[48] Skowhegan celebrated with a huge street party. More than three thousand well-wishers cheered as Margaret and Clyde jubilantly led the torchlight parade down Water Street and joined in the dancing. Bands played and speakers predicted a brilliant future in Washington.[49]

Clyde Smith went off to Congress with a staff of two—his old partner, Roland Patten, and his wife. Margaret kept track of Smith's appointments, briefed him on daily tasks, handled his correspondence, helped him with his speeches, gathered research data, mediated between governmental agencies and constituents, greeted and entertained visitors, and dealt with the press. In short, she "did everything in his office short of going to the committee room or to the floor of the House to vote."[50] Patten was listed on the congressman's letterhead as Secretary, but Smith referred to him in speeches as his "other secretary."[51] Margaret did the work and she insisted on the pay.[52] Mrs. Smith attracted favorable press both at home and in the capital as one of the few congressional wives actively working for her husband. They praised her strong business background, her skill, and her feminine charm. She told interviewers her relationship to the congressman was "a sort of a partnership."[53]

Although she found abundant and satisfying work as a congressional secretary and hostess, Margaret missed her connections to women's groups back home. She found a substitute in the Congressional Club, a social group composed of the wives of Congress members, Supreme Court justices, and the president's Cabinet. It was a friendly and efficient way to meet other congressional wives and, perhaps more important, to learn to negotiate the bewildering complexity of Washington social protocol. Congressional wives were to leave calling cards at the White House at the beginning of every year, and wives of new members called on the wives of incumbents. A club handbook precept declared: "The exchange of first calls should be made in person, and will cancel all official obligations, for so long as the two ladies are in the same position in official life." Specific days of the week were designated for calling upon Washington officials. Mondays, for example, were for Supreme Court justices, Thursdays for senators. Mastering these myriad laws of social decorum was part of the training for the congressional wife.[54]

Mrs. Brewster, whose husband then represented Maine's third district, offered to show Margaret the procedure. The two ladies traveled from house to house. No one was home, nor expected to be. "It just wasn't done to be there," MCS said. The two women waited in the car while Mrs. Brewster's driver left their calling cards at the door, right corners folded over to denote a personal call. It seemed easy enough. Margaret made the next round by herself, beginning at the home of Mrs. Hamilton Fish, wife of the congressman from New York. Having already folded the corner of her card, she rang the bell. She was startled and dismayed to be met by Mrs. Fish and invited in for tea and cake. Feeling unsophisticated and unsure—"We were just country folk"—she agonized over whether or not to remove her gloves. Mrs. Smith left a short time later, thankful that she had survived her first critical social event.[55]

When not traveling about in carriages and chauffeured limousines dropping off their calling cards, the women met in their opulent Beaux-

Arts club building for teas and receptions, bridge parties and dinner dances.[56] The Congressional Club's delight in fashion and ceremony was not wholly unlike Margaret's earlier experience with women's clubs. Though the social trappings attracted her, she felt more comfortable with her reputation as a "working girl." She became club treasurer and oversaw the funding and completion of a $200,000 club house renovation.[57] Although club duties significantly added to her workload, Margaret highly valued her association with the prominent women of Washington. MCS later credited them for easing her transition into congressional office. Her good rapport and reputation with the women insured a measure of respect from their husbands: "The men in the House were so nice to me because their wives probably told them to be."[58]

Despite her education in social protocol, Margaret continued to feel uncomfortable in formal situations, as did Clyde. Naive about the importance of social gatherings to the work of a congressman, Smith found Washington society a frivolity, exhausting at the cost of serious work. Eschewing all but the unavoidable, the Smiths preferred informal dinners at home. It was a point of pride to MCS, as well as to her husband, that she did not waste time while in Washington "going socially."[59] MCS later recounted, with more amusement than embarrassment, Smith's numerous social gaffes; many of these reveal her continuing sensitivity to issues of class and status. For example, a favorite story concerned the Smith's first dinner party after settling in Washington. The entire Maine delegation was there, including the "very proper" Mrs. Wallace White. Nonetheless, despite Margaret's private admonitions, Clyde encouraged his beloved chihuahua, Alice Betty, to take her dessert at the table as she always had.[60]

Freshman Smith quickly won assignment to one of the Seventy-fifth Congress's most important committees, the House Labor Committee, and immediately found himself embroiled in one of the most bitter fights of the late New Deal—the battle over wage and hour legislation that would ultimately become the Fair Labor Standards Act of 1938. Four months after Smith arrived in Washington, the Roosevelt administration submitted legislation to replace the recently repealed National Recovery Administration (NRA) codes regulating minimum wages and maximum hours and prohibiting the labor of children under sixteen.[61] The administration's bill (S.2475) passed the Senate largely unchanged, but foundered in the House Labor Committee, chaired by Representative Mary Norton (D-NJ), under attack from an alliance of Southern Democrats who feared wage equalization would eliminate their advantage over northern industry and labor leaders who feared that the minimum wage might become the maximum and that bureaucratic control of the wage structure would undermine union bargaining power. The bill staggered out of committee, after two tempestuous months, laden with 129 amendments. A strong coalition of Republicans and Southern Democrats on the House Rules Committee refused to discharge the bill. Congress adjourned without further action.[62] Determined to establish wage and hour standards, FDR called a special session in November. In a desperate effort to get the measure to the floor for debate, Norton and her committee feverishly gathered the 218 signatures necessary for a discharge petition, forcing the Rules Committee to turn the bill loose.[63] The House voted to recommit the bill, by now a "mush of concessions and a shining example of how not to prepare and pass federal law."[64]

The new Congress brought increasing pressure to resolve the wages and hours conundrum. In March 1938, Norton appointed a subcommittee, headed by Robert Ramspeck (D-GA), and including Smith, the sole representative from the industrialized northeast, to create a new bill. After three weeks of constant deliberation, the subcommittee deadlocked; another two months were consumed hammering out a compromise. Again the Rules Committee refused to act, voting 8–6 against discharge. Again the Labor committee scrambled for the necessary 218 signatures; this time they were obtained in just over two hours.[65] Once free, the Fair Labor Standards Act of 1938 prohibiting child labor and setting minimum wages and maximum hours passed handily.[66]

In the midst of this protracted labor battle, Clyde suffered a heart attack that put him to bed for six weeks. Minimizing the seriousness of his illness, he notified his constituents that "irregular eating and sleeping with so much attention to business [has] forced me to bed for repairs." He assured them his illness would not impair his congressional duties as he had arranged voting pairs, and Mrs. Smith was efficiently handling the office, "never failing to give attention to every visitor and not allowing a communication to remain unanswered more than one day."[67] Keeping in close touch with Maine was a high priority, particularly for a man who still hoped to be governor. Truth was, he hated Washington, hated finding himself for the first time in his political career a minor figure in a minor party, "day after day called upon to vote [his] convictions in the face of inevitable defeat."[68] Smith went home to Skowhegan in September, seemingly fully recovered. Curbing rumors that he might challenge the incumbent governor, he told four hundred party regulars gathered at his testimonial banquet that he wished to return to Washington to finish his work on the Wages and Hours bill, then "I would like to complete a career of 43 years of faithful service to the state and its subdivisions by being governor in 1940."[69]

The burden of Smith's labors in Congress, coupled with his fragile health, compelled him to spend increasingly more time in Washington and less in Maine. In his place, he sent his wife. She took the train to Maine once a month or so, made speeches, visited with party officials, and carried constituent concerns back to Clyde. She stood in for him at the Maine Republican Convention in the spring, assuring political leaders that it was his work, not his health, which kept him away from Maine.[70]

As Margaret traveled for her husband, she developed a voice of her own. No longer simply an emissary, on at least a few occasions she articulated a counterposition to Smith's. For example, she made frequent talks to women's groups about equal rights and her opposition to protective legislation for women, which Smith supported, and the necessity to increase military preparedness, a stance to which Smith was opposed.

In an instance that became legendary, Mrs. Smith addressed the Kennebec County Women's Republican Club on 27 October 1938. Her talk, entitled "The Experiences of a Congressman's Wife in Washington," began with a description of the rigid social formula required in the capital. Then she shifted to a more serious topic. Only thirty days before, in Munich, the British and French agreed to allow Germany to annex a piece of Czechoslovakia in an attempt to appease Hitler and prevent wider war. Having spotted war on the horizon, Mrs. Smith called for preparedness. This day was Navy Day, she said, and "development of our navy means self-preservation. Money spent in this direction, although from the viewpoint of many is expensive, maybe extravagant, is at all times an insurance . . . [and] the best insurance for peace is preparation for war."[71] It is likely that few, beyond the group of ladies who attended, paid any attention to the speech. Smith himself was unaware of her message. MCS remembered that he refused to help her prepare it and added, "probably he never would have suggested that I talk about the United States Navy."[72]

Indeed, Smith favored ironclad neutrality and opposed military expansion on moral and economic grounds. Just a few months before his wife's speech, he vehemently attacked proposals of the "big navy boys, sword rattlers and jingoists" to increase the tonnage of the U.S. Navy. His opposition to plunging money into munitions in the midst of a Depression was unequivocal: "When one thinks of the desperate need for funds for general well-being, or the tax relief that could be effected by omitting the cost ($70 million) of one battleship, it is easy to highly resolve that such folly must cease."[73]

Smith believed economic interests associated with the manufacture of armaments were bent on provoking war with unnecessary war-preparedness campaigns. The profit motive was a powerful impetus for the Great War, he said, and that lesson should not be forgotten.[74] Accordingly, Smith voted for the Neutrality Act of 1937, and two years later spoke in the House in favor of retaining unqualified neutrality, saying "America has no excuse for meddling, even to this somewhat limited extent, in foreign affairs, unless certain that the democracies of the world are being destroyed. . . . [I]t is wise to retain the embargo we have."[75]

In a state with a large shipbuilding industry, her position would seem to be the most politically adroit. The significance of her speech remained obscure until Margaret ran for political office herself. At any rate, no one remarked on the discrepancy at the time. Congressman Smith, the press pointed out, was very fortunate to have her for his deputy: "Mrs. Smith, who holds a directing influence on his course . . . is a helpmate whom Maine has every right to admire. If he should gain the nomination and be elected Governor, the State itself would indeed be fortunate in its first lady."[76]

First, though, Clyde faced a very tough reelection race for Congress. His opponent, F. Harold Dubord, characterized Smith as a pseudo-liberal bent on sabotaging New Deal programs, but this strategy backfired. Smith's lengthy record on labor and pensions for the aged appealed to those who still favored the New Deal in 1938, and his conservative call for fiscal responsibility in administering these programs appealed to those who did not. What's more, Smith had climbed aboard the crowded Townsend bandwagon.[77] The apparent deficiencies of the Democratic administration's Social Security Act and the recession of 1937–38 had reinvigorated the Townsend movement; over ninety Townsend Republicans were elected in 1938, that is, more than one-half of the entire Republican membership in the House of Representatives.[78] Smith won, but it was close; he captured only 48.9 percent of the vote.[79] His postelection speech reiterated his plan to run for governor in the following election and intimated his current victory presaged an equally certain triumph two years hence.[80]

Back in Washington, work consumed him. Long hearings and acrimonious debate in the House Labor Committee continued. Passage of the Fair Labor Standards Act had not ended disputes over wages and hours. The focus merely shifted from establishing standards to defining exemptions and enforcement. Within a year, no fewer than forty-two bills were pending to modify the law in varying degrees.[81] In addition, sit-down strikes, growing hostility to the labor movement, and the increasing strength of New Deal opposition, fueled efforts to dismantle or, at the least, limit the power of the National Labor Relations Board. The skirmishes over the Labor Board persisted throughout the Seventy-sixth Congress. Efforts to resolve them were "not only tiring but tedious, the constant succession of abstruse parliamentary strategies, the stream of amendments, the shouting and beseeching of members supporting or opposing the bill. Hour after hour and day after day." Smith noticeably worsened.[82]

In December, doctors confirmed what he must have known for a long time. He was in the tertiary (or final) stage of syphilis. It was now affecting virtually every system in his body, in addition to serious destruction of his heart. The technical terms were tabes dorsalis and tabes paresis: a chronic inflammation and progressive sclerosis of the spinal cord and a general softening of the brain that produced progressive paralysis and insanity. The diagnosis also contained advice: "to live as quietly as possible both mentally and physically . . . [and] to decrease rather than increase his political activities as so much of his future is intimately concerned with his manner of living."[83] It is impossible to know if he shared this information with Margaret. It is clear that he ignored the advice.

Smith could no more give up politics than he could stop breathing. He plunged into a gubernatorial campaign bent on countering "malicious statements" from his political enemies that he was seriously ill and unable to attend to his duties.[84] Friends returning from Washington reported Smith in fine condition: "He's in this fight and he isn't going to get out of it; that is positive."[85]

Come spring, in responding to questions concerning his commitment to a gubernatorial race, some equivocation crept into Smith's rhetoric: "May I emphatically say that until a man whose vision extends beyond politics and selfishness, comes forth for this great office, I shall remain in the contest to the end."[86] Apparently someone did. By fall, the Maine Republican Party had at least four more candidates for governor. Smith pulled out. His parting statement indicated that the entry of new candidates and the prospect for a "larger and more effective" Republican coalition in Congress made him prefer "to go back to the Nation's Capitol instead of to the Blaine Mansion."[87]

Rumors of his poor health continued to plague Smith's subsequent campaign for reelection. He splashed state newspapers with ads offering a "$50 Reward for [the] name of [the] person circulating insidious stories about me being ill. . . . My activities in Congress bespeak good health . . . [as I am] working night and day for my constituency."[88] Notifying his supporters that he was occupied "on the important Labor Committee that is holding daily sessions," Smith sent his wife to the Maine Republican convention in the spring of 1940.[89]

She was annoyed with him when she left. She knew how he hated these events, but he had promised to come this time. Then, at the last moment, he said he did not feel well, would she please go on alone. More angry than concerned—"he always seemed to find some illness to stop him from doing what he didn't want to do"—Margaret caught the late night flight to Portland.[90] She arrived exhausted, then hurriedly set up a hospitality room, patted her hair in place, and plunged into a long day of charming the delegates and constituents.[91] When her parents arrived from Skowhegan late in the evening, she left with them to drive back to Washington. Margaret was just too tired to go beyond Boston, so they stopped at a rooming house where she and Clyde had often stayed. The owner met her at the door. The state police, she told Margaret, had left a message for her: her husband was seriously ill and she should hurry home. Leaving her mother and father to follow later, Margaret tried frantically to find transportation. Finally, she hired a taxi to take her to New York where she caught a train for Washington.[92]

When she arrived, Dr. Dickens told her Smith's condition was critical, his chance of recovery forty-sixty, and not likely to survive a year.[93] For a couple of days, he seemed to rally. Concerned about the rapidly approaching deadline for filing primary petitions, Smith urged his wife to file for office in her own name.[94] Then he dictated a press release. He had suffered a coronary thrombosis, he stated, and "may be physically unable to take an active part in congressional affairs for an indefinite time." Therefore, "All that I can ask of my friends and supporters is that in the coming primary and general election, if [I am] unable to enter [the] campaign, they support the candidate of my choice, my wife and my partner in public life, Margaret Chase Smith. I know of no one else who has the full knowledge of my ideas and plans or is as well qualified as she is, to carry on these ideas and my unfinished work for my district."[95]

Like her husband, Margaret tried to keep Smith's options open. She told the press that, should he recover, she would gladly step aside; either way "the people of the Second District will have a Smith to vote for."[96]

Smith told his wife to call her sister in Augusta to pick up and begin circulating new nomination papers for her, then instructed her to call several of his Republican friends with the news and ask them for their support. "I spent all that Sunday evening, from 8 o'clock to 12 o'clock," MCS said, "calling those men." Finally, she sent the nurse out of the room and climbed into bed beside her husband. For a time he talked softly to her and told her how much he cared for her. Then he was gone.[97]

4 | On Her Own

Following a solemn obsequy in the House chamber, Margaret boarded the train bearing Clyde Smith on his last trip home to Skowhegan. "Countless friends in the community from all walks of life were inexpressibly grieved." Business was suspended, school dismissed, and curtains drawn in the sorrowful town. Hundreds filed past his bier, banked with flowers in the Smith's south parlor, "and looked for the last time on the remains of their friend, who had become a statesman." Memorial speakers honored him as "a magnetic orator," champion of the poor, and "valiant fighter for those who labor." Then the long funeral cortege wound slowly through the hills to the Pine Grove Cemetery in Hartland, his boyhood home.[1]

Margaret had little time to mourn. That same day, Governor Barrows announced a special election to choose Smith's successor.[2] Both the special primary and election for the nine-month unexpired term needed to be completed before the regular primary in mid-June. Mrs. Smith's nomination papers were already in circulation, spread by Smith's county chairmen and Margaret's network of women volunteers. She was challenged in the special primary only by perennial candidate Frederick Bonney, who was criticized for his "questionable taste" in doing so. Bonney countered that once installed in office, Mrs. Smith would be very hard to dislodge. Still, in light of Smith's stated preference that his wife succeed him, Republican leaders agreed to concede the unexpired term.[3] The vote was small; she captured more than 90 percent.[4] The day after the primary, she made a solitary pilgrimage to her husband's grave on what would have been their tenth wedding anniversary.[5]

Prior to the special June election, Democrats debated their appropriate strategy in this unusual campaign. They appeared split between those who favored gestures of gallantry toward Smith's widow and those who argued that it was not "good party politics to lie down and let the opposition party have things its own way, even if its leading candidate was a woman." Democratic candidate Edward J. Beauchamp made the final decision. He magnanimously pulled out, allowing Mrs. Smith the short term without opposition.[6]

Things were different, though, in the campaign for the full term. Clyde Smith's reelection had been certain; his death opened the field. The day of his funeral three Republican challengers registered their interest in the post.[7] Smith's stated wishes notwithstanding, "public office is not bequeathed, as is property," noted one political commentator. If Mrs. Smith wanted to return to Washington, she would have to fight for it.[8] Her decision to run for the regular term was never in doubt. She had made a promise to her husband she could not, would not, abandon. "I had to get ready for that election," MCS remembered. "I had to get ready to run for the next two years if I was going to, and I felt that I *had* to as long as I was in it."[9] Margaret campaigned on a combination of Smith's legacy and her own political experience. Her husband's deathbed imprimatur was a powerful epistle to his loyal supporters. They believed that "had his wife not possessed the ability necessary to equip her for the important work of a member of Congress, Clyde Smith would never have asked the voters to elect her to succeed him."[10]

During the ten years of their partnership, Smith taught his wife the intricacies of politics and the practical machinery of government, but his most important contribution to her education was his personalized, gregarious political style. Since his first campaign for the Maine legislature in 1898, when he made the rounds of his district on a bicycle, Smith recognized the importance of personal relationships with the voters. By his side, Margaret had acquired an intimate knowledge of her constituents' concerns, a positive public image, an established political organization, an acquaintance with important state and party political leaders, and a clear understanding of the demands and rewards of public office. Together, they had built a power base that automatically became hers when Smith died. Because of her pledge to continue her husband's work on pension and labor legislation, she inherited the enthusiastic support of Maine labor, Townsendites, and other New Deal partisans. These groups represented the heart of the Second District electorate. While her district contained scattered rural, and mostly conservative, villages, much of the voting population was within the capital city of Augusta and the industrial cities of Waterville, Lewiston, and

Auburn. These areas were strongly unionized and, in the absence of a competitive Democratic Party, tended to vote for liberal Republicans.[11]

In the 1940 campaign, however, issues of war and peace drowned out more prosaic concerns. Unlike her late husband's vigorous defense of neutrality, Mrs. Smith advocated swift preparation for war with Germany. America must give priority to armed power, she said. "We must immediately build up land, sea and air defense. . . . We must also mobilize the industrial genius of this country. . . . We must arrange to purchase and store at least a year's supply of every vital raw material. . . . We must increase our production to the maximum."[12] Her speeches reiterated her 1938 Navy Day message: military weakness leads to war; preparedness insures peace.

Hitler's forces were moving quickly and relentlessly across Western Europe. In the spring of 1940, Germany overran Norway, Denmark, the Netherlands, Belgium, Luxembourg and, by June, France. The surrender of Denmark directly threatened Greenland, Mrs. Smith said, and the capture of Greenland would place the Nazis a mere fifteen hundred miles from Maine. The "destruction of Maine," she warned, "would be the first objective of any attack" by the Nazis.[13] It was imperative that Americans, and particularly Mainers, prepare for war.

This sense of Maine's vulnerability, along with the fear that their proximity to danger was getting insufficient attention in Washington, animated the campaign. Rhetoric and editorials lamented that American indifference was leaving "peaceful Maine" defenseless as the "tides of European war washed in higher waves against American shores day by day."[14] Writers generally expressed approval of Mrs. Smith's assessment of the crisis and, more to the point, her ability to do something about it. One remarked: "It may be a long time until the war board gets around to Maine unless someone active and aggressive like Mrs. Smith is there to stir them up a bit."[15]

She did not disappoint them. Although Margaret Smith was officially seated in Congress only a week before the primary for the regular election, she immediately took advantage of her status as congresswoman-elect to announce her efforts to obtain new military bases for Maine, reporting she was fairly certain of obtaining an Army Air Corps training base and an auxiliary Naval base for her district, and was continuing efforts for a permanent Naval Air base on the Maine coast.[16]

From the start, she made a point of being on the job during the week. Smith told the electorate that, while she would like to be home campaigning, her first duty to them was in Washington.[17] But when she did come home, her weekends in Maine were a "political Blitzkrieg." Arriving on a midnight flight from the capital, she raced through a carefully choreographed itinerary. For example, her trip through Waldo County in August began at 4:00 a.m. with a bracing dip in the Penobscot River with a group of Young Republicans and ended nineteen hours later, after visiting all thirty voting precincts, making thirty-five speeches, attending a dozen meetings, and shaking countless hands during factory tours.[18] Her tirelessness did not escape notice. Patten, acting as her secretary, saw to it that her itineraries were published well in advance and in every district newspaper. Political columnists, particularly the women among them, wrote of her diligence and poise, her stamina and "quiet sincerity," and touted her candidacy as an important step for all women.[19]

Her opponents, apparently preempted on the defense issue and still reluctant to openly criticize Smith's widow, appeared baffled by the challenge of a woman competitor without a record they could assail.[20] One flanking maneuver ironically backfired. Rumors accusing her of trying to hide her French-Canadian ancestry indicated that her maiden name, Chase, was an Americanized version of the French Chasse. Smith produced her DAR paternal genealogy proving her Anglo-Saxon heritage, while neglecting to mention her maternal ties to Quebec.[21] Failing that, her challengers concentrated almost exclusively on her sex status which, unlike her ancestry, was impossible to deny.

As the election neared, the dominant question increasingly became "Is Maine ready for a woman in Congress [while] Europe totters and domestic affairs are in turmoil?" "Amazing as it may seem in these stirring times," columnist Dorris Westall pointed out, "it is a question of sex, not of ability, that the voters will decide June 17."[22] Despite Smith's resolute commitment to a firm national defense policy, her opposition, including a sizable contingent of women, persisted in contending that Congress was a man's job.[23] Her primary opponent, John G. Marshall, led the chorus, emphatically asserting that with a war coming on, the voters "want a militant Representative in Congress. A flick of the wrist and a smile won't do it."[24] Smith's supporters responded that their candidate was not likely to wilt in a crisis: "The comely but firm-jawed lady from Skowhegan . . . will boldly champion and espouse the rights of her people with absolute courage and fearlessness." Moreover, she was "better equipped in the mechanics of the job" than her opponent, having already learned her way around Washington.[25]

Though some women opposed her nontraditional endeavor and considered her overreaching her bounds, many others did not. Organized women's groups, notably the Maine BPW and DAR, although avowedly nonpartisan and nonpolitical, saw Smith as one of their own and volunteered, as individuals, to aid her campaigns.[26] They were joined by a group of activist Republican women Smith knew from the state committee who in concert with Republican male supporters formed the "Kennebec County Mrs. Smith Goes to Washington Club" to circulate nomination petitions, distribute campaign literature, register voters, and drive them to the polls.[27] Smith was as ambivalent about having women leading her campaign as she was about appealing directly to women and thereby emphasizing her sex even more. Her official announcement hesitantly used a double negative to justify her right to seek office. Since the "women of Maine and of the nation . . . have availed themselves of the privilege and have met the responsibilities of citizenship," she said, "It may not seem inappropriate that they should have an effective part in determining the policies of our government."[28] In midcampaign, she altered her campaign cards in an apparent effort to minimize her liabilities. The original carried a photograph of her looking grave and determined, with the message: "Vote for the One Who Will Vote for You! A Woman of Experience, Ability and Sound Judgement!" The new version had a more flattering photograph that minimized the grayness of her hair and eliminated the words "A Woman of."[29] Unable to counter accusations based upon her presumably inherent nature, Smith chose instead to emphasize her long association and considerable experience in the halls of government: "And now, my friends, I ask you if my desire to follow the policies of my husband who served you many years, my experience as his associate, and understanding of the needs of you citizens of the Second Congressional District are not more important in these critical times, than a man who must take months to become established."[30]

She won. Whether from sympathy, acknowledgment of her competence, or simply because she seemed the most likely to respond to the threat of war, Smith swept the Republican primary with 27,037 votes (her four opponents shared 15,319 between them), then triumphed over Democrat Edward Beauchamp in September.[31]

Returning to Washington eager to continue her husband's work, Smith requested appointment to his old slot on the House Labor Committee. Committees are the core of the legislative process, where the work gets done and reputations made. Smith, like all new members, wanted an assignment commensurate with her interests and those of her district. But with never enough choice seats to go around, newcomers must usually settle for minor committees. For the last few months of the Seventy-sixth Congress, her husband's unexpired term, she had been assigned to Elections, Invalid Pensions, War Claims, and Revision of Laws. None of these committees met during this period.[32] When the new Congress convened in early 1941, Smith thought she had a good chance, because of her nine months' seniority, to be named to at least one major committee.[33] Labor was again her first choice, Military Affairs her second.

The work of the two committees would be closely associated in the coming months, she told readers in her first weekly column "Washington and You," because labor was "integral to national defense, and therefore a place on Military Affairs would give me an opportunity of [sic] watching labor and national defense both."[34]

Obtaining a "good" committee assignment depended upon a complex and often extremely subtle mix of considerations, involving the influence of party leadership, committee chairs and minority leaders, seniority, precedent, district composition, party loyalty and, often, personality factors.[35] Smith had the support and encouragement of Labor Committee chair Mary T. Norton and ranking minority member Richard Welch.[36] She also had a powerful adversary on the committee. Michigan conservative Clare E. Hoffman adamantly opposed "another Smith" as well as "another woman" on the Labor Committee.[37]

Hoffman had resented Clyde Smith's rejection of "Republican principles" in favor of support for New Deal labor legislation. Moreover, he could never forgive Smith for deliberately misusing his proxy to save the National Labor Relations Board. In addition to writing his own amendment to abolish the Board, Hoffman had taken the floor no fewer than twenty-one times in the previous eleven weeks to denounce "this wrecker of businesses; this creator of unemployment; this conspiring, arrogant National Labor Relations Board."[38] Smith could hardly have misunderstood Hoffman's position. Yet, when called upon to vote whether to dismantle the Board or to add two members to it, Smith cast his vote, and Hoffman's proxy, for the increase. The result was a nine-to-eight vote saving the Board from extinction.[39] Smith died two weeks later.

Quite apart from his anger at Smith, Hoffman's rhetoric indicates he would have opposed Mrs. Smith's assignment to the Labor Committee based on her sex alone. He made no attempt to hide his aversion to women in public positions, frequently highlighting the connections between despised liberal policies and women's part in them. Primary targets of his attacks were Committee Chair Mary Norton and Secretary of Labor Frances Perkins.[40] Hoffman was also critical of the female reviewing attorneys for the National Labor Relations Board. They were, he said, "intelligent appearing . . . but the chances are 99 out of 100 that none of them ever changed a diaper, hung out a washing, or baked a loaf of bread." He did not state how those experiences might better have qualified these women to review labor board cases.[41]

When Mrs. Smith discussed her chances of being appointed to Labor with Maine senior Senator Fred Hale, he reminded her of Labor's thankless duties, suggesting she "work hard for it, and hope to heaven you don't get it."[42] She didn't. Smith was assigned to Education, Invalid Pensions, and Post Offices and Roads.

Debates about the nation's defense dominated the Seventy-seventh Congress. While many political leaders were concerned that the war in Europe not take precedence over domestic problems, others cautioned that American neutrality was likely to be an impossible goal. President Roosevelt tried to satisfy both camps by pursuing an isolationist policy while building up American military forces. Interventionists charged him with failing to provide leadership; isolationists accused him of cynical duplicity.[43] Clare Luce epitomized FDR's vacillation with the comment that all great men have a characteristic gesture: for Hitler, the upraised arm; for Churchill, the V-sign; and for Roosevelt, a wet finger raised to the wind.[44]

During the summer and fall of 1940, German bombs pounded London and the United States moved closer to involvement. In September, FDR circumvented neutrality legislation with an executive order trading fifty World War I destroyers to Great Britain for rights to build bases on British possessions. In October, a bipartisan majority approved a large increase in defense spending and established the first peacetime draft in American history. Not surprisingly, Congresswoman Smith supported both measures.[45]

This appearance of unity did not hold. Another draft law came up in August 1941, after the Roosevelt administration asked for changes to broaden and extend the Selective Service Act from one year to the duration of the national emergency and remove the 900,000 ceiling. Clashes in both Houses between isolationists and interventionists over the implications of expanding the standing army tended to split along party lines. Dissent in the Senate was led by Robert A. Taft (R-OH), who strenuously objected to indefinite extensions and eventually forced a compromise of eighteen months. The Senate passed H. J. Res. 222 by 37 to 19; the House by an incredibly close 203 to 202. Smith voted in the affirmative.[46]

Roosevelt believed the survival of Britain was key to American security. Mrs. Smith agreed, saying that aid to Britain was in America's own interest: the longer the British held out, the more time the United States would have to prepare for war.[47] Supplying arms to the British would not, the president maintained, bring the nation closer to war. He used the analogy of a garden hose loaned to a neighbor to put out a fire and getting it back when it was no longer needed. On the Senate floor, Taft used an antithetic analogy to convey his opposition: "lending arms is like lending chewing gum," he said. "You don't want it back."[48] Senator

Burton Wheeler (R-MT) bitterly likened lend-lease to the agricultural programs of the Depression. "The New Deal's triple-A foreign policy," he said, "will plow up every fourth American boy." The final vote ratified lend-lease by a wide margin. Both sides knew that it removed the last traces of American neutrality. [49]

Smith's unwavering support for FDR's foreign policy put her at odds with her own party a good deal of the time. Her party unity score—that is, the percentage of votes she cast with the Republicans—hovered around 50 percent.[50] "It has not been easy to make decisions on defense measures," Smith admitted to the press. But "by sticking to my principle of voting for everything which promises to better prepare us against attack, and for keeping us out of war by making us strong, I have been able to make up my mind in each case."[51] Smith's "courage" and independence found favor at home. The most powerful voice of Maine, the Republican Gannett press, repeatedly disparaged the isolationist proclivities of First District "Unrepresentative" James Oliver and the Third District's Frank Fellows, who, it charged, were blinded by partisan distrust. Only Smith recognized that Maine was "not the home of pacifism and isolationism."[52] After she became the only Maine representative to cast a vote in favor of repeal of the Neutrality Act in November, the *Portland Press Herald* observed, "The State has long since come to recognize in Mrs. Smith a clear-thinking, straightforward and completely honest Representative who is not to be diverted from what she believes to be patriotic service by any red herrings that may be drawn across the trail. Mrs. Smith, as good a Republican as any, was the only one to slice through to the core of the situation and to vote what Maine believes."[53]

Of course, the most persuasive indication of Maine's approval was Smith's success at the polls. As the 1942 election approached, commentators saw no hope for a rival of her own party and little enthusiasm from the Democrats for mounting a challenge to one so "solidly entrenched in the affections" of the voters. Moreover, that "the old cry 'I think it should be a man' has been virtually eliminated."[54] Smith ran unopposed in the primary and with minimal resistance from Democrats. In 1944 and again in 1946, Republicans declined to challenge Smith and Democrats lost to her every time by over 60 percent of the vote.[55] It is difficult to define precisely why Smith was so popular at home. She understood her appeal as graduational and earned. "I attribute my first election to sympathy. But in 1940, when President Roosevelt carried my district by 10,000 votes, I was reelected by 27,000. I say that victory was based on friendship. In 1942, I received 68 percent of the vote cast, and I claim that result was based on my record."[56] Second District Mainers took to her, at least at first, because they knew her and because her apprenticeship with Clyde Smith gave her considerable legitimacy. The novelty of a female leader also fascinated them. Her every move was interesting, giving her a unique access to media coverage and instant recognition, valuable tools for a politician. Her sex tended to place her, in public perception, outside, and frequently above, politics as usual. Women, as a group, have long been considered more moral and less competitive and self-interested than men.[57] The notion of Smith's "naturally" higher ethical standards and greater honesty were a distinct advantage. Moreover, this was enhanced by her avoidance of a strict adherence to party dogma because of the high value her constituents placed upon individualism and self-reliance. Mainers tended to choose their representatives for their *independence* from party allegiance.[58]

The qualities and personal characteristics that turn up repeatedly in local, state and national writings about Smith include plainspokenness, frankness, sincerity, independence, honesty, integrity, steadfastness, courage. From the beginning, she made conscience and firm resolve her hallmark. While the press took considerable pains to note Mrs. Smith's youth, petite stature, and "attractiveness," they also praised her ability to balance between genders, to discharge her duties "with the same businesslike manner as a man" while preserving "a womanly dignity, and without a single suggestion of any smattering of masculinity."[59] She was also celebrated for her frugality, for always spending significantly less than her opponents and accepting no campaign contributions because they might appear to compromise her integrity. Smith, then, held enormous appeal for her Yankee constituency because she seemed to share their values in ways her critics and rivals did not.

Her independence was underwritten by the quality of her relationship with her constituency at home. She set two basic goals for herself—to stay on the job in Washington and to keep close to the people in her district. In essence, she never stopped campaigning. Smith flew or drove home from Washington nearly every weekend when Congress was in session. The Second District of Maine was the largest east of the Mississippi, cutting across the center of the state from the Canadian border to the Atlantic Ocean, and Smith made a point to reach every precinct at least once a month. The traveling was often difficult, especially during the February recess, when she had to negotiate the treacherous frozen back roads of the northern counties. During the war, her perseverance in the face of gasoline and rubber shortages won her plaudits for "all but hitch-hiking" between gatherings.[60]

Besides scheduling numerous speeches, meetings, luncheons and dinners, she did just as Clyde had done: "I'd go into the little towns; I'd go into the schools; I'd go into church groups; I'd stop at stores. I went around shaking hands with everybody."[61] She "set up shop" in selectmen's offices, grange halls, post offices, and church basements, inviting everyone, regardless of party, to bring their troubles to her. Notices would appear in local papers a week or so prior to her arrival. A typical notice read: "Mrs. Margaret Chase Smith, congresswoman from Maine's Second District, is in this city to interview residents of the district who have matters on which they seek her advice." She did not know all the answers, she acknowledged, but "I am in a position to contact people and agencies who do, and I am always glad to do what I can."[62] Her secretary worked nearly full time responding to voters' concerns and running interference with the federal bureaucracy on their behalf. "Her office is a service agency for her constituents," said a Maine politician. "They know that if a pension check doesn't come through they can get in touch with her and she'll do something about it."[63] When a politician helps someone in a small town, everyone knows about it. "Have you ever asked her to investigate some local problem for you?" a Maine weekly asked. "No matter what question may be referred to her, an answer, specific and immediate comes back. And that isn't all. With all the duties of her busy life she has time to do the kind and thoughtful thing."[64] Another editorial noted, "In Mrs. Smith's case, it has been demonstrated beyond any doubt that a woman can be just [as] energetic and effective as the male of the species. . . . [A]ny request made to Mrs. Smith meets with prompt response and have been marked by successful results."[65] She answered every letter on the day it arrived. She remembered constituents' names and personal details about their lives.[66] In short, she seemed to care about them.

Smith also kept in touch with the home folks with a weekly column in local newspapers, a practice begun by her husband, though written by Roland Patten. When she began her own column, she insisted on writing it herself, so it would "sound like Margaret Smith."[67] "Washington and You" was a newsy letter home, dealing with the issues of the day and educating her readers about how government worked as she was learning herself. She chatted about the weather and how much she missed Maine, informed citizens how they could take advantage of federal programs, noted the names of visitors to Washington, and invited everyone to come see her.[68] In addition to her own writings, news of Smith's activities in Washington appeared almost daily in Maine newspapers. Gannett's Washington correspondent, May Craig, often functioned as Margaret's press agent. The two had been friends since Mrs. Smith first came to Washington with her husband. After Clyde died, Craig frequently visited Smith in Skowhegan; they accompanied one another on speaking tours of Maine, and celebrated major events and holidays together. Charmed by her friend's political success, Craig treated her readers to regular missives about Smith's activities and frequently trumpeted the respect she was earning in Congress.

The public perception of Smith's concern for the people of her district built for her a record of confidence and trust that could be cashed in at election time. At the same time, belief in her basic integrity afforded her a greater leeway in positions taken on controversial issues. Smith understood and shared her people's needs and desires. These did not, though, always fit into precise ideological categories. Like them, Smith seldom saw important matters of policy as party issues. She cared about security and defense, but also about labor problems and old age pensions, child welfare and education. Numerous speeches during this period argue for eliminating the national debt while in the same breath asserting the necessity for "adequate preparedness" and the continuation, even initiation, of additional relief programs for the unemployed and aged. Consistency is not a requisite for political office; indeed, the opposite is more often the case. In legislation and speeches, she gave voice to the often contradictory claims citizens demand of government—perfect security and benevolent support, guns and butter.[69]

Smith's high election tallies gave her legitimacy in Congress. Party leaders and other members respect those who consistently win big. They are "the favored ones who are escalated inexorably up the ladder of seniority. Those who must work the hardest to survive the political hurdles back home are least likely to surmount the barriers on the way to acquisition of power in Congress."[70] Election pluralities are taken into consideration for important committee assignments, privileges, and favor.[71] Smith also considered them a kind of shield against harassment. Large majorities, MCS said, "give you power. They won't mess with you. They know you will be there awhile."[72]

She had few illusions going in. Just after taking office, she endorsed James G. Blaine's description of congressional service: "There is no test of a man's ability in any department of public life more severe than service in the House of Representatives . . . no place where so little consideration is shown for feelings or failures of beginners. . . . What a man gains in the House he gains by sheer force of his own character, and if he loses and falls back, he must expect no mercy."[73]

Governed by lengthy and detailed rules and procedures, this institution also bound its members to a firmly established, although ostensibly informal, system of norms and traditions. Custom required the newcomer to serve a proper apprenticeship during which he was expected to work hard, develop an area of specialization, learn his way, and keep his mouth shut. The pressure for conformity even extended to dress and mannerisms. He was "advised not to draw attention to himself by unusual dress or attitude—only senior members can successfully defy convention."[74] The junior member extended tolerance and courtesy toward other members and deference to his congressional elders. The late Speaker of the House, Sam Rayburn, gave the same advice to each freshman class: "to get along, go along." While members valued dependability, intelligence, integrity, and dedication to the institution, the critical interpersonal norm was reciprocity, the willingness to trade votes and favors. Developing friendships and alliances with other members, then, was vital to accomplishing legislative business. Personal familiarity was enhanced in informal settings like the Democratic Study Group or the Republicans' Chowder and Marching Society where members socialized, exchanged ideas, and shared information. One of the most influential associations was the least formal, the House "gym group." Partly because it crossed party lines, and partly because of its extreme informality, the gym was the ideal forum for getting acquainted, developing rapport, refining cooperation, and demonstrating leadership ability.[75]

Clearly the gym was no place for a woman. A woman, by virtue of her sex, regardless of her personal qualities and abilities, could not conform to the male standard nor fit into the male domain. In informal gatherings, a woman's presence simply increased the discomfort level. In the absence of guiding standards for interaction in the legislature, men and women responded to one another in culturally determined but institutionally inappropriate ways.

Artful compliments to a "gentlewoman's" beauty, charm, and warmth are scattered throughout the *Congressional Record* of the Seventy-seventh Congress and beyond. Perhaps such gestures were simply intended to indicate respect for the ladies, a guileless exaggeration of the long-standing deferential tradition of congressional courtesy. Occasionally, though, the excruciating gallantry barely disguised hostility and condescension. One telling example, from Rep. Charles Gifford (R-MA): "The lady members we have today are extremely satisfactory to us. But they, like all women, can talk to us with their eyes and their lips, and when they present to us an apple it is most difficult to refuse. . . . These ladies are so attractive. They are dangerous in that they may influence us too much. Suppose we had fifty of them. Seemingly I note flirtations enough now, but what would there be with fifty of them?"[76] Gifford's remarks reveal prevailing assumptions about women and power: women are flirtatious, tantalizing, manipulative, and therefore, treacherous. Strength, force, authority over others—the requisites of power—were, and continue to be, considered unsuitable for females. If women were assumed to be self-deprecating and nonassertive, then exercising power without appearing to do so required manipulation with girlish charm, hiding strength behind mock helplessness. Unfortunately, the feminine ideal of appearing without power was as inappropriate for public office as its opposite.

Congresswomen generally accepted chivalrous attentions as honorable, or at least decided that retorts would be self-defeating.[77] Smith, a newcomer intimidated by the education and status of her colleagues, enjoyed the feminine perks and found the deference and gallantry flattering and fun. She became frustrated, though, when it was not accompanied by professional respect.[78] Upon entering her first meeting of the Committee on Education, Smith, embarrassed but pleased when every man stood up, blushed and said she hoped they would just forget that she was a woman and regard her as any other member.[79] It was not likely. Whatever the motivations for this treatment, the effect was the same—reinforcing difference and placing women outside the arenas of power. A woman's range of responses to this male culture was necessarily limited: she could choose to act like one of the boys and risk ridicule and rejection, or she could choose to ignore the isolation and try to work as though it did not exist. Smith chose the latter. "I had a way of hearing the things I wanted to hear," MCS said, "I ignored any discrimination. I never, never acknowledged it. Never."[80]

Like all members, Smith's power depended to a large extent upon being taken seriously by her colleagues. Political leaders who desired to limit women's participation and advancement often attempted to impose a sexual division of political labor, channeling women into fields considered to be of interest to women such as health, child care, and education. If women's place was in the home, then women's interests were assumed to be home issues. Some women agreed, whether or not they recognized an effort to keep them in their place.[81] Smith spent a brief period on the Education Committee, but when an opportunity for advancement came, she chose for herself a "hard" issue, one with strength—military defense—which, by its very nature, allowed her to create an image of forceful leadership. Her chosen area of expertise, adopted in the fortuitous circumstance of wartime, subsequently shaped her congressional career.

There were just eight women in the Seventy-seventh Congress—seven representatives and one senator. Senator Hattie Caraway (D-AR) was the first and only woman senator elected by popular vote. Of the seven in the House, two were Democrats: Mary Norton (NJ) and Caroline O'Day (NY), and five were Republicans: Edith Nourse Rogers (MA), Frances Bolton (OH), Jessie Sumner (IL), and Jeannette Rankin (MT). Given the importance of collegial networks in the functioning of Congress, and the likelihood that they were isolated from those formed among the men, it would seem probable that the women would associate with one another for their mutual benefit. Nonetheless, they did not. Individual friendships, such as that between Margaret Smith and Frances Bolton, blossomed and endured, but political alliances as women were anathema.[82] The very idea of a woman's bloc in Congress brought a sharp response from Mary Norton, who emphatically stated that she sincerely hoped that day would never come. "Nothing would indicate our weakness more."[83] Smith, too, believed women should always "avoid any tendency to . . . stand as one sex against another."[84] Female members, moreover, frequently denied that any common cause existed. Their interests and their constituencies were as varied and unique as those of male members of Congress, they asserted. "We women represent all the people in our district just as the men do."[85]

While the women in the House were indeed as varied as the men, they did tend to respond to their situation in similar ways. Constantly drawn into the debate on women's issues, their rejoinder was to define them broadly: no political or social issue existed that was not a legitimate concern of women. Moreover, congresswomen argued, their sex was irrelevant to their occupations as lawmakers. Yet, Norton's widely repeated remark, "I'm no lady. I'm a member of Congress," often taken to indicate the women's resistance to gender pigeonholing, at the same time seemed to acknowledge that the two roles were incompatible.[86]

The difficulty was in conveying a sort of gender neutrality. Most women then in public life, including Margaret Smith, repeatedly referred to themselves as human beings, not just women. It seemed axiomatic to them that "women are people" so "women deserve equal rights."[87] These assertions, though, were quickly followed by a denial of feminism. A slippery and loaded term, feminism had long been associated with radical suffragist women whose militant actions smacked of sex antagonism.[88] The movement's anger and single-minded zeal seemed selfish and unreasonable to women who believed in the virtues and rewards of individual achievement. "I definitely resent being called a feminist," Smith affirmed. "A woman's viewpoint should be objective and free of any emphasis on feminine interests."[89]

Congresswomen knew well the risks of professional and political derision from their peers for offering aid and comfort to other women. No politician, Smith believed, could afford to align herself with one-half of her constituency when the powerful half was threatened by that allegiance.[90] Yet, at the same time, these congresswomen clearly had a gender consciousness, an understanding of the prejudices against women. All of them worked on at least some major legislation designed to remove discrimination or advance opportunities for women, frequently crossing party lines to do so. Since the first congresswoman, Jeanette Rankin, introduced a maternal and infant welfare bill in 1918, women were instrumental in passing legislation men disregarded. Norton and Bolton, for example, worked to elevate the status of nurses; Smith and Rogers turned their efforts toward aiding women in the military; and all of them worked together on postwar measures for equal pay and child care. This work, however, was largely confined to the war years, a propitious historical moment for women in the public arena.

Despite their denials of allegiance, congresswomen were inevitably lumped together in the popular press where the public perception of them was shaped by powerful imagery of women in the home. Their views on national issues were infrequently solicited while an extraordinary amount of space was devoted to descriptions of dress and physical attractiveness, womanly attributes, and assurances of domesticity. Photographs frequently showed congresswomen in stereotypical female occupations—cooking, ironing, typing, talking on the telephone.[91] However political women felt about themselves, what seemed important to the journalists, and their readers, was whether or not women in the public sphere were authentic women, that is, that they conformed to cultural images of women as mother, sister, wife, or widow. Less flattering conceptions of women also flourished in 1940s coverage of the "petticoat contingent," one that seemed to be, in the telling, completely absorbed by fashion competitions and smoldering cat fights.[92] Though writers attested that "most of the petticoat tribe ask only to be treated like men," they assured this would seldom occur.[93] The congresswomen found it all a bit wearing and, when given the chance, protested that they had more important things to say. Likely as not, such complaints were buried in stories that continued to patronize them.

Perfectly conveying the ambivalence of congresswomen's gendered roles and their public images, Bolton dropped a note to gossip columnist George E. Sokolsky to tell him about the new girl in town, Margaret Chase Smith. "A hard worker and a fine investigator, she gives evidence of judgment and sincerity, of tolerance and understanding. . . . In addition to this she is charming and attractive and the men buzz around her like bees."[94]

5 | Naval Affairs

Buoyed by Maine's vote of confidence in 1942, Smith began the Seventy-eighth Congress with a request for one of the most powerful committees in wartime, the House Committee on Naval Affairs. While positions on Naval Affairs Committees (NAC) in both Houses were something of a Maine tradition, her freshman status was a considerable liability.[1] She was, however, able to demonstrate a long-time commitment to a strong navy (owing to her 1938 Navy Day speech), a stance appreciated by NAC Chairman Carl Vinson.[2] "Admiral" Vinson, who once declined the post of Secretary of Defense under Truman because he preferred to "run the Pentagon from here," was both feared and admired as an autocratic curmudgeon who would tolerate no dissension on his committee. Everyone knew he "owned the Navy. . . . [A]nyone smart enough to take on Vinson [was] too smart to do so."[3] Vinson told the press he considered Smith "one of the outstanding members of the House [and] her attitude on national defense and foreign policy have been right."[4] Given her reputation as friendly, cooperative, and "universally approved" by her colleagues in the House, Vinson probably considered her temperamentally, as well as philosophically, compatible with the group.[5] Ultimately, though, it was House Minority Leader Joseph Martin's (R-MA) political calculations that prompted him to name Smith to the NAC at the same time that he appointed Clare Luce to Military Affairs. Mindful of the publicity value of women members on the service committees, as well as the partisan capital to be gained in recognizing and symbolically "rewarding" all American women, Martin admitted to the press that "in singling out the women members for these assignments, the committee was guided by a realization that the women of the country take an important part in the war effort."[6]

World War II defined Smith's House career. While scholars disagree about the liberating effects of wartime for women, she definitely benefitted from an environment that heightened the importance of women in the public sphere.[7] As she worked on a variety of military and home-front issues, she represented her sex in the media, the committee room, and on the House floor, articulating the contradictions between women's new roles and aspirations and traditional attitudes about women's place. These same circumstances also enhanced Smith's ability to surmount contradictions of her own—the need to remain ladylike while demonstrating she was tough enough to handle the hard issues. Development of expertise in military affairs and consistent advocacy of a strong national defense policy affirmed that reputation. Through her experiences on the NAC during the war she established her specialty, learned the finer points of political efficacy, and met the single most important person in her life.

Within days of her appointment to Naval Affairs, Smith was named to a seven "man" subcommittee to investigate vice (a euphemism for prostitution) and a rising venereal disease rate in areas surrounding naval ports. Vice was apparently flourishing. Since the war began, the popular press released a host of incendiary articles chronicling such startling "facts" as "a diseased prostitute, receiving upwards of three dozen men in a night, could do far more damage than a 500-pound bomb dropped squarely in the middle of an Army Camp."[8] Smith, along with many other congressmen and public officials, fielded a flurry of concerned letters urging government action.[9] The Roosevelt administration responded with a host of new boards and committees under an umbrella agency headed by the crime-fighter Eliot Ness.[10] In July 1941, Congress passed legislation making vice activities near military installations a federal offense.[11] None of these efforts, though, seemed to make much headway against the problem. While armed with the power to police areas designated hazardous to the troops, the military seemed extremely reluctant to use it.[12] After months of inaction, Surgeon General Thomas Parren published a stinging attack on the military's perfunctory anti-VD policy. Calling venereal disease the "No. 1 saboteur of our defense," Parren's book contained lurid descriptions of "our country's newly organized panzer prostitutes."[13] The press gleefully reprinted portions of the Parren polemic, and public moral outrage forced an angry President Roosevelt to demand a full report from the Army and Navy. Subsequently, Secretary of the Navy Frank Knox met in closed session with the House Committee for Naval Affairs, and following the meeting, Vinson dispatched the seven-member subcommittee, including Smith, to Virginia.[14]

While vice and its impact on the progress of the war was the impetus, a whole constellation of desperate conditions in congested port cities soon prompted the subcommittee to broaden its focus. Over the next eight months, the group toured military installations, schools, neighborhoods, war industries, hospitals, and jails. Hundreds of witnesses came to complain, to explain, to justify, and to plead for help, poignantly revealing the scope and complexity of the problems. The Congested Areas Subcommittee had a front row seat on wartime America in its most extreme circumstances.[15]

In port cities, the streets were teeming with people, night and day, in a ceaseless pageant of arrivals and departures. Thousands of men in uniform jostled in the streets with coveralled war workers, male and female, rushing to catch overcrowded buses to get to jobs and home again. Streets leading from the harbor to downtown were lined with honky-tonks, juke joints, bawdy houses, and tattoo parlors, all vying for attention with bright neon signs and loud music. Long lines snaked down the sidewalks and into the streets—lines to get into restaurants, into movies, into taverns, into grocery stores. Men in uniform and in grimy work clothes slept in the streets, in their cars, in hotel lobbies, on park benches. Life in boomtown was, in short, "life on a more primitive level."[16]

As the hearings opened in Norfolk, Virginia, a parade of military and local health officials debated venereal disease rates and described their efforts to control prostitution. From testimony, it appeared that the net effect of closing these red-light districts had not been the elimination of prostitution, but its dispersal. No longer under the control and scrutiny of police and doctors, it had moved out of their reach into the jurisdiction of the county sheriff and a few scattered deputies. Taxi drivers acted as procurers, ferrying soldiers and sailors to the honky-tonk "hot spots" that had sprung up just outside the city limits.[17] Moreover, disturbing testimony made it plain that the prostitute's place as a major source of contagion was rapidly being taken by transient young girls, sometimes only thirteen to fifteen years old, who were assumed to be unable to resist a uniform.[18] A third group of women straddled the line between professional and amateur. These were chiefly waitresses in restaurants and beer parlors supplementing their meager wages.[19]

Legal definitions of prostitutes were intentionally vague to allow police to assume extensive discretionary authority, based on the underlying assumption that all women were potentially contagious. "Promiscuous," or simply unescorted, women were picked up, compelled to undergo degrading medical examinations for venereal disease and, if found infected, forcibly detained for as long as six months.[20] Ignoring obvious violations of constitutional rights, authorities believed repression and detention had proven to be "a practical and thoroughly effective police procedure for the control of venereal disease."[21]

Sitting at the end of the long table next to subcommittee counsel LTJG William C. Lewis, Jr., surrounded by a roomful of men, Smith felt distinctly uncomfortable with the topic of discussion and faint hearted about participating. In a perfect metaphor for their later relationship, Lewis wrote a question for her to ask on a slip of paper and passed it to her.[22] Realizing that if she did not use it, he would provide no more, Smith spoke up. He continued to supply questions and she became an active participant in the hearings, especially with respect to matters concerning women.

Smith tried her best to fit in, both in meeting rooms and out. As the only woman on the trip, she worried about the proper clothes to wear and the correct protocol.[23] She insisted on being the last to deplane because of her junior position on the subcommittee, despite the efforts of Chairman Ed Izac (D-CA) to place her first, and she always sat at the end of the table, according to seniority, next to Lewis.[24] Knowing that "the men on the committee didn't want a woman around all the time," MCS remarked, Lewis would frequently take her for a walk after dinner to remove her from their company. After a time, she enlisted Lewis's aid in gaining access to forbidden places. Disguising herself, she got him to take her to see a "hot spot." The other subcommittee members got wind of her plan, though, and caught up with her, turning it into "an official visit," not at all what she had in mind. She was disappointed anyway to find out it was "only a bar."[25]

Dismayed by reports of hundreds of women being rounded up and thrown into overcrowded facilities, Smith did manage to slip off alone, between sessions, to visit the Norfolk jail. There she found ninety-one women and girls were being held in space meant for twenty-five. Scattered mattresses lay about the floor, topped with filthy blankets. There was one lavatory and one table. Forced to wait weeks, even months, before being sentenced or diverted to their home authorities, the women, Smith told the press (who dubbed her the "vice admiral") "had absolutely nothing to do, not even a place to sit down."[26] Most of the younger girls had been arrested, she found, for being alone on the street, trying to find a brother or a boyfriend in the hustle-bustle of boomtown. Port towns were replete with large numbers of men in uniform; liberty parties averaged 70,000 to 80,000 in Norfolk. Married women told her of finding themselves stranded when their husbands were moved to another area, of being bored and lonely. They went out unescorted and were promptly arrested.[27]

Vice raids fell most heavily upon lower- and working-class women. Smith told the press and city officials that a girl in Norfolk could not survive waiting tables or working in beer parlors at starvation wages of only $10 or $12 a week (women working in war industry typically made three to four times that amount). Young women without skills, Smith asserted, often found prostitution an economic necessity.[28]

Throughout the hearings, Smith vigorously objected to the unsanitary and neglected condition of the female inmates, the wrongful detention of innocent girls, and the absence of programs for training and rehabilitation. While she favored detaining the women until they were well, she found it unforgivable that no one was making an effort to see that they were trained to make "a better kind of living." When Smith asked the Newport News city manager if anything was being done to "help girls coming in, without jobs or with jobs that don't pay enough, to contact them before they get into the hands of the police," he replied lamely that some social agencies tried to help, but usually the girls were picked up, then those not infected were turned back to their home authorities. "I can't think of anything less effective," Smith said sharply, "than sending them home at random."[29]

Discussions of vice were soon overwhelmed by an array of social disruptions brought about by the rapid expansion of war industry and military activities in the port cities.[30] Towns had been transformed from largely residential communities into overcrowded industrial centers almost overnight. Few municipalities registered population increases of less than 100 percent since the war began, and several on the west coast had exploded into boomtowns five and six times their normal size within two years.[31] In these areas, as many as fourteen people occupied a single room, sharing one toilet with twenty other families. Federal temporary housing projects, in those areas lucky enough to have them, contained no streets and no sewers, just flammable wooden shacks in a sea of mud.[32] Food shortages of monumental proportions resulted from rationing programs based upon prewar population figures. Grocery shelves cleared within an hour of opening in Virginia, and two hundred restaurants in San Francisco closed in 1943 after their food allowances were cut in half.[33] Manpower shortages left municipalities without adequate fire and police protection, transportation services, or garbage collection. Raw sewage flowed directly into beach areas, foreclosing recreation and polluting seafood sources. Communities threatened with epidemics of typhus, bubonic plague, and malaria reported critical shortages of doctors and hospital beds.[34]

Moreover, the perceived need for another full complement of city and military services for the "negro" population placed additional burdens on these communities. Race relations, always volatile, grew increasingly tense in the separate but unequal atmosphere of the cities. "Colored" housing was notably inferior to the worst whites had to bear and often built beyond the reach of public transportation.[35] Black soldiers had no access to USO or the other meager entertainments; black war workers, male and female, were assigned to the most menial chores and assumed to be infiltrated by "bad elements" who made trouble and were on the verge of being wildly out of control, having too much money to spend on liquor and drugs.[36]

The constellation of congested area problems was manifested in individual lives. The average male recruited to work in war industry would arrive to find no housing. He lived out of his car, or shared a "hot bed"—rotating an eight-hour sleep shift—in a stifling dormitory.[37] Since his ten-hour war job often took two or three hours to reach, he left too early to get breakfast at one of the very few restaurants that had enough food to open.[38] Come lunchtime, he could hope for a meager meal at work—the cafeteria at the Bethlehem Shipyards, for example, was issued exactly one-tenth of an ounce of meat per meal per man.[39] It was nearly impossible to get food after work because restaurants were constantly running out, and most food stores closed before workers could reach them.[40] The war worker was tired and he was hungry.

Women working in war industry had the same problems as the men, plus another full set. Working mothers were further burdened by stores that closed early, meal preparation complicated by rationing and shortages, inadequate child care arrangements, insufficient medical services, long lines, and shoddy merchandise. The subcommittee found the average woman worked thirteen days on, one day off, then worked six days on, one day off, followed by another thirteen days. Most had full responsibility for the marketing, the care of their homes, their husbands and children. They got their work done at the expense of their sleep and health.[41]

The impact of these problems was, while predictable, profound—absenteeism, often nearly 20 percent of the workforce, and labor turnover rates approaching 100 percent in most West Coast ports. Women's absentee rates were 50 percent greater and their turnover rate was more than double that of men.[42] Uncovering the reasons behind those figures was a major goal for Smith. A steady stream of war industry representatives complained that women were unreliable, often took a day off without warning, and frequently and capriciously quit their jobs.[43] What, Smith asked them, was being done to help women handle their dual responsibilities? Was part-time work available, and what about programs for child care? Part-time work was simply too complicated to offer, replied an employment manager in a typical response, and as for child care, "We have felt that should be handled outside the company," he said, referring obliquely to "undue obligations to employees."[44] At the same time, exit interviews and employee surveys indicated that as many as one-third of the mothers in a given work area would work if safe, convenient, affordable child care was provided.[45] Smith made it a point to get industrial representatives to admit that women who did have access to child care were dependable workers and insisted the record reflect that women's absenteeism was due to circumstances beyond their control; they were simply being asked to assume too much of the burden. She asked, "Shouldn't we be doing something to help?"[46]

Like most junior members of Congress, Smith's ability to influence her colleagues was limited. Her significance rested in her attempts to raise issues that would not otherwise have been addressed. Very few women testified at the Congested Areas Hearings—only 13 of 421 witnesses—and most of them appeared as representatives of federal, state or local authorities. No one spoke for working-class women—whether prostitute or aircraft welder—and no one spoke for women and children, except Smith. Her suggestions for child care, housing planned for families with two employed parents, more inexpensive housing for single women, flexible hours, and a recognition that working women worked at least two jobs, reflected a sensitivity to women's situations not apparent in the men serving on or appearing before the subcommittee. Also, her presence and persistence seemed to raise the consciousness of her colleagues. After a few hearings, Chairman Izac and Rep. John Fogarty (D-RI) started sounding like Smith, seizing the opportunity to point out to industry representatives that women war workers needed assistance, not blame.[47]

Smith continued to press for increased government-sponsored child care in the House, working with five other congresswomen, across partisan lines, to thwart Rep. John Taber's (R-NY) amendment to cut funding nearly in half in 1943.[48] In her very first speech on the floor of the House, Smith pleaded for recognition of the difficulties working mothers faced: "We found many women standing in line waiting for medical care, for themselves and their children. We found them waiting hours after work to get their groceries and other necessities. We found children roaming the streets and some even locked in automobiles, not only because their war-working parents were absent from home but also because of the lack of child-care facilities and schools. This is an emergency. We have waited altogether too long to meet it. . . . [W]e can economize, but not when it comes to the care of our children."[49] Opposing testimony by Clare Hoffman (R-MI) contended that public child care would be unnecessary "if some of these women, instead of going into beer parlors, would go home and take care of their children."[50] Taber's amendment lost by 5 votes, 59 to 64, but it was a meager victory. The line held but stiff opposition foreclosed any chance to increase funding.[51] At peak capacity, the child care program administered by the Federal Works Agency enrolled less than 3 percent of the children under fourteen of working mothers.[52]

Smith's sensitivity to gender discrimination, heightened through many years in the workplace, also led her to pursue a series of measures during and after the war to equalize opportunities for women. The first bill she submitted to Congress aimed to abolish the differentials in minimum ages for war work between men and women.[53] Later, she joined other congresswomen in attempting to codify equal pay for equal work. Wartime had not erased the boundaries between men and women's work, but in many instances, the boundaries were redrawn. Many male jobs were modified (most often simplified) into female ones, making unequal wage rates more easily explainable. However, when women began literally taking men's jobs, employers and unions were faced with a dilemma. To pay a woman at a man's wage undermined the barriers that divided women's work from men's, but to pay them below it undermined the value of the job and threatened men's wage scales when they returned to reclaim those jobs. Primarily because of their desire to sustain male wages, government and labor unions worked together to persuade management to equalize wages. In 1942, the War Labor Board issued General Order No. 16 permitting employers to balance wage and salary rates between males and females "for comparable quality and quantity of work." This was, however, only a suggestion.[54] In 1945, Mary Norton, as Chairman of the House Labor Committee, introduced legislation mandating equal pay for women. Vigorously opposed by management and Chambers of Commerce, the bill failed.[55] Two years later, Smith and Helen Douglas (D-CA) introduced equal pay bills. These measures also failed.[56] The modest gains women made in the workplace during the war were hard-won and short-lived. Once the emergency had passed, interest shifted to the re-employment of veterans, and women workers dispersed into lesser-paid female occupations or went home to rebuild war-shattered families.

By the same token, efforts on behalf of an equal rights amendment were intensified during the war years, but ultimately failed in the face of competing agendas. While the ERA had been proposed in every Congress since 1923, victory seemed more likely in the mid-1940s, in light of a new sense of women's economic and political importance. Stating simply that: "Equality of rights under the law shall not be denied or abridged by the United States or by any state on account of sex," the equal rights amendment, cosponsored by forty-two male members, was the first resolution introduced in the House in 1943. As the first congresswoman to publicly endorse the measure, Smith said, "Women gained the vote as free citizens of the United States in the last war period. It is fitting that the principle of equal rights should be recognized in this war period."[57] The ERA was reported out of the Senate Judiciary Committee in May, but failed to make it out of the House Judiciary.[58] At the beginning of the next Congress, Representatives Smith and Rogers resubmitted the amendment, becoming the first women to cosponsor the ERA, but passed it to a man to introduce it.[59] Both parties were on record in favor. Included in the Republican Party platform of 1940, the Democrats added it to theirs in 1944.[60]

An impressive combination of the National Women's Party and the Women's Joint Legislative Committee (a coalition of women's organizations) lobbied in favor of the amendment. But there was by no means universal approval among women, and the divisions were closely drawn along class lines. Women who supported the ERA, like Smith, were mostly business and professional women who prized personal freedom and accomplishment, values relevant to women who aspired to compete equally with men. They contended that protective legislation—any legislation that distinguished between the sexes—did more harm than good. Those opposed to the ERA, by and large working-class women and their champions led by the Women's Bureau and women's labor groups, had no intention of surrendering hard-fought gains provided them in protective legislation for some abstract notion of equality.[61] The division among women was mirrored in Congress, with liberals tending to support labor and protective laws for working women. The ERA made it to the floor of both Houses in 1946. Cosponsored by twenty-four senators, the measure passed the upper House by a heartening 38 to 35 in favor, but well short of the two-thirds needed.[62] The measure never came to a vote in the House. The moment had passed. The postwar shift toward a resumption of "normal" life mitigated against the struggle for women's legal equality. It would be a long time before the ERA gained strong support again.

Controversies surrounding the issues of equal rights, equal pay and government-sponsored child care, reflect the ways in which women's social progress during World War II depended upon the exigencies of war need. They also illuminate the boundaries of acceptable women's roles, and the limits to the power of a handful of female representatives. Smith had more success in her efforts on behalf of military women, partly because she had gained increased power within the committee, partly because others more powerful than she desired the same ends, and partly because she had learned to make skillful use of the process.

Just prior to American entry into World War II, Edith Rogers, who had experienced the problems of civilian women working with the Army in the last war where she served as a Red Cross nurse, proposed legislation to establish the Women's Army Auxiliary Corps (WAAC).[63] Smith testified in support of the bill, and like Rogers, she preferred a woman's corps that would be "a regular part of the Army in every way, excepting of course, actual combat."[64]

Four basic themes were stressed by proponents of the WAAC bill, in these as well as in subsequent discussions about women's military service—the efficiency of employing women in times of manpower shortages in order to free men for combat; women's "natural" abilities that made them better suited for some occupations, notably those that required finger dexterity and involved a significant amount of tedium; the justice of providing women the opportunity to exercise their rights and responsibilities as citizens of the republic; and pledges that women's duties, authority, and length of service would be strictly limited and, unlike civilian volunteers, could be strictly controlled.[65] Despite assurances that the Army expressly did not "advocate the creation of an Amazon contingent to supplement combat forces," opposition in Congress rested primarily upon concerns for increased costs and rhetorical defenses of sacred American womanhood.[66] Congressional resistance delayed passage of the WAAC bill for several months, even after the Japanese attack on Pearl Harbor provided the final, decisive push into the war. Prodded by the Secretary of War and Chief of Staff George C. Marshall, Congress finally approved a women's auxiliary as adjunct to the army, but not in the army.[67]

In this ambiguous position, the WAAC limped along for a year until Rogers pushed legislation changing the WAAC to the more integral WAC (Women's Army Corps) in 1943. Similar women's divisions were created in the naval services: Navy WAVES, Women Marines and Coast Guard SPARs.[68] While women's military status still remained somewhat ill-defined, the purpose of the women's corps was unambiguous: their service was to be in an auxiliary capacity, in a fixed number of occupational categories, to release men for combat duty. Women's units, mirroring American society, were racially segregated. [69] Their numbers and their authority were strictly limited, their military rank to top out at one colonel or captain in the position of the Women's Director, and their length of service for the duration of the emergency plus six months.[70]

During the congested areas investigations, as Smith inquired about military women, she uncovered great reluctance to make use of them.

Besides citing the difficulties involved in providing housing for the women, military commanders complained most about the mandate to release a trained man within thirty days of acceptance of a presumably untrained woman.[71] As long as women were considered temporary help, Smith believed, this situation would continue. She filed a report with the NAC urging future consideration of a permanent corps of women in the peacetime military.[72]

Just before Christmas 1944, Smith made an extensive inspection tour of the Pacific war theater with members of the NAC, covering 24,527 miles in seventeen days.[73] She watched carrier battle exercises from the bridge of the U.S.S. Saratoga with Pacific Fleet Commander Admiral Chester Nimitz and discussed with him the need for WAVES in the Pacific.[74] She ate at mess with enlisted men, dodged sniper bullets in Saipan, and inquired about Maine boys so she could call their families when she got home.[75] At every stop, she toured hospitals and interviewed nurses. She was appalled by the conditions under which they worked, with shortages of the most rudimentary supplies and living conditions best described as crude. Nurses told her, though, that their biggest problem was their job's precariousness: if they got sick or hurt as a result of such duty, they were simply sent home.[76]

Military nurses held temporary status and relative rank (that is, the pay but not the command authority), a compromise made to prevent them from exercising command over male officers. Convinced that women needed regular permanent status in order to have the stability of a military career and respect as equals, Smith came home to propose such legislation for nurses. But not until she obtained her own subcommittee with jurisdiction over medical services three years later was she able to make significant progress on this matter.[77] Teaming with Representative Bolton, who introduced a companion bill for army nurses to match Smith's legislation for the navy, and aided by reports of severe nursing shortages, Smith guided through legislation resulting in the Army-Navy Nurse Act, granting nurses in both services permanent status and regular rank as commissioned officers with commensurate pay and benefits.[78]

Obtaining regular status for nurses was comparatively easy; nursing was regarded as fundamental to the physical and emotional well being of the military. Considerably more resistance met efforts to broaden roles and benefits for other military women. It took, for example, three tries to pass legislation to simply permit women in the WAVES and Marines to serve overseas. Despite the fact that WACs were stationed in North Africa and the European Theater and nurses had already seen action in Bataan and Corregidor, House debate on the WAVES measure was characterized by male demands that American women be defended, hallowed, and kept home. Smith withdrew the bill in the face of certain defeat.[79] Her second try fared better, at least in the House, probably because of increasing pressure from Admiral Nimitz, who indicated he needed five thousand WAVES immediately to release men for combat duty.[80] The Senate, however, refused to condone overseas service. Senate Naval Affairs Committee Chairman David J. Walsh (D-MA) twice stuck the overseas clause (Smith got it through the House in 1943 and again in 1944). "The Navy, to my mind," Walsh told WAVE Director Mildred McAfee, by way of explanation, "is a male organization."[81] A compromise measure, finally approved in September 1944, allowed women to serve only in the "American area" (North and South America, Hawaii, Alaska, the Canal Zone, and the Caribbean).[82]

The imperative to give permanence to women's military status had little support until the end of the war. The process of demobilization, with its massive clerical requirements, heightened the need for women, as did the continuing necessity of support for occupation troops. Under increasing pressure to resolve the question of women's peacetime participation in the Navy, the House NAC met in May 1946 to consider a proposal to establish a permanent women's naval component. At issue was whether to create permanent regulars and reserves for women, as the men were organized, or restrict women to reserve status only. Men on active duty were designated within the regular navy; those men on reserves were kept in readiness to be called in case of an emergency. Vice Admiral Louis E. Denfeld, Chief of the Bureau of Naval Personnel, testified that the Navy planned to assign "an appreciable number of officers and enlisted women to active duty in peacetime . . . [but] whether we have them in the regular navy or the reserves does not matter." For the record, Capt. Jean Palmer, director of the Women's Naval Reserve, stated the obvious: "The women would rather be in the regular navy." Chairman Vinson made it clear, however, that he intended to establish a permanent women's reserve, subject to unlimited active duty and sent home at the discretion of the naval secretary; there would be no women regulars. Using women only when the services needed them, he decreed, was the "happy solution."[83]

Smith did not see it as a happy solution at all. Using large numbers of women on active duty, while designating them as reserves, was unfair and dishonest. A permanent reservist, Smith contended, was a contradiction in terms. "There is no such thing as a service career for a reservist."[84] To her the issue was simple: "The Navy either needs these women or they do not." If they did, then women should be made regulars as well as reservists, and if they did not, then the matter was settled. She offered an amendment to provide "the authority to appoint enlisted women in the Regular Navy and Regular Marine Corps in the same manner under the same circumstances and conditions as such laws or parts of laws apply to the appointment of enlisted men." Surprisingly, Smith's amendment passed, 10 ayes to 2 noes. But it would not hold. Vinson refused to call a vote on the bill, and the Seventy-ninth Congress adjourned without taking further action.[85] A similar WAC bill was reported out of the House Military Affairs Committee during the same session and met the same fate.[86]

Legislation concerning women's integration into military service was resurrected in the Eightieth Congress, where the measures, following unification of the Naval Affairs and Military Affairs Committees, were considered by Armed Services Committees (ASC) in both Houses.[87] Again, hearings were held first in the Senate, and all the big guns the military could muster testified, including Chief of Staff and General of the Army Dwight D. Eisenhower; Fleet Admiral Chester W. Nimitz; and the directors of the women's branches: WAC Col. Mary A. Hallaren, WAVE Capt. Joy Bright Hancock, and Marine Col. J. W. Knighton. With little variation, they explained that the initial reluctance to accept women in the military had rapidly given way to open admiration and greater reliance upon them. Testimony provided abundant documentation of need and deployment, praised women's striking capacity for patience, attention to detail, and enthusiasm for monotonous work, and stressed the importance of a nucleus of highly trained women in the event of a rapid remobilization. Military leaders were simply recognizing that clerical work was women's work in civilian life and therefore logical that it should be so in the military. Their motive, as Eisenhower put it, was "plain efficiency"—women cost less and did the job better. From their point of view, anything short of permanent status was not an option "because it would be impossible during peacetime to attract the right kind of women for a period of two or three years on reserve status. . . . [T]hey would not be willing to leave [their civilian jobs] for some short period, when there was no security and no retirement benefits attached to them."[88]

After the hearings concluded, the Women's Armed Services Integration Act granting women regular military status was reported out of the Senate ASC on 16 July 1947, and passed the full Senate on a voice vote a week later.[89] But when the bill was sent to the House, ASC Chairman W. G. Andrews (R-NY) and Vinson, now second in command, refused to consider it. Following six months of inaction, Smith angrily confronted Andrews. She had learned that, as a result of "behind-the-scenes, off-the-record" executive sessions with some unnamed members of the Navy Department, an agreement had been reached to jettison the Senate bill. She reiterated the need for women to have permanent regular status or none, urging him to be forthright and to publicly vote yes or no "and not a dodging 'maybe.'"[90]

Meanwhile, the apparent need for women in the military increased. By 1948, it had become abundantly clear that the emergency was not over; the war had merely shifted from hot to cold. In the face of a potentially dangerous civil war in Greece, a Communist coup in Czechoslovakia, and Russia's threat to cut off access to Berlin, came a reconsideration of a peacetime draft, and the realization that the services could not afford to turn away women volunteers.[91] Nevertheless, Chairman Andrews made a vigorous appeal for postponing the issue, asking the service representatives to consider creating a Women's Reserve Corps in which all the women could be held in abeyance until they were needed. Eisenhower responded yet again that he thought that it would be a mistake to keep women in the reserves where they would have no permanence and no future. Secretary of Defense James Forrestal concurred, saying that without "the appeal of coequal status," the services could not attract and hold competent women. In short, the military repeated once again that they needed the women and to keep them they had to be able to offer them equality and permanence. Yet, the bill came out of the subcommittee just as it had gone in—for reserve status only.[92]

Hearings before the full House ASC hardly resembled hearings at all. During the brief discussion, in which the service representatives in attendance were not called upon to testify, several members of the committee indicated that they believed the Senate version of the bill could not prevail because of significant opposition in the House to giving women equal rank in a regular military. The final vote was 26 ayes and Mrs. Smith: no.[93] Chairman Andrews, determined to get the matter out of the way quickly, listed it on the consent calendar, a method usually reserved for noncontroversial bills that are reported out of committee unanimously approved. Smith objected to the legislation being "railroaded through on the consent calendar." The bill as reported out, she stated, was "grossly misleading," containing as it did only a temporary one-year reserve clause that discriminated against women. It was better, she said, to have no legislation at all. Smith's objection to the bill prevented its quick passage by the full House without debate. They had no choice but to bring the issue to the floor.[94]

The floor debate was lengthy and intense.[95] ASC Chairman Andrews announced that his committee had arrived at the only acceptable alternative, a "compromise" between the two extreme views: that of rejecting the women totally or "injecting" them into the regulars. Their bill would authorize enlistment and appointment to a woman's reserve, placing no limit on the number of these reserves who could be called to indefinite active duty. This "compromise" bill passed the House without objection. Smith, in a standing vote, supported Adam Clayton Powell's (D-NY) amendment barring racial discrimination in the women's armed forces; it fell 63 noes to 12 ayes. Then, in a strategic effort to limit the bill's detrimental effects, Smith proposed three amendments of her own. The first was to change the name of the bill to reflect its true intent, from the misleading "Women's Armed Services Integration Act" to "the Women's Armed Services Reserve Act." It carried.[96] Her next amendment gave members a chance to change their minds. Essentially the Senate bill altered to reflect changes necessitated by the unification of the Armed Services, it stimulated further debate that ultimately foundered over women's presumed excessive health care costs, and was rejected 66 noes to 40 ayes. Her last challenge was to amend to strictly limit the number and manner in which women could be utilized on active duty—to a maximum of ten officers and twenty-five enlisted women and for two years. The issue had not changed, she said, the services either needed the women or they did not. If they did, then they should be taken into the regular military organization. If they did not, then there could be no objection to such limitations. The amendment was rejected 41 noes to 21 ayes. From there the bill went to a joint conference with the Senate to thrash out a compromise.

Smith had scored a tactical victory by forcing the issue to the House floor where it could be fully debated, then turned over to joint conferees, at least half of whom supported women's integration. Not content to let the matter rest uneasily with this group, Smith contacted Secretary Forrestal, demanding he investigate and expose the collusion behind efforts to scuttle the bill. "This, to say the least," Smith wrote, "is duplicity that gravely questions the integrity of the administration of the National Military Establishment." Forrestal responded with emphatic messages of support for the Senate bill to members of the joint conference, who hammered the two bills into one favoring regular status.[97] Public Law 625, The Women's Armed Services Integration Act, was signed into law by President Truman on 12 July 1948.[98]

Because policy is collectively made, it is often impossible to assess the impact of one member of Congress on the progress of a particular piece of legislation. This instance is the exception. And in the process, Smith demonstrated a mastery of important lessons in the art of politics. She had proven she could play hardball. It was time to move on to the major leagues.

6 | No Place for a Woman

Rumors that Maine's senior senator, Wallace White, was planning to retire had been circulating for several years, fueled by gossip about his ineptitude and ill health. By the late 1940s, White was majority leader in name only, taking signals from Robert Taft so frequently that sympathetic reporters offered him a rearview mirror.[1] Governor Horace Hildreth and former Governor Sumner Sewall seemed the likeliest contenders for Wallace's seat. Both men were popular and interested. Hildreth, who had been elected with the highest percentage of Republican primary votes ever given a gubernatorial candidate, was assured the support of the regular Republican organization. Sewall, a man who had never lost an election, had been a popular governor from 1941 through 1945. Considered a maverick and a liberal, Sewall was believed likely to split the party, attracting labor support and that of veterans.[2]

Almost no one speculated that Smith would try for the U.S. Senate. Although there were rumblings that the Maine GOP was grooming a strong challenger for her next bid in the Second District, many conceded that she could stay in Congress as long as she chose.[3] Despite her secure position in the House, though, Smith had become increasingly discouraged about her ability to climb to leadership. The ascendancy of a Republican majority following the 1946 elections had not translated into greater power for her.[4] With the merger of the service committees, Smith had enough seniority to stay, but slipped in rank to thirteen of twenty members. When she attempted to win appointment to the more powerful Appropriations Committee, she paid for her ideological independence. Conservative leaders passed over her request in favor of five newcomers with less service, including one freshman.[5] Still, the odds against her winning a Senate race, and the risks to her political career, were great. No woman before her had successfully run on her own—that is, without a previous appointment to the Senate— and Smith had to forfeit her House seat in order to try.[6]

On Sunday, 1 June 1947, halfway through her fourth term, headlines announced: "Senator White to Retire; Mrs. Smith Will Seek Seat."[7] Citing her seven years' experience in national government and her desire for a "wider opportunity" to serve the people of her state, Smith claimed that it was a "logical step" for the senior House member to move into the Senate when a vacancy arose. Owen Brewster had done so, as had Wallace White. "There was no reason," Smith said, "to think that simply because I was a woman . . . I should not take that step."[8]

Editorials generally wished Smith well, but few were optimistic about her chances. While it might be possible she could benefit in the likelihood that Sewall and Hildreth would split the Republican vote, her statewide appeal was untested and unlikely to be as strong as that of either governor. "Nobody in Maine gets into the Senate without a political machine, fat campaign funds, the right business connections, and the help of the powers that be," said the experts.[9]

Smith was extraordinarily popular in Maine and not just in her own district, a factor that Republican leaders and political pundits seldom acknowledged. In her second term, she began active constituent service for people outside her district who, disgusted with their own representatives' lack of concern for their problems, had turned to her.[10] Further, while on Naval Affairs business—hearings, ship launchings, speeches and follow-up efforts—she attracted favorable attention in Portland, Maine's largest city, and across the state, notably through glowing reports in the Gannett press. Guy P. Gannett's approval—earned by her advocacy of a strong military and a firm foreign policy—reached all corners of Maine along with his newspapers.

Smith's biggest asset going in, and likely the one that tipped her decision to run, was the encouragement and able assistance of Bill Lewis. From the day he first suggested questions to her during the Congested Areas hearings, Lewis and Smith worked closely together. The son of two attorneys, William Chesley Lewis, Jr., was born in Wilburton, Oklahoma, in 1912. After graduating with a law degree from the University of Oklahoma and an MBA from Harvard, he worked as a prosecutor for the Securities and Exchange Commission in Washington, investigating public utilities' illegal campaign contributions. While on active duty with the Naval Reserve during the war, Lewis served on the staff of Assistant

Navy Secretary James Forrestal, who lent him to the House Naval Affairs Committee as a legislative assistant. There he worked for Vinson, eventually becoming Chief Counsel, and began his association with Smith.[11]

Traveling with the subcommittee and spending professional and leisure time together cemented their friendship. In official photographs, Smith and Lewis are frequently side-by-side, perhaps reflecting as much about their status on the subcommittee as their amity. A pair of more casual photographs in MCS's personal collection reveals first Lewis, then Smith, reclining on the same picnic blanket—the apparent result of them swapping places to smile into the camera held by the other. MCS recalled warm evenings while the subcommittee was in California: "By that time, Bill—he was awfully cute about it—was across the courtyard from my room, and would play his 'tonette' in the window. I suppose he was as lonely as I was."[12] Soon, she began to bring Lewis home with her to Skowhegan. Just five months after they met, he was there for a Chase family reunion. In the fall of 1944, when she returned to dispose of the property Smith had left her, Lewis came, too. She sold her business blocks downtown and transferred her lovely mansion, which had grown too burdensome to maintain, to two doctors who promised to transform it into a hospital in memory of Clyde Smith.[13]

By war's end, Lewis had become a part of her family celebrations and a close friend of her sister and brother-in-law, Laura and Joseph "Spike" Bernier, at whose home he established legal voting residence in 1946. It appears that Lewis (and likely Smith) planned a long-term relationship, one that might require his official residency in Maine. Given Mainers' historic distrust of outsiders (people "from away"), it made sense to try to defuse an issue that did, in fact, arise after she became a senator and hired Lewis to work for her. Long before that, though, she had come to rely on Lewis's education, expertise, and encouragement.[14]

After the service committees merged in 1946, Lewis lost his assignment as counsel. He resigned his naval commission to accept a comparable rank in the Air Reserve, and joined his father, a colonel in the Army Air Corps and director of the Air Reserve Association, in vigorously lobbying for unification of the armed services and the establishment of a separate and equal Air Force.[15] Smith collaborated with that effort.

To be sure, she had advocated the idea of unification, in the interests of economy and efficiency, as early as 1941, but association with the Lewises intensified her convictions and channeled her energies.[16] It was Lewis to whom she turned to help her prepare to chair her first hearings on permanent status for military nurses, which resulted in the Army-Navy Nurse Act, the first measure to unify army and navy legislation.

And it was Lewis who worked as liaison between Smith and his father to enlist her support for a package of legislation designed to make the Reserves more attractive in pay, benefits, and recognition.[17] Working together to bring the unification bill out of committee, Smith lobbied colleagues and promoted the issue in speeches and public forums, while Lewis organized letter-writing campaigns to pressure congressional leaders to consider the measure before the session ended.[18]

Right in the middle of the final push for unification legislation, which was also concurrent with her fight for regular status for women in the military, Smith announced her plans to run for the U.S. Senate. While it is impossible to discern precisely when she made her decision to run, or whether it was a joint decision, Lewis was certainly central to the process. He later characterized himself as "perhaps the first one to tell her that she should run for the Senate and to present a convincing analysis (based on her 1946 reelection campaign) of her excellent chances of winning."[19]

National security provided the final impetus for resolution of the armed services' merger. While the debate over the military raged, President Truman embraced a policy of containment against mounting Soviet aggressiveness in Eastern Europe and the Middle East. To a joint session of Congress in March, the president warned of the gravity of the Russian challenge and declared that "it must be the policy of the United States to support free people who are resisting attempted subjugation by armed minorities or by outside pressures." This determination to contain Russian expansionism by the "adroit and vigilant application of counter force" required a strong and unified military, intelligence and national security organization. Just before recess in July, Congress passed the National Security Act of 1947, creating a coordinated military establishment and a National Security Council with a Central Intelligence Agency.[20] Economic aid to war-torn Europe was corollary to American security. In announcing his plan for European Recovery, Secretary of State George C. Marshall asserted that wretched postwar conditions, exacerbated by drought and severe winter weather, left the region ripe for totalitarianism. Without assistance for reconstruction and rehabilitation, Europe would "face economic, social and political deterioration of a very grave character."[21]

Several groups of congressmen subsequently journeyed to Europe to investigate the postwar situation for themselves. In September, Smith joined with a special subcommittee of the House committees on Armed Services and Appropriations for a five-week trip to Europe and the near East.[22] Before she left, Smith and Lewis drafted press releases based on her State Department briefings to be mailed from eleven countries to every radio and newspaper in Maine to exploit what Lewis considered a "definite political advantage for her." He wrote his mother that "we not only had drafted press releases from eleven of the European places where she will be, but we also have them mimeographed and the envelopes addressed to all radio stations and newspapers in Maine. . . . I hope that press releases prepared weeks in advance . . . will hold up and that events in between will not alter them too much."[23] Featuring topographic and industrial comparisons with her home state, the homogenized reports made only vague references to "trouble spots" or "problem areas" without further elaboration. While many of the weeklies printed these pieces without comment, at least one sarcastically criticized the banality and shallowness of Smith's European dispatches. What's more, she cheated herself with the pre-written reports. As the only woman on the trip, she attracted extraordinary attention from the press wherever she went and attracted much better publicity than her own. The national press described her addressing the House of Commons in London, querying Italian officials about the degree of participation of women in their government, conferring with the Egyptian Minister of Health about the current cholera epidemic, and tossing 500 lollipops she carried in her satchel to hordes of tattered children.[24]

It is interesting to note the ways this anecdote was used to make different points in its retelling. For example, as May Craig reported, Smith distributed lollipops to children who had never seen one before so Rep. Dewey Short (R-MO) demonstrated how to unwrap and lick a lollipop to the apparent delight of the children. Another reporter, George Dixon, said Smith "threw" them at a crowd of children who just stared at them, whereupon "Mrs. Smith began to cry as she saw her gifts lying in the street" until Short came to her "rescue. . . . Mr. Short became the most popular man in the area." Later in the campaign, Smith's opponent Albion Beverage criticized her as a frivolous woman who would take lollipops to a starving Europe.[25]

After the committee's visit to Iran, where Smith addressed the Iranian Parliament, Ambassador George V. Allen's cable to the State Department, citing a "particularly enthusiastic" response to "Mrs. Smith, not only because of her personal intelligence and charm but also as representative of American womanhood . . . [whose] visit may have a far-reaching beneficial effect on the position in public life of Iranian women," was widely quoted in the press.[26]

Then, on the trip home, Smith became a genuine heroine. About four hours out of the Azores, the plane on which the group was traveling lost its number three engine, then the other engine on the same side began to falter. The plane turned back for the Azores into a headwind, raising concerns about the fuel supply. "It was," Flight Chief Luke Quinn admitted, "a bit of a sweat." As the congressmen were donning their "Mae Wests" in preparation for a possible ditch into the briny, Smith remained calm and confident. She produced three harmonicas she had purchased in Switzerland for her niece and nephews and persuaded the others to join her in singing. Quinn remarked, "Everybody was scared. Everybody was aware of the danger. Congresswoman Smith showed remarkable poise and cheerfulness. . . . Her calmness was reassuring to passengers and crew alike."[27] Safely on land, Short departed the plane praising Smith as "the best soldier—and sailor of us all," and Admiral Swanson crowed, "An amazing woman—don't know how she stays single." Later, Rep. Gordon Canfield (R-NJ) sang her praises for the *Congressional Record*. "She can take it," he wrote, "and those who have seen her under fire can bear witness."[28] Joining the chorus back home, newspaper editorials effusively praised her mettle: "It is a real test of courage to remain poised and at least outwardly cheerful when deadly peril threatens . . . then the instinct is to give way to blind panic; but courage and strength of character . . . enabled Maine's Rep. Smith to show, during four long hours of the touch-and-go race between life and death last Friday, the poise, the cheerfulness and calmness . . . [that gave a lie to] the bigoted phrase . . . 'no place for a woman.'"[29] Smith responded modestly. "I was just as scared as the rest of them," she said, "only as a woman I couldn't have the luxury of showing my fear."[30]

She came home with two and one-half months left to campaign before Congress reconvened, enriched by her renown as an imperturbable statesman in touch with international concerns and comfortable deciding grave matters of state. Smith toured Maine describing the devastation and chaos she had witnessed and, like her fellow travelers, forcefully endorsing the European Recovery Plan as a "major counter-offensive" in the Cold War and one that must be stiffened "with realistic armed power . . . we must back up our Marshall Plan dollars with arms. The surest way to prevent war is to be ready to go to war."[31]

Smith had returned from abroad armed with colorful stories and tales of wrenching misery for the campaign trail. Then, just as she began her tour, wildfire raced through western and southern Maine, causing the worst disaster in the state's history. A dry summer followed by a parched autumn precipitated the conflagration, driven by winds that reached eighty-seven miles-per-hour and challenged only by desperate men, armed with brooms and wet burlap bags, shovels and hand pumps. The blaze cut a swath from the New Hampshire border to the down east coast, leveling thousands of acres of timber and hundreds of farms, fine old sea captains' homes, and gracious summer cottages, driving residents into the sea.[32] Rows of blackened chimneys rising out of the smoking ash looked little different to her from war-torn Europe. Faced with Maine's own distress, she canceled the rest of her tour to return to Washington to try to obtain federal aid for both Maine and Europe. In her speech before Congress, Smith compared the forest fires in Maine to the "smoldering political fires interspersed throughout Europe ready for open flames if fanned by Europe's shifting political winds and fed by Europe's hunger drought."[33]

Smith's diligent pursuit of relief for Maine stood in sharp contrast to that of Governor Hildreth, who was slow to respond to the emergency and reluctant to extend state aid to damaged communities. After President Truman authorized federal monies and direct aid, Hildreth made a much publicized journey to the White House to say thanks. This effort to buttress his standing with the voters backfired, however, when columnist Drew Pearson pointed out that it was Smith who had mobilized federal relief, forcing a defensive Hildreth to respond that he was paying a "simple courtesy call" on the president after he had granted assistance that, by law, only a governor could request.[34]

Until snow brought an end to the drought, rivers were low and power short. Electricity throughout Maine had to be rationed, encouraging renewed interest in the Passamaquoddy Tidal Power Project. Abandoned some ten years before, the plan to harness the twenty-seven-foot tides of the Bay of Fundy for power generation again seemed a viable solution to the development of cheap and reliable power and, not incidentally, the economic rehabilitation of the chronically depressed eastern Maine region. Designed by hydroelectrical engineer Dexter Cooper in 1919, some $7 million had been expended in surveys and studies during the New Deal before the project foundered over costs, feasibility problems, and Canadian objections (they shared sovereignty of the waters) that disruptions of plankton dispersal would harm herring fisheries.[35]

The prospect of major power shortages resulting from the drought prompted Smith to sponsor a bill in early 1948 commissioning the president and State Department to negotiate with Canada to use the waters of Passamaquoddy Bay, and authorizing $100 million for a federal project to harness the tides to produce low-cost electrical energy.[36] Governor Hildreth, apparently preempted, announced an alternative plan for a Joint International Boundary Commission to study feasibility and admonished Smith for making Quoddy a "political football."[37] She countered that the project must not be "resurveyed and restudied to death . . . my bill calls for action." She was, she said, concerned primarily with the site's utility in national defense; the power project would have the capacity to supply the great quantities of power needed for heavy industry in times of war.[38] She was, however, not unmindful of its potential for stimulating the Maine economy—and for stimulating her Senate campaign.[39]

Smith was off to a good start but her early lead was expected to evaporate in the face of her opponents' lavish campaigns. Hildreth and Sewall were both well connected and personally wealthy.[40] But what she lacked in resources, Smith and Lewis made up for in organization. Over the years, beginning with the names she inherited from Clyde Smith, she had amassed a core group of committed volunteers, though most of these were in the Second District. Meticulous office records of people who had expressed interest in her candidacy, previously volunteered to help, or had sought her aid at some point, were mined for names that might be persuaded to circulate petitions throughout the state.

Beginning with the official launching of her campaign on January 1, Smith and Lewis mailed thousands of blank primary petitions, along with lists of her qualifications and Speaker Joe Martin's endorsement of her party loyalty. While state law required a maximum of thirty-six hundred voter signatures to get on the primary ballot in 1948, the plan was to acquire as many signatures and addresses as possible to support their "grassroots" strategy. Smith volunteers gathered more than twenty-five thousand signatures, complete with addresses. Following through, Lewis organized the massive project. Tapping into his family resources, he enlisted the aid of his mother and father, who used their office's "addressograph" to label twenty-five thousand envelopes and more than twice that many penny postcards. Every signee was mailed a "personal" thank you message that said: "I do not have sufficient finances for paid professional workers. That is why you are so important to me . . . and why *we* will win." A second set of postcards were mailed halfway through the campaign with messages aimed at specific groups emphasizing Smith's votes on their behalf. For example, cards mailed to Grange officials cited her votes for parity, soil conservation, and price supports; those mailed to veterans and reservists emphasized her sponsorship of reserve legislation, and so forth. Local organizers were provided with preaddressed postcards to announce meetings, pamphlets listing Smith's voting record and commendations, pledge cards for volunteering to make speeches, phone calls, and/or provide transportation to the polls, and "Smith for Senator" bumper stickers.

Lewis directed a very personal organization, overseeing every aspect of it. County chairs reported directly to him, and he kept meticulous records of who was responsible in each area, who signed primary papers, who could be counted on to call meetings, who got out the vote. He also established a network of "reporters" to keep him abreast of rumors and polls in each area, and targeted speeches and press releases accordingly. An unpaid volunteer, Lewis preferred the background. He enjoyed the cloak-and-dagger aspects of covert action, referring to himself as "the phantom campaign manager" and using his anonymity to "infiltrate" crowds and eavesdrop for comments about "Margaret." Smith and Lewis worked to keep his role clandestine, even from close associates, while publicly maintaining that she did not have a paid campaign manager (which of course was true) "lacking the resources of the opposition," as her literature put it.[41]

Such a complex campaign, even with abundant volunteer help, cost money. For the first time in her political career, Smith decided to solicit and accept campaign contributions. In December, she announced that Clifford Carver, wealthy shipping magnate and a man with considerable contacts, prestige, and influence among Maine Republicans, would serve as her financial manager.[42] First to contribute to "Smith for Senate" was Rep. Frances Bolton, who kicked off the campaign with a check for $500. Lewis followed shortly with a check for $1,000.[43] While Smith received a few more contributions this large, most were for five or ten dollars, many for as little as one dollar or two.[44] The "Smith for Senate" contribution that brought her the most for the least was a $1 donation from an eighteen-year-old girl whose accompanying note she circulated throughout the campaign: "I regret only two things: that this must be merely a token contribution to your senatorial campaign and that I am not yet old enough to vote."[45]

Smith's was a shoestring campaign, and she made the most of it. As penny postcards peppered the state, stories of her supporters' innovation and thrift captured the popular imagination. Her local workers in Bangor, for example, dropped pennies in newly expired parking meters around town, leaving a flyer on the windshield attributing their public service to the "friends of Margaret Smith."[46] She was counting on Maine voters to be offended by the large amounts spent by her challengers, sharpened by continual references to herself without funds in a fight against big money machines. She might be short on monetary wealth, said her campaign literature, but she had "a wealth of experience, a wealth of ability, a wealth of congressional 'know-how' and a wealth of nonpaid friends supporting her."[47] Her record in Congress, while important, mattered less than her reputation for hard work, integrity and affability. She met with as many people as possible, as she had always done during her years in office. Few were new to her, or she to them; she had been to their grange hall, church basement, club meeting. Her frustrated opponents angrily challenged supporters to "name one thing Mrs. Smith has ever done to represent the Second District—and don't try to tell us that she always answered her mail!" But that of course was precisely what folks remembered. Constituents valued small favors of a "purely personal nature" to a far greater degree than some extrinsic "contribution to the public welfare."[48] Smith enhanced that intimate connection with voters in the simple yet powerful message of her campaign: I do not have the resources my opponents have [I am like you]; I am not the tool of machine politics in Maine [I am like you]; but I do have you and together we can prevail.[49]

Then came what Smith later called her "lucky break." On Friday, the thirteenth of February, just four months before the hotly contested primary, while racing from one speaking engagement to another, she slipped on the ice and fractured her right elbow. Rushed to the hospital, she had a cast set and without missing a beat, dauntlessly charged ahead to keep afternoon and evening speaking engagements. MCS recalled that she felt especially pressured to continue as she was due at a men's luncheon in Rockland followed by a "big men's meeting" in Portland; neither group had ever been formally addressed by a woman.[50] The press loved the imagery of Smith meeting constituents and making speeches with her arm in a fashionable print sling. Stories and editorials made much of her "unwomanly" qualities, frequently pairing this anecdote with her heroism aboard the crippled plane over the Atlantic to demonstrate her courage and perseverance and to chide those who alleged that the Senate was no place for a woman.[51]

Awareness that women constituted 64 percent of Maine's registered voters, and the assumption that they might vote for a woman on the basis of gender, encouraged political activity by Maine women "unmatched since the women gained the franchise." Both her opponents' wives made unprecedented public appearances on behalf of their husbands, Mrs. Sewall asking, "Why take a woman to Washington when you can get a man?"[52] Women's groups took their place beside Rotary and Kiwanis as important forums for political speeches and debates; the question inevitably arose: "Is the Senate a place for a woman?"[53]

The first women's organization to take a partisan position in the campaign, the Maine State BPW, declared their support for Smith a week after her announcement, promising "to endorse and help [her] in every way possible."[54] The Women's Christian Temperance Union soon followed suit.[55] Then the DAR, while carefully avoiding the appearance of partisanship, hosted a tribute to Smith at their National Defense Breakfast in Washington.[56] In speaking to these groups, Smith both lobbied for their support and encouraged them to participate more fully. She domesticated politics by suggesting that the management of public affairs was similar to the management of the home—government as housekeeping writ large. Far from colliding with their roles as homemakers, Smith insisted, politics was the best possible exercise of the lessons that women had learned from it: "Women administer the home. They set the rules, enforce them, mete out justice for violations. Thus, like Congress, they legislate; like the Executive, they administer; like the courts, they interpret the rules. It is an ideal experience for politics."[57]

As far as holding office was concerned, Smith averred gender was both irrelevant and central. "I am proud to be a woman," she told audiences, "but I want it distinctly understood that I am not soliciting support because I am a woman. I solicit your support wholly on the basis of my record of eight years in Congress." Her official statement declared: "While she is a champion for the women, she is no feminist for she believes that a woman's viewpoint should be objective and free of any emphasis on feminine interest."[58]

Women journalists were thrilled that Smith's candidacy seemed to be "awakening a community of interest among the women." Doris Fleeson, Josephine Ripley, Helen Henley, and May Craig, among others, traveled with the candidate, wrote often of the campaign, and speculated about what the election meant for women. Intrigued by the possibilities, they eagerly predicted that if "modest, hard-working, just plain Margaret Smith" won, soon half the senators would be women.[59] Two months before the primary, the Women's National Press Association named her Woman of the Year for Politics in hopes the award would "help boost [her] political stock with the State of Mainers."[60]

After receiving some criticism for her frequent absences from Congress while she was campaigning (she had missed over half of the session's roll calls), and considering the coming vote for European Recovery and the Women's Press Club ceremony, Smith skipped the Maine Republican convention and returned to Washington, citing the press of official business. She recruited her sisters, Evelyn and Laura, to take her place. "What a shame you had to miss the convention," Evelyn wrote her, "Laura and I were congressmen for a day if we never are again. . . . Everyone in general felt that you were doing the right thing by staying there in Wash." Indeed, the press praised Smith for "loyalty to her job" and lavishly covered President Truman's presentation of the Woman of the Year Award to her.[61]

All this activity on the part of women in the press, organized women, and Smith's huge cadre of female volunteers seemed to justify men's worst fears of "petticoat rule." That men felt vulnerable to women's imminent usurpation of the political realm is perhaps best exemplified by a cartoon in wide circulation during the campaign. Entitled "Indication of a Busy Leap Year," the cartoon places a glamorous woman, labeled "Smith, aspirant to the Senate," approaching a white-whiskered sea captain, designated "Maine," proffering a "Political Marriage Contract." Asks she, "Aw, who's afraid of a woman?" The captain looks startled and dismayed, while, in the background, another salty type tells his cronies, "Gosh, if he's landed, none of us is safe."[62]

Smith's female attributes and the "women's vote" were only part of conservatives' concern. The widespread perception that she did not adhere to party ideology, but considered each issue on its own merits then voted with her convictions, made her enormously popular with the voters, but deeply worried the GOP. Smith called herself a "moderate," which she defined as "somewhat more liberal and somewhat less conservative than . . . 'middle of the road.'"[63] But the press mostly emphasized her liberalism. The *New York Times* commented that "if she had been born in any other state except Maine she'd be a Democrat. . . . She has a mind of her own and uses it." In short, "she is a party all by herself."[64]

During the war, Smith had profited from her strong stand on defense, and had not retreated from that focus in the face of cold war with Russia. Military legislation continued to define her career, especially bills for Reserves and the Women's Armed Services Integration Act, which was passed as the campaign entered its final days.[65] It was in this same spirit of concern for preparedness that she made her most noticeable deviation from party regularity, an act that hit the headlines in mid-campaign. Smith was the only Republican to vote against slashing Truman's 1948 budget by $5 billion. She voted against her party, she said, because she feared mandated cuts might come from military budgets which would be "false economy and impair our real national security."[66] Perhaps, though, voters were less concerned with national issues than with those closer to home, especially her record on labor and social welfare measures that found favor with Maine's working class. Smith endorsed federal aid to education, increases in low cost medical care, social security, and old age assistance.[67] More troublesome was her position vis-à-vis labor. Her voting had been ideologically ambiguous, a curious mixture of liberal and conservative positions, but, on closer inspection, had an internal consistency. In every case, she chose a middle ground as closely as she could discern it.

Organized labor in Maine applauded her opposition to the despised War Labor Disputes (Smith-Connally) Act in 1943, even though her postvote statement made it clear that she opposed it not because it was an antilabor measure but because she found it both redundant and dangerously permissive. It provided for a strike vote while a "no-strike" pledge was in effect, and she did "not think there should be a law that even admits the possibility of a strike . . . for the duration," she wrote.[68] Whether or not they thought she had the right reason for voting as she did, Maine labor urged her reelection in 1944 on the basis of that vote, finding her "a real friend of the working men and women in this country."[69] Again, during the postwar labor turmoil in 1945 and 1946, when Congress moved to curb union power, Smith voted "right" for labor, believing that punitive measures, written in the heat of anger, were inappropriate.[70] For this, Maine unions again endorsed her reelection, seeing her as "a lone and shining star in the Maine firmament. . . . Mrs. Smith is the best man we have in Washington."[71]

The impulse to control labor unions accelerated when the 1946 elections returned a Republican majority to both Houses. Seventy antilabor bills were introduced in the House alone. While Smith had consistently opposed revision of labor laws supported by House Republicans, in 1947 she drafted a series of bills she said were designed to balance the needs of all parties, providing for checks on management as well as labor, and for congressional veto of presidential seizure. "The crux of this whole matter," Smith testified, "is the abuse of power—and measures must be taken to safeguard against this whether it is labor, management, the president or the Congress."[72] Smith's bills fell into the soup with the others. In the end, after lengthy and acrimonious debate, Congress passed the Labor-Management Relations (Taft-Hartley) Act of 1947. Passed again over Truman's veto, the measure asserted the primacy of the national interest over the claims of either management or labor, although it shifted the balance of power decidedly toward management.[73] Smith voted for the Taft-Hartley Act and for the override, contending that it set the proper equilibrium. "The Public comes first," she said. "My voting record on labor legislation has been 100 percent for the public, rather than exclusively for either Labor or Management."[74]

As the 1948 campaign got underway, organized labor debated whether to endorse Smith for the Senate. She had voted for some measures they liked, but she had supported the detested Taft-Hartley Act. Maine Federation of Labor President Ben Dorsky withheld official endorsement while acknowledging she had done better than the rest of the congressional delegation. Her record on labor was, he said, "not perfect, but it's not zero. We regret that she voted for the Taft-Hartley Act."[75] It was an open question whether outright endorsement would help or hinder her senatorial candidacy. Since Smith was being criticized by her own party for being too liberal toward labor, it might be to her advantage if labor leaders did not endorse her, thereby inhibiting that allegation while doing little to change the minds of rank and file supporters.[76] Smith's campaign material played it both ways. In an advertisement addressed to "Labor," she stated that the opposition intended to defeat her because she was prolabor. "What will be your answer June 21?" To her critics, she denied she had labor's support because she had voted for the odious Taft-Hartley.[77]

Smith's independence also fueled speculation that Maine Democrats were considering backing her. While such a move would not help her in the primary, it could give her a second chance at the post in the general election. Although the party chairman denied the possibility, the notion apparently had some appeal.[78] As it happened, Smith was a frequent write-in candidate in the Democratic primary, for Senate and a host of other county and legislative offices.[79]

As the primary neared, and Smith's lead widened, the Republican opposition turned venomous. Anonymous smear sheets accusing her of some serious, and some silly, misdeeds, most aimed at her sex and her liberal record began circulating. Some accused her of "carrying on with men," and of breaking up her husband's first marriage. Adversaries tried ethnic slurs. One had her changing her name from Chasse to hide her Canadian ancestry, another had her changing it to Chasse to attract the French-Canadian vote.[80]

The worst of the charges were contained in a three-page document, mailed to hundreds of households in Maine, that apparently required considerable research and gave the appearance of a factual and objective analysis of her voting patterns. Smith was accused of being soft on Communism, a traitor to the Republican Party and, in league with American Labor Party Representative Vito Marcantonio of New York, a tool of organized labor. The document's appraisal of 242 measures in the past five Congresses revealed that 29.3 percent of her votes were in opposition to her party and 44.2 percent of them were the same as Marcantonio's.[81]

Smith wanted to respond to this allegation immediately, but Lewis persuaded her to wait until he had time to research the record and craft an equally devastating refutation. MCS said Lewis told her that "'if you want me to help you, you'll have to do it my way.' And, of course, he was right. He was always right." When she did respond, she chose to do so first to the women in her hometown. "It was not easy to do," MCS admitted, "to have to clear your name before your own townspeople. I didn't think I could do it, but Bill said, 'of course you can do it.'"[82]

In late May, Smith faced the 200 members of the Somerset County Women's Republican Club in the Federated Church parlor in Skowhegan and told them that she was being attacked on the basis of her sex and with a distortion of her record in Congress. "I have avoided making the status of being a woman an issue in this campaign," she told them, "for I truly believe that one's sex should not be a determinant in the selection of public officials." But, since her opponents had engaged in a "whispering campaign that the Senate was no place for a woman," that message, she asserted, "is a direct challenge to every woman in Maine." Her opposition, she said, had resorted to the distribution of "anonymous printed lie sheets that charge that I am a Communist and a traitor to the Republican Party." While these were "so ridiculous and so patently a pack of lies that they [did] not warrant the dignity of recognition," she resolved to answer them point-by-point, lest anyone misinterpret her silence. Demonstrating both the distortion of the numbers, in that the author had chosen to analyze only 242 votes of more than 1,500 cast during her tenure in the House, and further revealing the votes chosen to analyze her "alliance" with Marcantonio were also in accord with an "imposing array of Republican leaders," Smith concluded that the smear sheets simply betrayed "the desperation of my opponents."[83]

Whether the charges were true or not, and few believed them to be, columnists and editors assailed the moral bankruptcy of those who would resort to anonymity. The "dirty in-fighting" of Smith's challengers, they reported, offended voters' "Yankee sense of fairness and decency" and had "resulted in awakening otherwise apathetic voters to the place where they are determined to see that Mrs. Smith stays in Washington."[84] "Margaret Chase Smith, champion of the people is roaring out front as the senatorial parade comes down the stretch . . . because the common folk adopted her."[85]

Smith's final mailing of 25,000 postcards, sent to arrive the last delivery date before the primary, were targeted by sex. Cards sent to the approximately 15,000 male signers carried two slogans: "Don't Trade a Record for a Promise" and "Fight Money Politics and Smears." To 10,000 women went the message: "The Opposition Says That Margaret Smith Must Be Defeated Because She Is a Woman. ANSWER THIS CHALLENGE."[86]

In her radio address the night before the primary, Smith spoke eloquently of herself as "a symbol of a 'grassroots' protest against political machines, money politics and smears." She wanted to win, she said, for "the rank and file of the people of Maine," for that eighteen-year-old girl who donated one dollar to her campaign, for the mill worker who jeopardized her job to support Smith, for the housewife who went door-to-door, for the veteran, the granger, the insurance salesman, the woman farmer, the state employee, the small businessman, the longshoreman and the teacher, for all those who "have courageously resisted political intimidation, who have denounced and fought smears, and who have put their hearts and souls in my campaign because they were convinced that I was their symbol of protest against such things. . . . We will win because we have an inspiring cause to fight for. . . . The issue tomorrow is clear. It is the rank-and-file against the paid professionals."[87]

Smith's victory was stunning: she amassed 63,786 votes, a plurality of 4,675 votes over the combined totals of her three opponents.[88]

Two days later, she stood before the Republican convention in Philadelphia, grinning broadly before thousands of cheering Republicans responding to Joe Martin's question: "Have you heard the news from Maine?"[89] Before Smith spoke, Frances Bolton warmed the crowd with an impassioned speech on the importance of women to the nation and to the Republican Party. "All hail! Margaret!," she cried, "we women rejoice that your judgments will be a part of Senate consideration of the great problems of the future."[90] When her turn came, Smith affirmed her nomination as evidence that the Republican Party was "willing and able to expand the role of women in public office" and offered them "real hope for greater political recognition." More than that, she said, hers was "a grassroots victory." She admonished her party to eschew its reputation as the party of privilege, and to "demonstrate by its platform and its nominees . . . that the Republican Party is the party of the rank and file—that it is the grassroots party."[91]

Though hardly a grassroots agenda, a reasonably progressive platform emerged from the convention that nominated New York Governor Thomas Dewey for president and California Governor Earl Warren as his running mate. Limiting criticism of the Truman administration to a short paragraph, the document outlined the party's proposals for the future, including a bipartisan foreign policy, a progressive program of civil rights that opposed segregation in the armed forces and the poll tax, and favored antilynching legislation, federal housing aid and slum clearance. The GOP held their ground on labor and the controversial Taft-Hartley labor law, while favoring equal pay for equal work regardless of sex as well as a constitutional amendment providing equal rights for women.[92]

For the rest of the summer, Smith joined the traditional whirlwind tour of Maine, campaigning for Dewey-Warren with the rest of the Republican ticket. The group spent long, hot, dusty days "campaigning, hand-clasping, stair climbing, driving over good and not-so-good roads" and, in a typical day, visited "five wood products plants, two shoe factories, a woolen mill and a pulp mill," holding impromptu rallies in town squares and speaking in Legion halls, then repeating the drill in each of sixteen counties.[93] Asked why she assumed this arduous task in light of her unassailable victory, Smith told the press: "I know I'll win, but I want to meet my people. I want to find out what they want. I want them to ask me questions. They have a right to know what I am doing and why."[94]

Smith made the cover of *U.S. News and World Report* with her landslide victory in September.[95] "As Maine goes . . . " was apparently signaling better times ahead for women and Republicans, who saw it as an omen portending a dramatic victory of their own in November, despite the fact that such prognostications had faltered in the past. This time, sober reflections on the meaning of Smith's election could find little cause for optimism on the national level. She was clearly not the usual case, having won as the result of a firm hold on the imagination of Maine voters and the built-in support of a Republican majority. As her Democratic opponent, Dr. Adrian Scolton—a dermatologist whose campaign was based upon his belief that since it was a sick world, America needed doctors in government—rather sourly put it, "For the Republicans to have won Maine again [was] like the Dutch taking Holland."[96]

Encouraged by all the polls and backed by a well-oiled machine, Governor Dewey acted as though he were already president. Pompous and cold, he ran a desultory campaign that ignited little grassroots enthusiasm. He failed to respond to Truman's attacks or to delineate a program of his own. President Truman, beginning barely seven weeks before the election, launched a strenuous whistle-stop tour, contending Republican hostility to labor and the failures of the "do-nothing" Republican Congress. He called them into special session before the election, daring them to implement their progressive platform. Stalwart conservatives led by Senator Robert Taft refused, exposing the sharp split in the GOP between the progressives behind the nominee and the conservatives in control of Congress. In one of the more dramatic elections of the twentieth century, President Truman defeated Governor Dewey and carried with him a striking reversal of the Republican majority in both Houses. Republicans lost seventy-four seats in the House and nine seats in the Senate in 1948, but picked up their first woman senator.[97]

7 | Joan of Arc

On January 3, the opening day of the Eighty-first Congress, women from across the country converged on Washington—by auto cavalcade, planes and two special trains—to celebrate Margaret Chase Smith's entrance into the "most exclusive men's club in the world." They jammed the galleries of the U.S. Senate, bursting into applause as the new woman senator came into the chamber. Despite a warning gavel, they cheered again as she proceeded to the rostrum on the arm of her colleague, Senator Owen Brewster, to swear her solemn oath to support and defend the Constitution of the United States. It "seemed to me," wrote reporter May Craig, that "all the women in the world were there."[1]

The "Tribute Train" arrived the day before, carrying nearly 500 representatives from the National Federation of Business and Professional Women's Clubs around the country. They staged an elaborate series of celebrations for Smith and all the women of the Eighty-first Congress. Another train, the "Woman-for-Public-Office-Special," brought over 100 delegates of the Multi-Party Committee on Women, Inc., representing thirty-six state and national women's organizations. Led by Judge Lucy Somerville Howorth, this group came armed with a specific program for training women in public service, lobbying for appointive positions, and encouraging bi-partisan gender unity. The Multi-Party Committee intended to harness the energy and optimism surrounding Smith's victory to launch a million dollar campaign to promote women for public office. "The powder was there," Howorth noted, "and this seemed to be the spark it was waiting for." Senator Smith was, she said, a "shining example of the purposes the Multi-Party Committee hopes to accomplish" because Smith had won her high position on the basis of her own ability, yet recognized that women needed one another in order to correct the inequities of American democracy.[2]

Jubilation reigned at the huge gala luncheon sponsored by the BPW in the ornate Congressional Room of the Hotel Statler. As the new senator took her position at the podium, waiting for the clink of dishes and murmur of elated voices to gradually hush, she smiled widely, savoring the moment. Then, swallowing the lump of pleasure and nervousness in her throat, she began to tell the more than five hundred women, a few dozen men (most of them top government and military officials) and her mother, what this day meant to her and what she thought it should mean to them. Her achievement, she said, was not simply a triumph for her, but "a victory for all women, for it smashed the unwritten tradition that the Senate is no place for a woman." Echoing Howorth's twin messages of individual achievement and gender solidarity, Smith said her success irrefutably demonstrated "that ability and proved performance, rather than sex, are the best standards for political selection." She then announced she "gladly accept[ed] the unofficial responsibility of being senator-at-large for America's women." With cheers and applause ringing in her ears, Smith hugged a "bouquet" of 225 congratulatory telegrams while press cameras flashed. It was a rousing start to an optimistic two-day celebration of the political power and purpose of women, and a provocative debut for the new woman senator.[3]

From the day Senator Smith took her oath of office, she was "Exhibition Number One" in Washington.[4] Everything she did was news, but her changed status did little to alter the press' conception of a political woman. Her pronouncements and speeches, her activities and votes, got less copy than her appearance. It began with abundant speculation about what she would wear opening day, apparently on the assumption that her fashion statement would set the tone for her tenure in the U.S. Senate. Her friend, May Craig, left little doubt about the importance of Mrs. Smith's physical features to her effectiveness as a senator. While her colleagues surely admired "her industry and her political sagacity and her poise and her common sense, [they] also have an eye for the friendly blue eyes and the shiny gray hair and the slim ankles. Men are the same the world over. An attractive woman—is an attractive woman."[5]

Responses to the new woman senator from the press and her colleagues ranged from the laudatory to the diminutive, sometimes both in the same breath. Columnists took particular note that she occupied the "Number One" seat in the Senate, inferring that this honor bespoke the high esteem of her colleagues. The distinction, though, came by chance. Three seats were available on the floor, and she won first choice by lot. She picked number one because it had once been the desk of Maine Senator and Lincoln's Vice President, Hannibal Hamlin.[6] When Smith took the gavel from Minority Floor Leader Kenneth Wherry during a civil rights filibuster early in the session, it was clearly her gender that made the act remarkable. Wherry bragged to reporters that it was the "first time a woman ever served as floor leader—got to bring her up right."[7]

Dozens of societies, schools and women's organizations rushed to present her with tokens of their esteem and bask in her reflected glory. Honors from her first year ranged from honorary doctorates to the American Women's Association Award for Vision, Integrity and Valor to the Kentucky Chamber of Commerce's Key to "My Old Kentucky Home." Even Hollywood joined the chorus. Sylvia Sidney starred as Congresswoman Margaret Wyndham Chase in *Mr. Ace*, with George Raft as a political boss who falls in love with her but refuses to support a woman's candidacy. Another film adopting the Smith persona was Billy Wilder's *A Foreign Affair*, with Jean Arthur as a prim and strait-laced congresswoman from Iowa. Arriving in Berlin with a congressional committee to investigate the morale of American occupation forces, she is shocked by public displays of affection until swept off her feet by a kiss from an American G.I. and, giddy with love, determines to marry him and take him home to Iowa. Katherine Hepburn and Spencer Tracy played married lawyers on opposite sides of the case of a woman who shot her philandering husband in 1949's *Adam's Rib*. Hepburn's role was exceptional for its depiction of a successful professional woman who also enjoyed an equitable relationship with a man. Prominently displayed behind attorney Hepburn's desk was a large portrait of the woman who had come to symbolize successful professional women, Senator Margaret Chase Smith.[8] Smith took it all with good grace, hoping the attention would soon wane, yet fearing that it might. Free publicity, except in the most negative of contexts, was always welcome.

Smith soon acquired a national audience, not only for her "attractiveness," but for her political opinions as well. Her weekly column, "Washington and You," became a daily with the United Features Syndicate, which also carried Eleanor Roosevelt's "My Day." Distributed to thirty-four newspapers in eighteen states, it remained, like her original weekly, "as conversational as an over-the-back-fence chat," covering subjects she knew well, from politics to military legislation to advice on how to keep cool during summers in Washington. While it added significantly to her workload and required careful writing so as not to commit herself to positions on pending legislation nor irritate her colleagues, the column also gave Smith the opportunity to communicate her ideas without the filter of the national press.[9]

The Senate was a perilous place for a woman, a place of wary alliances, competitive infighting and jockeying for position, and an institution that fiercely defended its traditions against the onslaught of newcomers and outsiders.[10] The smaller size and the less formal procedures of the Senate tended to heighten the importance of interpersonal relationships, built upon shared experiences and common values. Mrs. Smith was fifty-one years old, with no college degree, when she took her seat among some of the most highly educated and powerful men of her time. Despite her lengthy apprenticeship in the House, Smith was again a freshman and, as a woman, inescapably an outsider.

Eager to establish herself in a manner that insured the respect, if not the affection, of her ninety-five male colleagues, Smith took care not to upset gender stereotypes. For many years, she had adhered to a set of self-imposed rules for success, the first was "be feminine," followed by "don't demand special privileges" and "be friendly, but not too friendly."[11] Her reasonableness and acceptance of the conventions that bound her sex (despite often being frustrated by them) led to her being "universally approved and liked by her colleagues" in the House.[12] But she had to begin all over again in the Senate. Carl Vinson, her mentor on the Naval Affairs Committee, tried to ease her transition. In recommending her appointment to the Senate Armed Services Committee, he gave her his highest praise, pointing out that her priorities were in the right order: "While Mrs. Smith retains her charming femininity . . . she never insists upon feminine prerogatives or privileges. She is an exceptional woman—but she is an extremely effective champion of National Security before she is a woman."[13]

Smith's moderation, while perhaps less appealing as a political persuasion, was a welcome personal characteristic, particularly her insistence upon absolute equality while eschewing what she called "feminine privileges." In the House, for example, she quickly learned to arrive early for meetings to avoid having a room full of men stand up when she entered. Smith insisted on taking her place strictly according to seniority, often in the face of the insistent gallantry of male members.[14] She had a reassuring businesswoman's style in manner and dress, taking care with her grooming. As one woman columnist noted, "The statesmen can get away with unpressed trousers and dandruff, but Mrs. Smith ignores a run in her stocking at the peril of having attention called to it on a nationwide hookup."[15] Her dark suits were chosen "so as not to be too masculine, but not too unlike the rest of them." The one feminine touch

she allowed herself was a fresh rose on her lapel, which soon became
her trademark. She began wearing one initially, she said, "to take people's
attention away from my limited wardrobe."[16] Smith lived simply, avoiding social affairs. Any sense of the importance of social gatherings in
the work of a senator was negated by her discomfort as a single woman.
"I was not good at small talk," she said, and more to the point, "a woman
unescorted is conspicuously alone." Seldom invited to bring a companion of her own choosing, she "often regretted to the White House" because she had no escort.[17]

As a woman in a unconventional career, Smith found it necessary
to choose between a private existence and a life of public service. Despite persistent rumors that she might marry one of any number of "eligible bachelors," it was all just gossip. Smith had little time and no
interest in romantic entanglements. "My life," she firmly believed,
"was not compatible with a woman's life. That is why I never married
again. It would not have been fair to any man not to have a home life."[18]
The traits necessary for her political success—self-absorption, relentless
drive for approval, intense ambition—plus a tremendous investment of
time and energy, militated against close family ties. Though she sent birthday cards and regular letters to siblings, her focus was always on politics.[19] "I have no family of my own, no hobbies. My job is my life," she
once said. "I often wonder why I work so hard. And then I will walk
down to the town square and shake some hands and hear my name called
out, and I will know why all over again."[20]

Smith was fortunate to find a partner who shared her enthusiasm
for politics, someone whose skills and temperament complemented hers.
Bill Lewis provided the counterbalance to her career, the stability to her
life. While his role in her Senate campaign remained intentionally obscure, almost as soon as the ballots were counted she officially named
him as her administrative assistant. Lewis had the legal education she
lacked. He did all her research, prepared her for hearings, outlined
speeches, and helped her draft and decipher legislation. Smith's reputation for competence and sagacity owed much to Lewis' careful briefings. "I played the game," MCS said, "I didn't let them put anything over
on me. I was very fortunate to have Bill Lewis with me. . . . He gave me
the courage and support that I needed."[21]

Lewis set up Smith's Senate office and ran it with military efficiency.
Staffed with young Maine women, most of them fresh from high school,
her office was "the nerve center and backbone of my daily contact with
the people of Maine."[22] Smith took a maternal interest in her "girls,"
looking after their health and requiring them to phone their parents from

the office once a week. From them she expected strict decorum, hard work, and complete loyalty. Smith insisted upon same-day responses to an average of over 200 letters a day. Beyond that, she left the details to Lewis who, assisted by her brother-in-law Spike Bernier, instituted a regimented office procedure and maintained a strict schedule.

Spike picked up the mail early in the morning, long before regular delivery to Senate offices. He had it sorted and distributed before the staff arrived, ensuring that their inquiries to government agencies would be made before other offices received their mail. For letters demanding her personal attention, Smith typed out her responses on small slips of recycled paper in order to keep her responses brief and save dictation time. Secretaries typed them in final form. Her Senate office was simply a larger, more complex version of her House office. Constituent service continued to be the crux of her business.

Though temperamental opposites, Bill and Spike had long been friends and worked well together. Bernier seldom suppressed his sense of fun and relaxed attitude, serving as a foil for the sterner Lewis. A lean and thoughtful man, Lewis affected an imperious persona in the office and was frugal to a fault. He preferred mashed potato sandwiches to steak, and complained about the cost of twenty-five cent coffee. He wore shirts with tattered collars and cuffs, which he turned himself. "We were surprised," one former employee said, "when we learned that he was one of the richest men on the Hill." Another surprise was how different Lewis was away from the office. Once a year he and Smith held a picnic and pool party for the staff at his home in Silver Spring. There Lewis was casual, friendly and funny; "he always laughed that day."[23]

Besides his duties as office manager, chauffeur, press secretary, political strategist, and chief confidant, Lewis acted, somewhat over-eagerly, as gatekeeper and lightening rod for Smith, one who took the heat and deflected it, enabling her to challenge and match her opponents while remaining a lady. "One of the things I've been," Lewis once said, "is her S.O.B. Everyone in public service needs an S.O.B. There are things that have to be said, sometimes, and she held an elective office and I did not."[24] He kept meticulous files of correspondence, lists of Maine and non-Maine citizens "for" or "against" her, lists of those she had done favors for and the nature of that help, lists of rumors and their perpetrators.[25] Lewis scrutinized press coverage, indulging a tendency to assign malicious intent to misunderstandings. His suspicious nature and well-honed powers of outrage, combined with his unswerving loyalty to Smith, led him to conduct correspondence, particularly with the media, as a forum to expose personal slights. "Any newspaper reporter who made a factual error, no matter how minuscule, in a story involving Senator Smith," wrote a Capitol Hill correspondent, "would soon be overwhelmed in correspondence by a mountain of data underlining the mistake."[26]

Lewis was proud to take that role for his boss, whom he perceived as a lone voice of virtue, often rising in vain against the venality of others. He told friends of his great admiration for her "determined independence and indomitable courage," her willingness to "speak up and fight for what she thinks is right and decent," and the prices she paid "in political loneliness [and] tremendous hard work."[27] Loyalty and admiration at that level were very significant in sustaining her. She knew his allegiance was unequivocal and felt profoundly lucky to have him. MCS summed it up this way: "He was so devoted to me. He had complete faith in me. He would not do anything that was not right for me. He would never allow me to get into something where I might get hurt."[28]

Conventional models of female-male relationships seem inadequate to describe that of Smith and Lewis. Lewis was a true friend, giving her counsel she trusted absolutely. Over the years, he became an indispensable part of who she was. Many years later, at the end of her life, MCS admitted she loved Lewis deeply. "We loved each other," she said, "[but] I could not marry a younger man, and I could not marry and keep my job. I wish that I had made more time for love."[29] Yet theirs was a relationship so close, a mutual respect so keen, a marriage of the minds so complete that, like an old married couple who finish one another's sentences, it becomes impossible to define them separately. They shared a deep and abiding partnership that went beyond romance. Their passions were reserved for politics.

Aside, perhaps, from his unusually close personal relationship with his boss, Lewis' duties differed little from those of the typical administrative assistant (AA). Because of their immense workloads, all senators relied heavily on their AAs, who behaved as "alter egos" on routine matters. For that reason, "relationships of mutual respect and cooperation [of a] very personal nature" were the norm, and AAs valued above all for their loyalty and their willingness to serve anonymously.[30] Lewis clearly preferred his position behind the scenes. He relished the "intrigue" and the game aspects of politics, and his role in facilitating her accomplishments.[31] What was different here, of course, was that this was a man working for a woman. MCS attributed Lewis' apparent comfort with having a female boss in a time when such relationships were very rare to the legacy of his mother, Nelle. Smith was a kind of surrogate for Nelle Lewis, an attorney like her husband and son, who was politically ambitious but thwarted by poor health.[32]

Whatever private life Smith enjoyed was inextricably linked with

Bill Lewis. He and his parents had been pivotal in her senate campaign and the experience made them fast friends. Soon after the election, General and Nelle Lewis built a home in Silver Spring, Maryland, and invited Smith to live in their lower level apartment. She gladly left her efficiency flat on the Hill to join them in the suburbs.[33] The Lewises, along with Smith's sister, Laura, Spike and their son, John, provided an affectionate family environment, a haven from the stress and anxiety of her work.[34] Another member of the Bernier family, Spike's sister Blanche, had worked for Margaret since 1937, as cook, seamstress and housekeeper. A reporter once had Senator Smith, exasperated after a trying day full of conflicting demands, declaring, "What I need is a wife!"[35] The combination of Blanche and Bill came closest to meeting those needs for creature comforts and warm regard.

The Eighty-first Congress opened with "a hard-punching, shin-kicking scrap for control of the Republican Party . . . raging in the cloak-rooms, on the floor and behind deliberately closed doors on the Hill."[36] The power struggle for head of the Senate Republican Policy Committee and, by extension, head of the GOP leadership, was being fought between conservative forces backing Robert Taft and rebel progressives behind Henry Cabot Lodge. Both leaders had presidential aspirations and "both sides were wooing Mrs. Smith."[37] In an unusual display of courtliness, Taft dropped into Smith's new office to welcome her to the Senate. Whether or not she was swayed by the senior senator's charms, she once again confounded those who saw irreconcilable differences between her liberal ideology and Taft's conservatism. She believed that "Mr. Republican," was, like she, a moderate or at least an inconsistent conservative. Both of them favored public assistance programs in housing, slum clearance and federal aid to education. Since his opponents, she said, had not committed themselves to any liberal legislation, she "preferred Taft's specificness." Despite the necessity of a rule change to keep his position, Taft prevailed as chair; his durability at the helm of his party ensured, Smith's references to his liberal legislation notwithstanding, the vitality of the Republican right.[38]

Just what kind of Republican was Mrs. Smith? Called a radical liberal by conservatives and a reactionary conservative by liberals, she was generally assumed to be allied with liberal New England Republican senators like Lodge, George Aiken (VT), Irving Ives (NY) and Charles Tobey (NH). But because she seemed to rely entirely upon her inner convictions for counsel, she remained an enigma. In the House, Smith had wandered comfortably around the middle of the political spectrum, truly unclassifiable as either liberal or conservative. Her party unity score had risen to 87 percent in the Eightieth Congress after bottoming out at 41

percent in the Seventy-ninth.[39] Speculation about her ideological proclivities became entangled with remarks about feminine unpredictability.
Who could divine how a woman would vote? Her colleagues were not
comforted by her cryptic message that she intended to remain "independent" while hoping "to go along with the Republican Party as far as
I can."[40]

Smith saw herself as a conciliator, her mission to heal the split in
her party. Smith staked her claim to the middle ground and urged her
party to follow. Echoing her earlier remarks to the Republican National
Convention, she prodded them to eschew their identification with the
"upper crust" to become "champions of the average man and woman,"
a reputation, she averred, that the Democrats had successfully deployed
for far too long. Decrying the "uncivil war" among Republicans and citing polls revealing that "rank and file" Republicans were more liberal
than their leaders in the Eightieth Congress, she claimed that "the hope
of the Republican Party is to nominate liberal . . . [rather than] conservative candidates." Smith predicted that the party that identified itself
as moderate, which she defined as "a blend of true liberalism with intelligent conservatism," would ultimately triumph.[41] Taking this concept a step further, she urged enhancing bipartisan cooperation in foreign
affairs by suggesting that President Truman appoint his defeated Republican opponent, Thomas E. Dewey, to Secretary of State. Such a move,
she wrote Truman, "would be the most convincing evidence that this
country is completely united in foreign policy and on efforts to achieve
a lasting peace." The Truman administration did not acknowledge her
suggestion while conservative forces denounced it as hopelessly naive.[42]

Despite their uneasiness with her ideological ambiguity, Old Guard
Republicans perceived the need to both control and exploit their female
exemplar. So they "swallowed hard" and admitted her to their advisory
group. Under considerable duress by the leadership, Brewster magnanimously stepped aside to offer Smith his seat on the Senate Republican
Policy Committee, in what appeared to many to be a quid pro quo for
her support of Taft.[43] Usually reserved for senior party members, the
move was a tribute, Brewster said, to Mrs. Smith's achievements and
evidence of the Republican Party's commitment to "full and equal participation by women in political affairs."[44] This was the party that, only
the year before, had fired RNC Vice-chair Marion Martin for suggesting
women deserved exactly that.[45] Knowledgeable readers "gagged a bit"
over the chivalrous rhetoric in the press release, recognizing that it was
"just plain good politics not to hide such assets from the public gaze,
particularly from the gaze of women voters."[46] Nor was Smith fooled
by Brewster's oily graciousness. The two Maine senators had long main-

tained a level of wariness toward one another. She considered him du-
plicitous and deceitful; he considered her petulant and unreasonable.
Early in their relationship, in the guise of a sympathetic friend, Brewster
had attempted to dissuade her from seeking Clyde Smith's unexpired
term in 1940, while covertly aiding one of her opponents. More recently,
Smith believed Brewster, a zealous Hildreth supporter, had been behind
the smear campaign against her senate candidacy. Brewster, one of the
Senate's narrowest conservatives, privately and publicly complained
about his female colleague, accusing her of being "a New Dealer" ever
since she had come to Washington.[47]

For the moment, though, the courtship of Smith was underway. At
a pre-inauguration dinner given for her by the Brewsters, Taft toasted
her as the "Joan of Arc of the Republican Party, who may well lead us
out of the morass of defeat."[48] Behind Taft's hyperbole was the message
that Smith held great symbolic value to the Republican Party, just as she
did for America's women.

Smith had hardly settled into her new office when rumors began
circulating that she was under consideration for vice-president. Launched
by gossip columnists, the astonishing notion gained increasing legitimacy,
reflecting both the public fascination with a woman in high political office
and the desire of Republican leaders to promote her for political advantage. Broadway columnist Dorothy Kilgallen broke the story that top-
ranking Republicans were "dead serious" about promoting Smith for the
vice-presidency in order to capitalize on her "political sex appeal" and
her ability to give the party the "jazzing up" it needed.[49] Columnist Jack
Lait added more details, describing "a secret confab" in New York between the GOP hierarchy and Smith to cement her candidacy in an "attempt to stampede the feminine voters."[50]

Rumors of vice-presidential possibilities escalated into presidential
fantasies. Imagine a woman president. . . . Would she require a "lady secret service?" Would she have the presidential plane redecorated in char-
treuse and pink? Would romance bloom in the White House between
the president and vice president? and if so, who then would be the real
president?[51] Smith had fun with it all, too. When NBC commentator
Robert Trout asked her, "What would you do, Senator Smith, if you woke
up some morning and found yourself in the White House?" she replied,
"I think I'd go right to Mrs. Truman, apologize, and go right home."[52]

Despite the levity of the public discussion, or perhaps because of
it, interest in women in politics, and in the nation's highest office, seemed
to be intensifying. The latest Gallup Poll reported that 48 percent of voters
were willing to support a qualified woman for president; the percentage had climbed from 33 percent in 1937.[53] What was significant about

Smith's possibilities, observed a Maine daily, was that "hard-headed pols" were considering the matter. "Whatever the outcome of this discussion, it is a real tribute to the political acumen and the demonstrated ability of Mrs. Smith."[54]

Soon even Brewster climbed aboard the "Smith-for-Something" bandwagon, telling reporters that the new senator "would make a very attractive candidate on the national Republican ticket," and assuring them that he spoke not of Mrs. Smith's "physical charm alone, but also her demonstrated capacity to get votes."[55] Doris Fleeson added that Senator Smith was "available. All her actions since she entered the Senate prove it. . . . She is writing a daily column. . . . She has offered her party a formula, very sensible, too, for the cure of its ills. . . . The Republicans are hardly in a position to snub any assets and an asset she is."[56] The esteem Taft had earlier expressed seemed, in light of the current discussion, portentous. On the spot, he somewhat reluctantly conceded that Mrs. Smith would make an ideal candidate for vice-president, although, he hastily added, he knew of no efforts toward that goal.[57] The press ran with it: Taft and Smith would balance conservative and progressive, business and labor, male and female, "ability and magnetism."[58] Under the same scrutiny, Smith politely disavowed any aspirations for higher office, but expressed gratitude for friends' approbations: "It's nice to be flattered and talked about. In that way, perhaps, I am more woman than senator."[59]

The talk did not die out with Smith's denials, however. Indeed, she added her own spark to the speculation when she remarked during a radio address that she believed women should fight for a spot on the national ticket—either president or vice-president. "By the objective standards of sheer merit and capability," Smith said, "there is no reason why a woman can't hold either of the two top offices of this country" and, she added, the "party that nominates a woman for vice-president or president will win the 1952 election." Since she was the only apparently eligible woman on the horizon, her quick disclaimer that she was not seeking such a seat herself but would fight for other qualified women candidates, seemed disingenuous.[60] Despite the self-serving remark, Smith was politically savvy enough to know that she was "not acceptable as a nominee on the ticket to those who presently control the Republican Party."[61] Much too unpredictable and liberal for the acknowledged leaders, Smith had little to offer the GOP ticket other than her sex, which she rightly believed was not enough. The women's vote was too ephemeral to count on, and likely to be won by less drastic means.

Smith knew her position as the Republican's "woman" was being exploited, but she genuinely believed that she could use it to modify perceptions about women in politics and to influence the direction of her party. She took the opportunity to deliver some well-aimed barbs at the powerful men who denied women's equality and controlled their political access. In testimony before Senate Rules, considering a direct presidential primary, Smith stated flatly: "The election of a woman president would be a miracle under our present system, not because the people would not elect a woman but because it is so highly improbable that the political parties would nominate a woman." Moreover, she would not have been elected to the senate were it not for Maine's direct primary system, which allowed her to nominate herself. The very fact that the GOP was currently toying with the idea of placing a woman in candidacy for the vice presidency provided a graphic example of how nominees are chosen "by a monopolistic political minority, rather than the people themselves." A national primary was needed to wrest power from this group and bring party organization under popular control. Only then would women have a fair chance at the nation's highest office.[62]

Smith's election to the Senate and public discussion of her suitability for the vice presidency stimulated a national debate that took the idea of women in high political office seriously, but it did nothing to alter the fact that Smith was again on the bottom rung of seniority. Her area of expertise, military defense, remained her first priority. She lobbied hard for assignment to Senate Armed Services while continuing to make tough speeches on preparedness that attracted national and international attention. "Russia has left us no other choice but to rearm," she said, in a characteristic speech, even at the "risk of economic insecurity. . . . We should make it crystal clear to the Politburo that we will back up our firm talk. . . . We should extend the olive branch with an eagle, instead of a dove carrying it to the bear."[63] Bernard Baruch, financier and hardline architect of American atomic policy, praised her speech as "full of good sense," while Moscow's *Literary Gazette* listed her among their rogues gallery of "warmongers" and "pen gangsters" plotting war against the Soviet Union.[64] But it failed to move ASC Chairman Chan Gurney. Smith would have to wait for four years, and Gurney's retirement, for that prize. Instead, she drew the Committee on Expenditures in the Executive Departments and the freshman's bane—the District of Columbia Committee.

Smith shared both of her committee assignments with Senator Joseph McCarthy of Wisconsin. They had known each other casually since being introduced by their mutual friend, May Craig, at an informal dinner party in 1947. Now when she asked McCarthy, the ranking Republican on Expenditures, for assignment to the Permanent Investigations Subcommittee, a plum for a freshman, he agreed.[65] For the first few months of the Eighty-first Congress, the subcommittee, headed by Sen. Clyde R. Hoey (D-NC), concerned itself with the activities of "five-percenters," men who had allegedly used their influence to secure government contracts for clients in return for a five percent commission. What began as a minor concern soon blossomed into a major scandal. The subcommittee's preliminary witness, lobbyist John Maragon, implicated several influential officials, among them James V. Hunt, a former Army officer and War Assets Administration consultant. His testimony, in turn, incriminated presidential aide General Harry Vaughn, who subsequently confessed to using his position to obtain favors for friends, and to accepting seven deep freezes which he passed along to First Lady Bess Truman, Chief Justice Fred M. Vinson and a host of lesser officials.[66]

When the subcommittee's three Republicans—McCarthy, Karl Mundt (SD), and Smith—met to discuss strategy, Smith pressed for a strong condemnation of the administration. In addition to her disgust with evident corruption, she was dismayed that press photos of Hunt's office revealed her autographed portrait among several dozen on his wall. Though innocently given, the photograph imparted a suggestion she was eager to discourage.[67] McCarthy and Mundt favored a milder reprimand, apparently reluctant to come down hard on John Maragon, who was later convicted of perjury for his testimony to the subcommittee. Maragon, a lobbyist for a sugar refiner and soft drink company, had inspired McCarthy's zealous pursuit of the end of sugar rationing, an effort that earned him the sobriquet "the Pepsi-Cola Kid."[68] Smith would not budge and after she threatened to file a minority report, her two colleagues gave in. And they further agreed not to publicly acknowledge their discord. Smith was furious, then, when McCarthy told reporters that she would hold a press conference about the closed meeting.[69] This violation of committee confidentiality shocked Smith, and she angrily vowed she would not trust his word again. Some weeks later, McCarthy asked her to speak on his behalf to a group of women in Milwaukee. Smith found it necessary to regret the invitation, sending instead a neutral note, couched in the language of senatorial courtesy, citing only McCarthy's "ability to get things done."[70]

At the conclusion of her first year in the U.S. Senate, Smith was still pushing toward the center. She predicted that "the Number One national development in 1950 [would be] an emphasis and growth of moderation and a trend away from the extremes that have marked the recent years . . . [involving] the development in the Republican Party of a moderate middle group between the extremes of 'me tooers' to the left and 'aginers' [*sic*] to the right who oppose everything the Democrats have done, including the good things."[71] In that same spirit, Smith objected to the flamboyant overstatement and negative language of the Republican's twenty-five hundred-word "Statement of Objectives and Principles" drafted by the conservatives for the 1950 mid-term elections. "We have to get away from the formal, legalistic language," she wrote Committee Chairman Taft. "We have to use the language of the common man. . . . The Republican Party must humanize itself in the eyes of the American voters." She advised the statement be reduced to a short list of major issues upon which "the conservatives, the liberals and the moderates of the Party can agree in complete unity."[72] In a nationally broadcast Lincoln Day speech, Smith praised the GOP for holding a "dollar-box-lunch affair—a common man's affair, not a $100-a-plate rich man's affair" to raise campaign funds. Then she presented her own rendering of the Statement of Principles, reduced from twenty-five hundred words to eighty-nine. Couched in "common, everyday words of the average man in the street," her version emphasized economic issues, including a balanced budget and reduced taxes, while minimizing ideological appeals.[73] The National Republican Senatorial and Congressional Committees later released this as a "digest" of their statement of principles.[74]

Party leaders seemed to value her views, but only up to a point. Moderation was a dirty word and independence anathema to party regulars who blamed Republican liberals and moderates for disharmony and defeat. One Maine editorial fretted that Smith's suggestions for compromise between the divergent views of "arch conservatives and liberal partisans" could easily "balance the Republican Party right out of the picture again."[75] Frustrated by twenty years of failure and powerlessness, cheated of presidential victory in the recent election, conservative leaders listened impatiently to Smith's counsels of moderation and bipartisanship.[76] At the very moment she was making her Lincoln Day forecasts of unity and conciliation, another junior senator was making the rounds in the Midwest. And Senator Joseph McCarthy was assuredly not advocating moderation. The issue he launched in his Lincoln Day speech in Wheeling, West Virginia, would eclipse all others in the next several Congresses and turn his party irreparably to the right. Never one to shrink from challenging her opponents, Smith would ultimately learn the price of taking on McCarthy and the conservatives.

8

A Declaration of Conscience

"I have here in my hand a list of 205 Communist agents in the Truman Administration," Senator Joseph McCarthy told the Ohio County Women's Republican Club in Wheeling, West Virginia. These men "have been named as members of the Communist Party and members of a spy ring ... [who are] known to the Secretary of State and who nevertheless are still working and shaping the policy of the State Department."[1] This bombshell, repeated in various mutations to the press as McCarthy made his Lincoln Day speech tour, launched what came to be called "McCarthyism," a steadily escalating spree of charges, innuendos, and smears, aimed at alleged Communists and designed to destroy the Democratic hegemony in Washington.

From Wheeling to Salt Lake City to Denver to Reno, McCarthy declared that there were 205 (later he said 57) "active Communists" or "card-carrying Communists" in the State Department. The more press attention he got, the louder and more vehement his assertions. In Salt Lake City, McCarthy offered to provide the names to the Secretary of State; in Reno, he dispatched a telegram to President Truman demanding the State Department's loyalty files be reopened lest the Democratic Party be labeled "the bedfellow of international Communism."[2] Upon his return to Washington, McCarthy triumphantly announced that he had penetrated "Truman's iron curtain of secrecy" about subversives in his administration.[3] A week later, in a rambling, sometimes incoherent and constantly contradictory eight-hour speech on the Senate floor, he again recited his charges. His speech was punctuated by frequent interruptions from Democratic Majority Leader Scott Lucas, in a futile attempt to force McCarthy to straighten out his numbers.[4] Still, the issue was so explosive that only two days later, the Senate created a special subcommittee of the Foreign Relations Committee, chaired by Millard Tydings (D-MD), to investigate McCarthy's charges.[5] Along with her colleagues, Smith listened to those allegations with alarm. Impressed by the force of his presentation, convinced by his apparent possession of specific information, she thought, at least at first, that he "was onto something disturbing and frightening. . . . I made it a point to go to the Senate floor repeatedly to listen to his speeches."[6]

It is easy to see why McCarthy's assertions captured public attention. Though American concern about subversion has a long history, reaching back at least to the Russian Revolution of 1917, never had the threat of worldwide Communism loomed larger than it did in the five years since the conclusion of World War II. By the time McCarthy made his speech in February 1950, the Soviets had extended their "iron curtain" across Eastern Europe, Mao Tse-tung brought Communism to China, major Communist parties were established in France and Italy, and the Russians had exploded their own atomic bomb. At home, one astonishing headline after another attested to widespread disloyalty and espionage. More than a thousand classified documents had been discovered in the offices of the left-wing magazine *Amerasia* in 1945, and despite repeated conservative attempts to investigate and exploit the matter, it remained unresolved.[7] The following year, Canada exposed several rings of Soviet spies engaged in sending atomic secrets and uranium to Moscow. And the year after that, in 1947, the House Un-American Activities Committee (HUAC) under J. Parnell Thomas (R-NJ) claimed Americans were being brainwashed by Reds in the motion picture industry.[8]

The fear of radicalism had long been easily exploited for partisan ends. Martin Dies, a right-wing demagogue from Texas and first chairman of a Special House Committee on Un-American Activities, honed it into a key political weapon in the late 1930s when he turned allegations of Communism in government into a bludgeon against the liberal New Deal policies of the Roosevelt administration.[9] After the war, the deterioration of American-Soviet relations and the effort to uproot domestic subversion led to an escalating game of partisan charges and countercharges. Anti-Communist hyperbole, long a staple in Republican platform oratory, took center stage. During the 1946 campaign, for example, the chairman of the Republican National Committee tagged Democratic policy with "a made-in-Moscow label."[10] That November, Republicans won control of both Houses of Congress for the first time since 1928. Two years later, the Republican platform contained a plank pledging "to expose the treasonable activities of Communists and defeat their objective of establishing here a godless dictatorship controlled from abroad."[11] Sensing a winner for the 1950 campaign, the GOP's adoption of the motto: "Let Us Get America Out of the Red . . . and the Reds Out of America" demonstrated its intention to again make Communist subversion a major campaign issue. Their Statement of Principles threw down the gauntlet, condemning "the failure of the administration to recognize the full implications" of the Communist conspiracy, deploring "the dangerous degree to which Communists and their fellow travelers have been employed in important government posts" and pledging "immediate action to bring about the prompt elimination of all Communists, fellow travelers, and Communist sympathizers from our federal payroll."[12]

Nor was the rhetoric milder on the Democratic side. President Truman employed a declamation of fear to build public support for his extraordinary, and extraordinarily expensive, containment policies. Further, to counter Republican charges of waffling on Communism, he issued Executive Order 9835 creating a federal employee loyalty program designed to eliminate "security risks." His attorney general, Tom Clark, ominously warned that Communists "are everywhere—in factories, offices, butcher shops, on street corners, in private business—and each carries with him the germs of death for society."[13]

Republicans had seized the upper hand in the most sensational espionage drama of 1948. Testimony before HUAC from former Communists Elizabeth Bentley and Whittaker Chambers linked numerous prominent Americans to a Communist cell inside the government. The GOP contended that the FBI had refused to investigate and that domestic subversion was undermining American foreign policy. Chambers alleged that Alger Hiss, a former State Department official involved in planning the Yalta conference, and then head of the Carnegie Endowment for International Peace, had passed military secrets directly to the Soviets. Hiss sued for libel. Orchestrated by a young Republican congressman from California, Richard Nixon, charges and countercharges dominated the headlines for months. On the defensive, prominent Democrats, including Secretary of State Dean Acheson and Adlai Stevenson, vouched for Hiss's integrity. President Truman angrily dismissed the charges as "a red herring" fabricated by the Republicans.[14] In the end, Hiss was convicted of perjury, the statute of limitations having expired for an espionage conviction.

As the Hiss case unfolded, a Justice Department employee, Judith Coplon, was arrested and convicted of passing secrets to the Soviets. Then the British government announced the arrest and confession of Dr. Klaus Fuchs, a physicist who had worked on the Manhattan Project during the war, of delivering atomic information to the Russians. His testimony led to the arrest and execution of Julius and Ethel Rosenberg as Soviet spies. Republicans could hardly contain themselves. As historian Robert Griffith writes, "Here at last was meat and substance for the Republican charge of Communism in government. Here was confirmation of their worst suspicions and their fondest hopes."[15]

Three weeks after the Hiss conviction, Joe McCarthy made his speech at Wheeling. At the same time, Richard Nixon's Lincoln Day speech contained a warning of secret forces intent upon imposing the "slavery" of Communism upon the United States.[16] McCarthy's use of anti-Communist rhetoric, then, was right in step with his party. What made him different was the ruthless, unrelenting ferocity of his attacks. As the press reported his sensational charges, McCarthy's public popularity grew. His explanations for America's dilemma made sense: the "fall" of China was caused by traitors in the State Department; the Soviet development of atomic weapons was due to spies in the Manhattan Project; the core of American government was riddled with traitors. Five months after his Wheeling speech, opinion polls showed widespread support, and letters to the Senate were strongly pro-McCarthy.[17]

Conservative Republicans, motivated by a mix of conviction and political opportunism, were content to let McCarthy take the lead on the anti-Communist front. The Senate's most powerful Republican, Robert Taft, equally committed to removing Communists from the State Department and restoring Republicans to Congress, urged Joe to "keep punching." Figuring that the law of averages would eventually pay off, he counseled his colleague: "if one case doesn't work, try another."[18] Taft's friend and Smith's Maine colleague, Owen "Me, too" Brewster, joined in vocal support of McCarthy, excoriating the Truman administration for its lax security procedures and charging the Tydings Subcommittee with attempting to "whitewash" the Communist-riddled State Department.[19]

Democrats, while emphasizing their commitment to "observing at all times the constitutional guarantees which protect free speech, the free press and honest political activity," hastened to demonstrate that they, too, were not soft on Communism.[20] The Tydings Subcommittee "debate" quickly deteriorated into partisan hostilities. While McCarthy denounced the "egg-sucking phony liberals" allied against his crusade to drive out the "prancing mimics of the Moscow party line in the State Department," Democrats jumped into the fray with similar rhetoric.[21] Freshman Senator William Benton (D-CT), for example, denounced McCarthy as a "hit-and-run propagandist of the Kremlin model."[22]

Regardless of their opinions about Senator McCarthy's mission and methods, members of both parties were wary of directly confronting him.

The Democrats assumed that the Republicans were obligated to curb a member of their own party; the Republicans assumed that Democrats were obligated to disprove McCarthy's contentions. Moderate Republicans like Smith squirmed. Personally offended by his loud and boorish behavior, so counter to the senatorial courtesy she respected and cherished, Smith was growing increasingly distressed by the breadth and virulence of McCarthy's charges. She also entertained serious doubts about his veracity. She asked to see the papers he waved about as he made his charges on the Senate floor. The "photostatic copies" he showed her looked authentic, she thought, although they did not seem particularly relevant to his assertions. Still, as a nonlawyer, Smith felt she lacked the expertise to determine their validity. But the more she listened and the more she read those papers, the "more I began to wonder whether I was as stupid as I had thought."[23] In April, she expressed her misgivings by inserting the remarks of Vice-President Barkley and an editorial critical of McCarthy into the *Congressional Record*. Barkley had argued that, given current standards, Tom Paine might be found guilty of subversion; the editorial sardonically suggested McCarthy look into the matter.[24]

Smith recoiled when McCarthy accused Dorothy Kenyon of being a "security risk," who belonged to "at least twenty-eight Communist front organizations."[25] Smith knew Judge Kenyon and could not believe the charges were true. The New York judge was a prominent "patroness" of the Multi-Party Committee on Women, Inc., which had celebrated her election to the Senate, and a strong supporter of women in public life.[26] As had happened so often before and after, McCarthy's "verbiage outran his evidence," and his case against Kenyon fell apart. He quickly rebounded, hurling new charges at ever more prominent State and Foreign Service officials, such as U.S. Ambassador-at-large Philip Jessup, China Foreign Service officer John S. Service, State Department liaison officer Esther Brunauer, and Far Eastern policy adviser, Owen Lattimore.[27]

Smith deeply resented McCarthy's bullying Kenyon and his intimidation of anyone who disagreed with him. She was particularly sensitive to accusations of leftist sympathies forged in her recent campaign. She knew what it felt like to be unjustly accused and how difficult it was to disprove public perceptions. At the same time, Smith believed the Truman administration had been criminally lax in security, despite its loyalty program, and that national security depended upon the elimination of internal subversion. While she was as terrified as anyone of the insidious Communist menace, though, she abhorred the ways in which McCarthy's investigations trampled civil liberties. The most egregious sin, as far as she was concerned, was the destruction of individuals' reputations under the sanctity of congressional immunity for selfish political gain. Well before her experience with smears in her 1948 campaign, Smith demonstrated her discomfort with the transparent political agenda of HUAC. While she supported the fundamental goals of the anti-Communism committee, she voted against establishing a permanent HUAC and opposed funding its probes, suggesting that the FBI would be a more appropriate agency to investigate subversion.[28] During her first year in the Senate she backed efforts to define a "code of fair procedure" for investigating committees that placed restrictions on investigating procedures and gave witnesses procedural rights that were routine in criminal trials. In discussing the resolution in her column, Smith cited past abuses of congressional immunity and seemed to demonstrate a prescience about future investigatory hearings. She suggested that "the safest and surest way to minimize and avoid abuse is to appoint the most judicious and conscientious members to the investigating committees, to rule out the 'headline hunters,' to appoint members who are interested in facts rather than publicity—who want to investigate objectively rather than publicize passionately."[29] Such members were hard to come by in the 1950 Senate.

Every evening, as she left the floor, Smith returned to the office and complained to Bill Lewis that McCarthy was taking a legitimate issue and making a mockery of it. Someone should do something, she said; someone should protest against the partisan abuses of the Communist issue on both sides of the aisle.[30] But everyone seemed to be frightened of McCarthy. Several friends, notably journalists Ed Hart and Doris Fleeson, suggested her independence and rectitude made her "the ideal person to speak out and challenge Joe McCarthy." Still, she was extremely reluctant to do so. "In the first place, I was a freshman senator—and in those days, freshmen senators were to be seen and not heard, like good children." Second, like other Republican moderates, she felt that the Democrats should challenge him, but they were making a miserable mess of it on the Tydings Subcommittee. "Increasingly, it became evident that Joe had the Senate paralyzed with fear." And it became evident that if anyone was going to "do something," it would have to be her.[31]

Smith and Lewis prepared a statement. They discussed releasing it as a petition, to be placed on the speaker's desk and available to anyone who wanted to sign it. But she was convinced that if any of the conservatives knew of her plan, they would use Senate procedure to thwart her. She decided instead to privately ask a small group of moderates to join her, choosing only those she could trust to honor her confidence. She began with her friend from Vermont, George Aiken, and together they chose five others who agreed to sign: Charles Tobey of New Hampshire, who had been a friend of Clyde Smith's; Wayne Morse of Oregon, then a liberal Republican, later a Democrat; Irving Ives, a moderate from New York; Edward Thye of Minnesota to represent McCarthy's own region; and Robert Hendrickson of New Jersey.[32]

Smith and Lewis drove home for the Memorial Day weekend, discussing their strategy on the way. Despite her timidity, Lewis convinced her to make a speech to effectively introduce the statement. "I wanted him to write it," MCS remembered, "[but] I didn't ask and he didn't offer. . . . [H]e wanted it to be mine." So, as Lewis drove, she jotted notes about what she needed to say. Then they sat down together at her dining room table and drafted the most important speech of her life.[33]

Back in Washington, under tight security, Lewis mimeographed two hundred copies of her speech and held them in his arms as they headed for the floor. She instructed him to withhold release of the copies until after she began to speak.[34] Just prior to the afternoon session, Lewis asked the chamber's presiding officer, one of her cosigners, Irving Ives, to recognize Smith at the beginning of the session as she had an important speech to make. Ives probably assumed she intended to read the statement into the record; neither he nor the other cosigners knew of her intention to make a major address.[35]

Her voice trembled as she began: "I would like to speak briefly and simply about a serious national condition. . . . I speak as a Republican. I speak as a woman. I speak as a United States Senator. I speak as an American." Smith reminded her colleagues that they had all sworn to uphold and defend the Constitution, yet "those of us who shout the loudest about Americanism . . . are all too frequently those who, by our own words and acts, ignore some of the basic principles of Americanism— the right to criticize; the right to hold unpopular beliefs; the right to protest, the right of independent thought." The exercise of these rights, she continued, "should not cost one single American citizen his reputation or his right to a livelihood. . . . Freedom of speech is not what it used to be in America. It has been so abused by some that it is not exercised by others."

The Communist menace was real, she said, but instead of joining together to fight back, "Republicans and Democrats alike are playing directly into the Communist design of 'confuse, divide and conquer.'" As a result, she said, the Senate had become "debased to the level of a forum of hate and character assassination sheltered by the shield of congressional immunity . . . [and turned into] a rendezvous for vilification, for selfish political gain at the sacrifice of individual reputations and national unity."

There was little doubt among her listeners that most of her criticisms were aimed at McCarthy. Still, Smith did not spare the Democrats. The administration, she said, had "pitifully failed to provide effective leadership [on this issue]. . . . Yet to displace it with a Republican regime embracing a philosophy that lacks political integrity or intellectual honesty would prove equally disastrous to this nation. The nation sorely needs a Republican victory. But I don't want to see the Republican Party ride to political victory on the Four Horsemen of Calumny—Fear, Ignorance, Bigotry, and Smear."

When she had finished, Smith placed what she called the "Declaration of Conscience," endorsed by her six colleagues, into the *Record.* Making essentially the same points as her speech, though with considerably less passion, the document accused the Democratic administration and "some elements of the Republican Party" of contributing to "the growing confusion that threatens the security and stability of our country" for reasons of "selfish political exploitation."[36]

McCarthy sat white faced, two rows behind her as she spoke. Smith sat down, bracing herself for a rebuttal. But McCarthy said nothing, just stood up, and quietly left the floor.[37] If she had hoped that her fellow senators would respond with applause and congratulations, she was sorely disappointed. Only a couple of brief comments about her "inspiring and thought-provoking" address followed. Afterward, Smith slipped out to pack, then caught the midnight train to New York and then on to Florence for the Fifth Session of the General Conference of UNESCO meeting. Along with Sen. William Benton (D-CT), she had been appointed congressional advisor to the meeting, a gesture toward a bipartisan foreign policy and, perhaps, a gesture toward the female half of the population. Smith's participation was relatively insignificant, and might have gone unnoticed had it not had some utility in partisan attacks that followed her speech.[38]

Neither Taft nor Brewster had anything to say to the press. Even McCarthy, in a rare demonstration of reticence, made no official comment. The next day on the Senate floor, he resumed his demands for expulsion of Communists from government and indirectly responded to Smith: "Let me make it clear that this fight against Communism, this attempt to expose and neutralize the efforts of those who are attempting to betray this country, shall not stop regardless of what any individual or group in this Senate, or in the Administration may say or do."[39] He supposedly told his friends that he would not reply to "the spanking" she gave him because she was a woman. "I don't fight with women senators," he allegedly said.[40] Ridicule was always his weapon of choice; he quickly dismissed the tiny group of moderates as "Snow White and her Six Dwarfs."[41]

While Smith was on her way to Florence, her speech exploded in the press. The reactions were predictable: progressives loved it, conservatives

hated it. Hundreds of letters poured into her office; dozens of prominent Americans including historians, publishers, judges, business leaders and journalists wrote privately to praise and thank her. Typical was
author Herman Wouk's remark that "the national conscience has spoken from your throat. By one act of political courage, you have justified
a lifetime in politics."[42] Bernard Baruch commented that had a man made
the speech, he would be the next president of the United States.[43]

Many newspapers printed the entire text accompanied with florid
prose. The *Chicago Sun-Times*, for example, effusively lauded her courage
as part of an American tradition: "It has in it the ring of Lexington and
Valley Forge, of the Gettysburg address, of the American classroom, of
the American home, the American Sunday school and the American
church. This is a better Sabbath because of Margaret Chase Smith."[44]
Newsweek put her on their cover with the caption: "Senator Smith: A
Woman Vice President?" and commended her for wielding "her precise,
reasoned phrases . . . as neatly as a broom sweeping out a mess."[45] Harold
Ickes offered "orchids to Senator Smith. . . . If women had not already
made good on their right to vote," he wrote, "the granting of the franchise would have been fully justified when Margaret Chase Smith, Senator from Maine, spoke as she did in the Senate on June 1."[46]

Across the aisle, Westbrook Pegler found her "a nominal Republican . . . [who] took advantage of the special privilege of her sex . . . [to
engage in] selfish, harmful criticism of the party which elected her. She
and the six other Republicans . . . do not understand what a Republican
should be."[47] To the *Saturday Evening Post*, she represented "the Soft
Underbelly of the Republican Party."[48] Others more nastily assailed her
as an "egg-sucking" liberal, part of that "Moscow-loving, one-world, global
thinkers and planetary do-gooders" cabal of New Dealers. She had used,
they charged, "noticeably less vehemence" in criticizing Democrats and
her remark about the four horsemen of calumny provided valuable campaign material for the enemy.[49] The general message from the conservatives was that Smith was wrongheaded to interfere with patriot Joe, and
her remarks played right into the hands of the Democrats, if not the Reds.

The Washington Post called the speech "a seething indictment. . . .
Although she did not mention his name, it was clear her principal tar-
get was Senator McCarthy."[50] Numerous commentators made much of
the fact that she did not use his name. She could not; she was treading
on the thin ice of senatorial courtesy. Rules prohibited "direct personal
criticism toward another congressman [or any attempts to] question his
motives, his character, or his honesty."[51]

Smith's home-state newspaper notices were largely favorable. With one important exception, previously friendly papers remained so. The two major independents, the *Daily Kennebec Journal* in Augusta and the *Bangor Daily Commercial*, praised her for delivering "a public document of great significance . . . [that represented] statesmanship of the highest order." Other Maine papers crowed that Smith had "more than made up for her handicap of sex with courage and political acumen" and likened her speech to "a fresh breeze in the fear-ridden atmosphere" of the Senate.[52] Her previously enthusiastic booster, publisher Guy Gannett however, could not contain his disillusionment. Her Declaration of Conscience had done more harm than good, he wrote, because it "gave the administration a weapon which helped it to whitewash the State Department."[53] The loss of Gannett's support was a serious blow to Smith's standing in Maine; several years would pass before his editorials praised her again.

Smith's speech was a two-edged sword, though many chose to remark upon only one edge, that one unmistakably aimed at Joe McCarthy. The central message of Smith's speech, lost in the clamor over McCarthy, was that the Senate as a whole had ignored "some of the basic principles of Americanism" and allowed itself to be "debased to the level of a forum of hate and character assassination." The danger lay not in Senator McCarthy alone, but in the failure of respectable members to put a stop to him. It is difficult at this distance to comprehend the climate of fear and distrust that McCarthy personified. One measure is the disinclination of members of both parties to join Smith's call for patriotism and integrity in government. Those who valued individual freedoms should have; those who abhorred McCarthy's methods could have. Only twelve of the fifty-four Senate Democrats spoke out against McCarthy; only eight Republicans cared to repudiate him.[54] All but one who signed on with Smith's Declaration of Conscience quickly recanted. Most Republicans kept silent, preferring, as Taft did, to covertly encourage McCarthy while keeping a prim distance from his methods. Instead of welcoming her plea for ethics and honesty, the president tossed off a flip response, asserting he would not want to say anything that bad about the Republican Party.[55] Historians attest that the Declaration of Conscience was politically insignificant, with little or no lasting influence upon McCarthy or McCarthyism. Yet, the failure of Smith's statement to have a lasting impact is less a criticism of the statement than an indication of the strength of McCarthyism and its value to the Republican Party.[56]

Before the month was out, four of the six dwarfs "ran like ants from a burning log."[57] Apparently feeling the heat of negative reaction at home and fearful of retaliation, they explained that their enthusiasm for Senator

Smith should not be interpreted as any reflection on Senator McCarthy. Senator Thye protested that he had no intention of criticizing McCarthy and was just as eager as his fellow senator to see subversives routed from the State Department. For the record, he added, "I should like to say that the distinguished senator from Wisconsin . . . has performed a service to his country and to his state by what he has done."[58] Ives took the floor to assure McCarthy that he was "in full sympathy with the attitude of the senator from Wisconsin" and to commend him "for the excellent presentation he has made, for the constructive approach he has offered."[59] Senator Tobey, the only signer up for reelection in 1950, caved in after McCarthy attacked his politics and his manhood, calling him a "coddler of Communists" and a "man who speaks through a petticoat."[60] Tobey hastened to contain the damage by assuring his constituents that he had "not disavowed Senator McCarthy," on the contrary, he believed his "objectives are good."[61] Hendrickson, too, capitulated under McCarthy's withering hostility, hastening to imply that he had been pressured into criticizing his colleague. George Aiken remained Smith's friend, but distanced himself from her statement. He was really, MCS explained, "a conservative at heart," and a politician who preferred "popularity to principle." Only Wayne Morse held fast.[62]

In July the Tydings Subcommittee concluded, as everyone who had watched the partisan bickering expected, that McCarthy had perpetrated a "fraud and a hoax" on the Senate and the American people. The subcommittee charged him with "perhaps the most nefarious campaign of half-truths and untruths in the history of this republic."[63] McCarthy alleged the report was "a signal to the traitors, Communists and fellow travelers in our Government that they need have no fear of exposure."[64] After "the meanest Senate debate in recent memory," the report was accepted on a straight party vote.[65]

Congressional attention shifted, at least for a time, to foreign policy with the invasion of South Korea by Communist North Korea. American leaders including Smith believed the move a direct Soviet challenge to American security, one that must be resisted immediately and with all possible force.[66] Eschewing a declaration of war or even congressional approval, President Truman opted instead to work through the United Nations in committing U.S. troops to stop the North Korean advance. By the time the Americans arrived, Communist forces had pushed the South Koreans to the Pusan peninsula on the southern tip of Korea. There they dug in and held through the summer.[67]

Stalemate in Korea reinvigorated the anti-Communist issue and fueled Republican attacks in the 1950 campaign. Congress scrambled to pass a bill, almost any bill, to demonstrate their anti-Communist credentials before the November elections. The Internal Security (McCarren) Act, requiring the registration of "Communist action groups" and providing for their detention in times of "national emergency," passed over Truman's veto in September. Opponents claimed the bill not only violated basic constitutional liberties but would merely drive Communists underground. Supporters, like Smith, believed it a necessary countermeasure in view of the peculiar nature of Communism. One must, she said, be prepared to "fight insidious methods with insidious methods."[68]

What might appear to be moral equivocation bespoke Smith's central dilemma. On the one hand, she was firmly committed to civil liberties and civility in public debate; on the other, she believed Communism to be "an alarming menace that has taken full advantage of the constitutional rights of free speech and personal protection guaranteed by our free republic." While she trusted that it was possible to balance "the protection of civil rights and the protection of national security," the line had to be drawn against the "spies and traitors who would betray our country." Therefore, "relentless exposure and eradication of Communism here should be one of the top objectives of our government."[69]

In the fall, McCarthy interjected himself in campaigns to defeat two Democrats who had badgered him in recent hearings: Scott Lucas of Illinois and Millard E. Tydings of Maryland. In Illinois, McCarthy stumped for Everett McKinley Dirksen, pounding away at Lucas with the Communists-in-government issue. Dirksen won easily. But it was in the Tydings campaign that the perception of McCarthy's "political invincibility" took shape. Tydings was standing for his fifth consecutive term against a Baltimore attorney, John Marshall Butler. In what a Senate subcommittee report would later describe as "a despicable 'back street' type of campaign," McCarthy and his staff tapped wealthy campaign contributors (including $1,000 from Owen Brewster), produced a campaign tabloid called "From the Record" including twisted statistics and a "composite" photograph of Tydings listening intently to Earl Browder, head of the American Communist Party.[70] At the same time, Richard Nixon was also successfully parlaying his anti-Communist reputation into election to the Senate against Helen Gahagan Douglas in California. Tarring her with leftist ideology as well as gender, Nixon repeatedly referred to her as the "pink lady" and circulated tally sheets lining up her votes with those of Vito Marcantonio that looked suspiciously like those used by Nixon's friend, Owen Brewster, against Smith two years before.[71] The 1950 election brought in twenty-eight new Republican representatives and five new Republican senators, proving that riding with the "four horsemen of calumny" paid off.

In Korea, the "police action" continued. In September, Commander Gen. Douglas MacArthur launched an amphibious flank attack at Inchon, on the west coast, and rolled the North Koreans back into their own territory, crossing the 38th parallel by October. The war to save South Korea was over; the war to liberate North Korea had begun. What had started as an American attempt to preserve the government of Syngman Rhee and restore the boundary at the 38th parallel was transformed into a war against international Communism and an attempt to unify the two Koreas by force. Likening Russia to a "big bully who cries and runs the very first time he gets his nose bloodied," Smith applauded the new American aggressiveness and predicted easy victory.[72] But when MacArthur recklessly pushed on toward the Yalu River, challenging the Chinese Communists, the bully did not run. Chinese troops cut through the center of the American line. This was no time for timidity, Smith responded, the Communists respect only force. The United States must be willing to use any means necessary, including the use of atomic weapons, "for the preservation of peace." Frustrated by the concept of limited war, she equated it with appeasement, making an analogy between Korea and the events at Munich that resulted in the propitiation of dictators and culminated in global war.[73]

The situation in Korea was hardly analogous to Munich in 1938, yet wars are always fought from the lessons of the previous one. The ghost of Neville Chamberlain haunted the discourse on Korea. President Truman, in his address to Congress in July, equated Korean aggression with Communist expansionism and talked more about Hitler and Munich than about Korea.[74] To Smith, as to many leaders who had learned the lessons of World War II, anything short of total commitment was "nothing more than surrender on the installment plan."[75] Korea was a test of courage and no time for partisan bickering. Smith urged the president to "reorganize his entire Cabinet into a wartime coalition," and called on her colleagues for "unity on everything that is vital to our country . . . and forget politics. . . . We must convert . . . to war production as soon as we can."[76]

Rather than with unity, however, the U.S. Congress responded to the war crisis with more charges and countercharges. McCarthy continued unabated. In confirmation hearings for Anna Rosenberg for Assistant Secretary of Defense, McCarthy and his minions once again impugned the reputation of a Democratic official, although this time, in relatively short order, the charges were proven groundless and Rosenberg confirmed. But Smith was not satisfied; she reiterated her anger at unfounded and malicious charges, and she called upon the Armed Services Committee, which had handled the hearings, to "finish the job . . . to investigate thoroughly how those charges first arose and who is responsible. . . . It is not enough merely to clear a person so maliciously smeared with false accusations. . . . Perjury convictions should work both ways. . . . It is not only a matter of ethics and moral codes now—it is a matter of sabotage of our national security. For to undermine the confidence of the people with false malicious accusations in the very technique of that big lie so ruthlessly exploited by the Communists themselves is nothing short of treasonable psychological sabotage."[77] Her suggestion was treated as so much empty rhetoric. McCarthy was simply too hot to challenge.

Amid rumors that she was about to get a "political spanking" from the Republican organization, Smith requested a place on the Armed Services Committee.[78] In a detailed letter, she cited her past experience in military affairs, noted she was one of only two Republican senators without a major committee assignment, and complained that she had been passed over for major committees by senators with less seniority. Seniority was critically important to Smith in petitioning for increased power—it was, she felt, the single irrefutable security she possessed. She offered to relinquish her position on the Republican Policy Committee to Brewster, provided she was appointed to the ASC.[79] But the Republican organization brooked no deals. Though she retained her place on Executive Expenditures, Smith was dismissed from the Policy Committee, dropped from the District of Columbia Committee, and named to Rules and Administration. This was a lateral move; Rules was generally considered a minor committee, dealing primarily with "housekeeping" matters, although it did have jurisdiction over election and campaign practices (through its subcommittee on Privileges and Elections), a concern that soon had important consequences for Smith.[80]

Outraged and frustrated, Smith drafted a letter to Brewster fuming about the way the Republican leadership treated her: "kicked around on committee assignments," exploited by Taft "to attract the votes of women," and ignored in Policy councils. "If refusing to be dictated to on how I vote and the public position that I take on matters like McCarthyism is to bar me from committee assignments and allow others with less seniority to walk over me," she concluded, "then we might as well know it now."[81] There was more to come. Late one afternoon in January, one of McCarthy's staffers slipped a memo under Smith's door informing her that she had been summarily dismissed from the Investigations Subcommittee, replaced by freshman Sen. Richard Nixon, because of his "great background of experience in investigative work."[82] Smith took her protest to committee chair John McClellan (D-AR), arguing on the basis of two points: that she had considerably more investigating experience than either Senator Nixon or Senator Mundt (the other Republican freshman, and HUAC graduate, appointed to Investigations) and that the move violated custom and precedent concerning whether a member once assigned to a subcommittee could be removed over that member's protest. McCarthy asserted his authority as minority leader; McClellan declined to intervene.[83]

Ironically, a few days later, Smith's other committee, Senate Rules, named her to the Subcommittee on Privileges and Elections (P&E), along with Robert Hendrickson, Mike Monroney (D-OK), and Thomas Hennings (D-MO), to investigate charges of corruption, primarily involving Senator McCarthy, in the Butler-Tydings election in Maryland. After three months of public hearings, and four more dithering over drafting the results, Senate Report No. 647, though exposing transgressions, made no specific recommendations involving either Butler or McCarthy. Instead, it urged the full Rules Committee to formulate specific guidelines for contesting the election of a senator and for disciplining any senator whose election conduct rendered him "unfit to hold the position of United States senator."[84]

Over the weekend, Sen. William Benton (D-CT), concerned that the Maryland Report would simply be filed and forgotten, dropped Smith a note. He had discussed the Rules Committee meeting (at which the report had been released and agreed upon) with his wife, he wrote, and "I am sitting here trying to decide whether to make a speech on the subject next Monday. I rather think I will."[85] Benton did more than make a speech; he proposed that the Senate expel Senator McCarthy on the basis of the Maryland Report.[86] The Senate, traditionally reluctant to discipline its own, had never expelled a member. Moreover, expulsion required a two-thirds vote. Benton himself entertained no real hope of getting McCarthy kicked out of the Senate; his best bet was possible censure with the resulting publicity causing McCarthy's defeat for reelection in November. Smith was unhappy with Benton's impetuosity and, like many of their colleagues, thought his resolution was a tactical disaster.[87] During the week following the Benton Resolution, not a single senator spoke in its favor, and none came forward to defend Benton against McCarthy's predictable counterassault. Dismissing the Connecticut senator as "a little mental midget . . . [acting as] a megaphone for the Communist party-line type of smear," McCarthy aimed his barbs primarily at the two Republicans on P&E, Smith and Hendrickson.[88] Since they had, he said, already gone on record against him with the Declaration of Conscience, these two "puny politicians" should have disqualified themselves from the Maryland investigation.[89]

Hendrickson rushed to defend himself, claiming that the Declaration of Conscience had nothing to do with the issues involved in the Maryland Report, that at any rate, he never intended a direct criticism of McCarthy, and that he had been forced to make concessions and compromises in drafting the Maryland election report in order to expedite the matter of Senator Butler's status in the Senate. Had he written the report himself, Hendrickson said, "it would have probably taken on a much different appearance."[90] Smith then took the floor, and she was far from conciliatory. She faced McCarthy squarely and said, "Opposition to Communism is surely not the exclusive possession of the junior senator from Wisconsin. Nor does differing with him on tactics automatically make one a Communist or a protector of Communism. . . . [I]t would appear that the basis for disqualification is disagreement with the junior senator from Wisconsin. . . . [However] I shall not permit intimidation to keep me from expressing my honest convictions." Then she defiantly placed the text of her Declaration of Conscience once more in the *Congressional Record*.[91]

More committee shuffling followed the death of Senator Wherry in December. Smith seized upon the chance to escape P&E and its distasteful investigation of Benton's charges. She moved to Wherry's spot on the Rules Subcommittee and tried to make it sound more like a promotion than a lifeline.[92] Meanwhile, P&E Chairman Guy Gillette offered McCarthy an opportunity to respond to Benton's charges, but McCarthy declined: "I have not and do not intend to even read, much less answer, Benton's smear attack." He characterized it as the type of material found "in the *Daily Worker* almost any day of the week."[93] In a barrage of letters McCarthy impugned the motives of the subcommittee and challenged its jurisdiction in typically intemperate language. The "obvious purpose" of the subcommittee, he said, was to dig up campaign material for "the Democrat [*sic*] Party." Therefore, "the committee is guilty of stealing . . . picking the pockets of the taxpayers and turning the loot over to the Democrat National Committee."[94] Gillette sought a showdown, taking the matter to the full Senate and challenging McCarthy to make a formal motion to discharge the Subcommittee from further consideration of the Benton Resolution. McCarthy declined.[95] So Senate Rules Chairman Carl Hayden did.[96]

In three hours of debate, no senator rose in support of McCarthy's charges nor to advocate the discharge of the committee. The best his friends Dirksen and Bourke Hickenlooper could do was to make light of the matter, saying that committee members were too "thin-skinned" in resenting his charges. Smith rose to her feet to respond. One observer described the setting: "It was a scene to remember—the most dramatic scene the final session of this congress has produced yet. A roomful of men senators sprawled at their desks, most of them sheepishly silent . . . [as] a little woman from Maine . . . [stood] speaking the conscience of the Senate in a clear, ringing voice."[97] She focused her irritation on the hapless Hickenlooper, interrupting him several times to ask if he had ever been called a thief by a colleague, and why he thought the charges were unimportant. Then she said bluntly: "I say to the members of the Senate that Senator McCarthy has made false accusations which he cannot and has not had the courage even to try to back up with proof. . . . Any senator who votes 'nay' and against the resolution is saying unequivocally . . . that he believes that the charges of Senator McCarthy against Senators Gillette, Monroney, Hennings, Hendrickson, and Smith of Maine are false and without foundation." Before he hastily left the hall for a "previous engagement," McCarthy indicated that he, too, was prepared to vote against the resolution to discharge the committee. Thus, McCarthy was put in the peculiar position of saying he would have voted not to believe his own lies about the committee. The Senate unanimously rejected the resolution to discharge.[98]

More than eight months later, on the last day of the expiring Eighty-second Congress, P&E finally released its report. Though a substantial portion of the account dealt with McCarthy's questionable financial dealings, the report was predominantly a detailed indictment of McCarthy's "disdain and contempt for the rules and wishes of the entire Senate body, as well as the membership of the Subcommittee on Privileges and Elections." In an aggrieved and exasperated tone, the subcommittee described the "magnitude of the unpleasantness" they were required to sustain and "the inescapable conclusion that Senator McCarthy deliberately set out to thwart any investigation of him."[99] The report concluded without making recommendations. Instead, the "issue raised is one for the entire Senate . . . a matter that transcends partisan politics and goes to the very core of the Senate Body's authority, integrity and the respect in which it is held by the people of this country."[100]

In March 1952, just as Smith was breathing a sigh of relief at being freed from P&E, she was broadsided by the publication of a book called *USA Confidential,* "a full-scale, full-bodied, uncensored, unafraid account of the shockingly corrupt under-life of America."[101] It was the latest blockbuster from authors Jack Lait, managing editor of Hearst's *New York Daily Mirror,* and Lee Mortimer, a *Mirror* gossip columnist. The pair had developed a successful formula for sleaze, churning out four bestsellers that leveled sensational charge after sensational charge at "Bare Babe" establishments, corrupt elected officials, racketeers, "queers," and subversives. Their assertions might have been laughable had they not been so vituperative: "New York dope-dealers are imported from Puerto-Rico to sell junk and vote for Marcantonio;" "white girls are recruited for colored lovers" by means of jazz music; lesbianism resulted from "Marxist teachings" and "the examples of women in high political and social places;" the State Department, "despite denials and purges, is considerably more than thirty percent faggot," and so on.

Among the dozens of celebrities and public figures slandered, they included Senator Smith. In a chapter entitled "Reds in Clover," covering "Commies, pinkos, welfare statists, progressives—whatever they call themselves they smell the same," Lait and Mortimer listed her among the nation's "stunted visionaries" and "left-wing apologists," about whom a "Senate doorman remarked, 'There's too many women in the Senate!' She is a lesson in why women should not be in politics. . . . She takes every opposing speech as a personal affront and lies awake nights scheming how to 'get even'. . . . She reacts to all situations as a woman scorned. . . . She is under the influence of the coterie of left-wing writers and reporters who dominate Washington and they praise her so assiduously she believes it." Assertions that she was prone to the female sins of oversensitivity to criticism and susceptibility to flattery then gave way to charges of being a fellow-traveler: "Maggie is pals with Esther Brunauer and made a trip to Europe with her, fare paid by the State Department. Mrs. Brunauer is now under suspension from the department as a security risk."[102]

An outraged Smith immediately contacted her attorney, Richard Wels, and filed a million-dollar libel suit against Crown Publishers, Jack Lait and Lee Mortimer, claiming that parts of the book "contrived to injure" her by holding her up as an "object of hatred, contempt, scorn, derision and aversion among her neighbors, associates and constituents . . . as one who had cooperated with and been associated with pro-Communists and fellow-travelers, and as an incompetent, irresponsible and faithless public servant."[103]

She was not alone in feeling aggrieved. By June, four months after publication of *USA Confidential,* five libel suits totaling $11.5 million were pending, including one from Neiman-Marcus whose models and saleswomen were allegedly "call girls," their dress and millinery designers "fairies." Teamster's vice-president Dave Beck also sued, standing accused of using mafia-trained thugs to control union-sponsored pimps and prostitutes in Seattle.[104] Hundreds of other individuals chose not to sue, many no doubt dismissing the book as trash.

There was considerable expense involved in pursuing a libel suit. Despite Smith's attorney's assertion that the law required comment on the acts of public officials be backed by "a fair and honest and truthful statement of the facts," such defamation suits were notoriously difficult to prosecute. Politicians had long been considered fair game for attacks, whispering campaigns and vicious lampooning. Courts had generally adopted the "public official" rule, in which defamatory remarks were protected unless the charge was serious enough that, if true, would cause her removal from office.[105] Regardless of the ease or difficulty of such a suit, Smith could not let the slander pass unchallenged. Seemingly of a piece with McCarthyism, she considered the consequences to her reputation and to her political viability simply too great to risk.

Trial depositions established that Mortimer conferred with McCarthy and her inclusion in the book resulted from her Declaration of Conscience.[106] On the floor, McCarthy made a facetious reference to the matter, remarking that the book exposed an unnamed senator's involvement with accused subversive Esther Brunauer. This senator had decided to sue, he said, because "she thought her character was injured." Despite his unusual observance of senatorial courtesy in omitting the offended senator's name, there was no doubt who his referent was since Smith was the only "she" in the Senate.[107]

The Brunauer connection, as with all of McCarthy's accusations of fellow-traveling, was a tenuous one. An advisor for the 1950 UNESCO conference in Florence, Brunauer had arranged the senator's schedule and met with her a time or two for briefings. They did not travel together, nor see one another before or after this meeting.[108] Many of the other charges against Smith were simply ridiculous. In agonizing legalese, her attorney challenged the defendants to identify when and where the plaintiff "reacted as a woman scorned," and to specify the nights she allegedly "lied awake scheming how to get even."[109] The crux of the matter, of course, was her Declaration of Conscience—"The Mein Kampf of the Get-McCarthy-Bund"—taken by the authors as prima facie evidence that she was sympathetic to Communism.[110] For her trial deposition, Smith and Lewis prepared a detailed, line-by-line explanation of that speech that came down to simply this: "I have always approved of Senator McCarthy's objectives. I do not approve of his tactics. . . . I approve of getting the subversives out of government and out of the country. I don't approve of smearing innocent people to do it."[111]

Smith doggedly pursued the suit for four and a half years through tortuous delays and calculated obfuscations. Hundreds of hours, both hers and Lewis's, were spent in reconstructing voting records, researching speech notes, traveling to New York to testify, and contacting thirty-seven doormen, dozens of her colleagues, and numerous journalists to substantiate or refute the author's claims. During the period of the suit, the book sold nearly 180,000 copies, Lait died, and Mortimer exhausted two teams of attorneys, continuing his solitary battle long after Crown Publishers had agreed to settle. In the end, an embittered Mortimer charged that Smith, in her relentless pursuit of this "fraudulent lawsuit," had caused the deaths of his collaborator, his young wife, and his father and mother.[112] A month later, as Wels prepared Sens. Estes Kefauver and William F. Knowland to testify on Smith's behalf, the action was settled in the judges chambers.[113] A complete retraction of the statements made concerning Smith was published in all Maine newspapers and several major national ones. Assertions of the defendants, it said, "were mistaken and should not have been made."[114] She was also awarded a cash settlement totaling $28,500. Vindication was Smith's reward; she wanted nothing to do with the money. Lewis wrote Wels that his compensation had been "the sheer enjoyment I got in proving Mortimer such a damned liar and a damned fool so many times." Wels, insistent that Smith should have a tangible memento of the suit, fancifully suggested that she buy a mink coat, in the lining of which he would arrange to have the retraction silk-screened. "She can have a lot of fun when people comment on the coat," he wrote to Lewis, "flicking it open and showing the retraction in a silk fabric! The press girls would eat it up." Smith declined, saying "it would not be practical."[115]

Smith was growing justifiably weary of the battle. Almost since her first days as a senator, she had been in the vanguard of the McCarthy opposition. Often, when she looked behind her, there were no followers. "I was awfully tired of it, had no time to do anything else," said MCS. "I had to carry the blame for so much; I was very tired of doing it all alone."[116] Her demotion from the Investigations Subcommittee and removal from the Republican Policy Committee with Taft's tacit approval put her on notice that she could continue her crusade only at the risk of party ostracism. Support for McCarthy had become the test of party loyalty. Nonetheless, Smith felt so strongly that she could not back away from her enmity toward McCarthy and those who encouraged him.

The race for the GOP nomination for president in 1952, between front-runners Robert Taft and Gen. Dwight Eisenhower, offered Republican voters a clear choice between conservatism and moderation. It also offered a choice, in Smith's estimation, between those who wished to win in 1952 on legitimate issues and those who condoned the use of the smear and "the Big Lie."[117] While Eisenhower's position was less well known, Taft was clearly a condoner. And so, apparently, were his Maine supporters.

The Maine Republican Party, led by the state's senior senator, Owen Brewster, enthusiastically embraced Old Guard conservatism. As presidential hopeful Taft, with Brewster in tow, rallied the faithful in a preannouncement swing through Maine, Smith was the only member of the Maine delegation that did not attend, and her absence came in for some heavy criticism.[118] Guy Gannett's powerful voice thundered that "Most Maine Republicans are not moderate ones. They are Republicans to the last ditch. . . . Maine people take their Republicanism seriously . . . holding fast to old principles and philosophies in the face of the rising tide of liberalism. Mrs. Smith has not held fast with them. . . . Senator Smith's independence may not be as cherished as it once was."[119]

Although the state organization was ostensibly neutral until after the party's primary, they decided to circulate materials attacking Taft's opponents. The packet included a crude cartoon of Eisenhower receiving a hammer and sickle medal from Josef Stalin and a smear pamphlet charging Smith and a host of other "Republican renegades" with conspiracy in a "New Deal-Communist plot to . . . oppose the nomination of a real Republican."[120] Smith exposed the anonymous mailing on her radio broadcast and urged those receiving this "political trash" to send it back. Then she pushed RNC Chairman Guy Gabrielson and Senator Taft to repudiate such tactics before the Senate Elections Committee.[121]

Though she steadfastly refused to openly endorse either candidate, the charade was hardly worth the trouble. At every mention of Taft's name she included McCarthy's and frequently made reference to her abhorrence of smears.[122] She repeated that message once more on the eve of delegate voting and the Maine convention ended with eleven committed to Eisenhower, five to Taft. Many, including the Taft forces, credited her with swinging wavering votes to Ike. The matter stirred up fresh talk about her chances of being named his vice president, and fueled the increasing acrimony between her and Brewster, as well as the likelihood that the senior senator would eagerly work for her defeat in 1954.[123]

Smith's name turned up on several "dark horse" lists and straw polls, stimulating more wishful thinking from female journalists and a concerted effort from the BPW to place her name in nomination for vice president at the national convention. Smith responded that she was "highly honored."[124] In keeping with their bipartisanship, the BPW chose Texas judge Sarah T. Hughes for the Democrats.[125] While the GOP convention met in Chicago, she was at the bedside of her desperately ill mother in Waterville, Maine. Lewis fielded phone calls from the delegates at the convention and attempted to keep her informed of the unfolding events. The women had lined up about 110 votes for Smith on the first ballot, and designated Clare Booth Luce to make the nominating speech.[126]

Bitter battles in the bifurcated convention over rules and credentials ended with Eisenhower's nomination. Determined to avoid another split vote on the vice presidential nomination, Ike's forces sent word to

Luce and the BPW not to nominate Smith; Eisenhower wanted Nixon by acclamation. Accordingly, Luce announced that Smith, in the interest of party harmony, had requested that her name be withdrawn.[127]

The nomination of Smith would have been, of course, purely a symbolic act. No one, least of all she, harbored any real expectations of victory.[128] Nonetheless, she felt betrayed by Luce and betrayed once again by Republican leaders who denied her that acclaim. Luce wrote her a few weeks later asking Smith to correct the "misunderstanding" some harbored that "the men of the Convention prevented you from being put into nomination, and otherwise disparaged your candidacy."[129] Smith refused. She did not think people misunderstood. On the contrary, she understood it the same way. When Ike's majordomo, Sherman Adams, called to enlist her for the "campaign team," she begged off because of her mother's illness. Then she told him she was surprised at how warmly Eisenhower had "embraced McCarthy," whose friendship had been her "prime objection to Taft," and expressed her dismay that he had picked a running mate from the McCarthy camp.[130] Eisenhower persisted. He wanted her assistance, he told Smith, in "eliciting more enthusiastic support from the ladies." Against her better judgment, she agreed to write an article for *Woman's Home Companion* magazine urging women to vote for him.[131] "I am a Republican, but I am an American first," she began. She wrote that she supported the candidate who intended to "clean house in government . . . [through] objective Americanism instead of being soiled by partisan politics and political expediency." In a long paragraph about Communism, Smith compared her Declaration of Conscience to Eisenhower's opposition to the "tactics of smear and character assassination."[132] She complained in her transmittal letter to the editor about Ike's "surprisingly [*sic*] lack of definitiveness [on] vital issues," and her concern that his vague stances might solidify during the campaign in ways contrary to her interpretations.[133] She had hardly put the article in the mail when she read the announcement that Eisenhower would "endorse and campaign actively" for Senator McCarthy.[134] When the article came out in October, her paragraph on Communism had been deleted.[135]

While her mother remained gravely ill, Smith made occasional speeches for the Republican ticket in Maine, with a few journeys outside the state. But she continued to nurse her irritation with Eisenhower, and when he asked for more commitment, she put her foot down. "There are very serious differences between you and me," she told him, "in the manner in which you have compromised principles that I believe in and I thought you believed in. . . . [You] can't compromise those principles in Wisc. and [the] West and then try to forget them in N.Y. and N.E."[136] The irony is that Eisenhower told his audiences in

Wisconsin that while he agreed with McCarthy's aims, he could not agree with his methods.[137] This, of course, was precisely Smith's position.

She refused to make a major speech for Eisenhower until he "publicly and in nationwide pronouncement states his unqualified endorsement of my Declaration of Conscience."[138] On the eve of the election, RNC officials invited Smith to join Eisenhower in Boston for a nationally televised broadcast. On the condition that she would have the opportunity to ask Ike his position on her Declaration, she agreed to go. But as she prepared to leave for Boston, Smith's mother's condition worsened and she phoned her regrets. Mrs. Chase died that evening.[139]

Eisenhower's landslide took just enough Republicans with him to control Congress by the narrowest of margins (three in the House and only one in the Senate). In his message of condolence, the new president told Smith, "I have a feeling that we are both in the same philosophical camp," he wrote, "and I am anxious to discuss some of the current problems with you." She replied that she would like to get to know him better, too.[140]

Congressman and Mrs. Clyde H. Smith, 15 May 1937. *Courtesy Margaret Chase Smith Library*

Rep. Margaret Chase Smith with her mother, Mrs. Carrie Chase, receiving congratulations after Smith's victory in Maine's senatorial primary, 21 June 1948.
Acme Photo, Courtesy Margaret Chase Smith Library

President Harry S. Truman signs a bill to establish a permanent Army and Navy Nurse Corps, 16 April 1947. *Left to right:* Rep. Margaret Chase Smith; Col. Florence A. Blachfield, superintendent of the Army Nurse Corps; Lt. Comdr. Ruth B. Dunbar, assistant superintendent of the Navy Nurse Corps; Maj. Helen Burns, director of dieticians, U.S. Army; and Maj. Emma E. Vogel, director of physical therapy, U.S. Army. *Courtesy Margaret Chase Smith Library*

U.S. Senate Executive Expenditures Subcommittee, Five Percenter Hearings, 31 August 1949. *Left to right:* Sen. Walter F. George, Sen. Joseph McCarthy, unidentified, Sen. Margaret Chase Smith, William C. Lewis, Jr. Witness: General Harry Vaughn. *Courtesy U.S. Senate Historical Office.*

Sen. Margaret Chase Smith campaigning at the St. Croix Paper Company in Woodland, Maine, 28 September 1960. *Courtesy Margaret Chase Smith Library*

Presidential candidate Margaret Chase Smith arrives in San Francisco for the Republican National Convention, 12 July 1964. *Courtesy Margaret Chase Smith Library*

White House meeting with senior members of the Senate and House Armed Services and Appropriations Committees following the Tet Offensive in Vietnam, 30 January 1968. *Left to right:* C.I.A. Director Richard M. Helms, Gen. Maxwell Taylor, Sen. Milton Young, Secretary of State Dean Rusk, Sen. Carl Hayden, Sen. Margaret Chase Smith, President Lyndon Johnson, Rep. L. Mendel Rivers, Chairman of the Joint Chiefs of Staff, Gen. Earle G. Wheeler, Clark Clifford, Rep. William Bates, Rep. George Mahon, Sen. John Stennis, and Defense Secretary Robert McNamara. *AP/Wide World Photos.*

Margaret Chase Smith and William Chesley Lewis, Jr., in retirement, 1975. *Jean Moss, Photographer, Chicago, Illinois.*

9 | Smith versus Jones

Smith was at last a member of the majority party and Maine's senior senator as well, Owen Brewster having been defeated in a scandal-ridden Maine primary by Governor Frederick Payne. In the months before the vote, a series of exposés in Maine newspapers, repeated in the national press, detailed Brewster's long history of corruption and political legerdemain, involving fraud, illegal campaign funding, bribery, and influence peddling.[1] His loss was a bitter one, all the more so because his successor barely survived accusations that he had accepted bribes in exchange for access to state liquor distribution.[2] Still, to most, Payne seemed the lesser of the two evils. As Brewster went down to defeat, the *Washington Post* congratulated the state for "removing a carbuncle from the neck of the U.S. Senate."[3] Smith, though, was not particularly heartened by Payne's conservatism and affinity with McCarthy.[4]

In the Eighty-third Congress, Smith secured appointments to two major committees. Besides Government Operations, she was named to Appropriations and, at long last, Armed Services. On Appropriations, her subcommittees ruled on budget considerations for Armed Services and Foreign Policy. On the Armed Services Committee, Smith chose the Preparedness Subcommittee, and soon afterward, chaired a sub-subcommittee to investigate ammunition shortages in the Korean conflict. And, further increasing her visibility and influence, she was back on the Republican Policy Committee.[5] She was more powerful now, but so too was McCarthy, more arrogant than ever following his stunning reelection in Wisconsin.

Moreover, the GOP majority guaranteed he would suffer no further harassment from Privileges and Elections.

Since his defeat, Owen Brewster had been "wistfully hanging about the Capitol" petitioning for one administration post after another, in the State Department, the Maritime Commission, the Commerce Department.[6] In each case, the White House asked Smith if she would object to his appointment. Each time she said she would not. When asked if she would recommend Brewster, again she replied, she would not.[7] After the Eisenhower administration passed on nine requests, Brewster turned to his old friend, Joe McCarthy. Brewster wanted to be named counsel on his Government Operations Committee, replacing the departing Roy Cohn. Though Brewster was clearly unqualified for the post and "truly disliked on both sides of the aisle," his colleagues chose not to reject him outright. They instead "maneuvered to put Mrs. Smith in [that] position."[8] Conservatives predicated endorsement on the approval of Smith and at least half the Committee's Democrats. Smith signed on the condition that all of the Republicans and half the Democrats approved. The Democrats simply voted "present." Brewster was out.[9]

For the first few months of her term on the Senate Armed Services Committee, Smith was occupied chairing the investigation into ammunition shortages. Just before he retired as commander of U.N. forces in Korea, Gen. James Van Fleet touched off the inquiry by charging that shortages existed during the entire twenty-two months he commanded the U.S. Eighth Army. For Smith, the hearings were a welcome chance to earn national attention beyond internecine bickering with McCarthy. Just in time to help her in the 1954 elections, she became the first woman senator to direct a major investigation. Smith won considerable kudos for her firm but fair handling of the potentially explosive hearings. Thanks to Lewis, she was always well prepared. She insisted on decorum, advance prepared statements, and open hearings, which were among the first ever televised.[10]

The parade of witnesses revealed chronic interservice rivalry, divided authority, delayed production, and red tape and inertia in the vast military bureaucracy. Rationing began early as stores of World War II surplus rapidly dwindled. Even after the Chinese Communists entered the war, there was minimal effort to increase production, on the assumption that the conflict would end quickly. When it did not, ammunition ran dangerously low.[11] Affecting testimony from Gen. Matthew B. Ridgeway (who had assumed command in Korea after General MacArthur was relieved of duty) asserted "a direct relation between the piles of shells in the ammunition supply points and the piles of corpses in the graves registration collecting points. The bigger the former, the smaller the latter and vice versa."[12] The Pentagon countered that ammunition was adequate for defense, America's sole mission in Korea. Army Chief Gen. J. Lawton Collins said there was plenty for the men to protect themselves.[13]

Although the testimony centered around the availability of sufficient ammunition and the inefficiency of military procurement, the subtext of the hearings was the frustration with a limited war. MacArthur had been summarily fired for pushing offensive efforts. Van Fleet claimed he had been denied the means to rout the Communists. Ridgeway, too, was obviously frustrated. These generals had come home to tell Congress that the only way to end the Korean conflict was through total commitment to victory. As Douglas MacArthur put it in his letter to the subcommittee: "The overriding deficiency incident to our conduct of the war in Korea was not in the shortage of ammunition or other materiel, but in the lack of the will for victory."[14]

For the most part, the subcommittee agreed with the commanding generals, concluding that "there was a needless loss of American lives" in Korea because of ammunition shortages, and blaming the Truman administration for their "miscalculation and inability to plan for the defense and security of the United States."[15] Administration policy to run the war "without disrupting the civilian economy" was built on the false assumption that one could maintain, as Smith put it, "peace at home and war in Korea." She decried such partial mobilization as "costly and unworkable," and faulted the administration for making "foreign policy commitments which we are not ready to back up with military strength."[16] Going well beyond criticism of the previous administration, though, the final recommendations of the subcommittee for the establishment of clear lines of authority and responsibility, new business-like procurement methods, and top priority to rebuilding ammunition stocks and munitions plants on a standby basis, were in direct opposition to Defense Secretary Charles Wilson's plan to cut standby capacity and insure more economy in the Pentagon.[17]

Despite her misgivings about Eisenhower, Smith welcomed a strong military man in the White House. But she had become increasingly disenchanted with the president's decision to rely upon threats of "massive retaliation" with nuclear weapons to meet Soviet aggression while cutting conventional forces. Eisenhower called this "security with solvency," but Smith dismissed it as a "two-word catch phrase" that concealed a dangerous diminishment of American defense at a time when the Communists were threatening many parts of the world.[18]

Smith repeatedly called Secretary of Defense Wilson to account for proposed military budget cuts. During one confrontation over a five billion dollar cut in air power, she asked how Soviet strength had changed in a way that justified reducing American forces. Eleven times she asked the same question about whether the cut would compromise national security and eleven times Wilson refused to answer. Losing her patience, she tossed him a list of thirty-two questions and directed him to bring back written answers "from someone capable of providing them."[19] In the face of her hostility, the Eisenhower administration became increasingly wary of giving her specific information. When she requested "a complete reexamination of our overall defense and strategy," Secretary Wilson prepared a lengthy and complex reply for the administration only to have it aborted at the White House. Bryce Harlow, Ike's congressional liaison, indicated that "the president would not be well advised to write so much on this subject to Mrs. Smith." She just got a letter saying the matter was being investigated.[20]

As distressed as she was by stonewalling and unwise policies, Smith was also angered by her treatment by Defense Department and Pentagon representatives. "They treated me like a lady who didn't know anything, gave me a pat on the head. That's the way a lot of men did, so I had to keep asking, showing them," MCS explained. "I would ask questions the men wouldn't ask, but were glad I did. If I didn't get what I wanted, I'd ask for a special meeting, just me and the chairman and insist, pressure for answers. The men loved it when I went after Wilson, but they wouldn't do it themselves."[21] One committee staffer observed that "after awhile, the men at the Department of Defense and the Pentagon began to take her seriously because she demanded that they did. That didn't mean that they liked her, but they developed respect for her and the way she did her job. They knew they couldn't get away with doing anything less." Another remarked that "some of the men were pretty mean to her. They thought military affairs were not the proper place for a woman. She was tough, firm. She had to be. . . . She had her committee chair raised on little blocks of wood so she'd be as tall as the men. She did not want to look up to anyone or have anyone look down on her."[22]

Smith was proud of her feistiness, but also, after two years of confrontations with conservatives, she had become extremely sensitive to how easily her words and her motives could be distorted. Disturbed by Soviet challenges around the globe, and eager to prove her own anti-Communism credentials, Smith introduced two bills in early 1953 to curb the Communist Party. The first made membership a federal offense and the second prohibited the distribution of "Communistic propaganda."[23] These obvious violations of constitutional freedoms were justified, she said, because the Communist Party was "not a political party, but a subversive organization working to place us under domination of Communist Russia." To those who "indulge in nebulous theorizing on individual rights," she added, there was no right to "plot [the] murder of our country and to conspire to kill the very basic freedoms of our people." Though Smith criticized the "growing tendency among our people to say, 'I'm more patriotic than you' in order to try to convince their neighbors and their associates of their loyalty to their country," she seemed to be indulging in that very tactic in proposing these bills.[24]

As she well knew, many such measures had been advanced over the years and none passed. Hers was very similar, for example, to that drafted by Representative Mansfield the previous year, by Senator Reynolds in 1941, and many others in between. Besides its doubtful constitutionality, the act was redundant. Two other measures seemed to take care of the problem: the Internal Security Act (McCarren Act) required Communist organizations to disclose their membership, their officers, and their financial backing, and the Smith Act already made it a crime for anyone knowingly to support any group favoring the overthrow of the government by force.[25] Smith knew of those measures and the limits they imposed; still there was considerable symbolic and political capital to be gained by proposing to outlaw the Communist Party.

While some commentators accused her of "supporting repressive legislation which is totally out of character," they had failed to carefully read her Declaration of Conscience. She was as anti-Communist as anyone, and she was particularly eager to demonstrate that in light of her upcoming reelection campaign.[26] Lewis prepared a lengthy list of instances, meant to respond to potential critics, where she had spoken against Communism in her column and on the floor of the Senate.[27] She came out strongly in support of action against the leftist government of Jacobo Arbenz Guzmán in Guatemala, submitting legislation to boycott Guatemalan coffee in order "to crush the Reds" before their influence could spread.[28] Expressing her impatience with the State Department, instrumental in killing her bill in the Senate Foreign Relations Committee, Smith complained, "I don't understand this namby-pamby attitude of the State Department. . . . I think we should deal directly with these problems instead of beating about the bush with a lot of diplomatic talk. . . . We might as well do away with the diplomatic niceties and face the fact that the Reds have established a beachhead for subversive assault on the freedom of the Western Hemisphere. . . . How close do the Reds have to get before we stand up to them? How long are we going to wait to take a firm stand?"[29] In dealing with Arbenz Guzmán, the Eisenhower administration did, in fact, "do away with the diplomatic niceties" and launched a CIA-engineered coup in Guatemala that replaced Arbenz Guzmán with the more amenable Castillo Armas. This followed a similar

CIA coup in Iran that toppled Mohammed Mossadegh after he attempted to nationalize foreign oil interests, and restored Shah Mohammed Reza Pahlavi to the throne.[30] Given the limitations of massive retaliation, Eisenhower had drastically expanded covert actions to destabilize Communist regimes in the Third World without risking nuclear war. Since international law and "diplomatic niceties" were ignored by the Soviets, went the reasoning, such observances simply made patsies of the United States.

Smith's bills to outlaw the Communist Party died in the Judiciary Committee. But the Communist issue was by no means moribund. As the midterm congressional elections approached, members of both parties sought to "out-McCarthy McCarthy." Though Smith's was one of the first, in the Eighty-third Congress some nineteen measures specifically aimed at outlawing the Communist Party were offered. Several states also took action to bar Communists from elections.[31] Senator Hubert Humphrey (D-MN) stole the trophy at the eleventh hour when he offered an outlaw-the-Communist-Party amendment to an administration measure designed to penalize labor unions that permitted infiltration by Communists.[32] One pundit commented that the amendment had three purposes: (1) to outlaw the Communist Party, (2) to curb Communist-infiltrated labor unions, and (3) to reelect senators.[33] During deliberations, Smith at first argued that the measure should be debated as a separate issue. When that failed, she threw critical support its way in her typically succinct manner: "The question here," she said, "is very simple and direct.... Either we are completely... against the Communist Party, or we are not."[34] The measure passed the Senate 41 to 39 along strict party lines except for three Republicans who swung the vote—Smith, Kuchel of California, and Langer of North Dakota.[35]

Regardless of who received the credit, Smith was sincere in her eagerness to limit the Communists at every point. As negotiations to end the Korean stalemate began to break down, she suggested bluntly that, if war was resumed, "then drop the atomic bomb on these barbarians who obviously in their past atrocities have proved that they have no concept of a desire for decency.... We have tried everything else—maybe the atomic bomb will bring the Red barbarians to their senses as it did the Japanese. I know that some will protest that the atomic bomb is an immoral weapon. I agree that it is. But so are all other man-killing weapons of war.... When will we learn that you don't stop the Red murderers by merely playing tiddlywinks with them?"[36]

Just before the session adjourned, Smith again butted heads with McCarthy. When she prevented him from issuing independent reports from his Investigations Subcommittee during the recess on a procedural objection, he accused her of making it more difficult to get the "truth" to the American people, not to mention seriously curtailing his public relations.[37] As she headed home to Maine, McCarthy contacted his old friend, Owen Brewster, about a candidate to oppose Smith in the June 1954 primary. They settled on Brewster's former administrative assistant, Robert L. Jones, a political neophyte. Since Brewster's defeat, Jones had been working for Sen. Charles Potter (R-MI), a member of McCarthy's Permanent Investigations Subcommittee. As Potter's assistant, Jones frequently attended subcommittee hearings. In November, when McCarthy went to Maine for a speaking tour sponsored by the Veterans of Foreign Wars, he took Jones along. Smith's colleague Fred Payne served as escort. Jones sat on the platform while McCarthy spoke, and McCarthy always introduced him as "your Maine boy who is making a name for himself in Washington."[38] Though Jones denied any political ambitions, rumors circulated that Jones would oppose Smith in the primary and that he would do so with "Texas oil money" funneled through McCarthy.[39]

Jones continued to sit in for Potter on the subcommittee throughout the spring. Although it was contrary to Senate rules, McCarthy invited Jones to question witnesses during loyalty hearings involving a Camp Kilmer, N.J. dentist.[40] At one point he even introduced him as Senator Jones.[41] After the hearings, during which McCarthy savaged the highly decorated Brigadier General Ralph Zwicker as "unfit to wear the uniform," Jones issued a statement in Potter's name supporting McCarthy. Potter blew up and fired Jones, first because he filed the statement without authorization, and second, because he discovered that Jones, contrary to his denial, was indeed planning to oppose Smith, whom he highly respected.[42] Three days later Jones announced for the primary, saying he was planning "a bare-knuckles campaign."[43]

Washington was watching. Coming two months earlier than those in the rest of the country, Maine elections always attracted national attention anyway. But this one had the added element of the McCarthy factor, a matter of keen interest to members running for reelection.[44] *Newsweek* called it "the first clear test of how Republican voters feel about 'McCarthyism.'"[45] Though President Eisenhower's staff debated the advisability of his going to Maine on Smith's behalf, he ultimately decided not to go. Perhaps he did not think her seriously threatened or perhaps he was still trying to avoid a showdown with McCarthy—or with Smith.[46]

Jones was a virtual clone of his mentor from Wisconsin, adopting his mannerisms, his speech patterns, and his rhetoric. Reporters took to calling him "Junior McCarthy."[47] Powerful forces were against his running, Jones asserted darkly. "I am thoroughly convinced it is the handwork of devious, left-wing elements who are fearful of a bitter political show-down in Maine between the forces of Americanism and international liberalism." But he courageously chose to take them on because "Maine, indeed the Nation," according to Jones, could "ill afford to have a silent, puzzled, uninformed and weak-willed representative in the Senate when the ominous clouds of atheistic, international Communism overshadow every walk of life."[48]

Meanwhile, things were beginning to sour for McCarthy. Angered at the army's refusal to grant deferment to his staff aide, David Schine, McCarthy accused them of coddling Communists. When the army, apparently acting on orders from the president, refused to open their personnel records to his investigation, he charged them with incompetence and treason. Some twenty million Americans got their first look at the senator from Wisconsin during the dramatic televised Army-McCarthy hearings, watching as he viciously attacked anyone who resisted him.[49] Former supporters were outraged at McCarthy's behavior; conservative columnists like H. V. Kaltenborn complained that he had "become completely egotistic, arrogant, arbitrary, narrow-minded, reckless and irresponsible. Power has corrupted him."[50] McCarthy's favorable rating among the American people also took a precipitous slide, falling from a high of 50 percent in January to 34 percent by the end of the hearings in June.[51]

Accordingly, he had little time nor taste for the Jones campaign. As the Army-McCarthy hearings proceeded, McCarthy canceled a series of speeches he had planned to make in Maine.[52] Jones shifted to talking more and more about Maine issues and less and less about anti-Communism. As political observers warned against outside interference in the June primaries, Mainers began to wonder where Jones found the money to run against Smith. The father of four who had just left an $8,500-a-year job in Washington, Jones was obviously benefiting from an "apparent flood of out-of-state political slush funds and the swift spreading of the sinister shadow of Joe McCarthy."[53] Within a couple of months, a local newspaper broke the news that Jones's campaign was being financed by at least two Texas oil millionaire friends of the Wisconsin senator.[54]

Meanwhile, the Smith campaign quietly gathered momentum. She ran as she always had, speaking of her record and never mentioning her opponent's name, while Lewis methodically rallied the volunteers. Their only concession to this new opponent was in shifting Smith's campaign slogan from "Don't Trade a Record for a Promise" to "Don't Trade a Record for a Smear." Probably reflecting the coming election's national significance, Smith's Washington office fielded numerous requests from nonresidents offering to write letters or otherwise assist her campaign.[55]

Smith was mobbed when she arrived at the GOP convention in Bangor in April and received a standing ovation. Moreover, she was once again in good standing with Guy Gannett. As recently as the previous spring, he had reportedly been eager to find a viable opponent for her, but after her efforts on the ammunition shortages investigation and her tough anti-Communist rhetoric captured national attention, her home state newspaper of record came around, lavishly praising her as "gifted far beyond the ordinary . . . consistently [demonstrating] the courage of her convictions [and] steadfast devotion to her Country and the welfare of its citizens. . . . Mrs. Smith is a woman of character and conscience, she is a senator of competence and courage."[56]

Following Portland's lead, all the major papers in Maine supported Smith, drubbing her opponent with drollery. Columnists vied for the latest Jones's claims and held them up to ridicule. For example, Floyd Nute of Rumford described "another baffling gem" from Jones, who predicted he would capture the "great hidden vote in Maine." Nute wrote, "Who is responsible for hiding this vote? Are there persons in this state who have, in the past, or are now, hiding votes? We believe Mr. Jones may have at last found an issue here. A vast conspiracy of vote hiders."[57] In Maine, the contest appeared to be so overwhelming in Smith's favor that the biggest problem seemed to be local indifference.

Because of its national implications for McCarthy, though, the national media scrutiny, if anything, intensified as the primary neared. In June, Edward R. Murrow's "See It Now" turned the spotlight on Maine. Three months earlier, Murrow had taken on McCarthy directly, devoting his half-hour program to clips showing the senator browbeating witnesses, patronizing the president, and generally acting boorish.[58] This night, broadcast three weeks before the Maine primary, Murrow quoted affirmatively from Smith's Declaration of Conscience, remarking that there were those who said she must pay the price for her stand in the 1954 election. Murrow's clips juxtaposed Jones's McCarthyesque ranting with flattering clips of Smith's simple appeals to reasonableness and tolerance: "I believe that freedom of speech should not be so abused by some that it is not exercised by others because of fear of smear. But I do believe that we should not permit tolerance to degenerate into indifference. I believe that people should never get so indifferent, cynical or sophisticated that they don't get shocked into action. . . . I believe with all my heart that we must not become a nation of mental mutes blindly following demagogues." On June 21, Murrow concluded, "Mrs. Smith will learn the price or the reward of conscience."[59]

The combination of Jones's political inexperience, rumors of outside interference, and Mainers' increasing distaste for McCarthy, spelled doom for Jones. Smith defeated him by a five-to-one margin.[60] "She has raised the prestige of a Chamber where simple integrity and commonsense have too often seemed at a premium," commented the *New York Herald Tribune*.[61] But what did it mean? National newspapers debated whether the election was a true test of McCarthy's strength since he had not actively campaigned for Jones in Maine. Perhaps McCarthyism was of little concern to Maine voters, said the *New York Times*, "Yet there is not the slightest doubt that if Robert L. Jones had defeated Mrs. Smith his victory would have been considered a triumph for Mr. McCarthy."[62] An editorial in *The Christian Century* agreed, noting the denial of McCarthy's influence came only after the fact of Smith's victory. "His failure to stampede the Maine voters is one of the healthiest things that has happened recently in American politics. . . . Smith's overwhelming victory [should] put courage into her timorous senatorial colleagues."[63]

Shortly after her primary win, Brewster, never one to be short of brass, called on Smith to ask her to help out her defeated opponent. Poor Robert Jones, he said, had no job and no prospects; he owed $750 in campaign expenses and, worse, he owed Brewster $2000. Brewster told her he had turned to McCarthy for help, and the senator had promised Jones a spot on the professional staff of the Government Operations Committee provided that Smith would do the asking. When Brewster finished his tale of woe, Smith, likely stunned into speechlessness by this callous display, just looked at him in icy silence until he finally gave up and left her office.[64]

Meanwhile, things were beginning to go rather badly for McCarthy as well. In March, Sen. Ralph E. Flanders (R-VT) broke the Republican silence, adopting folksy humor to denounce his colleague's methods as mere "war whoops" and his prize "the scalp of a pink dentist."[65] Speaking again on June 1, the fourth anniversary of Smith's Declaration of Conscience, Flanders bitingly compared McCarthy to Hitler. The Communists, he said, could not have found a better tool than the senator who had spread lies and turned people into spying on one another, dividing his country, his church, and his party.[66] By the end of July, Flanders offered a resolution demanding McCarthy's censure for conduct "contrary to senatorial traditions" which tended "to bring the Senate into disrepute."[67] The denouement of McCarthy was at hand.

In other times, the Maine election would be all but over after the primary, but things were changing. In a state where people had always voted Republican by force of habit, independent candidates were coming forward and a resurgent Democratic party had been making serious inroads since 1952. Long plagued by ideological splits characteristic of single-party states, the Maine GOP had been seriously weakened by internecine battles, Brewster's piccadillos, Payne's liquor scandal and, in 1954, the political ineptitude of Governor Burton Cross. Winning the Republican nomination for governor in a three-way race with 40 percent of the vote in 1952, Cross had managed, in just two years, to alienate key supporters in nearly every part of the state.[68] Though Maine had not failed to reelect a sitting governor since 1910, the vulnerability of Cross spurred Maine Democrats to define a platform and choose serious candidates. Led by state Democratic Chairman Frank Coffin and Edmund Muskie, a Waterville attorney and three-term state legislator, the Democrats launched an aggressive effort to recruit alienated Maine voters. By April, they had written a platform critical of the economic situation in Maine and the "cold-blooded attitude" in Augusta, and settled on a slate of candidates, including Muskie to challenge Cross and Colby College history professor Paul A. Fullam to take on Senator Smith.[69]

The fall Senate campaign focused primarily on national defense and foreign policy. Fullam contended the Republican Party lacked a strategy for dealing with the Communist menace. Though he called for "aggressive containment," he found Smith too eager to resort to nuclear weapons and therefore unfit to "play the role a senator must play in preserving us from the horrible specter of atomic mass destruction."[70] She complained that she had been attacked in the primary as a liberal left-winger and was now being attacked in the general election as a "reactionary isolationist." She stayed with familiar themes: we must be as strong militarily as the "Reds" and find ways to stop them without getting involved in another limited war like Korea. She said she was particularly concerned with "Indo-China" where the people were "forced to make a decision between the evil Communism they fear and the French colonialism they detest." The U.S. must not, she said prophetically, "get sucked into fighting a war almost alone in an even worse place to fight than Korea."[71]

Toward the end of the campaign, Fullam, doubtlessly frustrated by his inability to provoke much public support, delivered an inflammatory critique of Smith in which he rhetorically asked her, "Are you proud? Are you proud of your state . . . with its rising unemployment rate? Proud of your vote for. . . ." His litany went on for several minutes, working its way through her voting record, and concluding, "I don't think this constitutes a record of which to be proud, but a record to hide behind generalizations."[72] Smith had Lewis check all the votes that Fullam mentioned and prepare answers to each point. Then, as she had in 1948, she waited until the night before the election to deliver it.

Her televised rebuttal, done in Lewis style, contained fifty-five responses to Fullam's accusations. She accused him of lying about her record while she had tried to keep the campaign on a higher plane. Item by item she refuted Fullam until she came to her trump card. She produced a sworn, notarized Republican nomination paper for her candidacy. She held it as the television camera zoomed in on the signature of Prof. Paul A. Fullam.[73] Incredibly he had signed her primary papers in January as a Republican, and announced his intention to run against her as a Democrat in April.[74] Having no chance to rebut, Fullam made an angry postelection reply, characterizing her speech as a vicious attack, lamely claiming that he had signed her primary papers because he preferred her over Jones (though he had signed it before Jones announced), and proclaimed, "as sure as there is a God in Heaven your evil ways will not prevail."[75]

From the standpoint of the Maine voter, the race for governor was much more interesting than that for senator. Muskie was gaining ground beyond the Democrats' wildest dreams. "Republicans for Muskie" clubs sprang up in formerly Old Guard enclaves, rural weeklies began to come out in support of the challenger, and many talked of the need to teach the Augusta crowd a lesson.[76] By August, a mock election at the Bangor Fair had Muskie winning decisively.[77] Even the weather seemed to turn against Cross. A series of meteorological disasters struck Maine just before the election. Hurricane "Carol" on August 31 was the worst storm since 1938, killing three and costing farmers an estimated $5,000,000. Rather than offer assistance, Cross pronounced the damage less than expected. Then, the weekend before the election, Hurricane "Edna" struck the state, killing eight and causing another $7,000,000 in damages. Despite the turmoil, 248,000 voters, or more than one-half of those eligible to vote, slogged through the mud to the polls to usher in "Hurricane Muskie." Muskie defeated Cross by 22,000 votes, though he was the only Democrat that won.[78]

Smith soundly defeated Fullam, getting 59 percent of the vote. Nonetheless, this was seen as something of a setback, at least by the Democrats, as it was half the majority by which she won in 1948. State representative and national committeewoman Lucia Cormier, who would challenge Smith more directly in 1960, saw it as the beginning of a new era. She said Democratic party leaders were "just beside themselves with joy . . . not only at the victory for Muskie, but because of the dwindled margin for Margaret Chase Smith."[79]

10 Amazon Warmonger

As soon as the election was over, Smith left for an around-the-world tour to evaluate the Cold War climate. In the decade since the end of World War II, new nations were beginning to emerge from underdeveloped territories in the Third World. Nationalism was intense, politics unstable. Most American leaders, like Smith, conflated nationalism with Communism and assumed that much of the trouble was inspired by Moscow. She wanted to find out for herself the degree of Communist influence around the world. Official congressional fact-finding junkets had been less than satisfying to her in the past. This time she wanted to ask her own questions.[1]

Her trip was personal and unofficial, she told the press, and she was paying for it herself. Bill Lewis, working with the State Department, planned the journey.[2] Sometime during the process, Ed Murrow asked to send a camera crew along. Despite some early misgivings, she decided that televising her journey, as she told Murrow's TV audience, was a way to "share my seeing and hearing . . . [to] provide Americans with a better insight and feel of [sic] world affairs and conditions."[3] It was also, of course, great publicity.

She had only a brief window of opportunity to make the trip before the Senate considered McCarthy's censure. Hearings on the Flanders resolution were nearing completion, with full Senate debate to begin in November. Accordingly, she and Lewis divided what was to become a two-month trip into two four-week segments. The first, in October 1954, would take her to western Europe and Russia; the second, in the spring of 1955, would be primarily to Asia and the Mediterranean region. In all she toured twenty-three countries, exploring farms, nurseries, hospitals, factories, fishing villages, food markets, refugee camps, and schools. She talked with individuals, "typical" families, local authorities, and almost every major world leader.[4]

Smith's questions focused on a few major themes. Everywhere she went, she looked for evidence of stability, of friendliness to the United States, and of strength and perseverance in the face of Communist aggression. She asked leaders what their country was doing to fight Communism and how the U.S. could help in that fight, their assessment of the likelihood of war in the next five years and how it might be averted, and advice about how the U.S. could most effectively exert world leadership.[5]

Though she was sometimes criticized for unduly seeking personal publicity and butting into foreign affairs best left to the president and the State Department, Smith maintained that she was simply trying to enhance her ability to do her job well. Though a number of her interviews were televised, "See It Now" was not shown in Maine.[6] Instead, she sent home weekly reports, part chatty travelogue, part descriptions of the personal characteristics and leadership styles of world leaders, and part reassurances that America, liked and respected around the world, was winning in myriad contests with "the Russian bear."[7] She told amusing stories on herself, like her "horror" during her interview with French Premier Pierre Mendès-France, when she glanced to the floor and saw that she was wearing one black shoe and one navy shoe. "What did I do? I tried to put my best foot forward."[8] And she expressed surprise when she found Communists more personable and less "backward" than stereotypes had led her to believe. For example, when she met with the Soviet chargé d'affaires in Washington to obtain a visa, she discovered "not the gruff, silent, belligerent, suspicious person that we have come to picture Russians as being." Instead, he was "very attractive and one of the most charming persons I have ever met."[9]

Despite her incursions into a few of the world's hot spots and her want of security protection, only one tense incident marred her journey. While awaiting passage to the Soviet Union, Smith and her entourage crossed into the Communist sector of Berlin. Curious about consumer goods in Communist stores, she was walking along the Alexanderplatz, looking into shop windows as a CBS cameraman filmed her. Someone brushed past her and muttered "Verboten," and then a second man said in English that it was forbidden to take pictures there. Smith, cameraman Charlie Mack, and CBS newsman Richard Hottelet, hastily left the area, not realizing until sometime later that the occupants of their other car, including U.S. Information Officer Elmer Cox, sound man Robert

Hottenloch, and Bill Lewis, had been arrested by the People's Police. They were detained for about an hour until Cox produced State Department ID and Lewis his visa permitting him to visit Russia. The way Lewis told it, the police capitulated when he declared, "Khrushchev will not like this!"[10] When the U.S. Commandant in Berlin officially protested, sarcastically criticizing the "Soviet view . . . of freedom" and calling the incident a "definite violation of allied rights in Berlin," his Soviet counterpart curtly replied that "the incident was the result of a misunderstanding . . . [that did] not justify the crude attacks on the Soviet Union contained in your letter."[11] That apparently was the end of it, though the exchange reveals the testiness on both sides.

Undoubtedly, the highlight of Smith's fall journey was the six days she and Lewis spent in Russia, where she talked with Deputy Premier V. M. Molotov. She began her interview in her typical manner, explaining somewhat disingenuously that her visit was "unofficial in every respect." Smith did not seem to understand, or at least to acknowledge, that the reason she had access to world leaders had everything to do with the implied "official" nature of her inquiry and her station. As she asked Molotov's opinions on various world conditions, he replied that his views had been previously expressed in the Soviet Government's "Note" of October 23, and peevishly complained that the United States never published Soviet notes. Smith said he was mistaken, but she could not prove this because American newspapers were not to be found in Moscow. A heated exchange on press secrecy ensued. "In parrying the senator's well-aimed thrusts," as Ambassador Chip Bohlen later described the exchange, Molotov argued that his government allowed numerous outlets for American propaganda. Then he delivered a thrust of his own, asserting his government had to be cautious because of acts of subversion by the United States, for which her government had authorized $100 million. What did the senator have to say to this? She replied that she knew of no such subversion. Funds went simply, she said, to provide information about the American way of life. Then she retorted that while the United States permitted the existence of the Communist Party, the Soviet Union did not permit an opposition party. Molotov laughed, but gave no direct answer, saying only that "the people will have what they want." Pressing her point, she asked if his country would not try to force Communism on the United States; he responded, "Of course not." Repeating her question, she asked again, "Would you not encourage the spread of the doctrine of Communism in the United States?" to which Molotov replied, "We don't want to limit the free expression of any people in any country."[12]

At the end of their conversation, after expressing her thanks to

Molotov and receiving his permission to use the interview however she liked, Smith asked for a copy of his interpreter's notes. Molotov demurred, saying she had an assistant there who could have taken full notes. Angered by his refusal, as soon as she landed in Helsinki, she issued a public statement that she "would not be surprised if the relations between the United States and the Soviet Union were broken off at any time by either side." She said her Kremlin experience convinced her that Soviet leaders, "talk one way, act another." Despite his promise to cooperate in every way with the West, Smith said, Molotov turned down a request for cooperation he could have granted easily (she refrained from explaining further). Though she recognized, she said, that "a week in Russia is too short a time to form hard and fast conclusions," her trip neither increased nor diminished her view of the Communist menace. She continued to consider it "a grave threat." She summed up her impressions this way: "The Soviet leaders smile only with their faces—never with their hearts. The little people smile with their hearts—when they get a chance to do so."[13] Her conclusions from her other interviews were scarcely more insightful. Mostly, she found what she expected to find: the Communists could not be trusted, and America's friends, with aid and support, would stand fast against them.[14]

After a month on tour, Smith hurried back to the business of the Senate. The Watkins subcommittee recommended censure of Senator McCarthy, finding him to be "contemptuous, contumacious, and denunciatory, without reason or justification, and obstructive to the legislative process."[15] McCarthy refused the advice of friends, including Sens. Everett Dirksen and Fred Payne, that he head off censure by apologizing.[16] Dirksen even drafted a letter of apology to Hendrickson from McCarthy, regretting his "ungentlemanly remark" (this in reference to McCarthy calling Hendrickson a "living miracle in that he is without question the only man in the world who has lived so long with neither brains nor guts"). But McCarthy refused to sign it, telling Dirksen, "I don't crawl."[17] Payne also urged McCarthy to apologize. He later recounted what followed: "Joe went to the floor right after that and got up to talk. Bill Fulbright from Arkansas had just made a speech on the censure movement. Joe looked up to the balcony and said, 'The senator from Arkansas, Mr. Halfbright. . . .' Well, Jesus, I knew right then it was all over."[18]

An unrepentant Senator McCarthy threw down the gauntlet with his opening statement claiming that the Communist Party "has now extended its tentacles to the most respected of American bodies, the United States Senate. . . . [I]t has made a committee of the Senate its unwitting handmaiden."[19] During the following weeks of angry speeches and shouting matches on the floor, Smith had little to say, and there was no doubt about how she would vote. Certainly, she could not help but feel vindicated now, four years after her Declaration of Conscience, to see McCarthy on the defensive.

When the Senate voted on December 2, the resolution carried 67 to 22. Forty-four Democrats voted aye; the Republicans were split down the middle. McCarthy was "condemned" by his colleagues for obstructing the business of the Senate and for bringing the entire body into dishonor and disrepute, but he was not censured. Sen. Styles Bridges (R-NH) made certain that the word "censure" did not appear in the resolution; leaving out that word forestalled any attempt to have him removed from the Senate by a two-thirds vote as was mandatory under Senate rules.[20] McCarthy retained his right to speak, to vote, and to sit on committees, but he no longer had power. He remained, isolated and harmless, in the Senate until his death on 2 May 1957.[21]

Following the eulogies came attempts at resurrection. McCarthy's committee, Government Operations, drafted and approved a resolution saluting the late senator for distinctive service in conducting "a most aggressive and courageous fight against Communism, striving constantly to awaken our people to the threat of the international Communist conspiracy to our Government and the institutions on which it is founded." Though a member, Smith had not been present at the creation of this document and when asked to sign it, refused. "If the resolution were one of expression of sympathy alone," she told Chair John McClellan (D-AR), "I would have been happy to sign it. But it went far beyond that to include language to which I cannot conscientiously subscribe."[22] Smith's refusal prevented a unanimous expression by the committee and effectively halted any further effort, already begun, toward completely expunging the condemnatory vote from the Senate record.[23]

Before Smith left on the second leg of her journey in early 1955, she joined the debate on the Formosa Resolution. The Communist Chinese had been shelling the Tachen Islands and the islands of Quemoy and Matsu, occupied by Nationalist Chinese troops, since September. President Eisenhower considered these small atolls in the straits of Formosa to be strategically important to the defense of the Nationalists (the only Chinese government the U.S. recognized) primarily as symbols of American toughness. Should that island barrier be penetrated by "international Communism," he told Winston Churchill, in a variation of the "domino theory," "that whole region would soon go."[24] As the harassment continued, the situation became so tense that Secretary of State John Foster Dulles remarked, "If we defend Quemoy and Matsu, we'll have to use atomic weapons. . . . I believe there is at least an even chance that the United States will have to go to war."[25] In early 1955, the president asked Congress for authority to use American armed force to protect Formosa as he deemed necessary.

Smith called the Formosa Resolution "a reserve declaration of war," and questioned whether America had the necessary military strength to back it up. Nonetheless, she said, "we have no other choice than to give the president, by an overwhelming vote, the power he requests. . . . [If] the resolution were defeated, we would give the impression to the rest of the world that we did not have the will to resist Communist aggression."[26] Though it was an unprecedented step to authorize a president in advance to go to war, the Formosa Resolution passed easily, 409 to 3 in the House and 85 to 3 in the Senate, indicating broad congressional support for halting Soviet expansion in Asia.[27]

When the Senate recessed in February, Smith and Lewis headed for the Far East to continue her investigations of the strength of international Communism. Insinuating herself into the tense situation in Formosa, Smith held extensive talks with Chiang Kai-shek and reviewed Formosan troops, whom she pronounced "lean and hard and battle worthy."[28] While Smith was pursuing accord with the nationalist leader, the administration was in the midst of delicate negotiations in the region. Eisenhower, having earlier promised to "unleash" Chiang Kai-shek for possible future military action against the mainland of Red China, warned the Communist Chinese about "misjudging our firm purpose and national unity." As tensions mounted, he reinforced Dulles's earlier threat to use nuclear weapons, saying he considered them appropriate to use "just exactly as you would use a bullet or anything else." His message was intended to deter his opponents; he was counting on the reluctance of Russia and China to risk nuclear war over the matter.[29]

Chiang heard the same messages and assumed the U.S. was ready for war on his behalf. On Smith's "See It Now" broadcast, Chiang declared he intended to liberate his people "from the Communist yoke through counterattacking the mainland" and that he expected Americans to provide "moral support, sympathy, material and logistical support."[30] President Eisenhower quickly responded that the United States could promise no such aid. He dispatched two emissaries "to induce the Generalissimo to propose some solution . . . acceptable both to him and to us," that would resolve the crisis short of war. Chiang refused to compromise, and the talks stalled with war a distinct possibility. The crisis was finally defused when Chinese Premier Chou En-lai indicated that Red China had no intention of going to war with the United States and was ready to negotiate about Formosa.[31]

The administration refrained from criticizing Smith's intervention, but the Soviets wasted little time expressing their annoyance at her meddling. The USSR's armed forces newspaper, *Red Star*, denounced her as "a military amazon" who hides behind bouquets of roses. Pegging its story—headlined "Rosa and Formosa"—to Smith's recent proposal to make the rose the national flower, the Soviets complained that "Mrs. Smith combines her love for roses with suspicious sympathy for Formosa. . . . So, out of Madame Peacemaker, surrounded with bouquets of roses, Senator Smith has suddenly changed into a military amazon who . . . waves the atom bomb and calls for war."[32] Recalling her earlier characterization by the Soviets as a "warmonger," Smith combined the two "insults" and bragged that "the Russian Communist press calls me an Amazon warmonger hiding behind a rose." She wore the epithet like a badge of honor, polishing it before audiences for years.[33]

As she traveled through Asia, Smith discussed trade in Japan, American friendship and aid in Thailand, Vietnam, Burma, India, and Pakistan. She finished up her trip in the Mediterranean, speaking sympathetically with Nasser in Egypt about colonialism and finding Francisco Franco "far different from the saber-rattling, fierce militaristic fascist that he had been so erroneously pictured to the American public."[34]

Meanwhile, in Maine, her constituents were complaining, impatient with her absences from senate duties after she had made so much of her perfect attendance in the recent campaign.[35] Smith returned to give the home folks and the Senate another report. As before, her takes on world leaders were superficial, characterizing them as, in the case of Indian Prime Minister Nehru, "an able man [who] has the confidence of his people," or Chiang Kai-shek as "a very confident man who gives every appearance of restoring the confidence of his government," or Francisco Franco as "an able man, and a very good man in his place in Spain—one of the able and capable leaders of the world."[36] She called for a change in the basis and "approaches" taken in foreign policy, by which she meant increases "in boldness and firmness."[37]

After her senate report, President Eisenhower invited her to the White House to discuss foreign policy, a gesture of respect for the senator from Maine. Smith passed along a few recommendations, including that Spain be admitted to NATO without delay, and communications with Nehru be initiated in order to entice this "mystic-like neutralist" away from Communism. She also reiterated her message to "get tough" with the Soviets. She was not sure he accepted her advice, but she was pleased that he had asked.[38]

There had been a recent thaw between Eisenhower and Smith. Their prickly relationship, largely the result of her anger at the president's unwillingness to confront and restrain McCarthy, now seemed headed for rapprochement. They shared the moderate wing of their party and agreed on fundamental Cold War goals.[39] Responding to her complaints about the "paucity of patronage" in her home state, the president included one million dollars in his budget to initiate yet another survey of the Passamaquoddy Tidal Power Project, despite the Canadian government's insistence that development of tidal power would lead to "high cost to power consumers and damage to fisheries," despite the Corp of Engineers' discouraging lack of enthusiasm for the project, and despite his personal aversion to public power projects.[40] Eisenhower also announced that he was accepting her invitation to Skowhegan as part of his vacation plans.[41] These gestures, along with nascent efforts to "dump Nixon" from the 1956 GOP ticket, fueled a flurry of speculation about Ike's real reason for traveling to Smith's hometown.[42]

Following two days of angling for Maine's famous freshwater salmon, the presidential caravan swung into Skowhegan. Ringing church bells and howling factory whistles bestowed a highly audible welcome. The town had spent weeks in preparation; everything sparkled with spit and polish. A huge sign on a downtown building proclaimed: "Ike—Margaret—1956." Military bands and a crowd estimated at seventy-five hundred—more than the entire population of the town—waited in the hot sun at the fairgrounds for the first glimpse many of them had ever had of a president of the United States. Standing proudly at the podium with Governor Muskie and assorted dignitaries, Smith introduced the president as "the greatest man of peace in the world." He joked about the "cannibalistic tendencies" of Maine's black flies and briefly discussed the inseparability of peace and prosperity. Then the president and the senator climbed back in the convertible for a couple of turns around the fairgrounds race track to wave and grin to the crowd before heading up the hill beside the Kennebec River for a cookout in her backyard. Eisenhower broiled his own steak over the open coals while Smith scrambled to find enough lobsters to accommodate the 100 plus newsmen who rolled into town with the president. Before the party was over, Smith talked Ike into trying a Maine lobster, despite his doctor's orders that he avoid shellfish. Mainers gratefully reported that Ike ate the crustacean with obvious relish. In the late afternoon, the presidential entourage headed for Bangor and back to Washington.[43]

It was a grand event for the state of Maine, for the town of Skowhegan, and for Senator Smith, but what did it mean? Likely it meant that the president simply wanted to go fishing in Maine. And while he was there, he tended to GOP business by paying honor to Maine's top Republican.

Following Eisenhower's heart attack that September, his candidacy for reelection remained in doubt until February. When he finally announced he would run again, he refused to endorse his vice-president, saying he desired his party's convention to choose. This ambivalence further encouraged the "dump Nixon" movement within the party, and numerous "Nervous about Nixon" ads from the opposition.[44] Smith turned up on a few lists of substitutes, but her potential candidacy chiefly served political columnists' need for interesting copy.[45] Still, Maine Republicans resolved to propose her as a "favorite daughter" candidate should an opening arise.[46] Smith said she was "honored" by their gesture. She felt distinctly less venerated, though, when no one invited her to speak at the convention until the last minute. By that time, she told them it was too late, she was already committed to work for the campaign in Maine.[47] Besides nursing her pique with the party, Smith had good reason for staying home to campaign for the Republican ticket. If dissension in their ranks had allowed Muskie to take office two years ago, as conventional wisdom had it, then she and Payne were determined to pull together in a show of unity against a popular governor and an increasingly well-organized Democratic Party.[48] Despite a Republican majority of four-to-one in the state legislature, Muskie had managed, through accommodation and compromise, to get an impressive 70 percent of the bills he submitted passed into law. His initiative for a new Department of Industry and Commerce had brought abundant new jobs into the state. Even the potato farmers were having a good year.[49]

With few local issues to debate and criticize, and so much at stake, Smith put her personal prestige and popularity behind the Republican candidates, especially gubernatorial challenger Willis A. Trafton, Jr., asking voters, as "a personal favor to me," to vote for the GOP. Mainers criticized her for "inject[ing] her own personality into the campaign to an unreasonable degree," and said, "the inference is quite plain that you shouldn't like her and Ed Muskie, too."[50] Holding her course to the end of the campaign, Smith even took voters to the polls in her own car.[51] It didn't work. Ed Muskie was reelected by the biggest vote ever given a Maine governor, defeating Trafton by 56,000 votes.[52] And Democratic Party Chair Frank Coffin won the vacated Second District congressional seat, Smith's home district. The First District race was almost too close to call; Republican Robert Hale squeaked through by 29 votes. The only part of Maine the Republican strength held was in the Third District, mostly rural, mostly conservative.[53]

Despite the September debacle, the Republicans were not too worried about the chances Ike would triumph in Maine in November, so Smith turned her efforts to the national race. She could always be counted on to court the "woman's vote," and she did her usual yeoman job making speeches around the country. Her most difficult assignment this time was a debate with Eleanor Roosevelt on CBS's "Face the Nation." She was to speak in support of Eisenhower while Mrs. Roosevelt would do the same for Democrat Adlai Stevenson. Feeling intimidated by the loquacious former First Lady and hesitant to debate a good friend, Smith decided her best strategy was to present a "favorably sharp contrast" to her opponent. She elected to stick to brief answers and insisted on giving a closing summary.[54] Most of all, though, Smith was uncomfortable with having to defend Eisenhower's policies. She disagreed with his military strategies, which she saw as sacrificing national security to economics, and disagreed with his foreign aid initiatives, which she defined as appeasement and capitulation to blackmail. Moreover, the event came at a very intense time in both the campaign and the world, with simultaneous crises in Egypt and Hungary, the details of which were still sketchy at broadcast time. Smith had only some of the following information about the situation.[55]

Gamal Abdal Nasser had come to power in Egypt in 1952, instituted land reform and pledged to eliminate British control of the Suez Canal. A 1954 agreement, which London reluctantly signed, provided for a phased withdrawal, and the U.S., as part of a foreign aid offensive, promised to fund Nasser's dream of the Aswan Dam on the Nile. Though Nasser avowed "neutrality" in the Cold War, he attempted to secure aid from both sides. After the Egyptian leader recognized the People's Republic of China and signed an arms deal with Communist Czechoslovakia, Secretary Dulles took this as betrayal and abruptly withdrew the Aswan Dam offer in July 1956.[56]

From Smith's position on the Appropriations Subcommittee on Foreign Relations, she consistently opposed foreign aid as a diplomatic tool, arguing that countries that took American aid paid back with apostasy. She distrusted any nation that had dealings with the Soviet Union and found the Eisenhower policy of "buying" friends to be at best unwise and at worst appeasement. She fought against aid to Yugoslavia on the grounds that Josip Tito proclaimed himself a "neutralist" while being "tied lock, stock and barrel to the Kremlin."[57] Similarly, she was pleased when Dulles annulled funding of Aswan. "We had tired of being blackmailed by Colonel Nasser who felt he could play footsie with Russia and scare us into paying for his desired Aswan Dam. What a surprised man he was when he found that his blackmail and bluff didn't work and we told him . . . he could try Russia."[58]

Nasser seized the Suez Canal, intent on using its profits to fund the dam while the British plotted military retaliation with the French and Israelis, assuming the United States would stand firm with her allies in the altercation. But when the Israelis bombed Egypt, Eisenhower publicly upbraided them for taking military action, announced that his administration would abide by the 1950 Tripartite Declaration, one part of which pledged the United States to support the victim of aggression in the Middle East, and called for a U.N. resolution against the invaders.[59]

At about this same time, the Hungarians were returning Imre Nagy to power, whom the Soviets had deposed in 1955. On October 31, the day after the bombing of Egypt and a week before the election, Nagy announced that Hungary was withdrawing from the Warsaw Pact. In response, the Soviets sent troops to Budapest, and the Hungarians turned to the United States for help. Largely because of his commitment to "massive retaliation," the president could do little short of bombing the Soviets. So, America stood by as the Russians crushed the Hungarians.[60]

This, then, was the setting for the preelection debate between Smith and Roosevelt. Under questioning from the reporters on "Face the Nation," the two women took strongly partisan positions and disagreed sharply on the wisdom of U.S. policies in the Middle East and Eastern Europe. Roosevelt charged the administration with weakening NATO and encouraging the Soviet Union to move into Hungary. The war in the Middle East, she said, could have been prevented "if we had acted a long time ago." Smith countered that Ike had "done his level best" to ease the tensions and she did not believe that U.S. leadership alone could have prevented an outbreak of hostilities. Eleanor Roosevelt monopolized the debate, while Smith was terse and to the point. When there was silence to be filled, Mrs. Roosevelt filled it. In a familiar tactic, Smith waited until the very end, when her opponent could no longer respond, and delivered her best shots. In her closing summation, Smith hit hard, dismissing Roosevelt's position as naked partisanship. Democratic presidents, she pointed out, "chose Dwight D. Eisenhower to lead our nation to victory in World War II and to head up NATO to stop the spread of Communism . . . . It is strange to see and hear Democratic leaders now accusing him of not being a leader. Why the difference? It is clearly the difference between principle and politics."[61] After they were off the air, Smith attempted to shake Roosevelt's hand, but the former First Lady turned her back and walked away. It was the end of their friendship. Smith later expressed her regret as well as her frustration that Mrs. Roosevelt simply did not understand a cardinal rule of politics—that political disagreements should not influence personal feelings.[62] Smith tended to forget that rule as well.

After Eisenhower's victory over Stevenson, Smith resumed expressing her growing dissatisfaction with his defense and foreign policy decisions, his excessive concern with economic considerations at the expense of security, and overreliance upon foreign aid to win the hearts and minds of the Third World. Doubtless, Smith believed that her mastery of foreign affairs and military policy impressed her constituents, but many of them were likely more concerned with threats of Japanese imports to the Maine textile industry, price supports for potato farmers, pork barrel defense projects that went to other states, and whether Aunt Minnie got her Social Security check on time. Smith took care of those, too. By the late 1950s, with military facilities at Bangor, Brunswick, and Limestone, and the defense payroll in Maine at some $80 million, she took prideful credit that her state was "practically one big Air Base."[63] Smith routinely sponsored bills to protect Maine industry and agriculture, supporting "peril point" amendments to reciprocal trade agreements that would cut off imports when they threatened domestic industry, fighting for military contracts for Maine products, and spending dozens of hours of secretarial time, and her own, each month on constituent service.

One illustration of her efforts and tenacity in political combat was her fight to equalize pay rates at the Portsmouth Naval Shipyard in Kittery, Maine, with those at the Boston Navy Yard. Pay rates between the two had been relatively equal until 1947 when the Navy lowered those at Kittery, contending that labor was cheaper there. For ten years, Smith tried to get the navy to change them back. Finally, she proposed an equalization bill to force the matter. The Smith bill passed both Houses by voice vote after unanimous approval by both Armed Services Committees. But when it got to Eisenhower's desk, he vetoed it, claiming the legislation would upset the navy's formula for matching shipyard scales with rates paid in private industry in the neighborhood. Smith argued there was little difference between the neighborhoods, that many of the workers lived in between the two yards, yet were paid as much as 29 cents more per hour in Boston.[64] Smith made a motion to override the president's veto.

Despite its minuscule impact on the nation's economy, the issue was fraught with political complications. For one, the Democrats were looking for an issue on which to rebuke the administration and reassert congressional control. Ike had vetoed 107 bills without an override since 1953. Smith knew she did not have enough power to push the issue, but she had a powerful friend. At her request, Majority Leader Lyndon Johnson called a quick quorum while the Republican leadership was in a Policy Committee meeting, and delivered enough votes to override in the Senate.[65] The Navy immediately announced a salary increase at Kittery of fourteen cents an hour, likely forestalling the override vote in the House. The president's veto was sustained. Smith tried again to equalize pay scales in 1960 with a similar bill, but Eisenhower pocket-vetoed it.[66]

Another example of Smith's service to her constituents, a more private example, was the case of Eve Moertl, a Czech refugee on a Fulbright scholarship to the United States in 1951. She met and married veterinary student Henry D. Bither, but since she was on a student visa, she had to go home. She immediately applied for a visa as an alien wife of an American citizen, but she could not get a hearing until her husband, by then practicing in Maine, wrote to his senator. Suddenly, Mrs. Bither got a call from the consulate, whose secretary she had not even been able to see the previous three months. As she tells it, the consulate threw down a telegram from the State Department stating that Senator Smith, a ranking member of the Senate Armed Services Committee, requested he expedite the visa application of a wife of one of her constituents. Eve landed in New York a month later.[67]

There were countless others Smith helped in myriad ways. Particularly in a state like Maine, composed of hundreds of small towns and villages, when just one person was helped in some way, everyone else in town knew about it and such kindnesses were not forgotten on election day. In addition, this strong following based on personal service allowed her some ideological flexibility in Washington.

Consistent with her position in the moderate wing of the party, Smith supported a relatively liberal social agenda in the 1950s, standing behind federal aid to education, increased old age and disability supports, favorable labor legislation, and civil rights; on most of these issues, with the possible exception of the latter, she agreed with the Eisenhower administration and, apparently, the majority of her constituents.[68] At the same time, she embraced a markedly conservative approach to matters of military defense and national security, and it was defense strategies that engaged Smith the most. In 1958, Smith dropped her assignment to Government Operations and picked up yet another defense-oriented committee, Aeronautical and Space Sciences, formed in response to the shock of Sputnik. The successful launch of the Soviet satellite in October, 1957, jolted assumptions about American technological superiority and led to a reevaluation of everything from the educational system to national defense. Under the aegis of his Senate Preparedness Subcommittee, Lyndon Johnson launched an intensive inquiry into America's aerospace readiness, concluding that the Soviets had widened what came to be called the "missile gap" largely because of "our own shortcomings and complacency," the result of the Eisenhower administration's persistent cuts in research and development. Subcommittee recommendations, later codified in Johnson's National Aeronautics and Space Act of 1958, called for the creation of a National Aeronautics and Space Administration (NASA), with a civilian director and permanent oversight committees in both Houses.[69]

Johnson invited Smith to join his Senate Space Committee. Most of the members were other committee chairmen or, like Smith, members of the Armed Services Committee. She was a good choice as she enthusiastically endorsed NASA's mission to surpass the Soviet Union and consistently supported space appropriations. Justifying the ever increasing costs of the space race, Smith stressed the "spinoffs" of space research, maintaining that the real payoffs came in advances in communications, weather prediction, and medical miracles.[70] Still, her primary concern was with the impact of space on America's military preparedness. "It should be crystal clear to everyone by now that we have entered a crucial age when all of our past concepts of national security and national defense must be reviewed and evaluated and many of them discarded." Most of all, Smith declared, "there is no reason for us to cringe in fear." On the contrary, "the naked truth is that as individuals and as a nation, we must toughen up emotionally. We must make it clear to Russia that we will fight if necessary. . . . Too long now have we failed to take the initiative ourselves and act first. . . . Unless we are willing to fight—unless we are willing to draw the line and make a stand at some point, Russia will surely gobble up the earth merely by threatening to start a war and thus blackmailing the free world into compromise after compromise that in reality is nothing less than appeasement after appeasement."[71]

The difficulty, of course, was in finding the critical balance point between military security and economic stability. Eisenhower's solution was to cut conventional forces while relying on the threat of nuclear retaliation to keep the peace. Smith's solution, no doubt heavily influenced by her executive assistant's predilections, was to cut standing forces and make reserves the major component of the American military. Lewis wrote and she repeatedly proposed legislation designed to make reserves more attractive in pay, security, and recognition. At the same time, however, the Eisenhower administration worked to reduce Reserve levels against an unyielding Congress. The president argued that maintaining Reserve forces "are unnecessarily costing the American people over $80 million annually and have been too long based on other than strictly military needs"—an obvious reference to payrolls and armories and other local benefits from defense coffers.[72] It was, of course, just such spoils that political representatives, including Smith, defended.

Interestingly, the fact that she held a reserve commission (Lt. Colonel in the Air Force Reserve) or that Lewis put in his reserve time in the office of legislative liaison for the Pentagon, elicited little comment, although this would seem to be a conflict of interest for a senator on the Armed Services Committee.[73] Lewis, whose father headed the Air Reserve Association until his retirement in 1951, was also a member of the "Congressional Air Reserve Squadron," the 9999th, led by General Barry Goldwater, himself a member of the Senate ASC. It was not at all unusual for congressmen to hold reserve commissions; the 9999th included at least five other senators and a dozen representatives. The squadron, formed in 1961 to enable reservists who worked for Congress to fulfill their training requirements in Washington, held weekly briefings and pep talks by Air Force officers in the Senate Office Building. Little wonder Pentagon budgets passed easily.[74]

Her combative rhetoric notwithstanding, Smith's activities on behalf of military matters—considering weapons procurements, officer promotions, defense policy, and reservist equalization issues—normally did not get her much press, but one episode certainly did. The story had everything: the nation's only woman senator, a Hollywood movie star, a World War II combat general, a Senate investigating committee, charges and countercharges, and before it was all over, a complete shake-up in promotion procedures.

In February, 1957, the Air Force submitted for Senate ASC approval a list of eleven nominations for promotion within the reserve ranks. Smith examined the list carefully and objected to six of the eight nominees for brigadier general, including James Maitland Stewart, better known as the movie actor Jimmy Stewart. She said that reserve officers who did not keep up their training requirements should not be made generals. Stewart had served only nine days of reserve duty in the past eleven years (requirements called for fifteen-day tours annually). To do so, she said, would shatter the morale of the reserve forces. Rules were rules, Smith insisted, and everyone should be equally obliged to abide by them. Lt. Gen. Emmett (Rosie) O'Donnell, Jr. argued on Stewart's behalf that war experience and ability counted in promotions, not just reserve activity. Mr. Stewart, he pointed out, had been commander of a bombing wing in Europe in World War II; he had been awarded several decorations including the Distinguished Flying Cross. And, besides, his movies had been a great boost to recruitment. Well, if he was being rewarded for his role in the film *Strategic Air Command*, Smith exclaimed, then "why don't you make June Allyson a Brigadier General for playing the female lead!"[75] O'Donnell and Smith slugged it out over several other nominees. With her usual meticulous preparation, she repeatedly tripped up the general and sessions turned into shouting matches. The bitter recriminations on both sides made their way into the public record.[76] But Smith held her ground. Stewart and the others would have to meet the requirements. When his nomination reappeared two years later, after Smith and ASC Chairman Richard Russell insisted the Air Force downgrade his duty assignment from Deputy Chief of Operations at the

Strategic Air Command to Deputy Director of Information Services, Stewart finally got his star.[77]

But there was yet another round or two to go. When Eisenhower nominated O'Donnell to Commander-in-Chief, Pacific Air Forces, a post that carried a four-star rank, Smith disqualified herself from the hearings, stating her "serious reservations about the integrity, performance, and reliability of General O'Donnell . . . [in light of his] personal attacks . . . against my integrity and character."[78] Though the committee called O'Donnell and Secretary of the Air Force, James Douglas, to account for Smith's charges, when they disclaimed any intent to damage her in any way, the vote in favor of O'Donnell's promotion was twelve to one.[79]

All of the charges and the countercharges exposed the turmoil behind the promotion system. Russell called for a sweeping investigation, turning the matter over to Johnson's Preparedness Investigation Subcommittee. After a two-month investigation concluded that "there appeared to be no systematic order or logic in the selection of officers made admirals or generals," the subcommittee called for a full overhaul of the services' systems for promoting reserve generals.[80] The military establishment was clearly unhappy with Smith for blowing the whistle on time-honored procedures. But many of her constituents again applauded her "conscience" in facing down the power of the Pentagon. Our senator, editorials crowed, would not be intimidated.[81] And she was about to demonstrate that once again.

Over the years, Smith had tried to get along with the Eisenhower administration. Most notable was her support for the controversial Dixon-Yates energy contract in 1954. When Tennessee legislators asked to expand TVA to accommodate the power needs of the growing city of Memphis in addition to maintaining energy levels needed by the Atomic Energy Commission (AEC) facility at Oak Ridge, the Eisenhower administration refused. Ike contended that public power projects like TVA were prime examples of "creeping socialism" in that "taxes from all the country were used to subsidize a particular region," and he pledged to encourage private power company growth.[82] Accordingly, he authorized a contract between the AEC and Dixon-Yates, a company formed to build steam plants in Tennessee. Opponents in Congress, led by Sen. Clinton Anderson (D-NM), Chair of the Joint Committee on Atomic Energy, contended that the contract committed the AEC to buy power at a higher cost than that of TVA and that the AEC was being used to subsidize a private power plant in an effort to weaken the TVA.[83]

It was a classic battle between private versus public power. Smith had long been on record as favoring public power, having battled for the Passamaquoddy Tidal Power Project for years against the determined efforts not only of the Canadian government, but also of Central Maine Power. Logically, then, she might have opposed the Dixon-Yates contract. However, after Eisenhower called her from Camp David and asked her, as a personal favor, to support Dixon-Yates, she voted to approve. She later alleged that it was the one vote of her entire Senate tenure that she regretted.[84] Under the Republican majority, the Senate passed on the Dixon-Yates contract. But the matter was revisited after the elections in 1954 brought in a Democratic majority. From January to July, the Joint Committee and the Senate Subcommittee on Antitrust and Monopoly held hearings that revealed, despite AEC Chairman Lewis L. Strauss's testimony to the contrary, that the contract was fraught with duplicity and conflict-of-interest. After months of hearings, of contention and charges, Eisenhower ended up withdrawing the contract in July 1955, and the matter ended.[85] Or so it seemed.

Three years later, in October 1958, Ike nominated Lewis L. Strauss for Secretary of Commerce.[86] It appeared that confirmation would be easily granted. Although the Constitution required the Senate to consent, American political tradition held that the president should be able to staff his Cabinet with men he trusted. Despite considerable grumbling, for example, Eisenhower's entire initial Cabinet had been easily approved. In 170 years, 33 presidents submitted 450 Cabinet nominations; thus far the Senate had failed to confirm only seven, and then only in cases of gross incompetence or moral turpitude. Moreover, Strauss had met Senate approval three times before: for promotion to rear admiral during World War II, for appointment to the Atomic Energy Commission, and for chairmanship of the AEC.[87]

Nonetheless, things began to look troubling for Strauss almost immediately. Though it normally took only a few weeks to consider a nominee for a Cabinet post, the Senate delayed confirmation hearings for six months, until well after November elections brought a large Democratic majority that significantly changed the dynamics.[88] Hearings begun in March continued into May, while Senators Anderson and Kefauver (D-TN), who had earlier confronted Strauss over Dixon-Yates, resurrected a host of sins. They contended that Strauss was responsible for hounding Dr. J. Robert Oppenheimer off the Atomic Energy Commission after he failed to support the development of the hydrogen bomb by charging him with disloyalty, and was guilty of cronyism in his involvement with the Dixon-Yates electro-power scam, using the AEC for the personal gain of a private power company. Critical of his rigid approach to nuclear test ban negotiations with the Soviet Union, the senators accused him of lying about the dangers of fallout and riding roughshod over people who opposed him on the Atomic Energy Commission. Strauss's most grievous sin, though, appeared to be his conscious decision to withhold information from Congress. Anderson was incensed by what he called Strauss's "two hats." While he served as chairman of the AEC, answerable to the Joint Congressional Committee on Atomic Energy, Strauss also acted as the president's personal adviser on nuclear energy. As such, Strauss regularly refused to respond to congressional inquiries on the grounds that he could not violate his confidential relationship with Eisenhower.[89]

During the hearings, Strauss was his own worst enemy. He was, said Senator Warren Magnuson (D-WA), "a very arrogant fellow. He's the only guy I know who could strut sitting down."[90] Given the unusual courtesy of rebuttal, Strauss reacted to criticism with evasion, disdain and dissembling, repeatedly calling his own veracity into question, and doing it all with condescending self-righteousness. Even Strauss's supporters admitted he "skirted the truth with his oblique explanations of his behavior. . . . He was determined to prove that he had been right about everything."[91] After two months of debate, the Senate Commerce Committee somewhat reluctantly approved the nomination nine to eight, remanding it to the full Senate in early June.[92]

The length and acrimony of the hearings surprised the administration, and those who tried to make tallies of the votes to confirm found they followed very closely along partisan lines. Rumor had it that Lyndon Johnson had made it a party test vote, although he announced that the Democratic leadership would take no formal position on the nomination. The vote in the Commerce Committee was six Republicans and three Democrats to confirm, eight Democrats to reject. The tally for the full Senate, by June 1, appeared to be 48 for Strauss, 44 against, and 8 undecided.[93]

Smith was among the undecided, the only Republican no one was sure about. Smith never revealed her vote ahead of time, and senators on both sides of the aisle knew better than to lobby her. Still, Strauss came to see her, and Clinton Anderson dropped by her office. She made a commitment to neither.[94] When she learned that Vice-President Nixon's invitation to dinner for West German Chancellor Adenauer included only one senator—her—and only one Cabinet member—Strauss—she canceled.[95]

After another two weeks of debate, the final vote in the Senate took place on June 19, following a prolonged filibuster by Senator Goldwater, who held the floor for several hours speaking about Strauss's qualifications and the notion that the Senate ought to confirm the men the president desired; he was stalling until a few more Republicans could make it back to the floor. Finally, shortly after midnight, Vice-President Nixon took over the presiding officer's chair, ready to cast his vote for Strauss in case of a tie.[96] As the roll was called, the votes tallied as anticipated;

then an expectant hush as the clerk called Smith. "No," she said firmly. Her colleagues gasped, and Goldwater hit his desk with his fist, exploding, "Goddamn!" He added a muttered, "She won't get a damn nickel." The reference was to his control of campaign funds dispersed by the Senatorial Campaign Committee which he chaired; Smith was up for reelection in 1960. He later claimed the incident never happened, but it was widely repeated in the press at the time.[97] And, as it turned out, she didn't get a "damn nickel."

The vote against confirmation was 49 to 46. Smith was one of only two Republicans to reject the nomination. William Langer of North Dakota was the other. Had they voted with the rest of their party, Strauss would have been confirmed 48 to 47. Langer's vote was no surprise; he had revealed his position long before.[98] But why did Smith vote against her party, against her president, against Strauss? Most press speculation contended she was a vengeful woman, determined to punish her party for nonsupport. She was reportedly "fuming at the president" for vetoing a bill important to her, "infuriated" that her party colleagues refused to back her fight to deny a fourth star to the "swashbuckling" O'Donnell, "resentful" that the administration "does not pay enough attention to the only woman in the Senate." She allegedly made deals with Anderson, Lyndon Johnson, or Drew Pearson, to get even with the Republican administration.[99]

There may have been something to them, all of them. Perhaps she did trade favors with LBJ. He helped her override Ike's veto and she was plenty mad at the president for that veto. And, though no one mentioned it, she was still smarting over Dixon-Yates. She was angry that the Republicans ignored her accusations of malfeasance against O'Donnell, confirming him anyway, and on the same day as the Strauss vote. But what resonates the strongest when examining this episode are the themes inherent in the Strauss controversy itself. For Smith, they could hardly have been more telling—guilty of McCarthyism (in the Oppenheimer matter), guilty of withholding information on nuclear matters, guilty of lying to Congress. Smith was simply reacting according to her long record of distaste for secrecy, for arrogance, for smear. There was no way she could have voted for confirmation.[100] "Those looking for hidden motives in her defection are wasting their time," wrote the *Press Herald*, "as she had nothing to gain from going against the president."[101] Eisenhower called the rejection of Strauss "one of the most depressing official disappointments I experienced during eight years in the White House," and referred to Smith and Langer as "short-sighted Republicans."[102] Publicly, he blamed LBJ for making the confirmation a party matter and, perhaps, trading favors with Clinton Anderson.[103] Privately, he harbored abundant resentment toward Smith, even to the point of refusing to have his photograph made with her.[104]

As the Strauss matter unfolded, Smith was feeling somewhat besieged at home, too, where the Democrats were gaining ground. She was grateful that she was not up for reelection herself in 1958. In loyalty to her party, she campaigned for Payne against his challenger, Governor Ed Muskie, but with little enthusiasm.[105] Recent revelations of Payne's association with shady businessman Bernard Goldfine, whose gifts of vicuna coats had become a cliche for political corruption, made it difficult. Goldfine was cited for contempt of Congress and was instrumental in driving Sherman Adams from his position as assistant to the president, damaging Eisenhower's promise of an administration "as clean as a hound's tooth."[106] The issue of corruption in government, coupled with perceived failures in the president's foreign policies, particularly with respect to Soviet space and missile achievements, and a deepening recession, promised to hurt the Republican Party in 1958.

The association of the Republican Party with corruption was reinforced by news of a fund-raising dinner for House GOP leader, Joseph W. Martin, Jr. The uproar started when it was revealed that RNC committeeman Jack Porter of Texas had solicited dinner ticket sales by indicating Martin could be counted on to line up House votes on the Natural Gas Bill, which exempted independent natural gas producers from federal utility-rate control.[107] Senator Andrew Schoeppel (R-KS), then chair of the Republican Senatorial Campaign Committee, acknowledged Porter's move was "unfortunate," but said he would not refuse the funds, which amounted to more than $100,000.[108] Smith immediately tendered her resignation from the committee.[109] She remembered how Texas oil money had reached into Maine in the 1954 campaign. Some of the same figures were involved in sponsoring the dinner for Martin, as well as a similar one for Lyndon Johnson. Under the glare of media exposure, the Senatorial Campaign Committee decided to repudiate the fundraising method after all and, as if to make it all better, said the money would stay in Texas to meet campaign debts there. Although she made no public comment about her resignation, Smith was lauded in both the local and national press for her stance on behalf of ethical behavior and political morality, and against old-boy politics as usual. It was yet another exhibition of independence which some of the more orthodox Republicans no doubt found tiresome.[110]

The 1958 election brought the most dramatic Democratic victory since the Roosevelt landslide of 1936. Democrats gained fifteen seats in the Senate, increasing their majority to 64. Maine elected a Democratic governor, a Democratic senator, and two Democratic congressmen.[111]

Edmund Muskie won easily in his bid to replace Payne, capturing 60.8 percent of the vote.[112] Smith now led an all-Democratic—except for her—delegation.

Reacting to the ideological shift in the Senate, liberal Republicans, including Smith, moved to propose their own candidates for GOP leadership. But in the tussle that followed, Old Guard conservatives hung on to power. Everett Dirksen succeeded William Knowland as floor leader, Styles Bridges held his chair on the Policy Committee, and Goldwater took control of the Senatorial Campaign Committee. Goldwater then bitterly denounced the Republican opposition: "I'm not for any liberal. I wouldn't support anyone who is involved with the elements that want to tear the party limb from limb."[113] It's no wonder that he made certain to punish Smith after the Strauss vote by delaying funds for her 1960 campaign.[114]

As it turned out, she did not really need them. Her bid for reelection to her third Senate term in 1960 was a rout, notable most for its consequences to her relations with Ed Muskie and for the way the press played with it than for any sense of a true contest. Smith's relationship with her fellow senator had been prickly since he won Maine's governor's seat in 1954. They had a few altercations about state business, and the tone of letters between them indicate a certain level of enmity on both sides.[115] Nonetheless, despite their party labels, it could be argued that Muskie and Smith were not so far apart. Both had reputations for probity and conscience, and both were political moderates. Both supported civil rights, federal aid to education, and Quoddy. Indeed, during his challenge to Senator Payne in 1958, Muskie, in positioning himself in opposition to his opponent, frequently found himself in league with her, for she had often split votes with Payne. Still, neither was wont to acknowledge that; he was as intensely partisan as she.[116]

Despite their differences, though, once Muskie was elected, Smith was determined to be cordial. When he came to take his oath in the Senate, the six-foot-four junior senator was escorted down the aisle by the five-foot-three senior senator. After some discussion about whether he should take her arm or she his, the parliamentarian ruled the new member takes the arm of the colleague who escorts him, so Muskie slipped his arm through hers. Afterwards, she extended the unusual courtesy of escorting him across the aisle and introducing him to all the Republican senators.[117]

The cordiality did not last. Never comfortable around political enemies, Smith viewed her colleague with suspicion, and it seemed to her that he went out of his way to disagree with her on most issues. Most grievous of all to her, though, were his efforts to seek her defeat in 1960.

Assuming "the only way to beat a woman in politics is with another woman," Coffin and Muskie designated Lucia Cormier, twelve-term state legislator, minority leader of Maine's House of Representatives, and former national committeewoman for the Democratic National Committee.[118] Muskie launched Cormier's campaign with an invitation to Washington, making her the honored guest at a series of luncheons, and told the press that he had taken Cormier to the Senate floor to try out one of the chairs.[119] Smith considered this behavior sneaky and underhanded, at the very least a breach of Senate etiquette. She resented, she wrote a friend, "the manner in which Senator Muskie has gone out of his way here in Washington to try to embarrass me with members of the Senate by introducing her as the next senator from Maine."[120] And it remained Muskie who angered her, not Cormier. Smith believed Muskie meant to make a mockery of the process, setting the two women against each other. He was hoping, she said, "everybody in the country would be watching for us to scratch each other's eyeballs out."[121]

Cormier began her campaign in early March, engaging in the kind of campaign Smith found so effective, visiting factories, lumber mills, schools, county fairs, harvest dinners, ladies' teas, gas stations and post offices, determined to shake one thousand hands a day. A French-Canadian Catholic, Cormier was expected to attract the allegiance of the roughly 30 percent of Mainers who shared her ethnic and religious background. She also needed to appeal to the 117,000 Maine independents to balance the two-to-one advantage the Republicans had in registered voters. And, because the contest was between two women, the "women's vote" was also considered up for grabs.[122] Traveling with her on the county fair circuit, the immensely popular Muskie attracted voters to the Democrat's booth, where most people did not recognize Cormier despite her lengthy service in the state legislature. Encouraged by reporters to characterize his colleague's "whirlwind campaign," Muskie chose instead to praise her handshake. It was, he said, "just right . . . for a woman or a lobster fisherman. She lets a man know she's got a good grip."[123]

While Cormier stumped the state, Smith remained in Washington on the job. She got some very favorable press, however, as several papers featured stories about her strategies for coping with the nine-day civil rights filibuster. Photographs of her snatching catnaps on her office couch between quorum calls and admiring tales of her ability to show up on the floor looking chic and fresh at all hours of the night kept her constantly before the voters in Maine. Smith treated the whole matter cheerfully, saying there was nothing to gain by complaining and then, in a rare disclosure, she revealed that she planned to vote to close off debate and in favor of the civil rights bill. Though lacking a black constituency, Smith's support for civil rights was consistent and principled. She had spoken in favor of the Supreme Court's 1954 *Brown* decision, approved Ike's use of troops to force integration in Little Rock in 1957, and supported the 1957 Civil Rights Act (the first since Reconstruction) while complaining that it did not go far enough: "The guarantee of civil rights should not be limited to voting."[124]

Meanwhile, she and Lewis, as they had in previous campaigns, were preparing meticulously detailed organizational materials to distribute to her volunteers around the state. She sent along position information and advice on how to promote her. She urged her supporters not to confuse the voters with too much detail, but instead concentrate on two points during the campaign: she had stayed on the job and stayed close to the people. She had not missed a vote since June 1, 1955; her uninterrupted roll call tally was approaching nine hundred. She had come home to Maine for weekend speaking engagements and meetings for forty-three consecutive months, and for the past thirteen years had spent at least six weeks visiting every one of the sixteen counties of Maine.[125] As she had in previous campaigns, she followed up with personalized thank-you letters to campaign leaders when the election was over, praising them for their effectiveness in delivering the vote, referring to the winning margin "you gave me," expressing "my deep appreciation for what you did for me." Lewis's elaborate preparations and Smith's heartfelt thank-yous kept the same volunteer team working for her time after time. Essentially, Maine had three parties: the Democrats, the Republicans, and "the Margaret Smith people."[126]

Smith's apparent popularity with the voters was counterbalanced by her somewhat peevish relations with the press. When she came home to campaign, she turned aside NBC camera crews, reporters from *Life* magazine, the *Wall Street Journal*, the *New York Times,* and the *Ladies' Home Journal*, all of whom wanted to follow her state tour. She did not, she said, intend for them to take over her agenda nor interfere with her connection with the people.[127] Maine's political writers, in turn, conferred upon them membership in the "Order of the Wilted Rose," reserved for those who had fallen victim to her "tart tongue . . . tarter pen and extreme personal sensitivity" to criticism from the press.[128] The size of the Order was difficult to gauge, but over the years, Lewis had maintained, apparently with his boss' favor, a rich and intense correspondence with myriad representatives of the press, most of them mind-numbing chronicles of injustice, "deliberate misrepresentations," and "gratuitous distortions." For that matter, much of their correspondence, with fan and critic alike, was a forum for the exposure of personal slights and misunderstood righteousness. Smith wrote carping letters, too, but with a difference. While she tended to complain about misunderstandings and recall recent offenses in brief, pointed and terse prose, he cited chapter and verse of slights, real and imagined, for the past several years, as well as those made by the correspondent's local newspaper, political party, town officials, neighbors, friends or relatives. There is no evidence that she did not agree with his method; the letters went out over her signature.[129] Lewis also kept detailed lists of friends and enemies with descriptions of their virtues and sins. Particularly following the battering they took from "rabid McCarthyites" one just could not be too careful.[130]

Still, while the press sniped about her hostility to reporters and party elites, the voters were captivated by her warmth and keen personal interest in them. She would shake hands with scores of people and manage to remember individuals she had not encountered in years. With but a few seconds' hesitation, she would recall where they first met and inquire about their families and concerns since the last time. This talent seldom failed to impress.[131] Presidential candidate Richard Nixon acknowledged her political power to an audience in Bangor: "You've heard of people riding in on a candidate's coattails. Up here in Maine, we're just hanging on to Margaret's skirt and hoping to do the best we can."[132]

Right in the middle of the campaign season, international developments captured attention. Just before a much anticipated Paris summit of the Big Four was scheduled to begin, Soviet Premier Khrushchev announced that an American spy plane had been shot down over Soviet territory. Eager to save the summit and convinced that the plane and pilot had been destroyed, Eisenhower released a confused series of statements first denying any knowledge of the plane, then claiming the plane had strayed off course while doing meteorological research. After Khrushchev produced pieces of the U-2 plane and the pilot, who confessed to "aerial espionage" over the Soviet Union, the president was forced to admit he had authorized the flights for reasons of national security. Eisenhower was so depressed over the incident that he considered resigning. When the conference began on May 16, Khrushchev denounced the "spy flight" and demanded the United States issue an apology. Eisenhower refused Khrushchev's ultimatum and the summit was ended before it began. This failure was all the more tragic because of Khrushchev's recent affable visit to the United States and the first stirrings of disarmament talks.[133]

The U-2 incident became grist for election-year campaigning, and seemed to seriously erode voter confidence in Republican foreign policy.[134] Debate in the Senate took on a distinctly partisan tone as senators vied to place numerous editorials defending their positions into the *Record*. Muskie arose on the Senate floor to express the sentiments "from the Maine grass-roots . . . people who have no political axes to grind whatsoever," who found, he said, the president's actions "disgraceful and inept." Smith rushed to Eisenhower's defense, charging her colleague with drawing conclusions from a mere three letters while her office had received eighty-eight favorable ones, yet she would not presume to speak for Maine's grassroots. Muskie's retort defended the right of his constituents to express their opinions.[135] For all the fireworks, it was a minor incident in the campaign but a telling one, in that Smith seemed to be spending more energy fighting Muskie than his surrogate candidate. She wrote supporters that she needed to win reelection, most of all, "so that the junior senator will know that the people in Maine still think for themselves and will not take dictation from anyone. I was so disturbed to have him giving what he called documentation of the grassroots' feeling in Maine with respect to slurs on the president that I had to speak out."[136]

Meanwhile, the national media was trumpeting the first time in history that two women were contesting for the United States Senate. Personalities and gender—not issues—took the spotlight. *Time* put Smith and Cormier on the cover, describing the battle as between the "cool, silver-haired, sometimes tart-tongued Republican . . . a meticulous, hard-working woman who asks no privileges because of her sex, rewards her friends and punishes her enemies with the coolness of a big-city boss" and the "stocky, even-tempered spinster, an ex-schoolteacher and the proprietress of a Rumford gift shop . . . [who] proved in the rough-and-tumble school of state politics that she could outshine the men around her." The article supplied a short history lesson on the woman suffrage movement and a general treatise on women in politics, omitting any analysis of the issues or the relative strengths of the candidates. It concluded lamely that "no matter which of the ladies from Maine gets the toga, women permeate U.S. politics. . . . [T]hey will play a larger, more important role in the affairs of state in the 1960s."[137] For a history-making story, it was shaping up to be surprisingly boring.

As journalists tried to provoke some action into the tepid campaign, both women resisted. Smith and Cormier had known and respected one another for years, mostly through BPW activities. They knew that the press was looking for a "cat fight," and they were determined not to give it to them. Smith maintained that "to resort to hair pulling and eye scratching would tear down everything I—we—have built up for women over the years." She remarked that she had apparently done such a good selling job to disprove the notion that the Senate was no place for a woman that she had even convinced the Democrats, who picked their strongest candidate to run against her. Cormier admitted she had admired Smith for some years, but thought she was no longer in touch with Maine; "Mrs. Smith and I have been friends—not close, but friendly in the past and I don't see why we can't be now."[138]

There were, in fact, no burning issues between them. Smith, as usual, said she was running on her record; Cormier countered that if experience was to be the only criterion, then a senator should be elected for life. She also poked fun at Smith's trumpeting of her unbroken roll-call tally, noting that "you send your children to school and expect them to be in their seats, but just being there doesn't make them good students."[139] When they finally scheduled a TV debate on the eve of the election, commentators hoped for action, calling for Cormier to "verbally slug it out with Mrs. Smith."[140] They were disappointed, for the two candidates had more cause for agreement than dispute. Cormier found herself in the awkward position of fighting Smith's *party's* position on issues, not Smith's, attempting to identify her opponent "with Republican arrogance toward the voters."[141] After the TV debate, Cormier made it a point to deny that she had attacked Smith on such issues as federal aid to education and depressed area legislation: "I did no such thing. I have mentioned repeatedly my opposition to the stand of *her party* on those issues." A few sparks flew as the two women contended over labor support. Cormier said the Republican Party didn't care about labor; Smith said that was absurd and quoted at length from union leaders praising her record on labor legislation.[142] Smith seemed to have rhetorical support from labor; her opponent had financial support. Cormier spent nearly $20,000 on her campaign, slightly more than $12,000 of which came from labor; Smith spent $5,619, most of it her own.[143] In the end, Cormier's efforts fell flat. As a textile worker from Lewiston put it, "I'm a Democrat. I think Lucia is a smart gal and all that, but I haven't heard a single reason why we shouldn't send Margaret back to the Senate."[144] Smith won with 62 percent of the vote, carrying Nixon along on her skirttails with 57 percent.[145] Smith won by the highest percentage of all the GOP in a year that saw the Democrats take back the White House. Most important to her was that Muskie's protégée had lost. She crowed to the press that her victory was "obviously the voters' repudiation of attempted one-man political rule of Maine."[146]

11 | Dream Ticket

The Eighty-seventh Congress opened with two women senators, Smith and Maurine Neuberger, the widow of an old friend, Senator Richard L. Neuberger (D-OR). In his five years in the Senate, Neuberger had established a reputation for honesty and ethics, going out of his way to praise those politicians he felt acted with integrity, including Smith. The two senators, despite their party differences, frequently agreed on policy and enjoyed one another's company.[1] Like Smith, Maurine had been her husband's partner in politics. She was also a seasoned politician in her own right, having served two terms in the Oregon state legislature. When Senator Neuberger died suddenly of a cerebral hemorrhage, Smith urged Maurine to swallow her grief and run for his seat.[2]

On opening day, the two "lady senators" (senatress? senatrix? the press asked) joined their colleagues to take their oaths.[3] Traditionally, a senator is escorted to the podium by the other senator from the same state. Accordingly, Neuberger walked down the aisle with Wayne Morse. When it came Smith's turn, though, she turned to Neuberger to take her arm. She explained later that she wanted to mark the "historic occasion" when two women had been elected on their own to the U.S. Senate. Some observers believed the move was to demonstrate that there was no rivalry between the women. Others suggested Smith's behavior reflected her "undisguised dislike for her junior colleague," Senator Muskie.[4]

As Smith and Neuberger assumed the "distaff side" of the Senate, the presence of two women who renounced rivalry and partisanship fueled speculation that they might team up "to fight for their female rights."[5] But theirs was an ambiguous solidarity at best. Even leaving aside the minuscule power they might muster to engage in such a skirmish, the two women could hardly have been more different. Neuberger was too flamboyant, too ostentatiously female for Smith. While her husband was a senator, Mrs. Neuberger had scandalized Washington when she dared to show up in a swimsuit to judge a beauty contest.[6] "She always wore earrings and chewed gum," MCS later recalled with obvious distaste.[7] Moreover, while Neuberger demanded all the perks of office, including the use of the senate pool where the men typically swam "clothed only in the dignity of the office," Smith declined use of the facilities, citing their cost to taxpayers and immodestly claiming to be "the nation's most economical senator."[8] Indeed, Smith had patiently waited twelve years for a convenient restroom. The men's lounge was just off the Senate floor, but Smith had to stand in line for the public ladies room on the floor below or take a long subway ride back to her office. She finally gained enough seniority to warrant a second office nearer the floor, commonly referred to as a "hideaway," with an adjoining bathroom, in 1959.[9] When Neuberger got a connecting hideaway with access to Smith's bathroom, the press announced the move with a telling headline: "Chivalry Lives On; Senate Pampers Women."[10]

Beyond their joint quarters, though, the two women senators found they had little in common because, of course, politics did matter. Smith and Neuberger were on opposite sides of most issues, developed colleagues on opposite sides of the aisle. Neither of them had any intention of risking male alienation for the sake of representing their sex—whatever that was supposed to mean. But both did seek opportunities to encourage and praise one another as examples of the best of women in politics. Smith said her female colleague supplied "strong evidence that the Senate could very well do with more women members." Neuberger returned the compliment, lauding her colleague as a pioneer and leader.[11] Still, they were not buddies, and their colleagues likely heaved a collective sigh that they would not attempt a feminist coup in the Senate.[12]

Smith's tussle with Muskie continued, indeed escalated, during the Kennedy administration. They battled over the appointment of a postmaster in Rumford, which Smith charged Muskie had deliberately held up for reasons "of sheer partisan politics" since the nominee had been chosen by Eisenhower.[13] And she resented being elbowed aside on the Passamaquoddy Power Project. With a Democrat in the White House, he took the inside track on this popular but increasingly hopeless cause.[14] When the Kennedy administration gave Muskie advance notice of federal contracts, Smith cried foul. After several instances in which she received official notice after Muskie's announcements appeared in the Maine newspapers, Smith fired off a series of increasingly vitriolic letters to the Secretaries of the Armed Services, Secretary of Defense Robert McNamara, and the White House, angrily accused them all of favoritism and "playing politics with national defense."[15] This apparently set off a flurry of activity in an administration well aware of Smith's potential for destabilizing Armed Services Committee meetings. Legislative Liaison Larry O'Brien claimed the White House was out of the loop on notifications, that the armed services advised members directly. McNamara's assistant, David McGiffert, described for Smith an elaborate system of synchronized messengers informing all congressional representatives simultaneously.[16] Neither admitted it was official White House policy to reserve these "choice plums" for Democrats, and Muskie acknowledged as much when he shrugged it off as simply "a political fact of life."[17] When the *Wall Street Journal* revealed the mechanism for such early shenanigans—that every morning a messenger from the Pentagon brought advance word of defense contracts to the White House for dispersal to "favorite Democrats"—Smith decided to publicly confront McNamara.[18]

The Secretary of Defense had just returned from a tour of Vietnam with General Maxwell Taylor. He appeared before the Senate ASC to report increasing stability in the South Vietnamese government of Ngo Dinh Diem and the likely completion of America's military program to train the South Vietnamese army within two years.[19] At the conclusion of this optimistic assessment, Smith changed the subject and asked him flatly what time contract announcements went over to the White House each morning. He replied he was not aware of the practice. In a follow-up letter, she accused McNamara of lying and asked, "If you are not completely frank and honest [about] a matter as relatively unimportant as this, then how can I rely and have confidence in your answers on the far more important matters that come before my committee?"[20] Very upset at being caught in a lie, McNamara demanded his staff draft a reply which did not require him to again deny the practice.[21] But the Secretary's equivocal reply, which simply stated that the White House was entitled to information from the Defense Department, only added to her fury. She called his answer "the most gratuitous and presumptuous expression ever made to me in my more than twenty-three years in Congress." She had asked for an explanation of the chronology of transmission and instead got "an affront and insult to my intelligence."[22] Smith's impatience with McNamara's prevarications and condescending attitude would come to have significant consequences for the Senate battles over America's escalating involvement in Vietnam.

As for her competition with Muskie, why did it matter that he got the announcements before she? Such press releases were designed to give the clear impression that the politician who announced the award had something to do with gaining the contract, and what might seem to be a minor matter took on the trappings of a fight for her political life. The effect of Muskie's continual "scoops" was, Smith feared, to convince voters that she was doing little for them while he was accomplishing much.

Her perception that the Maine newspapers also gave him preferential treatment exacerbated her frustration with the situation. May Craig in particular, it seemed to her, had consistently taken Muskie's "side" in the controversy. So when Craig wrote in her column that "hard feelings" between Muskie and Smith had prevented a meeting of the Maine congressional delegation, Smith publicly denounced her for writing "untruthful" stories implying "personal pettiness" within the delegation.[23] Then, as if to prove those allegations, Smith accused the Maine media of a "concentrated campaign to hold me up to scorn and ridicule" by asserting that she "should be redesignated as Maine's inferior senator" instead of senior senator.[24] The vehemence of Smith's remarks may have seemed a bit out of proportion, but Muskie frequently received more abundant and more favorable coverage than she, to the point where at least one letter to the editor complained that the "people of Maine are forced to buy out-of-state newspapers to reveal the good that Senator Smith does."[25] Her clashes with the press and Senator Muskie reveal Smith's acute awareness of the importance of public perceptions to her longevity in office as well as her frustration with the power of the press to affect those perceptions.

The conflict with Craig, though, was more complex and had a long history. After their close personal ties during her House years when Craig had unlimited access to her office and often acted informally as Smith's press secretary, relations between the two deteriorated drastically after Smith went into the Senate in 1948. There were a variety of reasons for the change. First, Smith resented Craig's efforts to discourage her from attempting a senate race, telling her that she had already "reached her peak."[26] Then there was the clash over McCarthy with whom Craig was close friends and continued to defend to the end.[27] The primary reason, though, was Lewis's active opposition to their friendship. Fiercely protective of his boss and determined to be her sole advisor, Lewis gradually shouldered Craig aside, pointing out to Smith the poor coverage Craig provided and implying base motives.[28]

Smith's public image, always important to her, took on a new gravity in the 1960s and may have contributed to the intensity of her criticism of the press. Just as soon as she got back to Washington after her reelection in 1960, Smith had a long lunch with New York Governor Nelson Rockefeller to discuss the future of the Republican Party. The previous campaign had revealed serious schisms in the GOP that Rockefeller had no intention of bridging. Instead, he proposed an alliance between the liberal forces in the party and moderates like Smith to halt the Goldwater advance.[29] Since taking over as chair of the Republican Senatorial Campaign Committee in 1956, Goldwater had been using that position to consolidate a national reputation, denounce "Me, too" Republicans, and call for a conservative renaissance.[30]

Most Republicans and, indeed, most Americans supported an aggressive foreign policy. The battleground was social welfare and civil rights, in Goldwater's words: those "New Deal, Fair Deal schemes."[31] Smith was among the fifteen signers of the 1960 "Declaration of Purpose" put forth by the "mainstream of progressive Republicanism," calling for "positive domestic programs" in housing, education, medical care for the aging, an adequate minimum wage, aid to depressed areas, assistance for small businesses and the family farm. They proffered this plan to Nixon in hopes that it might strengthen his hand against the conservative pressures shaping the party platform. Caught in the middle and desperate to mend the splits in his party, Nixon, generally confident of conservatives' loyalty, tried to enlist Rockefeller as his running mate. Failing that, he met with the New York governor at a secret meeting just before the convention and struck a deal to embrace moderate priorities in the platform, including an express commitment to "aggressive action to remove the remaining vestiges of segregation or discrimination in all areas of national life."[32]

Far from healing the split, Nixon's deal widened it into a chasm. Goldwater condemned his "surrender" to the moderate faction, calling the agreement "the Munich of the Republican Party," and vowing to turn the party around.[33] Though he was nominated as a favorite son in 1960, Goldwater was not yet ready to launch a serious attempt at the presidency. He bowed out at the convention and threw his support behind Nixon. But before he surrendered the floor, he challenged his fellow conservatives to "grow up" and "take this party back."[34] It was the opening salvo for a much more concerted fight in 1964.

Smith did not attend the convention, though she had a cadre of supporters intending to stage a demonstration at the mere mention of her name. At the podium, Goldwater read off the names of senators up for reelection that year, but turned away from the mike without calling hers. A Maine delegate ran to the stage and shouted her name, triggering the demonstration. Goldwater immediately sent Smith an apologetic telegram defending his action as "completely inadvertent and stupid." Smith accepted his apology, but the incident seemed to further confirm her sense of rejection from the party.[35] It didn't help when, a year later, Goldwater traveled to Maine to speak to the Young Republicans in Bangor accompanied not by the senior senator, but her junior colleague and member of the opposition party, Ed Muskie. Watching from the sidelines, Owen Brewster remarked, "I am unable to imagine any possible ways in which this strange association could help Barry as at least Barry and Margaret agree 50 percent of the time while he and Muskie disagree 90 percent of the time. If this is the way Barry runs for the presidency I find myself baffled."[36]

Smith's meeting with Rockefeller, who probed for the secret to her success at the polls and asked her to "be on his team," seemed to energize her efforts to stake a position of leadership for herself. It was time to move if she was ever going to. She was nearly sixty-three years old, and, though she had written little legislation over the years—much of it reserve and military adjustments and a few bills in support of Maine industry and agriculture—she had developed a distinguished reputation for integrity and good sense. She had not ducked an issue nor missed a roll-call vote since all that criticism in 1955; the number now reached nearly one thousand. She had twenty years in Congress, twelve of them in the Senate, and had accumulated substantial seniority on the Senate's most prestigious committees, the Senate Armed Services Committee, Senate Appropriations, and Aeronautical and Space Sciences. No woman had ever seriously run for president (or vice president) before, but then no woman had ever reached her level of power before.[37]

Smith began the new decade by stepping forward and staking out her position. Where heretofore she seldom made speeches and most of her remarks from the floor concerned legislation or partisan debates, she made four major speeches in the Senate in the three years of the Kennedy administration, all of them sharply critical of his foreign and military policies.

Kennedy's campaign had promised aggressive pursuit of the Cold War. Americans, he said, were "uneasy at the present drift in our national course" and "disturbed by the relative decline in our vitality and prestige."[38] His avowal of a new determination to get tough with the Communists included a reorientation of military and diplomatic strategy away from a deterrence based solely on "massive retaliation." He moved to increase conventional military capability, giving special attention to counter-insurgency forces, to allow more flexible responses to Cold War challenges, something, JFK said, between "holocaust and humiliation."[39]

Once in office, he was quickly faced with a series of crises and confrontations with the Soviet Union that tested his mettle. Kennedy had been especially critical of Eisenhower's toleration of a Communist outpost just "eight jet minutes from the coast of Florida." During the campaign, he vowed that he would "strengthen the . . . anti-Castro forces in exile, and in Cuba itself, who offer eventual hope of overthrowing Castro."[40] The new president, then, had few reservations about going ahead with the CIA plan for an invasion of Cuba and coup d'état against Fidel Castro he inherited from Eisenhower, especially since he had been assured that it would be as easy and as successful as the 1954 coup in Guatemala. The strategy used to overthrow Jacobo Arbenz Guzmán—an invasion by a small force of exiles, aided by a handful of World War II P-47 fighters and a disinformation campaign that broadcast reports of a huge rebel army backed by the United States, with a concomitant "cover story" of a wholly indigenous rebellion for American consumption—seemed proof that covert action could roll back Communist advances at minimal risk and cost and provided the model for action in Cuba.[41]

According to CIA operatives, an invading cadre of anti-Castro expatriates, following a broadcast of encouragement to insurgents beamed from Honduras, would be welcomed as liberators by disgruntled Cubans. It did not happen. When the approximately fourteen hundred Cuban exiles landed at the swampy Bay of Pigs in April 1961, they were met not by euphoric Cubans but by Castro's forces who soon routed them. Although the concept of the entire mission was flawed by the unrealistic expectation that Castro would quickly crumble after a significant portion of the Cuban population rushed to join the counterrevolution, Kennedy made it worse by banning the Air Force from providing air cover for the invasion on the assumption that he could maintain "plausible deniability" about official American involvement in the mission. The Bay of Pigs fiasco was a major foreign policy disaster, especially coming at the beginning of his administration. It made the young president look foolish and inept, raising his anxiety about being perceived as "soft" and weak willed. The incident tightened Castro's hold on Cuba, reinforced his dependence on the Soviet Union, and increased anti-American apprehension in Latin America.[42]

Two months later, in Vienna, Kennedy met with Khrushchev for their first summit conference. During the tense and hostile meeting, the Soviet premier announced his decision to resolve the status of divided Berlin on his own terms. In the absence of American cooperation, he threatened to sign a separate treaty with East Germany ending postwar occupation rights. Kennedy was furious. Seeing the situation as a test of his courage and will, he declined to negotiate. Instead, he called for an immediate buildup of U.S. and NATO forces, and asked Congress for an extra $3.5 billion in military and civil defense funds. Khrushchev retaliated by unilaterally ending a three-year moratorium on nuclear tests and boasted of a 100–megaton nuclear warhead. As leaders threatened one another, German soldiers stretched barbwire across the city, soon replaced by concrete, halting the exodus from East to West. The wall secured the immediate interests of the Soviets in Berlin and diffused the crisis, but it was hardly resolved. Berlin remained a divided city for thirty years, a constant reminder of bitter Cold War tensions.[43]

Again, in Laos, having inherited a crumbling situation where the U.S. and USSR had been backing competing factions since the 1950s, Kennedy attempted to steer a course between intervention and retreat. When pro-Communist Pathet Lao rebels, supported by North Vietnamese guerrillas, appeared to be winning, Kennedy opted for a show of force—delivering an ultimatum to the Communists, ordering the Seventh Fleet into the South China Sea and five thousand Marines into Thailand. Unprepared to do much else, Kennedy settled for a weak coalition government that could not hold.[44]

Kennedy's retreat at the Bay of Pigs, the failed clash over Berlin, and his decision not to respond militarily in Laos significantly increased the importance of taking a firm stand somewhere. The president determined Vietnam would be the place to hold the line in Southeast Asia. Unwilling to abandon American commitment to a non-Communist South Vietnam, persuaded that only limited resources were needed to bolster the Diem government, and eager to forestall Republican critics in Congress, Kennedy dispatched Special Forces to Saigon.[45]

Smith was glad he finally seemed to be taking a decisive position. Reacting to what she saw as a whole series of Cold War blunders by the administration, Smith warned of "ominous signs" of renewed vigor from the Soviets. "What has happened," she asked, "that permits Khrushchev to act as he does?" The Soviets had become emboldened, she contended, because Kennedy had lost his nerve. "The primary determinant for overall military advantage today is the capacity for total nuclear war," she stated unequivocally, for which the United States fortunately held the upper hand. She therefore found it perilous and foolish that Kennedy would squander that edge in favor of increases in conventional forces for which the Soviets held a clear superiority. "I know of nothing in political or military history which supports the thesis that it is safer to be weak than strong," she argued. "The greatness of this country was not won by people who were afraid of risks." Kennedy had used strong words in the recent crises in Cuba, Berlin, and Laos, but failed to back them up with strong action. As a result, she asserted, Khrushchev was not afraid of America's nuclear strength because "he is confident we will not use it. . . .

[W]e have practically told him we do not have the will to use that one power with which we can stop him. In short, we have the nuclear capability but not the nuclear credibility."[46]

To many contemporaries, and later historians, Kennedy's tough rhetoric toward the USSR was needlessly provocative and obstructed diplomacy.[47] To Smith, his talk was appropriate but limited; Kennedy had proven himself not bold enough to finish the job. "The quickest way to get a war," she contended, "is to talk tough and then back down."[48] The nuclear arsenal only worked as a deterrent if both sides believed that it might ultimately be deployed, and to suggest that it would not, to Smith, was tantamount to treason.

The Democratic reaction to her speech was immediate. First, Sen. Stuart Symington (D-MO) asserted that the administration's policy of increasing conventional weapons was not equivalent to telling the Russians that the U.S. would not use nuclear weapons. On the contrary, flexibility did not come at the expense of nuclear superiority but in addition to it.[49] McNamara called it "absurd to think that we would have unbalanced the budget simply to strengthen a weapon that we had decided never to use under any circumstances."[50] Attorney General Robert Kennedy added his voice to the chorus, saying he hoped that Khrushchev had "come to the realization that the President will use nuclear weapons."[51] All of these reassurances "delighted" her, Smith said, finding in them "a glimmer of hope for the beginning of nuclear credibility."[52]

Smith heard the president himself, in speaking to the United Nations General Assembly a week later, indicate that same possibility when he, in her words, "forcefully stated that the United States would not hesitate to use its nuclear capability if necessary."[53] Kennedy's major premise to the UN, though, was not a justification of nuclear armament, but a plea for disarmament. "Mankind must put an end to war—or war will put an end to mankind," he said. "We in this hall shall be remembered either as part of the generation that turned this planet into a flaming funeral pyre or the generation that met its vow 'to save succeeding generations from the scourge of war.'"[54] Kennedy pursued diplomacy and disarmament; Smith pushed for strength in the face of an implacable enemy. She did not believe that anyone could negotiate with the Soviets and that disarmament was simply an instrument by which the Communists could win without firing a shot. For her, the appeasement of Munich was a central metaphor for capitulation to totalitarianism, a vivid example of the cost of timidity. She defended "the necessity for real firmness if we ever hope to achieve peace," and the deep conviction that the Soviet appetite for aggression would never be satisfied.[55]

What was all this about? Was it partisan sniping at the Democratic administration? Was it positioning herself for leadership? Was it genuine concern for America's willingness to confront the Communists on every level? It was about all of those things. Smith's differences with Kennedy were ideological and they were personal. She thought him a political lightweight who had treated his tenure in the Senate as a mere stepping stone to the presidency; his reputation had been more for absenteeism than for accomplishment. She still considered his campaigning in Maine for her opponent Paul Fullam in 1954 as a personal affront and a confirmation of his untrustworthiness.[56] And then there was the McCarthy business. Kennedy had seemed to support him, at least she knew his father did, and Kennedy had ducked out of the censure vote.[57] Friends of Joseph McCarthy could never be friends of hers. Mostly, though, she saw him as backing down from the tough rhetoric of his campaign and she called him on it.

Smith's speech inspired editorial attacks and defenses across the country. Some from the left accused her of purely partisan assaults on the Democratic administration, "another turn of the screw in the slowly unfolding Republican attack on the Administration as appeasement-minded."[58] Nixon called from California to express his praise, and Goldwater twice commended her for pointing out the dangers inherent in "ignoring the one type of weapon that Khrushchev respects." It took "the courage and forthrightness of the lady from Maine," he said, "to drag the New Frontier kicking and screaming into an attitude of nuclear reality" and demonstrated her "increasingly important position . . . in the eyes of Americans all over the country."[59] Others saw her "pointless pugnacity" as dangerously naive and irresponsible, "almost beyond the bounds of sanity." "This is not bravery and firmness she calls for; it is defeatism and hysteria," rebuked another. She was foolishly "playing into Khrushchev's hands" by enabling the Soviets to portray Americans "on the one hand as trigger-happy and on the other hand as unwilling to fight."[60]

Seeming to confirm this assessment, the Soviets responded vehemently to her speech, denouncing her as a "bloodthirsty little woman" exercising her "cannibal instinct."[61] Khrushchev used her remarks to justify his resumption of nuclear tests. Rejecting British pleas to reduce tensions with the West, the Soviet premier said he could not "remain calm and indifferent to such provocative statements as those made in the U.S. Senate by this woman, blinded by furious hatred for the commonwealth of socialist countries." She must surely be "Satan in the guise of a woman [who has] decided to beat all the records for bestiality."[62] The Soviet premier's wife also joined in. In response to a letter from

Women Strike for Peace asking that she join their crusade to move the world "back from the brink of war if humanity is to survive," Nina Khrushcheva affirmed her support for peace, but her country could not disarm, she said, in the face of "threats like those voiced by Senator Margaret Smith . . . to destroy our homes, to kill our husbands, to take lives [*sic*] of our children."[63] Smith's reaction to these attacks was satisfaction. She bragged that the "effectiveness of a statement can be measured by the severity of the attacks . . . and the identity of the attacker," and said she was pleased that her message "got through to Khrushchev loud and clear."[64] "Mr. Khrushchev isn't really mad at me," Smith told the press. "I am not that important. He is angry because American official expression has grown more firm since my speech." She advised Mrs. Khrushchev that if she "really wants peace and sane survival then she should have a heart-to-heart talk with her husband."[65]

Despite her ferocious rhetoric and unimpeded by the apparent contradictions, Smith was also publicly maintaining that peace was a woman's business. "Man has not made much of a success at achieving peace," she declared. "He seems to vacillate and alternate between the extremes of war and killing on the one hand, and the extremes of appeasement and softness under the guise of compromise and negotiation on the other hand. And both extremes prevent any real and lasting peace." Abstrusely implying there was some middle ground, she said she was not certain women could find it, but "I don't see how women could do any worse—and, of course, we will never know unless women are given a chance." "I am not a feminist," she hastened to add, "I do not say that women are superior to men," though she did believe women possessed a "moral force" in the service of peace. It was not accidental, she claimed, that the United States, "where women have a far greater government role than in any other nation of the world" was also the "peace leader of the world."[66] Smith's seemingly appositional rhetoric of morality and peace coupled with threats of nuclear annihilation was not so to her. Peace was the goal, and unflinching firmness in the face of "nuclear blackmail" was the means.

Having staked out her position on foreign policy and asserted the superiority of her sex with respect to peace, Smith began dropping hints at her annual Lincoln Day speech to the party faithful in Bangor. In a carefully crafted speech, designed to raise the suggestion and place herself at the center while never explicitly saying so, Smith opened with references to the "Vice-President from Maine" one hundred years earlier, Hannibal Hamlin. He was, she said, a symbol of courage and conscience, not needing to note that those two virtues were also often attributed to her. Then she launched a critique of the "faintheartedness" of potential presidential nominees who "don't think President Kennedy can be beaten." The Republican Party, she said, deserved a candidate that was not afraid to lose, and that person would have first dibs on 1964.[67] Spotting her trial balloon, one listener concluded that "she might be willing to make herself available for at least the vice-presidency and possibly the presidency."[68] Shortly thereafter Maine State GOP Chairman David Nichols dropped in to monitor Draft Goldwater Committee meetings to assess her chances of being the Arizona senator's running mate, and the Maine press began pushing her as "a logical choice."[69] Smith "quietly but firmly" denied she had any such aspirations, "yet almost in the same breath" she claimed to have been receiving a "surprising amount of mail" following her nuclear credibility speech suggesting she become a candidate for president.[70]

Will she or won't she? The answer seemed to be not just yet. But she had begun sounding like a serious candidate with that opening shot against Kennedy in September, and she continued to do so. She made a speech in Chicago in March about "Public Responsibility." It was an exploration of her record and her conscientious attempts to balance local with national interests, public opinion with her own beliefs, cooperation with her party with doing what she thought was right. Tracing the high spots of her career, she defended her Declaration of Conscience and her attacks on the mushiness of Kennedy's foreign policy, accentuated her own independence, and bragged about Khrushchev's denunciations of her. One has to expect criticism, she said, for "rocking the boat." For her finale, she told the audience that what she had not expected was "a barrage of letters" urging her to seek the 1964 presidential nomination, telling her "to put up or shut up by being available myself."[71] She followed this thread no further in this speech nor any other during this period. Throughout 1962 and much of 1963, she kept the speculation alive by frequently expressing her surprise at the "widespread urging from letter writers all over the nation" that she seek the presidency, usually followed by an unassuming remark like "but I'm not taking it seriously."[72]

Following a three-week swing through six countries in Latin America with the Appropriations Subcommittee on Foreign Relations, on which she was the ranking Republican, Smith made another major speech to the Senate. Castro's efforts to export revolution to other countries in Latin America was of major concern to the committee, as well as the efficacy of a half-billion dollars in Alliance for Progress aid programs. The subcommittee found, announced Smith, "deeply ingrained cynicism and growing lack of respect for the United States." This was largely due, she said, to "our dismal failure in the half-hearted, timid, straddling attempted invasion of Cuba," and no amount of federal largess would buy it back. Respect must be earned, Smith argued, by demonstrating that the U.S. has "the will, the courage and the determination" to stop Castro from "ultimately becoming the dictator of all South America." Arms and military assistance, not just money, were needed to resist the Communists and insure the stability of Latin America.[73]

Smith's "steady, systematic attacks" on the Kennedy administration attracted the admiration of Republican leaders who had long bristled at her independent ways. She was rapidly becoming a sought-after speaker for the 1962 election season, with RNC Chairman William Miller acknowledging that "we consider her a very popular commodity."[74] One of her biggest hits was "The Kennedy Twist." Playing with the metaphor of the recent dance craze, Smith compared candidate Kennedy's statements with President Kennedy's actions and accused him of doing some fifteen different versions of the about-face on domestic and foreign matters since taking office. His second thoughts on the B-70 bomber program, for example, were "the Kennedy Twist in Reverse Action," the Viennese summit "the Kennedy Twist in waltz time," and the Bay of Pigs represented "the Kennedy Twist done in agony with a Cuban beat." Kennedy had, she concluded, "talked like Churchill and acted like Chamberlain;" he had delivered "neither greatness nor leadership." The Republican National Committee liked the speech so much they printed it up to distribute as a pamphlet.[75]

Kennedy's failures in Cuba had become "a stick with which [his critics] would forever beat him."[76] After the Republican Campaign Committee announced that Cuba, "symbol of the tragic irresolution of the administration," would be the "dominant issue" in the 1962 midterm congressional elections, several senators, citing Cuban refugee sources, grabbed headlines with accusations that the Soviets were transforming Cuba into a military base.[77] Nixon, campaigning for governor of California, accused Kennedy of caving in to both Castro and Khrushchev and called for a blockade.[78] An incredulous Goldwater puzzled at being called upon "to make a case for victory" against an administration that chose "to live with Communism rather than risk a test of strength."[79] Smith joined the chorus on September 21, the anniversary of her "nuclear credibility" speech, asking, "When will we start winning?" Not as long as the U.S. foolishly adopts "wishful thinking as a substitute for hardheaded realism," she claimed. Having allowed the Soviets to transform "Cuba into a Communist arsenal" and Vietnam into a "more involved war," Smith lamented, "our beloved country is rapidly becoming a secondrater."[80] Keeping up the pressure, Sen. Kenneth Keating (R-NY) accused the administration of willfully withholding damaging information about the increasing Soviet presence in Cuba, and claimed that launching sites under construction would have "the power to hurl rockets into the American heartland."[81] Minority leaders Sen. Everett Dirksen (R-IL) and Rep. Charles Halleck (R-IN) pushed through a joint resolution, S.J. Res.230, modeled on the Formosa Resolution of 1955, declaring U.S. determination to prevent—"with arms if necessary"—the creation in Cuba of an externally supported military capability. It passed overwhelmingly, 86 to 1 in the Senate, 384 to 7 in the House. The only dissenters protested that the resolution was not strong enough.[82]

Congress adjourned October 13. Three days later, President Kennedy was handed aerial photographs taken by a U-2 spy plane providing the first hard evidence of a Soviet buildup. Although there is some indication that Kennedy remained unconvinced that the missiles in Cuba materially altered the balance of power in the western hemisphere, politically he had no choice but to react promptly and firmly. Calling the Soviets' "secret, swift and extraordinary buildup" of nuclear capability in Cuba "a deliberately provocative and unjustified change in the status quo," the president announced a blockade of all shipments to Cuba and warned that U.S. armed forces were prepared "for any eventualities."[83]

Tensions mounted as five Soviet ships approached the quarantine zone. Preparations for an American attack on Cuba were underway when Kennedy received a message from Premier Khrushchev offering to remove the missiles in exchange for a pledge not to invade Cuba. The next day, a more hostile message arrived, with an additional requirement that the United States remove missiles based in Turkey. The president responded to the first, ignored the second. Khrushchev did not press the issue, and the crisis that had taken the two superpowers to the brink of nuclear war was over.[84]

The problem for Smith and the Republicans was that Kennedy's non-invasion agreement had forever botched the opportunity to remove the Reds from Cuba. That December, she spoke at Guantanamo Naval Air Station and engaged in some wishful thinking. She told the troops that she did not think Kennedy's promise was binding, inasmuch as "such a commitment would be very tragic in view of Castro's continuous threats against the United States."[85] America could not claim to be "the leader of the free world," she said, as long as it was willing to tolerate "the presence of this festering infection so very close to home. . . . It must and it will be eradicated else we shall all fall victims to it."[86]

Smith continued to press for assurances that America's nuclear capability remained intact, and that the willingness to use it would not be forfeited. During a "hostile reception" before the Senate ASC, she pressed McNamara about whether the U.S. "means business" about nuclear weapons or was "afraid to use nuclear weapons for fear doing so would immediately and automatically escalate into a holocaust war? That's the impression I get," she said, "and I think it is probably the impression Khrushchev gets." She and Goldwater teamed up to vigorously protest McNamara's defense policies and badger him into admitting that it was "our nuclear superiority and will to use it" that had compelled the Russians to back down over Cuba.[87]

Though Smith and other Republican critics continued to advocate a rigid foreign policy, both Kennedy and Khrushchev seemed chastened by their terrifying brush with atomic apocalypse. Beginning with the installation of a "hotline" between the White House and the Kremlin to facilitate communication in time of crisis, the two leaders pursued a series of measures designed to reduce tensions and halt the arms race. By the end of July 1963, the United States, the Soviet Union, and Great Britain agreed to a nuclear test ban treaty, barring all but underground tests. Reported favorably from the Senate Foreign Relations Committee, both Majority Leader Mike Mansfield (D-MT) and Minority Leader Dirksen declared themselves in favor of ratification and predicted it would pass by more than the two-thirds required. Opposition had developed, though, in the Preparedness Investigating Subcommittee of the ASC, which had been holding hearings of their own. Following testimony from members of the scientific and military community, including physicist Dr. Edward Teller, Gen. Thomas Power, chief of the Strategic Air Command, and other military leaders, all of whom opposed the treaty and characterized it as unduly favorable to the Russians, Chairman John Stennis (D-MS) released a report that a six-to-one majority of the members believed that the treaty would result in "serious and perhaps formidable military and technical disadvantages" for the United States.[88]

On the opening day of debate, Smith took the lead in denouncing the "expediency and haste" in agreeing to a treaty with an antagonist that had "seen fit to abrogate virtually all the agreements and treaties it has ever entered into with other nations whenever it served its purpose to do so."[89] She acknowledged that her constituents, as well as most public opinion, supported the treaty and that its ratification was "a foregone conclusion." But, she said, based upon what she had been privy to, she believed that the seductive optimism embraced by the treaty's supporters, who assumed its implementation would end the arms race and usher in a bright new world of cooperation with the Soviets, was alarmingly wrongheaded. She therefore cast "a very troubled vote against the treaty."[90] Ratification passed 80 to 19. The 19 in opposition were Republicans and Southern Democrats, unabashed cold warriors, many of them on the Armed Service and Foreign Relations Committees that heard the secret testimonies.[91]

Smith's adamant rejection of the popular measure stimulated debate about her motives and about the limits of her celebrated "conscience." Columnist Drew Pearson complained that she had let her ambition for higher office substitute for her good sense. She voted with Goldwater against the treaty, he said, hoping to share the presidential ticket with him.[92] Her vote, though, was consistent with her convictions. Still, she did seem to react a bit too vehemently when yet another columnist, Chalmers Roberts, asserted that she had been "no friend personally or ideologically" of Goldwater's yet opposed the treaty to curry his favor. She denounced Roberts to the Senate for his "serious error. I consider Barry Goldwater to be a good personal friend of mine—and I certainly consider myself a friend of his."[93] Goldwater responded with a note warmly expressing his appreciation for her defense of their friendship, "a cherished possession that I pray nothing I ever will do will deny it to us." Whatever her motives, the letter went into the "Vice President" file in her office.[94] That file also included a copy of a letter Goldwater sent to columnist Ruth Montgomery after she published a column entitled "Barry and Maggie Called GOP Dream Ticket."[95] He wrote: "I just wanted you to know that I share your extremely high regard for Margaret Smith, and I might add that she bears out what I have always said that women do a better job for their constituents and their government at any level than do men in the same legislative bodies."[96] A few weeks later, Goldwater told a press conference in Concord, New Hampshire, that he would have no objection if a woman was nominated as the vice-presidential candidate on the GOP ticket.[97]

Each new headline, each new speech stirred increasing speculation about Smith's vice presidential possibilities. Smith, pundits said, was "a top-flight politician, a capable and learned statesman, and a personality that even the movies can't match. . . . She's got all that a masculine candidate has, plus she's a woman."[98] Statistics about how many voters were women and how likely they would be to cross party lines to support a woman were endlessly debated. Her presence on the ticket would surely upset politics as usual and, one commentator speculated, it could even cause Kennedy to "ditch" LBJ in favor of a woman.[99] Clare Williams, assistant chair of the Republican National Committee, acknowledged that a "groundswell" for Smith for veep was building. Lewis upped the ante a bit, telling the press that her chances were slight and she knew it. Still, he pointed out that she had taken on considerable challenges before and triumphed. Recalling her successful race for the Senate in 1948 against overwhelming odds, he added archly, "the vice presidency differs only by degree."[100]

A month later, on the same day that Rockefeller formally announced his candidacy, Smith—or rather, Lewis—announced that she, goaded by enormous quantities of mail urging her to run for president, was "seriously considering" entering some presidential primaries. Having described herself as "less liberal" than Rockefeller and "less conservative" than Goldwater, Smith would give GOP voters, he said, "a third choice." He made it clear that, should she decide to run, she would enter only "popularity contests" which did not involve the entry of delegate slates since she had no resources to finance campaign organizations and did not intend to accept contributions. She would also, for the same reason, skip those with large filing fees. When asked if Smith was "really" running for vice-president, he retorted, "Nobody runs for vice president—they are chosen." His boss would announce her decision on December 5, when she was slated to speak to the National Women's Press Club in Washington.[101] As Mary McGrory noted, Smith (and Lewis, too) had a "considerable flair for building up suspense about her intentions."[102] As the media pursued her, she steadfastly refused to acknowledge an interest in being anyone's running mate. She was running for president or not at all. Either way, she insisted, she had not decided yet.

The idea that a woman could run for president did appear to be an idea whose time might have come. Although a recent Gallup poll revealed that "one of the greatest prejudices still to be found in politics today . . . is not religion, but sex," results indicated that 58 percent of men and 51 percent of women would support a "well-qualified" woman candidate. Gallup concluded that two factors favored Smith: that she was regularly in the top ten of most admired women in America, and that women were more likely than men to vote Republican.[103] And, it seemed the more the press and Republican leaders took the idea seriously, so did she. Soon after her announcement to announce, two GOP officials from New Hampshire stopped by her office to discuss the primary. Former Governor Wesley Powell and former Senator Maurice J. Murphy, Jr. told Smith that neither Goldwater nor Rockefeller represented the views of the Republicans in New Hampshire, neither of them could defeat President Kennedy, and they were looking for a third choice. She made no commitment to them, nor to the two groups from Illinois—one all male and the other all female—who also sought her entry into their primary. She was still withholding a decision until December.[104]

During what turned out to be his last press conference, President Kennedy was questioned about Smith's chances in the New Hampshire primary. He replied that if he were a Republican candidate he "would not look forward to campaigning against Margaret Chase Smith. . . . I think she is very formidable, if that is the appropriate word to use about a very fine lady. She is very formidable as a political figure."[105] Those two imperatives—to be both a formidable candidate and a lady, both feminine and presidential—turned out to be impossible to sustain, as she was destined to prove.

A week later, President Kennedy was assassinated in Dallas; Washington and the nation were gripped by shock and sadness. A quarter of a million people filed past the candle-lit coffin in the Capitol rotunda; the world watched as it made its final journey to rest beneath the eternal flame in Arlington Cemetery. During the brief ceremonial session preceding Kennedy's funeral, as Senator Mansfield was delivering the eulogy and Republican leaders declaring a thirty-day moratorium on partisan debate, Smith entered the chamber, removed the rose from her lapel and placed it on the desk formerly occupied by the fallen president.[106] Though she had been critical of his policies and contemplated running against him for president, Smith was greatly shaken by the loss. She canceled her announcement and all other public engagements for nearly two months.

12 | Leave It to the Girls

She started out talking about extremism. While her audience at the Women's National Press Club luncheon was there to hear whether she was going to run for president, Smith kept them waiting until the very end. Advance copies of her talk omitted the conclusion. She began by staking her claim to the middle ground of American politics, confirmed by attacks from "extremists on both the left and the right." The "bigotry and hatred" characteristic of the 1950s was beginning to wane, she said, because the "vast majority of Americans" were not extremists and had "no use" for extremists. Instead, like her, they were moderates. And out there, among the multitudes, were countless citizens supplying her office with "a steady flow of mail urging me to run for president of the United States."

Those letter writers provided an inventory of reasons why she should run. Chief among them was her political independence, which she defined as freedom from "unlimited financial resources or a tremendous political machine." Another was her political experience—she had been in national politics six years longer than Nixon, twelve years longer than Goldwater, eighteen years longer than Rockefeller. What she found most persuasive, though, was the suggestion that she could "break the barrier against women being seriously considered for the presidency." Seeming to undercut her own candidacy even before she announced it, Smith added that she "would be pioneering the way for a woman of the future—to make her more acceptable—to make the way easier—for her to be elected president of the United States."

Arrayed against her candidacy was an equally weighty list. Foremost was that of her sex. Being a woman, she admitted, was a political liability, since so many believed "no woman should ever dare to aspire to the White House." More practical matters also mitigated against a race—the absence of those financial resources and political organization that marked her independence. "As gratifying as are the reasons advanced urging me to run, I find the reasons advanced against my running to be far more impelling. Because of these very impelling reasons against my running, I have decided that," she paused dramatically, "I *shall* enter the New Hampshire presidential preferential primary and the Illinois primary."

Her audience, confused by her contradictory logic, hesitated and then burst into applause. As a grinning Smith tried to explain why she thought she had a credible chance, she invoked the lessons of 1948 "when practically no one gave me a chance to win." The New Hampshire primary would be a similar "test of how much support will be given a candidate without campaign funds . . . without a professional party organization of paid campaign workers . . . who refuses to absent herself from official duties . . . [and] who will campaign on a record rather than on promises."[1] Smith pushed aside a reporter's question about whom she would support should her candidacy fail. "I am a candidate for president," she said, "I am not supporting anyone else." No, she repeated, she was not a candidate for the vice-presidency; one does not run for vice-president.[2]

Despite her denials of interest in the second office, Smith recognized that, for the loser in the presidential sweepstakes, the vice-presidency was the best consolation prize. If she managed to demonstrate her popularity with the voters, she might have a chance for the second spot. Years later, MCS vigorously denied that desire, claiming no office short of the presidency could compete with her position as the only woman senator.[3] But abundant evidence suggests otherwise. There was little doubt she would have taken it if offered—and she held out hope right to the end that it might be—but she would not or could not say that. Running for vice-president was like a girl telephoning for a date; it was too risky and there was too much on the line if she was rejected.

The mode of her announcement set the tone for her campaign, as it careened between a serious political agenda and gender theater. At the same time that she was asserting her legitimacy to pursue the nation's highest office, she affirmed her femininity by providing her favorite recipe for blueberry muffins and the muffins themselves to the Press Club luncheon. Placing her among her principal competitors for the office—Barry Goldwater, Nelson Rockefeller and Richard Nixon—the central image from her proclamation was a widely reprinted photograph of a grinning

Smith holding up a hand-lettered sign reading: "Barry stews, Rocky pursues, Dicky brews, but Margaret Chase Smith wows and woos with Blueberry Muffins!"[4]

Similarly, press coverage of the announcement vacillated between patronizingly dismissive coverage of the invariably "charming lady" and hand-wringing about what the entry of a woman candidate would do to the New Hampshire primary. *Time* cautioned those who would dismiss her decision as "frivolously feminine. They don't know Maggie. Feminine she is, but not frivolous."[5] Most writers generally found the "comely widow" with the "silvery locks . . . a refreshing change from the hogjowled Throttlebottoms" who usually ran.[6] There were Throttlebottoms aplenty in 1964. Behind the front-runners came Governors George Romney and William Scranton, Ambassador Henry Cabot Lodge, perennial candidate Harold E. Stassen, and now, Smith. Political pundits pondered the possibilities of sex solidarity, and wondered which candidate she would harm the most. In any event, she was one candidate too many. Single-handedly, she had "destroyed all hope" that the New Hampshire primary would "clarify the GOP presidential picture."[7]

She opened her campaign in New Hampshire at dawn in the diminutive village of Pittsburg, five miles from the Canadian border. It was 28 degrees below zero, a crystalline February morning so cold that frozen moisture in the air sparkled like glitter. Startling a couple of loggers loading pulp wood into a truck, she extended her hand and a warm smile. One of them said, "You've got a lot of zip to be up here this morning."[8] She and Bill Lewis had driven the thirteen-hour trip from Washington with New Hampshirite Bill Deachman, counsel for the Space Committee, who acted as guide. A couple of rookie Washington reporters, Elsie Carper and David Broder, shivered along behind.[9] They dropped into Baldwin's General Store, warming themselves around the wood stove while Smith chatted with the proprietor and a schoolteacher who happened to stop in. She introduced herself and discussed the weather, not mentioning that she was running for the White House. "People know why I am here," she said.[10]

Smith and her tiny entourage moved through New Hampshire over the next six days, stopping at every village and crossroads, shaking hands and chatting in barbershops, newspaper offices, diners, churches, town halls, banks, dry-goods stores, and post offices. Her approach was low-key and quiet, introducing herself and passing the time of day, accepting whatever invitations for meals, meetings, and lodging came her way. People like to see that candidates are human, she said. There was "nothing more effective than a handshake and a little conversation."[11] She asked about their concerns, willingly shared her opinions, and thanked them for their courtesy. She was polite, cooperative with the press, and apparently tireless. Smith traveled over 1000 miles, talking with perhaps 10,000 people on her journey across New Hampshire, yet she modestly seldom mentioned her quest for the presidency and never once asked directly for a vote.[12] Smith had been winning elections this way for a long time.

Deachman introduced her to government officials and local dignitaries. Lewis functioned as her "background man." Sometimes when an interviewer asked a question, he supplied the answer with the preface, "I have heard Senator Smith say. . . ." He also drove the car and kept up a steady supply of pimento-cheese sandwiches.[13] Smith made a few impromptu speeches to Rotarians, Women's Republican Clubs, Young Republicans, and groups of students. These gave her a chance to outline her positions. On foreign policy, she kept to a simple litany: If I were president, she said, I would have given air cover to the Bay of Pigs invasion or never approved the mission. If I were president, I would never have lifted the blockade of Cuba without on-site inspection of the missile sites. If I were president, I would push to win in Vietnam or get out. If I were president, I would discuss peace with Khrushchev only on our terms, and only after he tore down the Berlin Wall. Domestically, she favored LBJ's objectives in the war on poverty, broadening Medicare, labor's right to bargain, orderly gradual integration, and the 1964 civil rights bill.[14]

Despite policy statements and bold assertions, the muffin thing haunted the campaign. Along with flowered hats adorning elephants, the muffin tin was a favorite image of political cartoonists. Like other members of the media finding a limited array of templates upon which to cast a woman candidate, cartoonists settled, basically, on four—woman as temptress, woman as matriarch, woman as presumptuous interloper, and woman as laughably inappropriate for leadership. One defining cartoon showed the leading candidates aboard a streetcar called the New Hampshire Express. Goldwater holds a box in his lap labeled conservatism, Rockefeller a box labeled liberalism. Smith is mostly out of the frame; all that's left to represent her is a muffin tin and a portion of ankle and high-heeled shoe.[15]

Smith's one attempt to make light of the muffin image backfired. In a televised exchange, reporters asked how, as a woman, she would be accepted by world leaders. She responded by reminding them of Joan of Arc, Catherine the Great, and Queen Victoria. Then, to demonstrate her reputation for toughness, she ran through the list of labels awarded her by the Soviet Premier: amazon warmonger hiding behind a rose, cannibalistic little lady, the devil in disguise of a woman. Well then, how would she "make out in a kitchen confrontation with Mr. Khrushchev?" She airily replied, "if it was making blueberry muffins, I probably would win."[16] As one editorial put it, Smith "muffed the opportunity" to state why she felt she was qualified to be president. "It would be nice if . . . we could match our statesmen in nothing more dangerous than blueberry muffin contests. Alas, we can't, and that brings to mind the old saying that a woman's place is in the kitchen. But not with Khrushchev."[17] The gaffe hurt. But her efforts to deny she was running, "as some of my detractors say, on a blueberry muffin platform," had the unfortunate effect of enhancing rather than minimizing the damage.[18] So did Nelson Rockefeller's decision to short-circuit her cooking advantage by sharing his recipe for "really rich" chocolate fudge.[19]

Campaign coverage of Smith came in essentially two varieties. One took her for a serious candidate, at least after carefully noting she was slim and attractive, pointed out her consistent political success, and cautioned against underestimating her. Finding it difficult to place her on the political spectrum, most settled for declaring her, at best, independent, and at worst, inconsistent. While acknowledging her experience, her national reputation for integrity and courage, and her "Amazonian interest in military matters" that might suit a commander-in-chief, nonetheless most agreed her sex was an insurmountable burden for an ambitious politician.[20]

The other variety aimed for comic effect, ruminating upon the general incompetence and foolishness of women. "In this country still, thank heaven," a writer huffed, "some people are born strong and some are born girls. Some people are born intelligent and some are born girls. Some are born of good character and some are born girls." A woman in the White House would put "chintz in the oval office, perfume in the cabinet room, colored ribbons on congressional bills." Besides, everyone knew that "the female of the species undergoes physical changes and emotional distress of varying severity and duration." Simply put, "the fundamental emotionalism of women does not suit them for the White House."[21] Even more threatening than emotional instability was a woman's potential for destabilizing foreign relations with sexual politics. Various scenarios of Maggie and Nikita had her scolding, flirting, or ignoring him to swap recipes with his wife, rhetoric that exposed the anxieties of Americans who liked their presidents masculine and their foreign policy virile.[22]

Smith was in a contest with rules far subtler than she assumed. She defensively insisted that women were people, that she saw no reason why a qualified woman should not be nominated for president, and that she expected people to vote for her record while disregarding her sex.

She could not acknowledge the contradictions between this gender-neutral rhetoric and the very feminine image she encouraged by posing for photographs while cooking or primping in front of a mirror, by remarking that "nothing can clear the mind like vacuuming," by handing out muffin recipes.[23] These images confirmed the public perception that a woman must somehow "stay feminine and at the same time prove herself equal to the job" of president.[24]

The people of New Hampshire responded to her warmth and charm, men and women alike telling her that she was a fine example of American womanhood, that they were proud she was doing this. But they turned to each other after she had moved on to wonder why.[25] When reporters questioned her commitment, she retorted that people who say she's "not serious don't know me because I don't do anything unless I'm serious." She intended to prove, she kept saying, "that you don't need a million dollars to run for president."[26] Her campaign was certainly in stark contrast to those of her opponents, especially the two millionaire front-runners. While they were flying in and out, spending copious funds on pollsters and advance men, TV time and billboards, Smith had no money, no organization, no advance publicist, no committed delegates, no buttons, no posters, no bumper stickers, no campaign headquarters.

Money was beginning to come in to her office, contributions ranging from 50¢ to $1,000, but she couldn't decide, at least at first, what to do with it. Many amounts were modest, and often accompanied by letters telling her this was the first time they had ever contributed to a political campaign and offering to stuff envelopes, make phone calls. From a ten-year-old girl came a dollar bill stuffed in an envelope labeled: "This is my *own* money that I saved for you." A woman sent a silver dollar she won in a supermarket contest. Smith replied to all of them with heartfelt thanks, saying that it was the small contribution that meant the most, "because it usually brings with it confidence and interest in my candidacy and there isn't any substitute." She also told them she had not yet decided whether to keep the money. For the moment at least, she intended to go it alone.[27]

Smith returned for another weekend in February, passing out recipes for muffins and foreign policy, and enjoyed it so much she said she was tempted to just forget her roll call record and come back for a week or two. Goldwater even offered to share his plane with her for a trip back up. But in the end, she determined her duty required her to be on the job in the Senate and turned down his offer. "If I had the time," she told the press, "I could give the other candidates a run for their money."[28]

Despite her limited effort in the state, she expected to do well in

New Hampshire. She believed she had her well-wishers' support, was well known there and, after all, these were her kind of people, fellow New Englanders who would surely respond to a frugal and principled campaign. Her free-spending opponents had developed serious liabilities. Goldwater entered as the favorite; polls showed him with a three-to-one edge over Rockefeller, but he rapidly lost favor from his off-the-cuff remarks and his obvious disdain for politicking. "I'm not one of those baby-kissing, handshaking, blintz-eating candidates," he told reporters.[29] But it was Goldwater's intemperate language and guileless candor in calling for the abandonment of character-sapping welfare programs, withdrawal of recognition of the Soviet Union, and authority to use tactical nuclear weapons by commanders in the field, as well as his penchant for modifying his positions several times a day, that dismayed New Hampshirites and would beleaguer him throughout the campaign.[30] Perhaps Goldwater's biggest mistake was in leaving the state the Saturday before the election after commenting that he had it "in the bag."[31]

Rockefeller, champion of the progressive wing, could not overcome objections to his private life and personal ethics. Recently divorced from his wife of thirty-one years, he had too quickly married a much younger woman who, heavy with child, accompanied him on the campaign trail. He turned out to be the spoiler spending his capital pointing out Goldwater's weaknesses.[32] Nixon, having recently lost the governor's race in California and given his "last press conference," remained in the background, limiting himself to pronouncements about his ideological acceptability to all wings of the party and hoping for a creditable showing from write-ins. Ultimately, it was Ambassador Lodge, prevented by Foreign Service regulations from taking part in politics and the recipient of a vigorous direct mail campaign on his behalf, who provided New Hampshire voters a way out of their dilemma. Unwilling to vote for either Goldwater or Rockefeller and loath to support a woman of any ideological stripe for the nation's highest office, the voters chose Lodge. The final tally: Lodge: 33,007; Goldwater 20,692; Rockefeller: 19,504; Nixon 15,587; Smith: 2,812. Smith also received about 3,300 write-in votes for vice president.[33] Left alone on the high road, she consoled herself by claiming the moderate candidate won, and if Lodge had not been in the race, those votes would have gone to her.[34] Goldwater sent her a friendly note commiserating that neither of them did as well as they had hoped, and adding his congratulations for "proving in a substantial way that women are not things of passing fancy in politics."[35]

Smith told the press she was "frankly disappointed," but planned to go on to the primary in Illinois, where she and Goldwater were the only two candidates on the ballot.[36] Besides limited opposition, Smith also had some organization in Illinois. She had two organizations, but because they had different agendas and she made little commitment to either of them, they often worked at cross purposes.

Two self-selected groups made pilgrimages to see her after reading about her presidential deliberations the previous December. Inspired by a rumor that Jackie Kennedy was being considered for Johnson's running mate, a group of Illinois state legislators, led by Lewis Morgan, Jr., proposed that Smith run for vice-president. Making it clear that they supported Goldwater's bid for the White House, they proposed to balance the ticket with "a true middle-of-the-roader." Smith was the perfect solution—a woman and a moderate. Though Lewis adamantly opposed putting Smith's name forward for vice-president, she told them she had no objection. While certainly not exuberant approval, to Morgan's way of thinking she gave them "the green light" on the Illinois primary. He immediately staged a press conference to announce that, in response to a "sizable groundswell of public opinion favoring Margaret Chase Smith for vice president," he was forming the Illinois Committee on her behalf. "I must emphasize that Senator Smith is not, and I repeat, is *not* a candidate for president but is giving consideration only to the vice-presidency." Recognizing that a potential vice-president must demonstrate popularity and await selection, he predicted Smith would draw 10 percent of the vote, making her a serious contender for the second spot.[37] After Smith announced she was running for president—and president only—in January, Morgan continued to insist she was really running for vice-president; "Of course, she can't say that. But I can."[38]

Meanwhile, a group of young "matrons" (Smith's word) from La Grange had also approached her after her preannouncement wanting to form the Margaret Chase Smith for President Committee. She and Lewis liked this group better, not least because they proposed the top spot. However, Morgan clearly had more clout with the state organization, and Smith preferred to avoid foregrounding a woman-led effort on her behalf. She hoped somehow that the two groups would work together. Promising to spend two weekends in Illinois but little else, she told both groups that she was glad they were doing it, but indicating that they were on their own.[39]

The women's club network worked out of leader Vi Dawson's basement. Seldom numbering more than a dozen or so at a time, the "boiler-room girls" typed press releases, painted posters, and sent out mass mailings, primarily to other women's clubs, asking them to participate in their "ten-for-ten" program: call ten of their friends to advocate for Smith, and ask each of those ten to call ten more. Provided with copies of Smith's positions and pithy quotes, supporters were asked to make more copies, hold a "coffee" to distribute them to friends and neighbors, and send them to at least twenty-five more people, as well as to local media.[40]

The matter of funding turned out to be the trickiest. Under orders from Smith, all money coming in for her campaign was to be returned. After New Hampshire, she decided to send it all back. It was not enough to sustain her, and it was not enough to surrender the high moral ground she gained by turning it down. Every donor got a letter expressing gratitude and describing her effort as a test of whether she could make a viable showing given her self-imposed limitations.[41] While her supporters admired her for refusing to "compromise her principles even to run for president," her refusal to leave her job or take any money made it very difficult to run a campaign. Friends and husbands donated poster materials, printing, and transportation; the women were reduced to holding garage sales to get basic supplies such as paper and stamps. Legislators dug into their own pockets for filing fees and printing costs for petitions, a few bumper stickers, and "cheap brochures."[42] Morgan tried to schedule several events around the state, but Smith canceled, sometimes at the last moment, because a vote was imminent. She even turned down a chance to meet with Illinois delegates in Chicago, arranged by Senator Dirksen, because she might miss a possible roll call.[43] Smith made it to Illinois for two weekends in March. Morgan's team booked every moment of her time from early morning breakfast to late night coffee klatch, making no effort to include Vi Dawson's group in the planning or celebrations, although they attended some of the events on their own. The tension between the two groups accelerated as the primary neared. The women saw the men shouldering them aside, exploiting Smith to help Goldwater. The men thought the women were engaging in an amateurish and naive endeavor. Smith opted not to choose. She invested $85 in her Illinois campaign, the cost of one round-trip ticket from Washington to Chicago; a women's Republican Club paid expenses for her second weekend.[44]

She was surprised when she won over 26 percent of the vote and delighted with headlines that said "Goldwater Win Overshadowed by Senator Margaret Smith Showing." Goldwater ended up with 62 percent of the vote, but his victory was widely touted as a defeat. Most of the press took her tally as protest votes against Goldwater.[45] Oh no, Smith said, the protest vote stayed home, those votes were for her. Her press release congratulated Goldwater for his win, but reflected she felt like a winner, too. She had proven that her kind of campaign could work, and that people would, if given the chance, reject "political bigotry" and vote for a woman. It was more than a personal victory, she said, it was "a victory for every woman in the United States."[46]

Between the Illinois primary in April and the Republican convention in July, there were scattered flurries of activity for Smith for President—a few demonstrations, a few pictures in the papers, a sprinkling of votes.[47] One of the more interesting was in Oregon where the BPW gathered enough signatures to demonstrate Smith's viability, the only criteria for listing on the state's ballot. Women in Eugene, in anticipation of a Smith tour of the state, collected trading stamps to turn into cash for her campaign fund. "This will be," an organizer said, "a woman-to-woman campaign and the money will come from just about the only thing a housewife can call her very own—that little book of stamps." Smith equivocated about a tour, but affirmed she "would have no objection and would be pleased for them to go ahead and do what they wanted to do." She did not go to Oregon. Rockefeller's progressive message found favor there, and Goldwater decided to pull out in order to concentrate his efforts on the eighty-six delegates in the winner-take-all contest in California. Again, Smith finished a disappointing fifth.[48]

After that, aside from a few patronizing articles, Smith's candidacy was hardly noticed; she had become an amusing sideshow to an increasingly bitter contest. Along the way she acquired a campaign song, a kind of self-parody that perfectly captured the incongruity of a woman president. Presented to her by chanteuse Hildegarde, it was called "Leave It to the Girls":

> Leave it to the girls!
> Where there's a frill
> And a powder puff
> There's greater skill.
> Leave it to the chicks!
> They've got a million magic tricks,
> To change the course of history.
> Their know-how is a mystery.
> But leave it to the girls!
> They're heaven sent—
> It could be that our next president
> Will wear perfume and pearls,
> Be diplomatic in pin curls—
> For love and glory, leave it to the girls![49]

For most of the campaign season, Smith hurried back to Washington, or stayed there, because of the constant promise of a breakthrough on the civil rights bill. Since 1957, numerous such measures had fallen to Southern resistance. Smith was among the cosponsors of a bipartisan series of seven bills in 1961, for example, designed to implement reforms contained in the 1960 platforms of both parties, eliminating poll taxes and other property qualifications for voting, assisting school desegregation, and authorizing vigorous enforcement. The only part that made it through simply extended the Civil Rights Commission for two years.[50] Recent pressure generated by an organized civil rights movement, however, forced the issue to center stage. Scenes from Birmingham and Jackson, Greensboro and Greenwood, and two hundred thousand demonstrators on the Washington Mall, aroused Kennedy's call for Americans to address this "moral crisis" and Congress "to make a commitment . . . to the proposition that race has no place in American life or law."[51] His civil rights proposals, though, stalled in Congress until after his assassination.

Vigorously pursued by President Johnson, H.R. 7152 strengthened voting rights and school desegregation, and prohibited discrimination in federal programs, public accommodations, and employment. As the measure inched its way through the House, more than fifty amendments were proposed, some substantive, some niggling, during stupefying weeks of debate. Then segregationist Howard Smith (D-VA), holder of a lengthy record of stopping, delaying, and watering down progressive legislation, came up with a surprise, one that caused considerable hilarity among the men and energized the handful of women in the House. He proposed that "sex" be added to Title VII, the provision barring discrimination in employment on the basis of race, creed, color, or national origin. He had been motivated to include sex, he obliquely implied, by concern over an "imbalance of spinsters." Chanting "vive la difference," Emanuel Cellar (D-NY), who introduced the bill, asserted that women were not a minority in his household, although he usually had the last two words: "yes, dear." Once the laughter died down, Cellar, suspecting baser motives on Smith's part, attacked his amendment as "illogical, ill-timed, ill-placed and improper." Next on their feet were two female House members struggling to keep it alive. Martha Griffiths (D-MI) said that if there was any necessity to point out that women were a second-class sex, the laughter proved it; Katherine St. George (R-NY) argued that women were "entitled to this little crumb of equality. The addition of the little, terrifying word 's-e-x' will not hurt this legislation in any way."[52]

It was widely assumed that Smith added the "terrifying word" for the express purpose of making the provision so controversial that it would likely be defeated. In light of Cellar's opposition to civil rights and the jocularity with which he introduced it, this seems reasonable, but it appears his motivation was a bit more complex. A longtime supporter of the ERA, Smith desired that, should civil rights measures pass, women would be guaranteed the same protections as blacks. Thus it was that a coalition of women legislators, representatives sympathetic to the ERA, and civil rights opponents seeking to the scuttle the bill saved the sex provision in the House.[53] The bill then moved to the Senate where Sen. Richard Russell vowed that Southerners would fight it "to the last ditch—to the death." With twenty-one of the sixty-seven Democrats coming from the South, the administration needed the support of at least twenty-two of the Senate's thirty-three Republicans to invoke cloture against a Southern filibuster, and the cooperation of Minority Leader Everett Dirksen to deliver them. A longtime foe of integration, Dirksen was also a man skilled at gauging "the velocity of the political wind."[54] Capitulating to a combination of social turmoil, sharpening public opinion, presidential pressure, and the determined cajoling of floor manager Hubert Humphrey, the minority leader tackled the tough job of trying to reconcile the conservatives and the liberals in his party behind the bill. He would need to change it enough to make it acceptable to the conservatives, but not so much that it could not be passed before the July nominating convention.[55]

Meeting with the Republican leadership in early April, Dirksen announced his plan to propose forty amendments to Title VII (the section most objectionable to conservatives, including himself, because of its impact on private business), most of them designed to weaken federal enforcement.[56] Among his list of changes, though to him a minor one, was eliminating the inclusion of women. Arriving at the meeting just as Dirksen declared that the sex stipulation must go, Smith stopped and asked him to repeat what he just said. She told him that would be a reckless move especially in light of the coming election and that she would vigorously oppose it on the Senate floor.[57] Dirksen caved in, also abandoning several other amendments progressives in his party thought might cast doubt on support for an assertive civil rights bill.[58]

Despite Humphrey and Dirksen's agreement on a combined bill and with it, the hope of sufficient votes for cloture, the filibuster continued—through April, through May—becoming a source of embarrassment to the presidential campaign. Fortuitously, a cloture motion was delayed until just after the California primary, June 2, so the party's leading conservative did not have to be called to account. Goldwater's poor showing in the primaries in New Hampshire, his slippage in Illinois, and his loss to Rockefeller in Oregon made success in California imperative if he expected to go to the convention with the nomination assured.

California was also where Smith had her largest contingent of committed volunteers, despite her decision following the disappointment in New Hampshire that she could not afford to enter their state's primary. Her enthusiastic partisans did their best to drum up publicity on the cheap, hoping against hope to acquire a few delegates from other states at the convention in San Francisco. In a small rented office "equipped with two desks, a loaned typewriter and a mimeograph machine," and staffed by a handful of clubwomen, the California Committee for Margaret Chase Smith for President opened for business. Working with Vi Dawson in Illinois, using club contacts in forty-three states and the District of Columbia, they launched a nationwide "I Will" campaign. Boosters pledged to write letters, hold coffee klatches, solicit newspaper editors, implement the "ten for ten" program, and join the "March for Margaret," a coordinated effort to canvass all national delegates to the convention.[59] Again the Smith policy of returning all campaign contributions raised serious problems for her supporters who reported with growing frustration that this practice "created resentment and . . . cast suspicion on the committee which was trying to raise funds for the very same purpose." As the convention neared, the women held bake sales and sold roses and campaign buttons to raise money for a demonstration. But what the Smith for President Committee lacked in funds, they made up for in ingenuity. Without the $125 rental for a Cow Palace headquarters, they borrowed a model redwood cabin on a trailer base used by the Red-E-Cut Company to advertize its product at county fairs. Smith was the only presidential candidate to bring along her own log cabin.[60]

Three days before the California primary, Happy Rockefeller gave birth to Nelson Rockefeller, Jr. and effectively ended her husband's chances to win, though the vote was very close. Goldwater won by only about 59,000 votes out of the two million cast, but he won all eighty-six delegates.[61] He hurried back to Washington where Majority Leader Mike Mansfield, after 740 hours of Senate deliberation over 83 days, called the cloture motion on the civil rights debate.[62] It passed 71 to 29, four more votes than required. Six Republicans voted no, including Goldwater. Smith voted yes. Nine days later, the Civil Rights bill reached a vote. In the closing moments before the tally, Goldwater addressed his colleagues. Citing his long history of opposing "discrimination or segregation on the basis of race, color, creed, or any other basis," he complained about the "glaring defects of the measure . . . and the sledge-hammer political tactics which produced it." Announcing his intention to vote against H.R. 7152, he cited the absence of a "constitutional basis for the exercise of Federal regulatory authority" over such matters, contending that its passage would "require the creation of a federal police force of mammoth proportions . . . [resulting in] the destruction of a free society."[63] Goldwater's opposition was consistent with his conservative principles to set limits on federal power and keep government out of people's lives. Still, his remarks echoed those of the most reactionary Southerners.[64] The Civil

Rights Act of 1964 passed the Senate, 73 to 27—all senators present and accounted for, including Clare Engle (D-CA), dying of a brain tumor and unable to speak, who pointed to his eyes to signal an aye vote—one year to the day after Kennedy first sent the measure to Congress.[65]

Mobilized by Goldwater's callus reversal of the historic Republican support for civil rights, the dithering Stop-Goldwater forces finally came together behind Governor Scranton of Pennsylvania. Lodge resigned as ambassador to come home and help; Rockefeller swung his organization and funds to the Pennsylvania governor.[66] On June 12, only thirty-one days before the convention, Scranton announced he was entering the race under the banner of "progressive Republicanism."[67] It was too little, too late. Though faring poorly in the primaries, Goldwater had sewn up delegates using just the strategies Smith had publicly deplored: behind-the-scenes politicking at state conventions and party conclaves. He arrived at the Cow Palace with "770 votes for sure," far more than the 655 he needed to secure the nomination.[68]

For Smith, it was simply too little. As her campaign dribbled to a close, she could count on sixteen delegates—fourteen of them from Maine, pledged to her "as long as she is a factor." Held together only by their commitment to her, all expected to be released after the first ballot to vote as they pleased. The other two delegates were John Rouzie (chair for North Dakota) and Smith's cheerleader, Sen. George Aiken, who told everyone that "if she were a man with her ability she'd get the nomination on the first ballot."[69] Smith was pleased Aiken volunteered to make her nominating speech; she asked only that he not refer to her as a woman.[70]

Smith had no intention of sitting out the convention in her hotel room; she wanted to be there to witness the entire spectacle. "Not go to the Cow Palace!" she said to Jo Ripley, "Not be there to hear Senator Aiken put my name in nomination for president of the United States! If it's against tradition, that's just nonsense. Of course, I am going to be there."[71] Defying custom that dictated no candidate for nomination should make an appearance in the big hall before the balloting, Smith put on her brightest red dress and took her place in a box overlooking one of the nastiest conventions in recent times.

"Barry's Bully Boys" girded for war, establishing elaborate communications systems to monitor delegates and a buddy system of "signed in blood" delegates to shadow those who might be "stampeded, persuaded, given misinformation" by the stop-Goldwater movement.[72] Moderates, searching for a strategy to reveal their opponent as "impetuous, irresponsible and slightly stupid," decided to provoke a confrontation.[73]

Scranton forces drafted an inflammatory letter challenging Goldwater to a debate that indicted his philosophy and disciples. Defining "Goldwaterism" as a "crazy-quilt collection of absurd and dangerous positions that will be soundly repudiated by the American people," the letter charged his stalwarts with having "bought, beaten and compromised" enough delegates to win the nomination while treating them as "little more than a flock of chickens whose necks will be wrung at will." Furious at the attack, Goldwater deflected it from himself by distributing copies to all the delegates with the comment that he was disappointed Scranton would make such an attack on *them*.[74]

Rather than opening up the convention, the letter hardened conservative positions that held throughout a protracted platform battle. Proposed planks asserting sole presidential authority over nuclear weapons, denouncing the extremist ideologies of the John Birch Society and the Ku Klux Klan, and pledging vigorous execution of the Civil Rights Act were emphatically defeated. "This crowd," observed one delegate, "would reject a plank favoring motherhood and God in their present mood."[75] Smith remained above the fray, suggesting only that the party keep the platform brief and to the point. They should, she said, just delineate the basic differences between the two parties, but leave out all the troublesome details.[76] Refusing to join in the rancor over the finished product, she said only that it was "acceptable," though weak on domestic issues and civil rights.[77]

On Wednesday evening, eight candidates were presented to the convention. Dirksen nominated Goldwater, praising the Arizona senator for his "blazing courage" in taking unpopular stands, presumably including that against the Civil Rights Act that Dirksen had pushed through the Senate. Gold glitter showered from the ceiling, a huge banner dropped through a hole in the roof, and "real Indians" shrieked war cries while hundreds of placards bobbed throughout the hall. Somewhat more subdued, the demonstration for Rockefeller's nomination was accompanied by signs urging "Responsible Republicanism." Next named was Sen. Hiram Fong of Hawaii, the first Asian-American to be nominated for president, who eschewed any demonstration on his behalf.[78]

Then it was time for Aiken to nominate Smith. Calling her "one of the most capable persons I have ever known," Aiken said she was "ace high" in integrity, ability, common sense and courage: "courage to stand for the right when it may not be popular to do so—courage to stand for decency in the conduct of public affairs—courage to stand alone if necessary against formidable odds."[79] As he shouted his candidate's name, a small but spirited demonstration erupted on the convention floor. About 150 students in turtlenecks and turned down sailor hats pumped homemade red and white crepe pompons to the "Maine Stein Song" and "Everything's Comin' Up Roses." As the convention cheered and Smith-for-President signs bounced merrily in the aisles, the first woman nominated by a major political party for the presidency of the United States beamed from her box, "her eyes moist and her hand clutching a limp rose."[80] A Goldwater operative remarked, "It was a good-natured interlude, one of the few this acrimonious convention enjoyed."[81] A series of seconding speeches followed. Where Aiken had avoided saying "woman" or "she" until nearly the end of his speech, Frances Bolton highlighted "the tremendous contribution of this exquisitely feminine, politically experienced woman." Since Goldwater forces had earlier rebuffed a suggestion that, as a gesture to women, he give Smith one delegate vote from each state on the first ballot, seconder Betty Horne tried again, suggesting uncommitted delegates not waste votes Goldwater did not need, but to vote for Smith.[82]

It was after one o'clock in the morning before the roll was called. As Goldwater watched from his suite at the Mark Hopkins, the tally came in as expected on the first ballot: Goldwater: 883; Scranton: 214; Rockefeller: 114; Romney: 41; Smith: 27; Judd: 22; Fong: 5; Lodge: 2.[83] In the tumult that followed, Scranton stepped forward to ask for unity, a unanimous ballot. While several state delegations moved to the winner, the Maine delegation was in disarray. They split 8 to 6 in favor of climbing aboard the Goldwater bandwagon, but Smith had left the hall without releasing them. Governor John Reed and National Committeeman David Nichols held fast, contending that while Smith had made no attempt to dictate what they should do after the first ballot, they were certain she would be displeased if her own state abandoned her. Horace Hildreth grumbled that their hesitancy "smacked of poor sportsmanship." In any case, the final gavel fell before they reached a consensus. So Smith held on to her votes, ever after able to boast that she finished second only to Goldwater.[84]

As his team was preparing Goldwater's acceptance speech, the latest poll indicated that 80 percent of the electorate preferred Johnson. He suggested, only half joking, that instead of an acceptance speech, they write a rejection speech and "tell them all to go to hell."[85] In a way, that is precisely what he did. Clearly eschewing customary gestures toward party unity, Goldwater truculently accepted his party's nomination: "Any who join us in all sincerity, we welcome; those who do not care for our cause we do not expect to enter our ranks in any case. . . . And let our Republicanism, so focused and so dedicated, not be made fuzzy by any unthinking and stupid labels. *I would remind you that extrem-*

ism in the defense of liberty is no vice. And let me remind you also that moderation in the pursuit of justice is no virtue."[86]

His listeners, friend and foe alike, were shocked. Cliff White, the leader of the original Draft-Goldwater movement, was "stunned [at this] calculated rebuff to the moderates and liberals within our own party and to the millions we had hoped to draw to our cause." Nixon described himself as "almost physically sick" over the remark. He later said Goldwater not only did not bind the wounds in his party, but "opened up new ones and rubbed salt in them." Rockefeller expressed "amazement and shock," calling the speech "dangerous, irresponsible, and frightening."[87]

The day after his nomination, Goldwater named RNC Chairman William E. Miller, whose views paralleled his own, to be his vice-presidential running mate. Goldwater told a Republican state Chair's meeting later that day that he chose Miller because "he drives Johnson nuts."[88] Goldwater did not at any time, he later contended, consider Smith a possible running mate, and he was equally certain she never anticipated that he would.[89] His note to her after the convention reflected at least partly why: "You will never know what a real thrill it was for me to hear George place your name in nomination at the Convention. . . . I wish to God we had more like you wearing long pants instead of skirts. We'd have a much better setup."[90]

After San Francisco, she appeared with Phyllis Diller on the "Steve Allen Show" and addressed a BPW Convention in Detroit. For her the party was over, but most everyone was gracious enough not to ask why she had done it. Many years later, she resurrected three themes she had emphasized at the time to explain her motives: she ran because others had urged her to do so, because she wanted to break the barrier for women, because she wanted to be president for the same reasons that men did. All of them were true. She found the hand of destiny in all those appeals that she provide a "third choice." Breaking the barrier for other women was also a nicely feminine selfless act. Finally, she wanted to be president because it was the top job in her business, because it was the capstone to a lengthy and distinguished political career, because she loved the limelight, because she thought she could do a good job.[91]

At the time, and later, she complained that no one took her race seriously, but she did not seem to either. She short-circuited her self-assertion at the outset, covering herself with excuses going in. It would be, she had said, "a very uphill battle. [There are] many odds against me and I shall be grateful for every vote I get. I have learned that it is pretty difficult to compete with people with lots of money when you don't have any."[92] Smith was defeated before she began because she designed it that way, literally setting herself up to fail by placing the roadblocks in her path herself. Critics took her to task from not running "like a man," inadvertently summarizing why she could not. "Senator Smith doesn't have to increase her handicap by being female about it. Why doesn't she step in boldly, state her qualifications honestly, think positively instead of femininely, and run like a man? The American voter may accept a woman on the ballot, but he'd rather she didn't act exactly like one."[93]

On the one-year anniversary of her race, she acknowledged she should have done it differently. If she had it to do over again, she would organize in every state and go after the delegates, and she would do it at least two years in advance.[94] She thought that her biggest handicaps were her lack of money, organization, and time. But her biggest handicap was her sex. It is a fashionable cynicism to say that anyone so ambitious and self-confident as to put up with what it takes to be elected president is morally disqualified. This pervasive suspicion of ambition goes double for a woman. The aggressiveness and the conceit, the drive for power that sustains a candidate through the grueling, ego-bruising race had to be denied. While her presence in the race challenged assumptions about women and power, her appeal had to be consistent with the implicit acceptance of traditional female roles. The combination put her in an impossible bind. Her motivation had to come from outside, her goal redefined as an altruistic desire to break the barrier for someone else. Only after her motives were purified could she allow herself to take the risk, enjoy the challenge. Imprisoned by the assumptions of her time, she had to pursue the nation's most powerful position while seeming not to want it.[95]

The way Smith ran for president was, at best, a pragmatic approach to an impossible situation. She did not try harder because she believed that she could not win. She was right. She had no chance. But she also had nothing to lose—she spent no money, invested little time, did not risk her position—and much to gain in terms of status, publicity, a chance to encourage debate about women in politics, great fun, and a place in history.[96] Perhaps that is all she could have hoped for all along. Frances Bolton summed up her own, and many women's, frustration with the outcome: "After a bit, you know, you men are going to have a woman for president. It's just too bad you didn't take this one."[97]

13 | The Grand Old Lady

While she highly valued party loyalty and had swallowed her distaste on other occasions, Smith could hardly bring herself to stump for the Goldwater-Miller ticket. He put her "team spirit to the acid test," she told the Maine GOP, suggesting that it would be "best both for him and for me that neither he nor any of his organization request that I campaign for him." She would campaign for Maine Republicans, but "avoid the mention of the names of Goldwater and Miller." Invited to a Goldwater strategy breakfast in August, she told Bill to say she would not attend, to "give no reason and say nothing else." When they offered to adjust the date, she refused again.[1] Smith finally agreed to one "Brunch with Barry," part of a series of programs designed to mellow Goldwater's image, but that was her limit.[2] On the hustings she defended those things she could, like his aggressive foreign policy, avoided the issue of civil rights as much as possible, and invariably criticized his embrace of extremism.

Goldwater was on the defensive from the start; all opponents had to do was quote him. Notorious for saying the right things in the wrong places, he attacked Medicare in a Florida retirement community, TVA in Tennessee. He scorned the war on poverty in Appalachia and told North Carolina peanut farmers of his desire to end farm supports. The point seemed to be to exhibit political courage, but his unalloyed candor, even his supporters came to believe, amounted to a political death wish.[3] Moreover, many were frightened by his views on international relations. Impatient with containment, he called for rollback and ultimate victory, advocating a policy of immediate, aggressive, and uncompromising challenge to the Soviet Union, backed by nuclear intimidation.[4]

Goldwater's seizure of the far right surrendered moderation to Johnson, who characterized his opponent as "contemptuous toward the will of majorities, callous toward the plight of minorities, arrogant toward allies, belligerent toward adversaries, careless about peace."[5] One potentially serious administration liability—the uncertain course of the Vietnam conflict—was removed early in the campaign. On August 2, it was announced that an American destroyer, *Maddox*, on a routine patrol in the Tonkin Gulf off the coast of North Vietnam had been attacked and fired upon by three North Vietnamese torpedo boats. LBJ issued a stern warning, dispatched another destroyer, *C. Turner Joy*, and put forces on alert. Two nights later, August 4, it was reported that enemy forces in the Gulf had attacked both destroyers. The president, avowing that such "repeated acts of violence . . . must be met . . . with positive reply," ordered retaliatory air strikes against North Vietnam.[6]

Remembering Truman's error in Korea, he asked for swift congressional concurrence. With little debate and hardly an objection, both Houses of Congress overwhelmingly approved (416 to 0, 88 to 2) the Gulf of Tonkin Resolution on August 7, giving the president the authority "to take all necessary measures to repel any armed attack against the forces of the United States and . . . to take all necessary steps [to assure] peace and security in southeast Asia."[7] Retaliation had not come quickly enough for Smith, who criticized the administration's misreading of the first attack as isolated. "How wrong can they get? No wonder the Chinese Communists think the United States is a paper tiger" to be taunted at will, she said.[8] Neither Smith nor the rest of Congress realized that it was the United States that was doing the taunting, and lying about it. The U.S. Navy and South Vietnamese forces had been conducting secret military activities in the Gulf for several months specifically designed to harass and provoke North Vietnamese revanche. The resolution itself had in fact been drafted months earlier, held in abeyance until some "dramatic" occurrence made broad support inevitable.[9]

The Gulf of Tonkin Resolution simultaneously gave the president carte blanche to prosecute the war in Vietnam and effectively removed the issue from the 1964 campaign debate. Johnson's measured response successfully demonstrated firm leadership while avoiding a wider war, at least until the election was over. He won in a landslide. Goldwater turned electoral geography upside down, losing Republican strongholds in the Northeast and Midwest and winning only in his home state and five traditionally Democratic states of the Old South. Maine, once "the citadel of Republicanism," gave Johnson 68.8 percent, among the highest in the country, and elected a Democratic legislature for the first time in fifty-six years.[10]

Just a few months later, the beleaguered Maine GOP, hoping to capitalize on the immense popularity of their now favorite daughter, proposed a resolution, on the occasion of the twenty-fifth anniversary of Smith's first election, saluting her for having "worked tirelessly . . . and fearlessly for good government, a strong national defense and . . . to improve the American way of life . . . [bringing] credit to herself and honor to her State for her forthright stand on the great issues of the day and [respect] throughout the free world for her deep insight into international affairs."[11] After sailing effortlessly through Maine's lower House, the proclamation reached the state senate, which had changed from twenty-nine Republicans and five Democrats to the reverse in the last election, and where the passage of such laudatory congratulations seemed tantamount to a reelection endorsement. Senator Mary Chisholm, alleging that "no man could properly draft" an appropriate resolution, amended it to simply credit the state's "grand old lady" for wearing roses and making roll call votes.[12] After House Republicans staged a walkout, the assembly cobbled a compromise. The tribute to Smith's faithful and distinguished service became a recognition that she'd been in Washington a quarter of a century; her tireless efforts on behalf of good government changed to a mention that she was the first woman elected to the Senate on her own; praise for her forthright stands and insights into international affairs was altered to say that she "brought credit to herself and her State by being elected to the Hall of Fame for Women." All that remained from the original was congratulations on the occasion.[13] The modifications were clearly partisan, aimed at minimizing her impact on the 1966 campaign, but Smith, known to be "as sensitive to criticism as is a blister to friction," took them personally, as her opponents intended. She told friends that she was "deeply hurt."[14]

Maine Democrats, of course, had every reason to avoid exalting Smith, and the Republicans had every reason to fall in behind her, especially after polls indicated that an "incredible 79 percent of the voters were ready and willing to vote for the lady senator." Everyone knew that Smith would "run as long as she can breathe, and nobody can beat her as long as she runs."[15] Still, she was taking nothing for granted. She and Lewis mobilized their formidable volunteer corps, mailing out seventy thousands postcards to primary paper signers, urging phone banks and car pools and myriad other approaches to getting out the vote. Worried about voter apathy, she told the press, she was "running scared" as usual. Democrats suggested she was getting old—she was sixty-eight—and should retire. She never responded to the age issue during the campaign, but she seriously considered quitting. In September, she or Lewis drafted a statement of her intention to retire when her term ended in January 1967; it was never released. When the press later published a rumor that she intended to resign after she won reelection, she denied it as "false and malicious."[16]

Smith made her usual extensive campaign swing in June, the 110th consecutive month she had come home to Maine. Her speeches reflected her consistent compassionate support for social welfare and her passionate advocacy of a forceful foreign policy. She championed the sweeping social legislation of the war on poverty but deplored increasingly contentious civil rights confrontations with the remark, "I support civil rights; I do not support civil rioters."[17] She was similarly critical of students demonstrating against the Vietnam War, and "even more disturbed by the mounting evidence that our enemies—the Communists—are playing an important role in organizing and directing these youngsters."[18]

On the campaign trail and in the U.S. Senate, Smith praised President Johnson's "firmness" in the Dominican Republic, where he had sent the Marines to forestall a leftist coup. Johnson justified the intervention as necessary to prevent Communists from seizing the country, and Smith declared herself "proud of the very prompt manner in which he has acted" to prevent the rise of a "second Castro" in the Western hemisphere.[19] The prism of Munich continued to provide the metaphor through which Smith viewed the whole of international relations, and domestic ones as well. Whether the clashes were in Latin America, Vietnam, or on the streets of America, leadership required firmness and resolve. "Students should be heard," she said, "but not appeased." The "deplorable mess" in Vietnam resulted from American "vacillation," a failure of will, and she welcomed Johnson's recent move to augment sustained bombing of North Vietnam with combat troops in the South. Perhaps, finally, she was seeing a firm commitment to victory.[20]

As expected, Smith won reelection in a walk with 59 percent of the vote. Her Democratic opponent, state Senator Elmer H. Violette earned gold stars for "waging a responsible, but virtually hopeless fight."[21]

At the opening of the Nintieth Congress, Smith was elected chair of the Republican Conference, a position with appointive power and considerable status, and part of the bipartisan leadership for briefings at the White House. She also began her fourth Senate term as the top ranking Republican on the ASC and Defense Appropriations and in a commanding position to resume her disputes with the Secretary of Defense. After McNamara lied to her on federal contracts and she caught him at it, she seldom passed up an opportunity to publicly criticize him. Eventually this poisoned her relationship with the president, with whom she had long shared what Lady Bird called "a bond . . . a great respect and liking untrammeled by the difference in parties."[22] Shortly after he took office, Johnson ducked out of a commitment to present Smith with the prestigious Minute Man Award—for the citizen who contributed most to national security—from the Reserve Officers Association after she publicly denounced McNamara's "confused and contradictory" policies in Vietnam.[23] Smith was affronted by Johnson's "snub" and complained about it in a series of letters stretching over the next six years. She also sent the president detailed complaints about the practice of early notices every time it happened, meticulously delineating McNamara's equivocations and accusing him of "intellectual dishonesty." From the White House, McNamara suggested an artful reply: "To deny the practice would be untrue," he wrote the president, "to admit it unwise."[24] But evasions only inflamed her more. The dispute simmered throughout the course of McNamara's tenure, with Smith assuming that the secretary's prevarication on this matter was indicative of his habitual "sophistry. . . . This does not create confidence," she wrote Johnson, "for if the Secretary of Defense will be less than truthful to me on relatively small matters, how can I believe him on the really big matters?"[25]

The big matters were his consistent efforts to "downgrade our military strength to no more than that of a parity with Russia"—a move she derided as "a theory of peace through weakness"—while waging an increasingly demanding war in Vietnam.[26] She considered his plans to merge Reserves with the National Guard as particularly ill-conceived, and she set out to prove it, putting him on the spot in Preparedness Subcommittee hearings about the merger's impact on women and African Americans. Since there was no provision for women in the National Guard, she asked, what would happen to them? "He looked at me as though it was foolish for me to ask such a question," she reported to the Senate, then he stammered that "some arrangement" would be made. Well then, what about the fate of Negro Reserve Officers, especially in the South? When McNamara blandly asserted that the National Guard was fully integrated, "I could hardly believe my ears," Smith said.[27] Surely the Secretary should know that black officers and enlisted men constituted less than one percent of the National Guard, and none in the South. Smith told the Senate the Secretary's statement "would be ludicrous if it were not so tragically dishonest. . . . This is but another illustration of the great difficulty of the Senate Preparedness Investigating Subcommittee, the Senate Armed Services Committee, and the Senate Appropriations Subcommittee on Defense in getting forthright and accurate information from the Secretary of Defense and honest answers from him."[28] A frustrated McNamara challenged her assertions and wondered in a letter to her "whether it is possible to establish a relationship with the ranking Republican member of the Senate Armed Services Committee which will permit me to fulfill my responsibilities as Secretary of Defense."[29] Apparently it was not. Her response included a long list of his sins and this parting shot: "Mr. Secretary, you have not only been less than forthright and accurate in your statements to me—you have been arrogant and derogatory in your attitude toward me."[30]

In many ways, this debate became a surrogate for all the frustration Smith felt about McNamara and his Vietnam policies. She complained that he told one thing to the press and another to the Armed Services Committee, that he flip-flopped, sometimes during the same hearing, on his assessment of the war's progress. He dodged pointed questions, promised documentary evidence that never materialized, then came by her office hours later to correct a misunderstanding or apologize, off the record.[31] Personal animosities became inevitably entangled with political conflicts that escalated along with the war, and not simply with Smith. McNamara's dissembling was the operative strategy for an administration committed to effecting policy in a "low-keyed manner" to avoid a wider war with either the Communists or the Congress.[32] Consistent with his domestic priorities and his distrust for the military, Johnson approved McNamara's in-between war, one of applying just enough pressure to keep from losing Vietnam but not enough to provoke China. Military leaders, who found sympathetic ears in Congress, complained that McNamara was not pursuing the war vigorously enough, even with the massive escalation undertaken in 1965 to 1967, both in increased bombing and the introduction of nearly a half million troops. Moreover, they deeply resented that "whiz kids" using statistical calculations and systems analysis carried more weight than professional military judgment.[33]

By early 1967, the president was losing control of the war in Vietnam and in America. The bombing program was neither interdicting the flow of supplies nor persuading the North Vietnamese to the bargaining table. More and more troops were being sent and more casualties coming home, with no end in sight. Escalating military involvement combined with upbeat official reports had opened a yawning credibility gap and fueled a vigorous antiwar movement. Public support for the war was dropping sharply to below 50 percent, showing only slightly stronger support for increased military pressure than for withdrawal.[34] When President Johnson brought General Westmoreland home from Vietnam to deliver some good news about the war, the best he could say was that we had reached a threshold of attrition, finally killing more men than the enemy could replace. Despite this apparent "light at the end of the tunnel," he predicted it would take at least another 200,000 men and two years to win the war. But perhaps the worst news of all, at least to Johnson, was that Secretary McNamara had "gone dovish."[35]

A frustrated Congress, having abdicated its power to influence the course of the war with the Gulf of Tonkin Resolution, devolved into increasingly bitter confrontations. LBJ was beset by both sides in the Senate, the doves led by J. William Fulbright (D-AR), chair of Foreign Relations, and hawks on Armed Services, including his mentor, Richard Russell (D-GA), and chair John Stennis (D-MS), who also chaired the Preparedness Investigating Subcommittee. Ironically, that subcommittee, established and chaired by Johnson throughout the 1950s to exercise "continuous watchfulness" over all aspects of defense, soon became the scene of his defense secretary's undoing.

ASC hearings opened in January with McNamara testifying that bombing had not reduced the infiltration of men and material to the South. Gen. Earle G. Wheeler, chairman of the Joint Chiefs, said it had. McNamara asserted that he did not believe the North Vietnamese could be bombed to the negotiating table. Wheeler disagreed.[36] The stalemate held until midsummer. After the president accepted McNamara's recommendation to keep the bombing limited, the Preparedness Investigating Subcommittee decided to launch an exhaustive review of the war. At the hearings, Smith took the lead in choosing up sides, asking Chiefs of Staff and senior commanders identical leading questions like: "Could it not be stated that in all probability that a reduction or restriction of the bombing of the North would result in increased casualties of allied troops in the South because of the increased support the enemy would receive?"and "Would we in all probability have experienced fewer casualties in the South if the air campaign against the North had not been burdened with restrictions and prohibited targets?" Complaining bitterly about being shouldered aside by "meddling civilians" and denied "lucrative" targets, her respondents answered yes. During what McNamara later called "one of the most stressful episodes of my life," Smith asked him the same questions and got antithetical answers. He testified that no amount of bombing "could reduce the flow of men and supplies to the South below what was required to support the current level on enemy operations. Nor could any amount of bombing short of annihilation break the North's will to continue the conflict.... All you had to do was look at the numbers."[37] Smith bitingly faulted him for failure to make maximum use of the resources at his command. All five Chiefs of Staff and five senior commanders rallied with the subcommittee against the Secretary of Defense, finding him guilty of malfeasance and standing in the way of victory.[38] Under increasing public pressure and convinced that the stress of the office had rendered McNamara "an emotional basket case," Johnson eased him out, sending him off to head the World Bank.[39]

Like everyone around her, Smith was talking a lot about the Vietnam War, even writing lengthy articles for home newspapers, but she had nothing new to say.[40] To her, Vietnam was simply another arena in the Cold War—"we are in Vietnam to stop the Communists from conquering the world"—and that assessment never wavered. To her, the central problem was one of leadership. The administration's "half-hearted holding action,"caused by an excessive concern with world opinion, had encouraged the enemy in Vietnam and at home. As a result, the war was "chewing up our boys" without apparent gain, and dissent had "degenerated into violence and anarchy." This was no time for timidity and halfway measures. The solution was more bombing, not less, and full mobilization, including raising taxes and invoking wage and price controls. "Until controls are clamped on, the American people won't seem to realize what the real situation in Vietnam is," she said. And unless America could revive the spirit of the homefront, "the men in the Kremlin" could very well "complete a Communist conquest of the United States without . . . firing a shot."[41]

For the most part, it seems, her constituents agreed, although a few letter writers reflected a growing disenchantment with her bellicosity, calling her "a hawk among hawks," and reminding her that she was a member of the leadership she disparaged. Having hoped for a "careful, critical analysis . . . followed by a declaration as to what you think should be done," one wrote, he was instead "insulted by your simplistic and platitudinous rehash of the Vietnam worries that plague each of us and a feeling that your condemnation of the elected leaders sadly includes you among them."[42] Her demands for the bombing of Hanoi and Haiphong, the mining of the harbors and destruction of the industrial capacity of both cities, prompted a Brunswick editor to comment that calling "for the death of hundreds of thousands of North Vietnamese is not the sort of thing one thinks of when he thinks of the lady from Maine. . . . [S]he is so charming, so dignified and so modest that few of us ever pay much attention to what Mrs. Smith does in Washington."[43]

Westmoreland came home again in November 1967, to deliver another rosy assessment: "We have reached an important point when the end begins to come into view. . . . [T]he enemy's hopes are bankrupt."[44] Such pronouncements took on a bitter irony only two months later, when the Vietcong blasted their way into the U.S. embassy in Saigon, part of a sustained, coordinated attack against all major urban areas in South Vietnam. The Communists suffered enormous casualties during their Tet offensive; Westmoreland pronounced it an American victory. But back home, scenes of the chaos and destruction on the nightly news brought home the reality that this was a war America was not winning. By the end of March, Johnson had ordered a bombing halt and announced he would not run for reelection. This was the tragic heritage, Smith said, "of an administration that on the one hand overextended our military commitments around the world and on the other hand sacrificed on the altar of cost effectiveness the necessary military strength to back up those commitments."[45] "The American people yearn," she said, "for another Dwight D. Eisenhower to lead them back to real peace and security."[46] What they got was Richard Nixon.

Smith did not participate much in the 1968 campaign, although she did make a television spot for Nixon from her hospital bed.[47] For several weeks she had been forced to ride in an electric cart to get around the capitol, and by the end of summer the pain in her left leg had become unbearable. During the Senate recess in August, she had hip replacement surgery in New York that laid her up for four months and caused her to miss her first roll-call vote in thirteen years. The tally, standing at 2,941, had long been an obsession. Over the years, she skipped important travel and hearings, canceled presidential campaign obligations, and regretted to social functions, even at the White House, so she would not miss a vote. Though opponents belittled their importance, to her they were proof that she was doing her job and was willing to stand and be counted on every issue. With such a long unbroken string at stake, she and Lewis planned an elaborate strategy to get her back to Washington in time for a September vote. Despite a mad dash in an ambulance to a waiting plane, though, the weather and uncooperative Senate leadership thwarted them.[48]

Smith's surgery and the months of rehabilitation at Walter Reed made her feel old and tired. She was seventy and decided it was time to quit. She would stick it out for the next four years, she told Bill, but she would not run again.[49] Still she was not finished yet. Back on her feet, she returned to minority leadership in the Ninety-first Congress, this time with a Republican in the White House. His numerous courtesy calls at the hospital notwithstanding, Smith did not trust Richard Nixon. He was a McCarthyite and always would be. And she was not about to give up her hard-earned independence just because he was a member of her party. That quickly became apparent in the battle of the Supreme Court judges.

Early in his term, Nixon nominated Clement Haynesworth, chief judge of the Fourth Circuit Court of Appeals, to fill the seat vacated by the controversial Justice Abe Fortas, part of the Nixon Southern strategy to replace liberal judges with conservative Southern ones. Fortas had been named to the Court by LBJ in 1965, but denied promotion to Chief

Justice to replace the retiring Earl Warren because of charges of cronyism with the president, ultraliberal decisions, and financial improprieties. Fortas was forced to resign in 1969 to avoid impeachment.[50] Haynesworth, however, had a few ethical lapses of his own, including participation in decisions involving companies in which he held financial interest and documented hostility to labor and civil rights. Breaking her long-standing custom of concealing her position until the actual vote, Smith announced her opposition to Haynesworth's nomination. She opposed him for the same reasons she had opposed Fortas, she said, and rebuked the president for expecting a "political double standard."[51] She pulled hesitant Republicans with her. Confirmation was denied 55 to 45, including seventeen Republicans.[52]

Vowing vengeance on party members who "didn't stick with us," Nixon immediately named another judge with Southern ties, G. Harrold Carswell of Florida.[53] Cleared of financial improprieties in advance, Carswell nonetheless suffered from racism and mediocrity. Smith was particularly unhappy about his role in the privatization of a Tallahassee country club in 1956 to avoid integration. Investigators also uncovered a 1948 white supremacy speech and the 1966 sale of a lot with a restrictive covenant. Even those unconcerned with civil rights harbored doubts about his competence. His opinions had been reversed on appeal three times as often as his colleagues on the Fifth Judicial Court, all of whom refused to endorse him. Sen. Roman L. Hruska (R-NE), ranking minority on the Judiciary Committee, only made it worse by remarking that mediocre people were "entitled to a little representation on the Court."[54] Nixon invited Smith to the White House for a cautious chat while his counselor Bryce Harlow told waverers that she was with them on Carswell. Someone told Smith on the eve of the vote, and she quickly spread the word that it was not true. Confirmation failed by three votes.[55] Nixon angrily charged opposing senators with "bigotry and hypocrisy" and hinted at political reprisals against traitors in his own party, then named Harry A. Blackmun of Minnesota, who was quietly and unanimously confirmed in May.[56]

Smith also failed to come through on two weapons systems Nixon freighted with symbolic importance. The first was an anti-ballistic missile (ABM) system proposed and funded during the Johnson years but held up when McNamara simply refused to spend the money. Having been critical of the Democrats for this "security gap," Nixon made it a test of his ability to handle a Senate eager to exert control over military ambitions.[57] The second was debate over the SST, the controversial supersonic transport plane, a project Nixon held was critical to maintaining American "greatness" in its deadly competition with the Soviets.[58]

An avowed opponent of ABM from the beginning, Smith voted to gut it in 1968 and tried to abolish it by amendment in 1969. Failing that, she also opposed an amendment that would forbid deployment but fund research and development. She favored no money for ABM at all, but in helping defeat this last amendment, she paradoxically saved the system. It passed by her vote.[59] Similarly, she fought the SST, despite the arrival of a hand-delivered letter from the president on the day of the vote saying that an earlier decision to close Kittery-Portsmouth naval shipyard in Maine was being rescinded—or perhaps because of it. It was just a chronological coincidence, she said as she released the letter and then voted no.[60]

While the debate over this system, like that over the ABM, was a symbolic tussle over civilian versus military priorities, Smith opposed them both because she believed they would not work, not that they were too expensive and starving domestic programs. Her priorities were never in question. The nation's defense, she warned, had fallen to "a dangerous level . . . making the U.S. a second-rate power." There was "a desperate need for a wider public understanding . . . that our domestic and welfare priorities mean nothing if we grow so militarily inferior that the enemy takes over."[61] Indeed, Smith stood foursquare with the president in his approach to ending the war, a combination of gradual withdrawal and Vietnamization of the war in South Vietnam while escalating the war into neutral Laos and Cambodia. She remarked that she tried "three or four years ago" to get McNamara to do that. "If bombing supply lines is what they are doing in Laos," she said, "it's all right with me."[62]

Nixon's troop withdrawals began slowly with only twenty-five thousand men in 1969. In April 1970, the president promised 150,000 more would be coming home. Then, a week later, he sent thirty thousand American combat troops into Cambodia. Scores of college campuses erupted into waves of demonstrations against the sudden widening of a war that the president had promised to end. At Kent State, Ohio National Guardsmen opened fire on unarmed student protestors, killing four and injuring eleven. In the following week, protests and violence shut down 350 universities. Students from sixteen striking schools rallied at Colby College in Maine, held a two-day sit-in of the ROTC office, and sent a telegram to their senator: "Return home and address yourself to the people whom you represent."[63]

In what she later described as "the most unpleasant experience of my entire public service career," Smith endured ninety minutes of hostile grilling and withering defamation from some two thousand shouting students.[64] She told them she supported the president and tried to explain the purpose of the Cambodian incursion. It was to protect American troops, she said, "to ensure an orderly and safe withdrawal." She had been elected to represent them, one shouted, how was her mail running on the issue? She turned to Lewis; he said it was six to one against. Students were astonished she didn't know. "What about Laos?" another asked. "How could anyone trust a president who lied about the presence of U.S. troops in Laos?" There were no troops in Laos, she said firmly. At that point, an ex-Marine stepped forward to testify that he had been wounded in Laos fourteen months before. "In combat?" she challenged. When he answered yes, she turned away for another question.

Leaning heavily on a cane and in obvious pain, Smith waved off several attempts to cut the meeting short, determined to hold her ground until there were no more questions. Editorials awarded her points for "real courage," but berated her ignorance of what was happening in the war, her ignorance of her constituents' opinions, and her "essential lack of understanding of the reasons for the tumult of the young."[65] She did not understand. Smith felt violated by the young people's intemperate tactics and disrespectful challenges and confused by their rejection of authority. She concluded that the central problem with students was not the war but moral laxity and the seductions of extremism. "Vietnam and Cambodia are not the basis of all this," she said. "If all this were to be finished tomorrow the trouble would continue." The riotous dissenters would find "some other excuse for violence."[66] She decided to issue a call to moderation, to make a formal second Declaration of Conscience.

Smith delivered it on the twentieth anniversary of the first. Likening the atmosphere to that of a generation ago, she warned that extremism was again polarizing the nation. "Militant intellectuals" on the left, refusing to listen while demanding communication, had turned campuses into "rendezvous for obscenity, for trespass, for violence," while counter criticisms from the right went "beyond the bounds of reasonableness and propriety and fanned, instead of drenching, the fires of division." These excessive overreactions on both sides, she said, presented "a clear and present danger to American democracy," a danger that would ultimately come from the right. Americans, faced with a "narrow choice between anarchy and repression," would choose repression. Smith closed with an appeal to "the great center of our people" to muster "their moral and physical courage" and reject both extremes.[67]

Much like her first declaration, this one had something for everyone. She had criticized both sides, and each could find something to applaud. On the floor and later that evening at a "rose-strewn love-in" at the Shoreham Hotel, Smith's colleagues, liberals and conservatives, lavished her with praise for her frank call to reason.[68] Responding to their congratulatory letters, Smith nodded to modesty, saying she hoped the speech "was not too pious," then took credit for "a trend away from violent extremism" as a result and boasted that the "only sustained sour reaction . . . [came] from pro-McCarthy people, who will never forgive me."[69] The press was generally favorable, too, describing her as "among the most thoughtful and respected members of the Senate" and saluting her for "attempting to rally the country to moderation and good sense."[70] A few noted her reputation for courage and contentiousness, and nearly all of them mentioned her advancing age and frailty, reporting she relied on a motorized cart and read her speech from two-inch print.[71]

Smith got the scooter before her first surgery and started using it again in early 1970 when her other hip proved troublesome. Soon after the Colby College confrontation she had her right hip replaced. New surgical techniques, developed since 1968, shortened Smith's recovery from months to weeks. She was so pleased she had the left hip redone in 1971, hardly breaking stride. Unfortunately, though, advances in orthopedic surgery were not matched with similar advances in ophthalmology. Smith's central vision had been gradually fading for some time, and she had hoped to get the trouble resolved while she was laid up with surgery. She was sorely disappointed as well as considerably annoyed when doctors seemed dismissive in confirming an earlier diagnosis of age-related macular degeneration. She was just getting old, that's all.[72] So much focus on her age was getting tiresome. She felt fine. There would be no more talk about quitting, not now, not when a challenger was bragging that he had a million dollars to defeat her.

Robert A. G. Monks, Harvard Law, multimillionaire executive of Sprague Associates of Boston, moved to Cape Elizabeth in 1970, set up a series of well-staffed field offices across Maine, stocked them with Watts lines and computer banks, and launched his campaign against Maine's senior senator. He financed polls to reveal Smith's vulnerabilities, and hedged his bets by funneling $2,500 to the 1970 reelection campaign of four-term Second District Democratic Congressman and fellow Harvard alum William Hathaway who had already revealed his own intention to unseat Smith in 1972.[73] Amid growing speculation that, in light of this dual challenge, she would retire in 1972, Smith decided to end such talk six months earlier than usual, saying in June that she would be running again.[74]

Then, in early December, Smith suddenly disappeared. She missed thirteen roll calls in a row. After a week of fruitless efforts to reach her, reporter Don Larrabee got a call from Walter Reed Hospital. Bill Lewis has had a heart attack, she said, and his condition was critical. She intended to stay until he was out of danger; "Bill needs me and I need him." Larrabee asked if she was speaking for the record; she replied, "I don't care. Nothing matters if Bill doesn't live."[75] On December 19, Larrabee broke the story on the front page of the *Maine Sunday Times*, "Illness of Sen. Smith Aide May Shorten Her Career," and revealed "the special relationship of Senator Smith and General Lewis." For more than twenty years, Larrabee wrote, Lewis had been "a unique buffer for the only lady in a man's world . . . universally recognized as her alter ego without whom no major decision has been made . . . the master strategist behind every campaign . . . and the moving force behind her remarkable career."[76] Larrabee considered theirs to be "one of the greatest love stories on Capitol Hill," but Smith and Lewis felt violated and betrayed by his revelations and ceased all further communications with him.[77]

Smith spent her seventy-fourth birthday and the Christmas holidays at his bedside. Lewis came home before New Year's, expecting to fully recover. Concluding that Monks had left her no way to withdraw gracefully and Lewis insisting he was up to the task, Smith ended weeks of speculation with a brief announcement in February reiterating her candidacy.[78]

It was her first primary contest since 1954, and she was pushed hard. Monks hired public relations and advertising experts, used his computer system to track every registered Republican in the state and register thousands more, and spent nearly unlimited personal funds on radio, television, and billboards. He said she was old and out of touch. She took the state for granted while clinging to her precious roll call record and spending all her time in Washington. Despite her seniority on Armed Services and Appropriations, he said, she failed to bring home the bacon to shore up Maine's faltering economy.[79]

Smith depended on her volunteers and made an issue of his wealth, inexperience, and outsider status: Monks, Millions, Massachusetts. He was, in short, a carpetbagger. She did not believe a Senate seat should be for sale to the highest bidder, she repeated to audiences across the state, and expressed envy for those who had nothing better to do than campaign. She had been elected to do a job in Washington and that was her first priority. She would not neglect the people's work. She said her record spoke for itself, and extolled her closeness to the president and her pride in his efforts to end the war. Looking strong and elegant, she stood in endless receiving lines, chiding her opponent for calling her "frail and weak."[80]

Monks admitted spending $146,000, but campaign watchers guessed it closer to $300,000.[81] Mainers were still suspicious of people "from away" who charged in with too much money, too many bells and whistles. Smith was one of their own, and they closed ranks behind her. She beat him two to one.[82] But Monks had done some real damage, by splitting the party, by pointing out her weaknesses, and most of all by giving her such a hard race that her supporters thought the worst was over.

In the general election, Hathaway campaigned the way she always had, but did not this time. With all that surgery, she had not come home as often as she used to, and it had been a very long time since she had tramped the back roads and fishing villages seeking hands to shake. In his eight years in Congress, Hathaway came home frequently and concentrated on constituent service. While a lengthy session kept her in Washington during the campaign, her opponent, unconcerned about absenteeism, traveled the state, visiting every one of the 495 cities and towns, dropping into factories and sitting around country stores, and that still counted in Maine.[83]

Despite serious ideological differences between the candidates, the most obvious being their positions on the Vietnam war, issues were largely ignored. Like Monks before him, Hathaway emphasized her age and charged that she was ineffective in Washington and inaccessible at home. She, too, avoided discussing specific concerns, citing her "record" as speaking for itself and ducking debates. "I never reply to my opponents," she said, "and I never listen to them."[84] This tried and true method no longer worked the way it once had. One columnist derisively called it the Popeye Factor: "I yam what I yam."[85] "Perhaps 'people know' her record," said another, "but perhaps a lot of younger voters in Maine don't remember, because it has been so long since Sen. Smith has really done a heck of a lot."[86] Pressed by the Gannett newspapers to list her "accomplishments . . . made to benefit Maine directly," she modestly demurred, saying she found "personally claiming credit" for such deeds "repugnant."[87] When Lewis answered for her, constituents took her to task. Did she find answering the question "too strenuous? . . . or does Mr. Lewis really represent us? Will the real senator please stand up?"[88]

Though he had been there all along, her reliance on Lewis had become a central issue in her campaign. Many commented on his appearance, his health, his presence at her side, his answering the awkward questions for her. He was also dominant in a serious critique of her career published just before the election by the Ralph Nader Congress Project. Hastily constructed and riddled with voting and chronological errors, the report found her aloof and inaccessible, Lewis a "surrogate senator." Apparently piqued at her refusal to be interviewed by anyone other than Nader himself, the author used abundant quotes from negative press citing her faults and, though praising her Declaration of Conscience, wondered if a member of Congress should have more than one "finest hour" in thirty-two years.[89] Stung by the report and defensive about Lewis, Smith responded sharply during a televised debate with Hathaway to a question about her aide's influence: "He is a very helpful, able man. He has a college degree. I haven't. . . . Why shouldn't I rely on him?" In fact, she continued, she wished he were appearing on the program in her stead.[90]

Two efforts to bolster her stature backfired. She proposed a constitutional amendment to expel any member of Congress who missed forty percent of roll calls in a single session, saying the Senate was filled with moonlighters, junketeers, and presidential hopefuls more interested in their White House ambitions than in doing the people's work. The proposal attracted a good deal of national attention, much of it highlighting Muskie's lucrative lecture fees in pursuit of the presidential nomination.[91] At home it looked like a spiteful attack on a fellow Mainer whose presence in the Senate she had long resented and made no effort to conceal.[92] Smith's memoirs, *Declaration of Conscience*, edited and largely authored by Lewis, came out just as the campaign began. An angry and defensive book, it presented "a curious history of threats, intrigues, defections and disloyalty . . . a world sharply divided into friends, traitors and enemies, with the lady senator always vindicated (occasionally vindictive) and triumphant."[93] Instead of enhancing her image, the book revived a host of petty old disputes that found their way once again to the front pages. A clever retort by an old antagonist—that the days Smith could "depend on the three R's of roses, recipes and roll calls may be at an end"—got far more attention than it might have otherwise.[94]

Still more painful to Smith was the criticism that Maine women leveled at her. Where once they had been the mainstay of her campaign organization and the core of her most loyal supporters, a new generation worked actively to discredit her in 1972. Maine mothers for peace criticized Smith's stance on the war. Those who sought to tap what they presumed to be her innate female pacifism came away sorely disappointed. Far from moving to "stop the bloodbath in Vietnam" as they requested, Smith proved herself "unexcelled in condoning the slaughter. . . . Maine voters who believe in the value of life will not find Margaret Chase Smith worthy of their vote."[95]

After Smith lavishly praised Vice-President Spiro Agnew, whose inflammatory vitriol she described as "telling it like it is," Ramona Barth, president of the Maine chapter of the National Organization for Women, called a press conference to denounce Smith as a "warmonger," an "elitist," and a "token woman" who cared nothing for women's concerns. Maine's senior senator, Barth said, "represents everything women in the liberation movement want to eliminate."[96]

Smith was angered and embarrassed by activist women's unladylike tactics and vulgar confrontations, and profoundly disheartened by what she took to be a show of disloyalty. Arguments for women's rights, she believed, could only be strengthened by her example. She had redefined the possibilities; she had blazed the trail for them; she had proven that women could handle the rigors of public office. She had achieved what her generation of women had sought. Now was the time, she said, for "building on women of achievement," not tearing them down.[97] The Equal Rights Amendment, which she had been advocating for some thirty years, was close at hand, having passed through Congress in March. This should be cause for celebration and for appreciation of her efforts. But to radical feminists like Barth, who challenged the broad panoply of cultural definitions of male and female, the ERA, once considered the pinnacle of social change, was inadequate and beside the point. "The gut issues of women's liberation," Barth argued, "cannot be legislated away. . . . We want revolution, not evolution." Though Barth hardly represented mainstream feminists, her voice was the loudest, reaching via newspaper and television into every corner of Maine.[98]

Likely Smith's rejection by radical feminists had little impact on the outcome of her reelection campaign, but she remained wary of feminists ever after. Nearly twenty years later, she complained that they had not recognized her accomplishments nor realized the limits of her power. "Here I was, a woman with this background and this record—I cosponsored ERA throughout my Senate tenure, stopped Everett Dirksen from knocking the word "sex" out of the Civil Rights bill, got women full Regular status in the Armed Services, and championed many women causes in Congress—and they said I didn't do anything. NOW was calling for a male candidate to replace me while at the same time calling for more women in political office. They didn't like me because I would not join them, fight with them. But I could not have gotten elected if I did those things. Women just don't understand the political reality."[99]

As the campaign wound down and Smith finally broke free to come home in October, she tried hard to make up for lost time, hoping against hope that Nixon would lead a Republican sweep that would make her chair of Armed Services and cap her career. Nixon won by a landslide in 1972, but Smith lost in Maine, even in her hometown.[100]

The president did not campaign for her, and it was widely acknowledged that his operatives hoped to see him get a higher count than she in Maine.[101] She always thought that Nixon sabotaged her and maybe he did, but he did not need to.[102] She lost because she was getting old and tired; she lost because she was out of step with her constituents. As she became more conservative, they had become less so, and her once-lauded qualities—toughness, probity, tenacity—now seemed unyielding and reactionary.[103] She lost because she did not change, because she could not. If she had, she said, "everyone would think I was running scared. And I wasn't scared."[104] But methods that had served her well for so many years no longer did. She extolled her record and the power her seniority afforded her in an antiseniority year when younger politicians were kicking out older ones across the country, and eighteen-year-olds, voting for the first time, knew nothing of her record, only that she had made herself the enemy of youth. She never campaigned while the Senate was in session, believing her duty to the people of Maine was in Washington, but at seventy-four, it was more important than ever that she mount a vigorous campaign against the forty-seven-year-old Hathaway, and her absence gave credence to the charge that she took the state for granted. She accepted no contributions and spent little money, while Hathaway invested nearly $200,000, much of it in five-minute television spots on the eve of the vote. Bill Lewis, gaunt and haggard, surrendered the campaign to lieutenants, and no one cared as much as he did. Moreover, her aging cadre of volunteers, tired and self-satisfied after the primary, still assumed that, like in the old days, a primary win was a win and the election a foregone conclusion.[105]

Lewis faced the press alone the next morning and read her concession speech: "I congratulate my opponent and wish him well. I am deeply grateful to the people of Maine for their generosity in letting me serve and represent them for more than thirty-two years. I am even more grateful to my loyal supporters who worked their hearts out for me. I regret having let them down."[106] Then she and Lewis slipped quietly out of town and back to Washington, shunning friends and refusing to talk with reporters.[107]

14 | Senator Emeritus

They avoided the press for nearly three months, fueling rumors that she was bitter and brooding, having remained "a virtual recluse since her crushing defeat."[1] When she finally talked, she explained that she was not bitter, but had refused to grant interviews because "I had nothing to say except that I was disappointed to have lost and surely that wasn't news." She and Lewis, she said, had been very busy packing up thirty-two years worth of papers and memories in order to vacate her offices by January. The papers would be going to Skowhegan but she would not. Skowhegan's rejection hurt too much, she said. "And it's no use pretending it doesn't. I think it would be hard for me to live in Skowhegan right now, and it would be hard for many people in Skowhegan."[2] Yet she was determined not to be a "hanger-on" in Washington like so many of her former colleagues, haunting the halls of the Senate wistfully hoping for meaningful employment or selling their expertise as lobbyists.[3] She would have to find something else to do.

Using Silver Spring as their home base, Smith and Lewis traveled with the Woodrow Wilson National Fellowship Program for three years. For the most part she found respectful students who listened attentively to her laments about the erosion of public unity and civic confidence, the abandonment of "respectful and courteous persuasion" as approaches to securing women's rights, and the despicable dishonesty of Richard Nixon, a "crass pragmatist" overtaken by greed.[4] Lewis remained at her side, sharing discussions, writing her speeches, and sometimes reading them when the light was poor.

After a few years on the road, Smith was reconsidering her decision to avoid Skowhegan, while Lewis focused on the disposition of her papers. He gathered a host of well-connected friends, headed by former NASA administrator James E. Webb, into a foundation to preserve her records and legacy.[5] To be self-sustaining, they needed an academic affiliation amenable to Lewis's insistence that the resulting institution memorialize only Smith. He found that partner in Northwood Institute, a cluster of business management schools based in Michigan. Northwood accorded Smith an honorary degree, their Distinguished Woman Award, and the admiration and esteem they both thought she had earned. Working with the foundation, Northwood agreed to staff and manage her Library in exchange for her papers and her home; she retained a life tenancy.[6]

Smith came home in 1977 to a Skowhegan eager to "forget all the bad stuff." The governor declared Margaret Chase Smith Day and the town held a grand celebration, planted her a rose garden in Coburn Park, and named in her honor twin bridges over the Kennebec River. "We want her to know we love her and that we're proud of what she's done for Skowhegan," the organizer said.[7] Eventually they named an elementary school for her, a federal building in Bangor, and a ferry boat on Penobscot Bay. Curiously, the *Margaret Chase Smith* replaced the *Governor Edmund S. Muskie* on the crossing.[8]

Ground was broken for her Library in 1979 with Lewis directing every aspect of the project. It was his last great act of love for her. In the absence of a private life she had never cultivated, he knew she would need a public life to sustain her.[9] In the spring of 1982, with the Library nearly completed and set to open in August, Bill and Margaret took a short trip down to their side-by-side vacation homes on a peninsula near Cundy's Harbor. He dropped her off at her place and went to put down some new carpeting in his living room. When he did not come by for supper, she sent a friend to prod him. Bill was dead on the couch where he had stopped to rest. He had a smile on his face, they told her, and she tried to find that consoling. But the loss nearly overwhelmed her. Years later, still profoundly sad, she also remained angry that he had abandoned her, that he had died first when she had a fifteen-year head start. Had it not been for the Library, a reason to continue, she probably would have soon followed.[10]

The Northwood Institute Margaret Chase Smith Library opened on Women's Equality Day, 26 August 1982. The million-dollar facility housed a research center for scholars and a museum for the curious. At the far end of a long hallway lined with political cartoons, separated from the gallery by a red velvet rope, was the most extraordinary exhibit, Sena-

tor Smith herself, wearing her trademark rose and eager to visit. That is
where I found her in 1986.

In this sunny atrium, she greeted scores of callers who found their
way to this place, despite its location so far from major cities—people
who knew her in Washington, people who wanted to thank her for a
past favor, people who remembered her campaign for president. Stiff
military men with decorated chests and hats in hand came to thank her
for caring about them. Families asked to have their daughters' pictures
taken with "the first woman who. . . . " Streams of schoolchildren gaped
at photographs of her with the astronauts, the orange jumpsuit she wore
when she broke the sound barrier, the pennants reading Margaret Smith
for President. Then they gathered on the floor at her feet as she sat primly
in a low, straight-backed chair, responding to her obvious enjoyment of
them, her eagerness to joke and parry. What is it like to visit the White
House? Did she have children? "How does it feel to be named after a
school?" one asked. "It is a honor," she replied.

Smith continued to lead an active and rewarding life, reveling in
the renown and the sheer busy-ness of it all. Dedications, parades, rib-
bon-cuttings, commencements, town meetings, television appearances.
She served on numerous boards and foundations, continued to lecture
across the country, remaining vital and sharp well into her ninety-sixth
year, and taking ironic pleasure in referring to those who found her old
and feeble at seventy-four. But it was never enough. Through it all, she
never stopped being the politician. She never stopped campaigning, never
stopped worrying what people would think. She remained driven to the
end to keep up her mail, count audiences, assess honors, go where she
could hear applause, clip her notices, open her home to people who
would tell her how wonderful she was. She needed constant reassurances of her significance. It was vitally important to her to have the vali-
dation, the 2,941 roll calls, the 95 honorary degrees, that said "I've done
something, I mean something, I am somebody."

As the years went by, longevity began to erase "the dark edges of
her reputation."[11] Smith was gradually transformed from a querulous
old woman and washed-up politician into a living legend and a symbol
of all that was good about a Maine that was rapidly fading away. This
was never clearer than at the love fest the Republicans threw for her
ninetieth birthday. Everyone who was anyone in Maine politics rose to
lavishly praise her, including Sens. Ed Muskie and George Mitchell, possibly the only two Democrats in the room. Muskie reported Smith had
succeeded in public service "not because she was a woman but for her
integrity and strength [which made her] a match for any man." Rep. Olympia Snowe thanked "God for her pioneering spirit. . . . She showed women

could and should make a contribution to public office." Snowe wryly added that only 120 women were among the 12,000 persons who had served in Congress. "At this rate, we will receive majority by the year 3083." Sen. William Cohen, who had defeated her nemesis William Hathaway after a single term, said, "She is an oak tree and the rest of us are all just acorns at her feet." Governor John McKernan, Jr. pronounced Smith "the essence of the state," the embodiment of honesty, integrity, hard work, endurance, courage. "She is Maine."[12]

The press was no less effusive than the politicians. Endlessly recalling her Declaration of Conscience, local and national reporters praised her courage and integrity, seemingly more precious with each passing year. Her arrival at a local town meeting occasioned this description: She "walked with the quiet majesty of a Shaker eldress. We don't kneel for Maine royalty but every heart in the room swelled with pride. [It was] a homecoming and the heroine was quite old and quite beautiful . . . [b]attle-tested, valiant, pure. . . . She is every inch a Mainer."[13]

Toward the end, after we had spent dozens of hours together in life review, Smith was finally glad that I had been uncovering the contours of her life. As her memory failed, she would ask me to recall her past, for one more chance to savor it. We talked about death one day and about her legacy. She wanted no monuments, no funeral; she had been to too many. She would be cremated and her ashes placed in a bronze box in her living room overlooking the Kennebec River. Her obituary should simply say that she "gave her life to public service," she said. "My whole history in public service was determination to show that I was a woman and could do what a man could do without apologizing."[14]

She died 29 May 1995. Memorial Day. She died at home in the same bed her mother had, after eight days in a coma following a massive stroke. A simple memorial ceremony two weeks later reaffirmed the themes of her life and her place in history, as trailblazer, role model, icon of Maine. Sen. Olympia Snowe, who, like Smith, had made the transition to the upper House and who knew as well as anyone the difficulties Smith faced in her political career, said,

> I know that I and other women in public service have a very high standard to meet in her wake and some rather large shoes to fill as we walk in [her] footsteps. . . . She was an inspiration to millions of young girls and women all across the country who never before thought they could aspire to any kind of public office. She showed us through her talents, abilities, and energies that opportunities for women did exist and that the door to elected office could be unlocked and opened to all women. But

most importantly, what Margaret Chase Smith's life proved is
it is not necessarily gender which makes a difference in public
service, it is dedication, it is energy, perseverance, competence,
and the will to get the job done.[15]

Thinking of Senator Smith that day reminded Secretary of Defense and
former Sen. William Cohen of

an ancient Chinese proverb that says, "When drinking the water, don't forget who dug the well." We are carrying on a great
tradition which she helped us to create. We are all drinking from
the well of independence she helped dig. . . . Senator Smith's
legacy transcends her specific accomplishments as a legislator.
The whole is much greater than the sum of the parts. Throughout her remarkable career, she has endowed this state with a
legacy of grace, beauty, integrity and a fierce devotion to the values and principles that are Maine.[16]

In summary, said James B. Longley, Jr.: "She stands as a monument to
the power of simple Maine honesty and integrity and common sense.
She will be sorely missed, fondly remembered, and never forgotten."[17]

Notes

ABBREVIATIONS USED IN THE NOTES
General

AEC	Atomic Energy Commission
CHS	Clyde Harold Smith
CQ	Congressional Quarterly
CR	Congressional Record
MCSI	Margaret Chase Smith Interview
NAC	National Affairs Committee
S. Res.	Senate Resolution
H.R.	House Resolution
WCL	William Chesley Lewis
WHCF	White House Central Files

Repositories

CHP	Carl Hayden Papers
DDEL	Dwight David Eisenhower Presidential Library
EMDP	Everett McKinley Dirksen Congressional Research Center
ESMA	Edmund S. Muskie Archives
FDRL	Franklin Delano Roosevelt Presidential Library
HSTL	Harry S. Truman Presidential Library
JFKL	John Fitzgerald Kennedy Presidential Library
LBJL	Lyndon Baines Johnson Presidential Library
MCSL	Margaret Chase Smith Library
MNP	Maurine Neuberger Papers, University of Oregon
MTNP	Mary T. Norton Papers, Rutgers University
SCHL	The Arthur and Elizabeth Schlesinger Library on the History of Women in America
WMP	Wayne Morse Papers, University of Oregon

Newspapers, Maine

BC	Bangor Commercial
BDN	Bangor Daily News
BTR	Brunswick Times-Record
CH	Camden Herald
DKJ	Daily Kennebec Journal
FFR	Fort Fairfield Review
IR	Independent-Reporter
LCN	Lincoln County News
LDS	Lewiston Daily Sun
LE	Lisbon Enterprise
LEJ	Lewiston Evening Journal
PST	Portland Sunday Telegram
MST	Maine Sunday Telegram [after 1968]
MT	Maine Times
PA	Pittsfield Advertiser
PEE	Portland Evening Express
PPH	Portland Press Herald
RCG	Rockland Courier-Gazette
RFT	Rumford Falls Times
SR	Somerset Reporter
WMS	Waterville Morning Sentinel

Newspapers, National

BG	Boston Globe
BH	Boston Herald
BP	Boston Post
BSA	Boston Sunday Advertiser
CA	Chicago American
CSM	Christian Science Monitor
LAT	Los Angeles Times
NYHT	New York Herald-Tribune
NYM	New York Mirror
NYP	New York Post
NYT	New York Times
NYWT	New York World-Telegram
WSJ	Wall Street Journal
WES	Washington Evening Star
WN	Washington News
WP	Washington Post
WTH	Washington Times-Herald

In addition to other resources mentioned in the notes, the following records are located at the Margaret Chase Smith Library: Anecdotes, Scrapbooks, Statements and Speeches, and "Washington & You."

INTRODUCTION: DOUBLE VISION

1. MCSI, 17 October 1986.
2. Janann Sherman, "Margaret Chase Smith: The Making of a Senator" (Ph.D. diss., Rutgers University, 1993).

3. MCSI, 17 October 1986.
4. The holdings of the Margaret Chase Smith Library Center in Skowhegan, Maine provided the core materials for this book, including correspondence, documents, scrapbooks, statements and speeches, and many of the newspapers and federal records cited. Smith's office files make up the bulk of the collection; however, the original size and organization of the files is unknown. In the process of establishing the archives, apparently several individuals reordered the holdings and discarded an unknowable quantity. Some documents still contain traces of the old filing arrangements in the form of margin notations and headings. All these files remained volatile during the period in which I used them. The senator and her aides continued to move files and their contents about during her lifetime. Some were significantly diminished between my first viewing and later rechecking, most notably those relating to Senator McCarthy, the Vietnam War, and her 1964 presidential campaign. Others were reshuffled and, in some cases, increased as stored materials or new clippings were added to them. Unfortunately, since the collection has not, to my knowledge, stabilized, some of my file citations may no longer be accurate.
5. While not atypical of elderly persons, the rehearsed quality of Smith's recollections was accentuated by frequent interviews over time. Oral historians have amply demonstrated the tendency, in life recall, to rationalize experience, to overestimate causes to demonstrate outcomes as necessary rather than accidental, and to order remembrances in conformity with social and personal meanings. For an analysis of this process of "life review," see Paul Thompson, *The Voice of the Past* (New York: Oxford University Press, 1978), 100–113; Marianne Lo Gerfo, "Three Ways of Reminiscence" and John A. Neuenschwander, "Oral Historians and Long-Term Memory," in *Oral History: An Interdisciplinary Anthology*, edited by David K. Dunaway and Willa K. Baum (Nashville: American Association for State and Local History, 1984), 314–332.
6. The Constitution mandates that, while vacant seats in the Senate may be filled by appointment, elections to fill seats in the House of Representatives are mandatory. Kincaid found this widespread reluctance to see women as power seekers perpetuated by political scientists as well as the public. Diane D. Kincaid, "Over His Dead Body: A Positive Perspective on Widows in the U.S. Congress," *Western Political Quarterly*, fall 1978, 96–104.
7. MCSI, 9 March 1989.
8. Ibid., 16 March 1987.
9. Ibid., 13 March 1989.
10. In her analysis of female biographies, Carolyn Heilbrun asserts that women have been deprived of the words to describe and claim their desire for power over their own lives. Similarly, when Patricia Meyers Spacks reviewed the autobiographies of five politically active women—Emmeline Pankhurst, Dorothy Day, Emma Goldman, Eleanor Roosevelt, and Golda Meir—she found that, without exception, these women credited a public commitment, rather than a personal desire, as their prime motivation. Carolyn G. Heilbrun, *Writing a Woman's Life* (New York: W. W. Norton & Co., 1988), 11–31; Patricia Meyers Spacks, "Selves in Hiding," in *Women's Autobiography: Essays in Criticism*, edited by Estelle C. Jelinek (Bloomington: Indiana University Press, 1980), 112–132.

11. MCSI, 8 December 1989.
12. Ibid., 24 October 1992.
13. Leon Edel advised biographers to search out their subject's "life-myth," the individual's "hidden dreams of himself." Leon Edel, "The Figure Under the Carpet," in *Biography as High Adventure: Life-Writers Speak on Their Art,* edited by Stephen B. Oates (Amherst: University of Massachusetts Press, 1986), 18–31.
14. As analyzed here, Smith's narrative consists of the way she spoke about her life and career in 58 interviews and countless conversations with me over an 8-year period, enriched by her additional testimony in transcripts produced by other interviewers, and in a number of self-generated recollections in her files, collectively called "Anecdotes." My interview notes and transcripts will become part of the permanent collection of the Margaret Chase Smith Library Center upon completion of this project.
15. Don Larrabee, *BG,* 21 May 1972.

CHAPTER ONE: A SENSE OF PLACE

1. Louise Helen Coburn. *Skowhegan on the Kennebec* (Skowhegan, ME: Independent-Reporter Press, 1941), 1:xiii.
2. *Important Data on the History of Skowhegan* (Skowhegan, ME: Independent-Reporter, 1926), 6–7.
3. *IR,* 14 April 1910; Coburn, *Skowhegan,* 2:933–965.
4. *SR,* 28 July 1909; Robert P. Tristan Coffin. *Kennebec, Cradle of Americans* (New York: Farrar and Rinehart, 1937), 159.
5. Coburn, *Skowhegan,* 1:283.
6. *SR,* 6 July 1905.
7. Ice was a $2 million industry in 1890, and the Kennebec River was the source of 75% of Maine's ice exports. "Ice King" Charles W. Morse of Bath put together an ice-cutting and shipping empire worth $300 million at the turn of the century. Wayne Curtis, "Maine's Golden Decade," *Down East,* 1992, annual issue, 25; Ellen MacDonald Ward, "Notables of the Nineties," *Down East,* 1992, annual issue, 46; Coffin, *Kennebec,* 164–178.
8. Coffin, *Kennebec,* 159.
9. The mix was approximately two-thirds English to one-third French Canadian, with a few first-generation Irish, German, and Italians, at least one Chinese family and "occasionally . . . a negro." Coburn names several whom "benefactors" brought in to the state just after the Civil War. Schmidt makes reference to "less than twenty-four" African Americans in Skowhegan during this period. Coburn, *Skowhegan,* 198–200; Patricia L. Schmidt, *Margaret Chase Smith: Beyond Convention* (Orono: University of Maine Press, 1996), 20.
10. *IR,* 14 April 1910.
11. Ibid., 27 July 1911.
12. Examples and anecdotes about the Maine character abound in the popular press. For one attempt at a more scholarly analysis, see Charles E. Clark, *Maine: A History* (Hanover, NH: University Press of New England, 1990), 149–165.
13. These basic values surface frequently in MCS's recollections. I have taken them directly from interviews and anecdotes or inferred them from her narrative.

14. Anecdotes; MCSI, 6 June 1989; Gerald J. Brault, "The Franco-Americans of Maine," in David C. Smith and Edward O. Schriver, eds., *Maine: A History Through Selected Readings* (Dubuque, IA: Kendall Hunt Publishing Co., 1985), 384–396.

15. Coburn, *Skowhegan*, 1:196–198, 2:736.

16. MCS's mother is listed as Caroline Morin, daughter of Lambert and Marie Boulette Morin, on her 1896 marriage certificate, Scrapbook 7, MCSL. By 1905, John L. Murray headed the household at 81 North Avenue. Coburn's discussion of the Americanization of French names in Skowhegan by employers and teachers uses Morin to Murray as one example. H. E. Mitchell and Paul Davis, *Skowhegan Register* (Brunswick, ME: H. E. Mitchell Co., 1905), 18, MCSL; Coburn, *Skowhegan*, 1:198.

17. By the spring of 1855, the nativist "Know–Nothing" movement reportedly had 27,000 Maine members, with Catholics—Irish and French Canadian—as their chief victims. The fires of bigotry, never quite extinguished, flared again in the 1920s, this time in the guise of the Ku Klux Klan and again targeting Franco-Americans. Anti-French prejudice persists in Maine. The famous confrontation between Edmund Muskie and William Loeb, publisher of the *Manchester (NH) Union Leader*, during the 1972 presidential primary began when Loeb alleged that Muskie laughed at a "Canuck" joke. William Lemke, *Wild, Wild East: Unusual Tales of Maine History* (Camden, ME: Yankee Books, 1990), 101–106; David M. Chalmers. *Hooded Americanism: The First Century of the Ku Klux Klan, 1856–1956* (Garden City, NY: Doubleday & Co., 1965), 275–277; Rita Mae Breton, "Red Scare: A Study in Maine Nativism, 1919–1925" (M.A. thesis, University of Maine, 1972), 103, 206–207.

18. Anecdotes; Statements & Speeches, vol. 42, 3 January 1976. Murray's obituary, *IR*, 19 October 1922.

19. MCS was particularly proud that Salmon P. Chase, Abraham Lincoln's Secretary of the Treasury and the Sixth Chief Justice of the United States, was also a descendant of Aquila and Thomas Chase. *The Descendants of Aquila and Thomas Chase* (Derry, NH, 1928), MCSL; Statements & Speeches, Misc. 1925–1945, 17 July 1940, MCSL.

20. The farm was eventually acquired by the Rev. George Walter Hinckley to become a school for homeless boys. The Good Will-Hinckley Home-School-Farm for Boys, established in 1889, still functions as a rehabilitation facility for troubled youth and restored Smith's ancestral home as its visitor's center. "Geneolgy [*sic*] of George Emery Chase," Scrapbook 34, 3 Dec. 1945; Lawrence M. Sturtevant, *Chronicles of the Good Will Home, 1889–1989* (Hinckley, ME: The Good Will Home Association, 1989).

21. Anecdotes; MCSI, 7 September 1989.

22. Youville Labonte, compiler, *Marriages of Our Lady of Lourdes, Skowhegan, Maine (1881–1980) and of St. Peter, Bingham, Maine (1920–1980)*, (Augusta: Maine State Library, 1981), 39.

23. Raising doubts about MCS's given name, Patricia Wallace reports Smith's baptismal certificate reads Marguerite Mandeline (her original birth certificate was lost in a fire), implying some later anglicizing. Records indicate, however, that the church and their baptismal records burned in 1946. Moreover, given that her grandfather had already anglicized his surname, this French emphasis seems unlikely. More plausible is Smith's contention that

she was named for her paternal grandmother. Birth Records file, MCSL; Patricia Ward Wallace, *Politics of Conscience: A Biography of Margaret Chase Smith* (Westport, CT: Praeger Publishers, 1995), 5–6.

24. Anecdotes; Murray's obituary, *IR*, 19 October 1922; Margaret Chase Smith, *Declaration of Conscience*, edited by William Chesley Lewis, Jr. (Garden City, NY: Doubleday & Co., 1972), 169.

25. Statements & Speeches, vol. 42, January 1976, 3; Anecdotes; MCSI, 8 December 1989.

26. For at least part of her formative years, Margaret was raised Catholic. As an adult, she followed no formal religion, though on occasion she described herself as Methodist. Her youngest sister, Laura, remained a Roman Catholic throughout her life; their brother, Wilbur, chose Methodism. *IR*, 19 October 1922, 11 August 1938; MCSI, 6 June 1989.

27. 1920 Diary file, MCSL.

28. Anecdotes; MCSI, 9 January 1987.

29. Ibid., 8 December 1989.

30. MCSI, 9 January 1987.

31. Ibid., 6 June 1989, 7 September 1989.

32. Ibid., 28 January 1989; Pamela Neal Warford, *Margaret Chase Smith: In Her Own Words* (University of Maine, oral history project, 1989), 16.

33. This story has been retold countless times in biographical sketches and articles to demonstrate her early acceptance of responsibility and a strong work ethic. She first told it to me 9 January 1987.

34. MCSI, 22 April 1992, 3 September 1989.

35. Right after that remark, MCS quickly added, "I didn't have ambition, I was just thrown into it." The word seemed to carry too negative a connotation for her to allow it to stand. MCSI, 3 September 1989.

36. Skowhegan Class of 1916 motto: Labor Conquers All. Graduation program in Scrapbook 8.

37. The number of women working in clerical positions increased more than 140% between the 1910s and 1920s. First private then public schools responded with vocational training in office machines, filing, and stenographic skills. Sophonisba P. Breckinridge, *Women in the Twentieth Century: A Study of Their Political, Social and Economic Activities* (New York: McGraw-Hill Publishing Co., 1933), 177–184; Margery W. Davies, *Woman's Place is at the Typewriter: Office Work and Office Workers 1870–1930* (Philadelphia: Temple University Press, 1982), 158–162.

38. Anecdotes; Statements & Speeches, vol. 20, 12 January 1960, 33; pictures of the team on display at the MCSL.

39. Anecdotes.

40. MCSI, 1 April 1992; Helen Hight Brown and Reba Vail Eldridge, conversation with author, Skowhegan, 21 August 1991.

41. MCSI, 9 January 1987.

42. *IR*, 6 April 1916, 13 April 1916; Anecdotes.

43. Coburn, *Skowhegan*, 2:643.

44. Ibid.; Anecdotes.

45. *IR*, 22 June 1916, 29 June 1916, 10 August 1916.

46. Ibid., 19 April 1917.

47. Ibid., 3 May 1917.
48. Ibid., 26 July 1917, 2 August 1917.
49. Photographs of Margaret and friends, in Red Cross and World War I uniforms, in her personal photograph album, MCSL.
50. *IR*, 31 May 1917.
51. Ibid., 23 August 1917, 4 October 1917, 17 October 1917.
52. It is useful to note that in a small town families have many points of contact. Margaret's sister Evelyn married Harry's younger brother, Rexford, in 1930 (just a few months after Margaret married Clyde Smith). Harry was the oldest son of Grace and Michael St. Ledger, who shared a business with Clyde Smith's brother, Myron Smith, from 1914 until the 1930s.
53. *IR*, 3 May 1917.
54. Ibid., 8 August 1918; Coburn, *Skowhegan*, 2:617.
55. MCSI, 3 September 1989, 2 November 1989.
56. Ibid., 18 January 1989.
57. She carefully recorded wages earned during these years in Anecdotes.
58. The Chases did not own an automobile. Numerous photographs of Clyde, Margaret, Mr. and Mrs. Chase, and a variety of large shiny cars, in personal album, MCSL; MCSI, 26 July 1989.
59. Carrie Chase born 10 May 1876; Clyde Smith 9 June 1876.
60. Anecdotes; MCSI, 26 July 1989.
61. Anecdotes; *IR*, 29 June 1916.
62. Anecdotes; MCSI, 17 October 1986.
63. Ibid.

CHAPTER TWO: POLITICAL EDUCATION

1. Sixteen dollars was a fair salary in 1919. The average office worker earned $15.98 in 1921, although the Women's Bureau estimated that $18.38 a week was necessary for health and decency. While inadequate, it was above the wages of more than half the women working in manufacturing at that time. Living at home and in a small town likely kept Margaret's expenses more modest than average. Breckinridge, *Women in the Twentieth Century,* 223; MCSI, 2 November 1989.
2. As it turned out, Patten ended his career working for Margaret. In 1937, he went to Washington with the Smiths as Clyde's aide; Patten remained with her until 1948 when she moved to the Senate and he retired.
3. Anecdotes; MCSI, 28 August 1991.
4. *PPH*, 29 May 1924.
5. Warford, *In Her Own Words*, 24.
6. Coburn, *Skowhegan*, 2:880–890.
7. Anecdotes.
8. Croly was also the guiding force behind the organization of women's clubs under the umbrella of the General Federation of Women's Clubs. Breckinridge, *Women in the Twentieth Century,* 14–30; Coburn, *Skowhegan*, 2:882.
9. Karen J. Blair, *The Clubwoman as Feminist: True Womanhood Refined, 1868–1914* (New York: Holmes & Meier, 1980), 15–21.
10. Coburn, *Skowhegan*, 2:882; *IR*, 12 April 1917.
11. MCSI, 16 March 1987.
12. Geline MacDonald Bowman and Earlene White, *A History of the National*

Federation of Business and Professional Women's Clubs, Inc., 1919–1944 (Washington, DC: NFBPWC, 1979), 12–18; Lisa Sergio, *A Measure Filled: The Life of Lena Madesin Philips* (New York: Robert B. Luce, 1972), 32–36.

13. Ruth Sargent, *Gail Laughlin: ERA's Advocate* (Portland, ME: House of Falmouth Publishers, 1979), 111.

14. In 1957, the name was changed to the less controversial *National Business Woman*.

15. Coburn, *Skowhegan*, 2:885.

16. MCSI, 16 March 1987.

17. 1926 speech, BPW file, MCSL.

18. *IR*, 3 June 1926.

19. Anecdotes; MCSI, 13 March 1989.

20. Numerous scholars have explored women's voluntary associations as training grounds for political office, among them, Jeane J. Kirkpatrick, *Political Women* (New York: Basic Books, 1974), 69; Blair, *Clubwoman as Feminist*, 15–21; Susan J. Carroll, *Women as Candidates in American Politics* (Bloomington: Indiana University Press, 1985), 71–72.

21. Speech to the BPW upon her election to the U.S. Senate, "Our Senator," *Independent Woman*, November 1949, 335.

22. Contemporary magazines trumpeted female Horatio Alger stories of young women, armed with grit and ability, making it to the top of the business ladder, taking on and succeeding in unusual fields, and satisfying their personal ambitions while maintaining a happy home with Mr. Right. These stories were also a staple of *Independent Woman*. Patricia M. Hummer, *Decade of Illusive Promise: Professional Women in the United States, 1920–1930* (Ann Arbor: University of Michigan Research Press, 1979), 7–8; Dorothy M. Brown, *Setting a Course: American Women in the 1920s* (Boston: Twayne Publishers, 1987), 29–33.

23. MCSI, 26 July 1989, 5 September 1990.

24. *IR*, 26 March 1925, 19 May 1927.

25. Family Correspondence file, MCSL; telegrams in Scrapbook 9, 25 July 1924–28, May 1926.

26. *IR*, 4 April 1940, 11 June 1936; Smith obituaries in Scrapbook 6, 8 April 1940.

27. *SR* circa 1907–1908; MCSI, 18 January 1989.

28. Jim Brunelle, *The Maine Almanac* (Portland: Guy Gannett Publishing Co., 1978), 11.

29. Speech to Maine House, *PA*, Scrapbook 1, 12 March 1903.

30. *SR*, 29 June 1905.

31. *LEJ*, 1 November 1927.

32. Ed P. Page died 3 January 1908; the marriage took place 17 April 1908. *SR*, 9 January 1908, 23 April 1908.

33. *SR*, 14 May 1908, 1 July 1908, 5 November 1908, 17 December 1908; *IR*, 2 September 1909, 2 March 1911, 18 January 1912, 8 November 1934.

34. Coburn, *Skowhegan*, 2:508–511.

35. Though customarily reported in the newspaper with names and reasons for dissolution, the January 1914 divorce notice simply lists one without particulars, owing, no doubt, to Smith's association with the paper. *IR*, 29 January 1914.

36. MCSI, 18 January 1989.

37. The block included five stores with tenements and offices overhead on Water Street (the principal downtown thoroughfare), and on Court Street "stores, offices and restaurants, eight in number, with tenements on the second floor. . . . The consideration named in the deal is $44,000." This would be comparable to about $.5 million (in 1999 dollars). *IR*, 30 April 1914.

38. Smith either ran unopposed or had no serious opponents for most of his elections; he often won by majorities of 75% or more; vote tallies in Scrapbook 3.

39. MCSI, 2 July 1991.

40. *LEJ*, 7 March 1935.

41. MCSI, 8 December 1989.

42. Scrapbook 3, June 1918. Smith was in the House 1919–1923, Senate 1923–1929.

43. CHS file, MCSL.

44. Smith's salary as first selectman was less than $800 a year. *IR*, 11 March 1915.

45. Personal photograph album, MCSL.

46. 1920 Diary, 25 January, MCSL.

47. Ibid., 11 January.

48. Ibid., 9 January.

49. Ibid., 23 January.

50. Ibid., 1 February.

51. Ibid., 7 January.

52. Ibid., 11 January.

53. 23 December 1920, CHS file, MCSL.

54. Ibid., 6 January 1920; on February 2, she visited a friend with a new baby that was "too sweet for anything. Wish it was mine."

55. MCSI, 5 May 1992; clips in Scrapbook 9, 29 July 1925.

56. *IR*, 26 February 1925, 26 March 1925, 18 June 1925; *LEJ*, 7 January 1927; *DKJ*, 19 March 1927.

57. *LEJ*, 7 January 1927.

58. Dinner invitation, in Scrapbook 8, 18 March 1927; MCSI, 5 September 1990.

59. Minutes of the BPW state convention, 23 May 1927, BPW file, MCSL.

60. *IR*, 5 April 1928, 20 March 1930.

61. A shoddy mill was an early form of a recycling plant, making new textiles out of old rags that had been pulled apart and respun. Thanks to lobbying by the textile industry, the word and the product took on negative connotations.

62. Statements & Speeches, vol. 7, 1 July 1950; MCSI, 8 December 1989.

63. *IR*, 28 March 1930.

64. During the first half of the twentieth century, the Democratic Party was successful only in instances where Republican bungling stimulated a significant crossover vote. Whitmore Barron Garland, *Pine Tree Politics: Maine Political Party Battles, 1820–1972* (Ph.D. diss., University of Massachusetts, 1979).

65. This pattern was clear in campaign coverage throughout the period. Cummings later helped form the Page for Governor Club in 1934, *IR*, 17 May 1934; MCSI, 30 January 1989.

66. MCSI, 30 January 1989.

67. *IR*, 22 March 1930; *DKJ*, 20 March 1930; other clippings in Scrapbook 9, March 1930.

68. An informal survey of newspaper accounts reveals that only about half (19 of 41) of Skowhegan's brides between 1925 and 1930 wore white. Mrs. W. H. Cummings purchased the dress for her in Paris. "Wedding Memories" album, MCSL.

69. *DKJ*, 15 May 1930.

70. This spectacular house was featured in *LEJ*, magazine section, 3 August 1940; see also Coburn, *Skowhegan*, 2:663.

71. "Wedding Memories."

CHAPTER THREE: MRS. CLYDE SMITH

1. MCSI, 18 January 1989, 26 July 1989; letters in CHS file, MCSL.

2. MCS recorded memories of her marriage in an anecdote entitled "Employment," Anecdotes.

3. MCSI, 22 April 1992, 5 May 1992, 6 May 1992, 3 September 1989.

4. Ibid., 5 May 1992.

5. Anecdotes.

6. Ibid.; MCSI, 22 April 1992.

7. Letters in CHS file, MCSL.

8. Ibid.

9. MCSI, 18 January 1989.

10. Smith Correspondence, 9 December 1980, MCSL.

11. MCSI, 26 July 1989.

12. *LEJ*, 5 June 1930; *BDN*, 6 March 1929, 18 July 1930; Thomas L. Gaffney, "A Study of Maine Elections, 1930–1936" (master's thesis, University of Maine, 1968), 24–28.

13. *PEE*, 11 March 1930; *PST*, 8 March 1930; *IR*, 19 March 1930, 17 March 1932.

14. *IR*, 17 January 1929, 24 January 1929, 7 February 1929, 9 January 1930, 22 May 1930.

15. List of CHS health difficulties, CHS file, MCSL; *IR*, 5 February 1930.

16. *IR*, 12 November 1931, 23 May 1932, 18 May 1933, 16 November 1933, 10 May 1934, 18 October 1934, 16 November 1934, 2 January 1936, 14 May 1936.

17. For Maine political party structure and the importance of the local organization, particularly the women within it, in getting out the vote, see James Horan et al., *Downeast Politics: The Government of the State of Maine* (Dubuque, IA: Kendall Hunt Publishing Co., 1975), 117–120.

18. *IR*, 4 August 1938.

19. Ibid., 25 August 1932, 1 September 1932.

20. Ibid., 20 October 1932.

21. Published guest lists so indicate, though it must have been difficult in such a small town. Bunker remained active in the Republican Party and was elected to Margaret's former post, Republican State Committeewoman, in 1940, a post she held for four years. *IR*, 4 April 1940, 6 January 1944.

22. *PST*, 2 July 1935, *BDN*, 18 August 1936; Gaffney, *Maine Elections*, 52–57.

23. *IR*, 21 January 1932. The Executive Council was abolished by constitutional amendment in 1977.

24. MCSI, 26 July 1989.

25. Anecdotes; MCSI, 5 May 1992.
26. *IR*, 6 April 1933.
27. Smith medical history, clip from *BG*, 15 June 1947, in CHS file, MCSL.
28. Gaffney, *Maine Elections*, 113–119.
29. *NYHT*, 7 September 1934, cited in Gaffney, *Maine Elections*, 106.
30. *DKJ*, 11 September 1934.
31. Announcements were carried by all major Maine papers on the same date: *DKJ*, *BDN*, *IR*, 13 September 1934.
32. *PST*, 1 December 1935.
33. *LEJ*, 12 September 1934.
34. *DKJ*, 13 September 1934.
35. Anecdotes; MCSI, 6 May 1992.
36. Campaign Diary, MCSL.
37. MCSI, 26 July 1989.
38. Nichols interview, 23 March 1994; his father was a member of the group.
39. *LEJ*, 7 March 1935.
40. Prepared statement, CHS.
41. *BSA*, 23 February 1936, clip in CHS; *BDN*, 28 March 1936; *IR*, 18 June 1936.
42. Wallace, *Politics of Conscience*, 35.
43. An analysis of the press on this issue in Gaffney, *Maine Elections*, 157.
44. 1936 campaign speech, CHS file, MCSL.
45. Abraham Holtzman, *The Townsend Movement: A Political Study* (New York: Bookman Associates, 1963), 49–51.
46. Townsendite agitation prodded FDR to include old age pensions, along with unemployment insurance and federal grants for dependent children, in his 1935 social security plan. Edwin E. Witte, *The Development of the Social Security Act* (Madison: University of Wisconsin Press, 1962), 95–99; Alan Brinkley, *Voices of Protest: Huey Long, Father Coughlin and the Great Depression* (New York: Vantage Books, 1982), 222–224; John A. Garraty, *The Great Depression* (Garden City, NY: Doubleday & Co., 1987), 153–154.
47. *PPH*, 15 April 1936.
48. Gaffney, *Maine Elections*, 141; Congressional Quarterly, *Guide to U.S. Elections*, 2d ed. (Washington, DC: Congressional Quarterly, 1985), 938.
49. *IR*, 24 September 1936.
50. *BDN*, 22 January 1937; MCSI, 16 March 1987.
51. *BDN*, 28 September 1937.
52. MCSI, 26 July 1989.
53. AP story and assorted press clips, 1937, Scrapbook 9.
54. Congressional Club file, MCSL; 1937 Yearbook in Scrapbook 7.
55. MCSI, 11 August 1989.
56. Social Calendar, Congressional Club file, MCSL.
57. Despite the necessity to bend the club rules, she kept her post as treasurer into the second year of her first term in Congress. Wives of former congressmen were prohibited from holding office, but when Margaret tried to resign after Clyde's death the club voted to keep her in office until the renovations were completed. Congressional Club; Anecdotes.
58. MCSI, 6 May 1992.
59. Ibid., 13 March 1989, 18 March 1992.
60. Ibid., 11 August 1989.

61. The Supreme Court had struck down the National Recovery Administration in the 1935 Schechter Case. For the classic account, see William Leuchtenburg, *FDR and the New Deal* (New York: Harper & Row, Publishers, 1963).

62. Francis Perkins, *The Roosevelt I Knew.* (New York: Viking Press, 1946), 246–267.

63. *CR*, 75th Cong., 2d Sess., 13 December 1937, 1,386.

64. *WN*, 30 December 1937.

65. Perkins, *The Roosevelt I Knew*, 263; *PPH*, 13 May 1938.

66. *CR*, 75th Cong., 3rd Sess., 24 May 1938, 7,449–7,450; 14 June 1938, 9,178; 25 June 1938, 9,616.

67. Smith's message ran in newspapers throughout his district, clippings in Scrapbook 2, 1 August 1937.

68. Roland Patten, "Life of a Congressman," *IR*, 18 May 1937.

69. *IR*, 20 September 1937.

70. Ibid., 31 March 1938.

71. Navy Day speech, CHS file, MCSL; *WMS*, 28 October 1938.

72. Smith, *Declaration*, 66.

73. Smith, "Heard, Seen and Said at Washington," *IR*, 24 February 1938.

74. *CR*, 75th Cong., 1st Sess., 18 March 1937, 2,410.

75. Ibid., 29 June 1939, 8,310–8,311.

76. Clipping, Scrapbook 5, 15 January 1939.

77. *IR*, 8 September 1938; campaign ad, CHS file, MCSL.

78. Holtzman, *Townsend Movement,* 104.

79. *Guide to U.S. Elections,* 943.

80. *IR*, 15 September 1938.

81. "The Coming Wage-Hour Struggle," *United States News*, 29 May 1940, 30–31.

82. Craig, *PPH*, 7 December 1938.

83. Report, Research Institute of Cutaneous Medicine, 21 December 1938, to Smith's doctor, CHS file, MCSL; James H. Jones, *Bad Blood: The Tuskegee Syphilis Experiment* (New York: The Free Press, 1981), 2–7.

84. Political ad, "A Public Statement by Congressman Clyde H. Smith," Scrapbook 2, nd.

85. Ibid.; *IR*, 26 January 1939; *LEJ*, 8 March 1939.

86. Political ad, *DKJ*, 13 April 1939.

87. Clippings, Scrapbook 5; *BDN*, 5 November 1939.

88. Political ad, Scrapbook 5, 30 March 1940.

89. Political ad, asking supporters to call on Mrs. Smith at the convention, in Scrapbook 5.

90. MCSI, 24 July 1992.

91. *PPH*, 4 April 1940.

92. MCSI, 24 July 1992.

93. Dr. Dickens's remarks in CHS file, MCSL; MCSI, 8 January 1987.

94. Since the passage of Maine's Direct Primary Law in 1911, each candidate for office was required to file, with the secretary of state, nomination papers containing the signatures of qualified voters in his party in number not less than 1% nor more than 2% of the entire vote cast for governor in

the last preceding election in the state, district, or county wherein he sought election. Horan et al., *Downeast Politics*, 19–20.

95. Because of the weekend, the press release, dated Sunday, 7 April 1940, ran in many state newspapers alongside Smith's obituary. He died about 1:30 a.m. Monday, 8 April 1940.

96. *PPH*, 8 April 1940.

97. MCSI, 16 March 1987, 18 March 1992.

CHAPTER FOUR: ON HER OWN

1. *CR*, 76th Cong., 2d Sess., 8 April 1940, 4,158–4,159; *IR*, 11 April 1940.

2. *LEJ*, 8 April 1940.

3. *RCG*, 27 April 1940; MCSI, 16 March 1987, 24 July 1992.

4. Smith: 7,413, Bonney: 681. Data from MCSL.

5. *LEJ*, 14 May 1940.

6. Ibid., 15 May 1940.

7. *DKJ*, 8 April 1940.

8. *LEJ*, 8 April 1940.

9. MCSI, 16 March 1987 (emphasis hers).

10. Professor Herbert C. Libby to the newly formed "Mrs. Smith Goes to Washington Club," *WMS*, 11 June 1940.

11. Labor Legislation file, MCSL; 1940 campaign materials in Scrapbook 10; Garland, *Pine Tree Politics*, 74–81.

12. June 1940 speeches in Statements & Speeches, 1925–1945.

13. *PPH*, 25 May 1940.

14. *LEJ*, 18 May 1940; also *LEJ*, 5 January 1940, 2 February 1940, 7 May 1940.

15. *LDS*, 10 June 1940; also *LEJ*, 6 June 1940; *PST*, 26 May 1940.

16. *PPH*, 19 May 1940; Statements & Speeches, 1925–1945, May 1940.

17. *PST*, 19 May 1940.

18. Itinerary, Scrapbook 12, 23 August 1940.

19. Dorris A. Westall "Women in Politics," *PST*, 19 May 1940; Elisabeth May Craig, "Inside in Washington," *PST*, 6 June 1940.

20. *LEJ*, 5 October 1940.

21. These same accusations resurfaced in the 1948 campaign. Election 1948 file, MCSL; MCSI, 6 June 1989.

22. *PST*, 19 May 1940.

23. *LEJ*, 15 June 1940.

24. *PST*, 19 May 1940.

25. *LEJ*, 7 June 1940; *IR*, 6 June 1940; *LEJ*, 29 May 1940.

26. Maine DAR unanimously adopted a resolution "pledging their assistance, as individuals." *PPH*, 17 April 1940.

27. *WMS*, 11 June 1940; MCSI, 24 July 1992.

28. Statements & Speeches, 1925–1945, 13 April 1940.

29. Cards were her only campaign literature, Election 1940 file, MCSL.

30. Statements & Speeches, 1925–1945, June 1940.

31. Campaign data from MCSL.

32. *CR*, 76th Cong., 3d Sess., 1 August 1940, 9,806; MCSI, 30 January 1989.

33. Even small increments of seniority are considered; sometimes as little as a single day were pivotal. Joseph S. Clark, *Congress: The Sapless Branch* (New York: Harper & Row, Publishers, 1965), 176–177.

34. "Washington & You," 1 January 1941.
35. Charles L. Clapp, *The Congressman: His Work as He Sees It* (Garden City, NY: Doubleday & Co., 1963), 211–240; Donald G. Tacheron and Morris K. Udall, *The Job of the Congressman* 2d ed. (Indianapolis: Bobbs-Merrill Co., 1970), 164–173.
36. Mary T. Norton to MCS, Scrapbook 7, 27 May 1940; MCSI, 18 March 1992.
37. Conservatives regarded Smith "as almost un-Republican in his labor liberalism." *PPH*, 4 January 1941; MCSI, 7 August 1991.
38. *CR*, 76th Cong., 3d Sess., 10 January 1940, 226; A1,279–1,297.
39. *PPH*, 10 March 1940.
40. Criticism of Perkins, for example, in *CR*, 75th Cong., 1st Sess., 25 February 1937, 1,622; Hoffman's acrimonious debate with Mary Norton ran throughout deliberations of the Wages and Hours Bill. For her version, see Norton, unpublished autobiography, 139–159, MTNP.
41. *CR*, 76th Cong., 3d Sess., 12 January 1940, 302.
42. MCSI, 7 August 1991.
43. For a review of this material, see synthesis by John Patrick Diggins, *The Proud Decades: America in War and Peace, 1941–1960* (New York: W. W. Norton & Co., 1988). For more traditional approaches, see Robert A. Divine, *The Reluctant Belligerent: American Entry into World War II* (New York: Wiley Publishers, 1965); Robert Dallek, *Franklin D. Roosevelt and American Foreign Policy, 1932–1945* (New York: Oxford University Press, 1979).
44. Dallek, *FDR and American Foreign Policy,* 336.
45. H.R.10039, 11 June 1940; selective service, H.R.10132, 7 September 1940; *Voting Record By Roll Calls*, MCSL.
46. *CR*, 77th Cong., 1st Sess., 12 August 1941, 7,074–7,075.
47. "Washington and You," 14 February 1941.
48. David Brinkley, *Washington Goes to War* (New York: Alfred A. Knopf, 1988), 51.
49. H.R.1776; *CR*, 77th Cong., 1st Sess., 8 February 1941, 814–815; 11 March 1941, 2,178, 2,190–2,191; 17 March 1941, 2,297.
50. Party unity was 56% for the 77th; 52% for the 78th; 41% for the 79th; 87% for the 80th Congress, just before she ran for the U.S. Senate. *Congressional Quarterly* tallies, MCSL; J. Michael Sharp, *The Directory of Congressional Voting Scores and Interest Group Ratings* (New York: Facts on File Publications, 1988), 944.
51. *PPH*, 8 August 1941.
52. *PPH*, 2 July 1941. Guy Gannett Publishing Company owned the *Portland Press Herald*, the *Portland Evening Express*, the *Maine Sunday Telegram*, the (Augusta) *Daily Kennebec Journal*, and the *Waterville Morning Sentinel*, and functioned as the primary news source for a host of weekly newspapers. The other major newspapers in Maine were the *Bangor Daily News*, the *Lewiston Evening Journal* and the *Lewiston Daily Sun*. Gannett also owned WGUY and WGAN radio stations. Alan Robert Miller, *The History of Current Maine Newspapers* (Lisbon Falls, ME: Eastland Press, 1978).
53. *PPH*, 15 November 1941.
54. *LCN*, 4 June 1942; also see *CH*, 6 August 1942; *RCG*, 26 March 1942.
55. Data from MCSL.
56. *San Diego Union,* clip in Scrapbook 22, 5 April 1943.

57. Ruth B. Mandel, *In the Running: The New Woman Candidate*, (Boston: Beacon Press, 1981), 12.

58. Maine voters, conversation with author, Sabattus, ME, 24 June 1989; *PPH*, 21 February 1947.

59. *IR*, 20 April 1944.

60. Ibid., 13 August 1942.

61. MCSI, 16 March 1987.

62. *IR*, 13 August 1942; "Washington and You," 4 September 1941.

63. "The Gentlewoman from Maine," *Ladies' Home Journal*, January 1961, 111.

64. *LCN*, 4 June 1942.

65. *RCG*, 4 January 1946.

66. Film footage of receiving lines in MCSL.

67. Patten's remarks to Rotary Club, *IR*, 17 July 1941.

68. "Washington and You" ran as a weekly column from 1941 until 1948. After her election to the Senate, Smith's column became a syndicated daily, run in several hundred newspapers nationwide for five years. The complete collection is in MCSL.

69. See "Miscellaneous excerpts," Statements & Speeches, 1925–1945.

70. Douglass Cater, *Power in Washington* (New York: Random House, 1964), 121.

71. Clark, *The Sapless Branch*, 39; Tacheron and Udall, *The Job,* 167.

72. MCSI, 13 March 1989.

73. Statements & Speeches, 1925–1945, 29 June 1940.

74. Descriptions of norms, of course, use male members of Congress as their reference point, hence my use of male pronouns. Clapp, *The Congressman,* 14.

75. Ibid., 44–45; Tacheron and Udall, *The Job*, 134–135.

76. *CR*, 80th Cong., 1st Sess., 27 January 1947, 632; cited in Irwin N. Gertzog, *Congressional Women: Their Recruitment, Treatment and Behavior* (Westport, CT: Praeger Publishers, 1984), 61– 62. Reliance upon such "deference" was part of a pattern of putdowns that Kirkpatrick found alive and well in the 1960s; she called it "killing with kindness." Kirkpatrick, *Political Woman*, 109.

77. Gerzog, *Congressional Women*, 67–68.

78. MCSI, 2 December 1988.

79. Craig, *PPH*, 19 February 1941.

80. MCSI, 16 March 1987.

81. Duverger called this method the "functional theory of specialization," and deemed it "fundamentally anti-equalitarian, for it tacitly assumes that man's aptitudes are polyvalent, while those of women are monovalent." Maurice Duverger, *Political Role of Women* (New York: United Nations Press, 1955), 126.

82. The two women had been active together in the Congressional Club for several years. When Chester Bolton and Clyde Smith died within months of one another, their widows found solace in their friendship, as well as encouragement to go after their husband's congressional positions. Bolton-Smith Correspondence, MCSL, reflects their enduring friendship, which lasted until Bolton died in 1977.

83. *WES*, 5 January 1945.

84. *LEJ*, 23 June 1941.
85. Douglas Larsen, *NYWT*, 6 January 1945.
86. While frequently quoted in this manner, the remark was a bit different in context. It came at the end of a long and acrimonious debate with Representative Blanton of Texas over the passage of a series of bills by the District of Columbia Committee, of which Norton was chair. "He kept referring to me patronizingly as 'the lady.' Finally I reminded him that I was not 'the lady,' but a member of Congress." Mary Norton, unpublished autobiography, 107, MTNP.
87. Susan Ware's study of New Deal women described this same phenomenon. Ware, *Beyond Suffrage: Women in the New Deal* (Cambridge, MA: Harvard University Press, 1981), 15–16.
88. Nancy Cott, *The Grounding of Modern Feminism* (New Haven, CT: Yale University Press, 1987), 35–42.
89. Biographical sketch in Department of Labor, Women's Bureau Bulletin, "Women in the 80th Congress," Scrapbook 48, 15 September 1947; repeated twenty-five years later in Smith, *Declaration*, 85.
90. MCSI, 8 January 1987.
91. In order to pass the domestic test, women usually cooperated when asked for such poses; Smith's scrapbooks contain many such photographs. Norton, however, refused requests to pose before a stove, saying she would not be cooking in Congress. Maureen Rees, *Mary T. Norton,* 56, MTNP.
92. Egregious examples abound. For example, a profile of the women in the 77th Congress in *WP*, 29 December 1940, or *NYDN*, 13 March 1943.
93. *NYWT*, 6 January 1945.
94. Smith-Bolton Correspondence, MCSL.

CHAPTER FIVE: NAVAL AFFAIRS

1. Owen Brewster served on both the House and Senate Naval Affairs; Fred Hale on Senate NAC. Other Mainers served on the House Merchant Marine Committee.
2. Elected to the House in 1913, Vinson headed NAC from 1931 to 1947 when it was combined with House Military Affairs under the National Security Act to become the House Armed Services Committee. Except for a brief period that Republicans held the majority in the House, Vinson chaired Armed Services until he retired in 1964. Vinson biography in Georgia Congressional Delegation file, MCSL.
3. Eliot Janeway, "The Man Who Owns the Navy," *Saturday Evening Post*, 15 December 1945, 17.
4. *IR*, 28 January 1943.
5. Doris Fleeson, "They Wear No Man's Collar," *Nation's Business,* September 1946, 72.
6. *WES*, 19 January 1943.
7. Although it is generally conceded that fundamental attitudes towards women did not change, the debate centers on whether World War II constituted a turning point for women in terms of occupational opportunities and economic equality. William Chafe's "watershed" thesis has been challenged by a number of women historians who contend that World War II created only a temporary space for women to enter the public realm that closed follow-

ing the war, forcing women back to the private sphere. The debate itself illustrates the complexities of women's lives that render a simple tally of gains and losses impossible to construct. Major contributors to the debate include William H. Chafe, *The American Woman: Her Changing Social, Economic and Political Roles, 1920–1970* (New York: Oxford University Press, 1972); Karen Anderson, *Wartime Women: Sex Roles, Family Relations, and the Status of Women During World War II* (Westport, CT: Greenwood Press, 1981); Lelia J. Rupp, *Mobilizing Women for War: German and American Propaganda, 1939–1945* (Princeton: Princeton University Press, 1978); D'Ann Campbell, *Women at War with America: Private Lives in a Patriotic Era* (Cambridge: Harvard University Press, 1984); Maureen Honey, *Creating Rosie the Riveter: Class, Gender and Propaganda During World War II* (Amherst: University of Massachusetts Press, 1984).

8. Francis Sill Wickware, "National Defense vs. Venereal Disease," *Life,* 13 October 1941, 128. Similar articles: Irwin Ross, "Sex in the Army," *American Mercury*, December 1941, 661–669; Irwin Ross, "Sex in the Boom Towns," *American Mercury*, November 1942, 606–613; J. Blan Van Urk, "Norfolk— Our Worst War Town," *American Mercury*, February 1943, 144–151; Jonathan Daniels, "Soldiers' Saturday Nights," *The Nation*, 17 May 1941, 586; "Army Cracks Down on Vice That Still Preys on Soldiers," *Newsweek,* 31 August 1942, 27–31.

9. "Washington and You," 19 March 1941.

10. Bascom Johnson (Director of the Division of Legal and Social Protection of the Federal Security Agency), "The Vice Problem and Defense," *Survey Midmonthly*, May 1941, 142.

11. Modeled after a World War I concept establishing "moral zones" around camps, the May Act (named for its sponsor, Rep. Andrew Jackson May [D-NY], chairman of the House Military Affairs Committee), Public Law 163, signed in July 1941, provided for offenders to be fined up to $1,000 or sentenced to one year in jail or both. *CR*, 77th Cong., 1st Sess., 21 April 1941, 3207.

12. The May Act was invoked only twice, in Tennessee and in North Carolina. Allan M. Brandt, *No Magic Bullet: A Social History of Venereal Disease in the United States Since 1880* (New York: Oxford University Press, 1985), 167.

13. Thomas Parren and R.A. Vonderlehr, *No. 1 Saboteur of Our Defense: Plain Words About Venereal Disease* (New York: Reynal & Hitchcock, 1941); discussion of this book and its consequences in Brandt, *No Magic Bullet*, 162–164.

14. Letter, Frank Knox to Carl Vinson, 15 February 1944, NAC file, MCSL.

15. The subcommittee, chaired by Ed Izac (D-CA) included Winder Harris (D-VA), John Fogarty (D-RI), James Mott (R-OR), George Bates (R-MA), John Anderson (R-CA) and Margaret Chase Smith (R-ME). Melvin Maas (R-MN) later joined the subcommittee. LTJG William C. Lewis, Jr. accompanied them as special counsel. Hearings were held in the Hampton Roads, Virginia, Area, 24–27 March 1943 (Pt. 1); San Diego, California, 6–10 April 1943 (Pt. 2); San Francisco, California, 12–17 April 1943 (Pt. 3); Newport, Rhode Island, 11–12 May 1943 (Pt. 4); Portland, Maine, 18–19 May 1943 (Pt. 5); Puget Sound, Washington, Area, 25–27 October 1943 (Pt. 6); Columbia River Area,

2–3 November 1943 (Pt. 7); Los Angeles–Long Beach, California, 10–13 November 1943 (Pt. 8). U.S. House of Representatives, 78th Cong., 1st Sess., *Investigation of Congested Areas* (hereinafter ICA), by a Subcommittee of the Committee on Naval Affairs, Hearings pursuant to H.Res. 30, parts 1–8. From 16–22 March 1945, the Subcommittee held hearings in the Pearl Harbor-Honolulu Area, pursuant to H. Res. 154, 79th Cong., 1st Sess., Part 1–8. *ICA Reports*: Rpt. 66, Hampton Roads, 30 March 1943; Rpt. 91, San Diego, 3 May 1943; Rpt. 96, San Francisco, 17 May 1943; Rpt. 113, Newport, 24 May 1943; Rpt. 118, Portland, 7 June 1943; Summary Report 144, October 1943; Rpt. 164, Puget Sound, 5 January 1944; Rpt. 172, Columbia River, 25 January 1944; Rpt. 162, Los Angeles-Long Beach, 21 December 1943; Summary Report 272, November 1944; Rpt. 39, Pearl Harbor-Honolulu, 8 April 1945. President Roosevelt set up a parallel executive Committee on Congested Production Areas (CCPA), materials in President's Official File, OF 5298, FDRL.

16. *ICA Hearings*, Pt. 3, 1,001.
17. Ibid., Pt. 1, 24, 38, 72; Pt. 2, 409.
18. Ibid., Pt. 5, 1,169; Pt. 6, 1,316; Pt. 7, 1,619.
19. Ibid., Pt. 1, 225–226; Pt. 5, 1,174.
20. Ibid., Pt. 2, 413–414; Pt. 3, 786; Pt. 5, 1,170–1,173. FBI statistics indicated a 95% increase in the number of American women officially charged with morals violations between 1940 and 1944, but found only 17.3% of them infected. Anderson, *Wartime Women*, 104.
21. The Department of Justice endorsed regulations for compulsory examinations. ICA Hearings, Pt. 2, 599.
22. MCSI, 9 January 1987, 2 November 1989.
23. Ibid., 2 December 1988, 1 April 1992.
24. Photographs from hearings, MCSL; MCSI, 18 January 1989.
25. MCSI, 18 January 1989.
26. Robert H. Mason, "Girls Behind Norfolk Jail Bars," Scrapbook 28, March 1943; Craig, *PPH*, 6 April 1943.
27. *WP*, 27 March 1943; Statements & Speeches, vol. 2, 31 March 1943.
28. *ICA Hearings,* Pt. 1, 225–226.
29. Ibid., Pt. 1, 259.
30. Titles of the subcommittee's preliminary reports reflect this shift: Rpt. 66, " . . . Appointed to Investigate Vice Conditions in the Vicinity of Naval Establishments," 30 March 1943; Rpt. 91, " . . . Appointed to Investigate Congestion in Critical War Production Areas," 3 May 1943.
31. *ICA Hearings*, Pt. 3, 900–903; Pt. 7, 1,650.
32. Ibid., Pt. 2, 447, 491; Pt. 4, 1,137.
33. Ibid., Pt. 1, 294–296; Pt. 3, 684, 792.
34. Ibid., Pt. 1, 8, 113–119; Pt. 2, 605; Pt. 3, 651.
35. Ibid., Pt. 3, 1,013; Pt. 6, 1524.
36. Ibid., Pt. 3, 883, 1,013; Pt. 7, 1,637; Pt. 8, 1,764.
37. Ibid., Pt. 1, 97.
38. Ibid, Pt. 3, 754, Pt. 2, 468.
39. Ibid., Pt. 3, 895, 927.
40. *ICA Report* 164, 1,219.
41. *ICA Hearings*, Pt. 4, 1,126–1,128.

42. Ibid., Pt. 2, 462; *CCPA Report*, 2.

43. Ibid., Pt. 1, 272–276; Pt. 2, 462.

44. Ibid., Pt. 2, 462–466.

45. Ibid., Pt. 3, 775; *CCPA Report*, 2; *ICA Report* 39, 515.

46. Ibid., Pt. 6, 1,460–1,462.

47. Ibid., Pt. 4, 1,060; Pt. 6, 1,453–1,455.

48. Funding of childcare was set to expire 30 March 1944. Representatives Norton, Stanley, Rogers, Bolton, Luce and Smith issued a formal call for continued funding, submitted to House Appropriations, 24 February 1944, for *Hearings on H.R. 4346*, Scrapbook 25; *NYT*, 9 March 1944.

49. *CR*, 78th Cong., 2d Sess., 9 March 1944, 2,454–2,455.

50. Quoted in *Labor*, Scrapbook 25, 18 March 1944.

51. *CR*, 78th Cong., 2d Sess., 9 March 1944, 2,457.

52. Peak enrollment reached 130,000 children in 3,100 cities, while the Census Bureau estimated that 2.75 million working women had 4.5 million children under the age of 14. Federal funding ended 1 March 1946. Susan M. Hartmann, *The Home Front and Beyond: American Women in the 1940s* (Boston: Twayne Publishers, 1982), 84.

53. H.R.3332, *CR*, 77th Cong., 1st Sess., 13 February 1941, 996.

54. In heavy industry, the war increased instead of decreased sex segregation in the workplace. Even at peak, women held only 4.4% of skilled jobs and supervisory positions. Ruth Milkman. *Gender at Work: The Dynamics of Job Segregation by Sex During World War II* (Urbana: University of Illinois Press, 1987), 9; Alice Kessler-Harris. *Out to Work: A History of Wage Earning Women in the United States* (New York: Oxford University Press, 1982), 289.

55. H.R.526, *CR*, 79th Cong., 1st Sess., 21 June 1945, 27.

56. Statements & Speeches, vol. 5, 13 February 1948.

57. *WP*, 23 February 1943.

58. *WP*, 3 January 1944.

59. H.J. Res. 1, Rep. Louis Ludlow (D-IN); *CR*, 79th Cong., 1st Sess., 3 January 1945, 30. The bill later acquired 76 cosponsors (including Smith and Rogers). Smith considered it more effective for men to sponsor the ERA; women doing so, she said, made it appear that women were seeking special privileges. *NYT*, 25 April 1945; MCSI, 3 September 1989.

60. CQ, *Guide to U.S. Elections*, 94–98.

61. Cott, *Modern Feminism*, 12–28; Cynthia Harrison. *On Account of Sex: The Politics of Women's Issues, 1945–1968* (Berkeley: University of California Press, 1988), 6–11.

62. *CR*, 79th Cong., 2d Sess., 19 July 1946, 9,405.

63. *CR*, 77th Cong., 1st Sess., 28 May 1941, 4,531–4,533.

64. U.S. House of Representatives, 77th Cong., 2d Sess., Committee on Military Affairs, *Hearings on HR.6293*, "to Create the Women's Auxiliary Army Corps," 20 and 21 January 1942, 51.

65. *CR*, 77th Cong., 2d Sess., 17 March 1942, 2,582–2,608.

66. *Hearings on HR.6293*, 20 January 1942, 43.

67. Public Law 554, 77th Cong., 1st Sess., signed into law 15 May 1942.

68. WAVES, an acronym for Women Accepted for Voluntary Emergency Service; SPARs, from the first letters of the Coast Guard motto and its translation:

Semper Paratus—Always Ready." There was no designated acronym for the Women Marines. Though Smith is sometimes called "the Mother of the WAVES," legislation was submitted by Melvin Maas; her contribution chiefly rests on her efforts to obtain their full integration.

69. Limited to 10% of the WAC, 6,520 black women served in the Army in segregated units. Barred from the WAVES and SPARs until October 1944, only 72 black women became WAVES and four SPARs by the end of the war, though they were integrated into the corps. Women Marines did not accept black women. Data from Women in Military Service to America.

70. *CR,* 77th Cong., 2d Sess., 2 July 1942, 5,923; *CR,* 78th Cong., 1st Sess., 27 May 1943, 4,992–5,002.

71. *ICA Hearings,* Pt. 5, 1,190; Pt. 7, 1,686–1,698.

72. House of Representatives, Naval Affairs Committee, Rpt. 271, *Covering Various Assignments Pertaining to Women in the Naval Services,* 24 November 1944; *NAC* file, MCSL.

73. Itinerary in Scrapbook 28, December 1944.

74. "Washington and You," 18 January 1945.

75. *WMS,* 24 December 1944.

76. MCSI, 30 January 1989.

77. A Republican House majority in 1946 and the Legislative Reorganization Act of that same year requiring the merger of the committees of Naval Affairs and Military Affairs into the Armed Services Committee resulted in Smith's chairmanship of the Hospitalization and Medical Subcommittee.

78. H.R.1943, *CR,* 80th Cong., 1st Sess., 12 March 1947, 1,998–2,014. The Army-Navy Nurse Act, Public Law 36–80C, signed into law 16 April 1947.

79. Debate in *CR,* 78th Cong., 1st Sess., 22 April 1943, 3,709–3,728.

80. Committee on Naval Affairs, Rpt. 119, *Hearings on H.R. 2859* "to Amend the Naval Reserve Act of 1938 As Amended," 4 June 1943, 973–987; see also *WN,* 23 April 1943.

81. *NYT,* 16 June 1943.

82. *CR,* 78th Cong., 2d Sess., 18 September 1944, 7,862–7,863.

83. U.S. House of Representatives, 79th Congress, 2d Sess., Naval Affairs Committee, *Hearings on H.R.5915,* "to Establish the Women's Reserves on a Permanent Basis," 9 May 1946, 3,319–3,339.

84. Ibid., 3,338.

85. Ibid., 3,334–3,335; "National Affairs: The Admiral," *Newsweek,* 3 June 1946, 30.

86. House Report. 105, H.R.3054, "to Establish the Women's Army Corps in the Regular Army. . . . ," 12 April 1947.

87. In the Senate, the bill for naval women was combined with a bill to do the same for Army women. Designated S.1527 and S.1103 respectively, these bills were combined into S.1641, Title I of which referred to the WAC, Title II to women in the Naval services and Title III to establish women in the Air Force (this last was added as an amendment in House ASC hearings, 23 March 1948) to meet the requirements for joint legislation after the unification of the Armed Services.

88. U.S. Senate, 80th Cong., 1st Sess., Committee on Armed Services, *Hearings on S.1103, S.1157 and S.1641,* "The Women's Armed Services Integration Act of 1947," 2, 9, 15 July 1947.

89. *CR*, 80th Cong., 1st Sess., 23 July 1947, 9,793.

90. Smith to W. G. Andrews, 14 February 1948, in *CR*, 80th Cong., 2d Sess., 6 April 1948, A2,152–2,153.

91. Another factor in women's favor was a positive shift in public opinion toward women's participation in a peacetime armed services. An August 1947 Gallup Poll revealed 52% of men and 54% of women supportive. George H. Gallup, *The Gallup Poll: Public Opinion, 1935–1971* (Wilmington: Scholarly Resources, 1972), 667.

92. House ASC, Subcommittee #3, *Hearings on S.1641*, 18 February 1948, 5,569–5,579.

93. Ibid., 23 March 1948, 5,833.

94. Consent calendar bills almost invariably pass without debate or further amendment. For that reason, a single objection negates the consent. Oleszek, *Congressional Procedures*, 100. *CR,* 80th Cong., 2d Sess., 6 April 1948, A2152–2153.

95. *CR*, 80th Cong., 2d Sess., 21 April 1948, 4711–4720.

96. A version of this name change accompanied the bill into the joint conference where the original name was restored.

97. ASC file, MCSL.

98. Regular status had been achieved but not full equity for women. The measure limited them to 2% of regulars, capped ranks, and forbid women to serve aboard ship or aircraft involved in combat missions. Issues involving pregnancy and women's command authority were left to the discretion of the service secretaries. *CR*, 80th Cong., 2d Sess., 4 June 1948, 7,154.

CHAPTER SIX: NO PLACE FOR A WOMAN

1. Susan M. Hartmann, *Truman and Eightieth Congress*, (Columbia: University of Missouri Press, 1971), 13; Ross Baker, *Friend and Foe in the U.S. Senate* (New York: The Free Press),186.

2. *LEJ*, 28 September 1946; *PST*, 10 December 1947.

3. *PPH*, 25 January 1946; *LEJ*, 28 September 1946.

4. Reversal of majority status in the 80th Congress had been dramatic, upsetting a 16-year Democratic rule, changing from 242 Democrats and 190 Republicans to 245 Republicans and 188 Democrats. CQ, *Guide to Congress*, 896.

5. *WES*, 18 January 1947; "Washington and You," 15 January 1947.

6. All eight women who had served in the Senate had been appointed to fill unexpired terms. Only Sen. Hattie Caraway (D-AR) won election following the end of her appointment.

7. *PST*, 1 June 1947.

8. *New Brunswick Sunday Times*, 14 August 1949, Scrapbook 75; *DKJ*, 14 June 1948.

9. *LEJ* , 28 September 1946; Beverly Smith, "Senator from the Five-and-Ten," *Saturday Evening Post*, 11 September 1948, 36.

10. *PPH*, 2 September 1943.

11. WCL file, MCSL.

12. Personal photograph album, MCSL; MCSI, 5 September 1990.

13. For purposes of probate, the estate was estimated at less than $25,000, including several pieces of real estate, some heavily mortgaged. The Smith

mansion on Fairview Avenue was not included in his estate because, by the time of his death, he had transferred it to her (one-half on her birthday in 1931 and the other half on their fourth wedding anniversary in 1934). The Clyde Smith Memorial Hospital opened in December 1945, but remained financially unstable. In 1952, it was sold and reincorporated as the Fairview Hospital. Extensive renovations masked, then replaced, the original structure. The Fairview merged with the Redington Hospital in 1968, and the Redington-Fairview Hospital still operates on the site. After Smith sold her house, she moved back in with her mother until after her election to the Senate in 1948, when she built the house on Norridgewock Avenue in which she lived until she died. Property transferred reported in *IR* clippings in Scrapbook 27 and 33, 7 July 1944, 2 October 1944, 12 October 1944, 26 October 1944, 25 November 1945; other property records in CHS file, MCSL file.

14. Visits during those early years documented in *IR* "Locals" column 1943–1947; clippings in Scrapbook 23–40, 26 August 1943, 3 September 1943, 12 October 1944, 14 June 1945, 25 October 1945, 6 June 1946, 8 August 1946, 26 September 1946; see also MCS Datebook, vols.3–7, 1943–1947, MCSL.

15. Lewis's service records, Form DD13, WHCF, Box 402, LBJL; this material absent from MCSL.

16. *DKJ*, 3 July 1941.

17. Of Smith's 29 general bills submitted in the first session of the 80th Congress, 19 dealt with military issues, eight of those were reserve bills drafted by the ARA. WCL, *ARA Contact*, June 1948, Scrapbook 56.

18. Smith, *Declaration*, 69–81.

19. *WCL Notes*, 138; MCSI, 2 November 1989.

20. Leaving aside the myriad problems associated with the National Security Council and its Central Intelligence Agency, the unification of the armed services was only an illusion of unity. The plan retained separately administered departments of the Army, Navy and Air Force with coordinating Joint Chiefs of Staff under a Secretary of Defense with limited authority. Joint Chiefs retained control, as well as direct access to the president, and interservice rivalry continued unabated. Thomas G. Paterson, *On Every Front: The Making of the Cold War* (New York: W. W. Norton & Co., 1979), 57–60; Walter Mills, ed., *The Forrestal Diaries* (New York: Viking Press, 1951), 117–147.

21. Walter LaFeber. *America, Russia, and the Cold War, 1945–1984* (New York: Alfred A. Knopf, 1985), 58–61.

22. Itinerary in Scrapbook 50, September 1947.

23. 20 September 1947, WCL file, MCSL.

24. Statements & Speeches, vol. 4, September and October 1947; clippings in Scrapbook 48, 9 October 1947, 26 October 1947, 28 October 1947.

25. *PPH*, 26 October 1947; *WTH*, 28 October 1947; Beverage quoted in *PPH*, 18 June 1948.

26. Statements & Speeches, vol. 4, 29 September 1947; *WTH*, 28 November 1947; *PPH*, 25 November 1947.

27. AP story, 18 October 1947, Scrapbook 50.

28. Quoted in Craig, *PST*, 19 October 1947; *LCN*, 23 October 1947; *CR*, 80th Cong., 2d Sess., 26 February 1948, 1,812.

29. *PEE*, 20 October 1947; other clippings in Scrapbook 52.

30. Statements & Speeches, vol. 4, 20 October 1947.

31. Committee report, Statements & Speeches, vol. 4, 18 October 1947; remarks, Statements & Speeches, vol. 5, 13 January 1948, 17 March 1948.

32. Nine communities were completely destroyed and four more suffered major damage; approximately 3500 people were displaced, 2500 left homeless. For the full dramatic story of the fires of 1947, see Joyce Butler, *Wildfire Loose: The Week Maine Burned* (Camden, ME: Down East Books, 1987).

33. Statements & Speeches, vol. 4, November 1947; MCSI, 24 October 1992. Despite some opposition by hardline isolationists, the European Recovery Plan passed Congress in March, spurred by the loss of Hungary, Rumania, and Czechoslovakia, and was signed by Truman 3 April 1948.

34. *PEE*, 17 January 1948; Hildreth denial, *LDS*, 20 January 1948.

35. Harold L. Ickes, *The Secret Diary of Harold Ickes, Vol.I, The First Thousand Days, 1933–1936* (New York: Simon & Schuster, 1933), 188–190; Gertrude S. Cooper, "History of the Passamaquoddy Tidal Power Project," Passamaquoddy Tidal Power Project file, MCSL.

36. H.R.5821, 80th Cong., 2d Sess., 11 March 1948.

37. Craig, *PPH*, 22 March 1948; *BDN*, 16 March 1948; Statements & Speeches, vol. 5, 16 April 1948.

38. *PPH*, 12 March 1948; Statements & Speeches, vol. 6, 10 December 1948.

39. Washington County was in the conservative Third District, where Smith, according to Lewis's analysis, was least likely to win in 1948. Smith's sincerity about Quoddy, however, can hardly be questioned in light of her long commitment to the project. Her first act as senator was to introduce S.233, a Passamaquoddy authorization bill. She pursued the measure throughout the 1950s, frequently getting it passed in the Senate, only to have it stall in the House. After a personal campaign to force the measure out of the House Rules Committee, the Smith Act finally became P.L. 401 (84th Cong., 2d Sess., 19 January 1956). But the fight for funding the authorization continued. The Kennedy administration resurrected Quoddy, and it subsequently became a major partisan issue during the 1960s, with both parties (primarily Smith and Edmund Muskie) wrangling for credit. In the end, the Passamaquoddy Tidal Power Project, opposed by the Canadian government and private power interests in Maine, was "resurveyed and restudied to death." Smith finally abandoned the effort in 1966, with regret. She continued to believe that the project would have worked and been good for Maine. Materials related to Smith and Passamaquoddy in President's Personal File and President's Official File, HSTL; WHCF, Official File, Box 838, DDEL; WHC Subject Files, Box 650, JFKL; Congressional File (Pre-Presidential Material), Box 54, LBJL. MCSI, 24 October 1992.

40. *WES*, 25 February 1948; *BDN*, 25 April 1948; *PST*, 13 June 1948.

41. Election 1948 file; *WCL Notes*, 120–125, 301–305; Henry interview, 10 July 1991 and Gosselin interview, 27 August 1991; MCSI 9 March 1989, 30 August 1989, 2 November 1989.

42. Carver had a distinguished career in foreign service and the military. During the First World War, he was secretary to Col. E. M. House during the Wilson administration, also assistant to Bernard Baruch on the Council for National Defense; following World War II, he chaired a Norwegian relief

agency. Political commentators during the 1948 election speculated that Carver was interested in a post in the Dewey administration and had agreed to back Smith over Sewall, a former associate, because he thought her chances of winning were better. Statements & Speeches, vol. 4, 30 December 1947; *BDN*, 5 September 1948; Elections 1948 file, MCSL.

43. Photocopies of Bolton check, 23 June 1947 and Lewis check, 27 June 1947, Scrapbook 56.

44. Conclusions about precise contributions and expenditures are impossible, given the sparse and incomplete documentation in the files and the phased destruction of official campaign expenditure statements by the Maine Secretary of State's office. See Election 1948 file, MCSL.

45. Note from Helen Bernstein, Scrapbook 56, 14 June 1948; one example of its publicity value in Helen Henley, *CSM*, 20 June 1948.

46. *BC*, 17 June 1948.

47. Political ad, Scrapbook 55, 5 June 1948.

48. *LE*, 22 January 1948.

49. Election 1948.

50. *BC*, 13 February 1948; MCSI, 31 March 1992.

51. *PEE*, 14 February 1948; other clips in Scrapbook 55, February, June, 1948.

52. Quoted by Fleeson, *WES*, 25 February 1948; *PST*, 7 March 1948.

53. *PST*, 7 March 1948; *PPH*, 21 May 1948.

54. The Maine Federation petitioned for an official exception of the BPW's nonpartisan rule. Smith also secured the endorsement of the District of Columbia BPW. Rawalt, *History of the NFBPWC*, vol. 2, 11–12; *DKJ*, 8 June 1947; Statements & Speeches, vol. 5, 16 February 1948.

55. Maine Women's Christian Temperance Union file, MCSL; *IR*, 11 May 1948.

56. *IR*, 27 April 1948.

57. Statements & Speeches, vol. 4, 10 April 1947.

58. Statements & Speeches, vol. 5, 5 June 1948; campaign statement, Scrapbook 55, 5 June 1948.

59. Austine Cassini, *WTH*, quoted in *IR*, 3 February 1948; other examples: *WES*, 18 January 1947, 25 February 1948; *CSM*, 8 March 1948, 12 June 1948; *WTH*, 28 November 1947; *CSM*, 18 June 1948; *BG*, 20 June 1948.

60. Note from Jo Ripley, Scrapbook 53, 1 April 1948.

61. *WCL Notes*, 193; Voting Record, MCSL; *PPH*, 20 March 1948; *IR*, 6 April 1948.

62. *Chicago Daily Tribune*, Scrapbook 50, 9 December 1947.

63. Smith used this characterization many times over the years; early example: Statements & Speeches, vol. 6, 8 January 1949.

64. *NYT*, 20 May 1948; *Trade Union Courier*, 4 July 1949, clip in Scrapbook 74.

65. Craig wrote a long, laudatory article concerning Smith's efforts on behalf of military women that ran in many daily and weekly papers in Maine just prior to the primary. *PPH*, 5 June 1948.

66. *IR*, 27 February 1947; *WES*, 21 February 1947; Maine reactions in *PPH*, 22 February 1947; *LCN*, 24 February 1947.

67. *PEE*, 8 March 1948; *BC*, 12 March 1948; *PPH*, 18 June 1948.

68. Press release, 26 June 1943, Labor Legislation file, MCSL; "Washington and You," 14 July 1943.

69. Jonas McBride letter, 17 March 1944, Election 1944 file, MCSL.

70. Statement, *Labor Legislation*; David A. Morse, "Truman's Assistant Secretary of Labor in Heller," *Economics and the Truman Administration*, 37–49; Robert H. Zeiger, *American Workers American Unions, 1900–1985* (Baltimore: The Johns Hopkins University Press, 1989), 104–106.

71. *Maine CIO News*, February 1946, Scrapbook 35; CIO score sheet, 19 August 1946, had Smith voting "right" eleven of the twelve vital measures, far better than other members of the Maine delegation (First District's Hale voted wrong nine of twelve, Third District Fellows all twelve), Labor Organizations file, MCSL.

72. Statements & Speeches, vol. 4, 10 March 1947.

73. *CR*, 80th Cong., 1st Sess., 17 April 1947 (roll call) and 20 June 1947 (override), 3,670–3,671, 7489 respectively.

74. Answer to Charges of Abridgement of Labor's Rights," Labor Legislation file, MCSL.

75. *LDS*, 22 June 1948.

76. James McVicar, chairman of the Democratic State Committee, suggested labor leaders could withhold endorsement without altering labor's support of her, *PST*, 12 October 1947.

77. Campaign ad, Scrapbook 56; Election 1948 file, MCSL.

78. *LEJ*, 14 June 1947; *PST*, 15 June 1947, 1 August 1947; denial, *PPH*, 21 July 1947.

79. *PST*, 11 July 1948; Paul A. MacDonald, conversation with author, Wiscasset, ME, 10 August 1990.

80. Election 1948 file, MCSL.

81. Already a staple of Republican campaign oratory, smear techniques like those used against Smith were attempted against Estes Kefauver's bid for the Senate from Tennessee. After reading that Memphis boss E. H. Crump made similar charges against Kefauver, Smith forwarded a copy of her defense. Note this was the same guilt-by-association Nixon employed against Helen Gahagan Douglas in the 1950 California Senate race; he circulated "pink sheets" listing parallels between Douglas's voting and that of Marcantonio. Smith to Kefauver, 9 July 1948, Tennessee Congressional Delegation file, MCSL; Ingrid Winther Scobie, *Center Stage: Helen Gahagan Douglas, A Life* (New York: Oxford University Press, 1992), 265–266.

82. MCSI, 24 October 1992.

83. Statements & Speeches, vol. 5, 21 May 1948; Election 1948 file, MCSL.

84. *IR*, 25 May 1948; *LCN*, 27 May 1948; *BC*, 4 June 1948; many others in Scrapbook 55.

85. Talberth, *PPH*, 13 June 1948.

86. *WCL Notes*, MCSL, 304; copies in Scrapbook 56, June 1948.

87. Election 1948 file, MCSL; Smith, *Declaration*, 114–117.

88. Election data from MCSL.

89. Official Proceedings, MCSL, 197.

90. Ibid., 72–75.

91. Ibid., 198.

92. Ibid., 187–193.

93. The tour was considered mandatory: "If this year's candidates shied away from the grueling task, they might be branded political sissies." *LEJ*, 21 August 1948.

94. Quoted in *Boston American*, 22 June 1948, clip in Scrapbook 59.
95. "Significance of Maine Election," *U.S. News and World Report*, 24 September 1948, 14–15.
96. Election 1948 file, MCSL; *IR*, 21 September 1948.
97. David McCullough, *Truman* (New York: Simon & Schuster, 1992), 651–652, 668–712.

CHAPTER SEVEN: JOAN OF ARC

1. *PPH*, 6 January 1949.
2. Despite the great expectations of its founders, the Multi-Party Committee ran into financial difficulties almost immediately. Problems making up the $400 deficit from the "Special" prompted the committee to abandon their national effort to raise a million dollars. Brochure for MultiParty Committee 1948 in Scrapbook 67. Materials concerning the Committee in Somerville-Howorth Collection, Box 9, Folder 204 and Box 7, Folder 141, SCHL.
3. Statements & Speeches, vol. 6, 3 January 1949; press coverage: *NYT*, 3 January 1949; *WES*, 4 January 1949; *WP*, 4 January 1949.
4. *WES*, 14 September 1949.
5. *PPH*, 2 May 1950.
6. Anecdotes.
7. *WES*, 9 March 1949.
8. *Mr. Ace* reviewed in *WMS*, 26 October 1946; Marjorie Rosen, *Popcorn Venus: Women, Movies and the American Dream* (New York: Avon Books, 1974), 207–211; Molly Haskell, *From Reverence to Rape* (Chicago: University of Chicago Press, 1987), 203, 227.
9. "Washington & You."
10. The Senate as a closed society, with firmly established folkways and norms, was examined by William S. White and Donald R. Matthews in the 1960s. Interestingly, these authors, when faced with the presence of a woman senator, chose to ignore her presence (White) or dismiss her as an anomaly. William S. White, *Citadel: the Story of the U.S. Senate* (Boston: Houghton Mifflin Co., 1968); Donald R. Matthews, *U.S. Senators and Their World* (Chapel Hill: University of North Carolina Press, 1960), 13–14.
11. The others were: Get yourself a "no" man; Get on with the press; Don't orate; Identify yourself with a dramatic issue; Don't hold grudges; Take care of the home folks; Campaign all the time. Lilian Rixey, "Mrs. Smith Really Goes to Town," *Colliers*, 29 July 1950, 42.
12. Doris Fleeson, *Nation's Business*, September 1946, 72.
13. 6 December 1948, Georgia Congressional Delegation file, MCSL.
14. MCSI, 1 April 1992.
15. *WES*, 11 February 1949.
16. Smith, interview by Judith Burton-Norris, Northwood Videotape No.2, MCSL.
17. MCSI, 8 December 1989.
18. Ibid.
19. Anne Herrin, interview by author, Canaan, ME, 22 June 1994.
20. Helen Markel, "Twenty-four Hours in the Life of Margaret Chase Smith," *McCall's*, May 1964, 161.
21. MCSI, 18 July 1992.
22. Statements & Speeches, vol. 14, 22 April 1957.
23. Jane Anton, Dorinda Putnam, and Louise Marsh, interview by author,

Scarborough, ME, 20 July 1990; John M. Bernier and Charlotte Bernier interview by author, Carrabassett, ME, 9 October 1992; Bouchard interview, 11 June 1993. While Lewis' net worth is unknown, he and his parents had considerable investments in Texas and Oklahoma oil. Lewis left all his property to Smith when he died in 1982. WCL file, MCSL.

24. Lawrence F. Willard, "The Lady from Maine," *Yankee*, November 1977, 148.
25. *WCL Summaries*; materials in Election files, MCSL.
26. Samuel Shaffer, *On and Off the Floor: Thirty Years as a Correspondent on Capitol Hill* (New York: Newsweek Books, 1980), 186.
27. Lewis to Bolton, 10 December 1953, Bolton-Smith Correspondence, MCSL; this is also a very strong theme throughout Smith, *Declaration*, which Lewis authored as well as edited.
28. MCSI, 6 June 1989.
29. MCSI, 3 September 1989.
30. Matthews, *Their World*, 85; Harrison W. Fox, Jr. and Susan Webb Hammond. *Congressional Staffs: The Invisible Force in American Lawmaking* (New York: The Free Press, 1977), 87–90, 145–149; Kenneth Kohmehl, *Professional Staffs of Congress* (West Lafayette, IN: Purdue University Studies, 1962), 167–170.
31. Bouchard interview, 11 June 1993; Gwendolyn Angell and Patricia Angell, interview by author, Chicago, 4 November 1991; MCSI, 13 March 1989.
32. MCSI, 30 August 1989.
33. Anecdotes.
34. Bernier interview, 9 October 1992; MCSI, 3 September 1989.
35. *WTH*, 21 July 1949.
36. *WTH*, 2 March 1949.
37. *WMS*, 3 January 1949.
38. Statements & Speeches, vol. 6, 8 January 1949; Baker, *Friend and Foe*, 185.
39. Sharp, *Congressional Voting*, 944.
40. *Meet the Press*, Statements & Speeches, vol. 6, 10 December 1948.
41. Statements & Speeches, vol. 6, 8 January 1949; also in *CR*, 81st Cong., 1st Sess., 10 January 1949, A77.
42. The suggestion was not that far-fetched. In June 1940, FDR had appointed two prominent Republicans to his cabinet: Henry L. Stimson as Secretary of War and Frank Knox as Secretary of the Navy, in an effort to form a coalition government and present a united America to a world at war. Telegram, 3 November 1948, in Official File, HSTL. Smith referred to dismissal of her suggestion by both parties in Statements & Speeches, vol. 8, 8 January 1951.
43. *LEJ*, 15 July 1949; *BH*, 5 June 1950; Rixey "Mrs. Smith" 44.
44. *PPH*, 5 January 1949.
45. Hired by the Republican National Committee to be vice-chairman and director of women's activities in 1936, Martin established a federation of Republican Women's Clubs and pushed through a "fifty-fifty plan" for male and female representatives from each state. Elated by GOP success in 1946, she gave credit to women's role in the victory and expressed the hope for twice as many women delegates in 1948. Within a few days, Taft's handpicked RNC chairman, Carroll Reece, asked for Martin's resignation. Clare B. Williams, *History of the Founding and Development of the National Federation of Republican Women* (Washington, D.C.: Republican National Committee, 1962); *WES*, 18 January 1947.

46. *BC*, 19 January 1949.

47. *PPH*, 2 October 1948; *WCL Notes*, 242–246, MCSL; MCSI, 5 September 1990, 22 September 1992.

48. *WES*, 30 January 1949; *PPH*, 20 January 1949.

49. *WTH*, 26 March 1949.

50. *NYM*, 7 September 1949.

51. Clippings, Scrapbook 76, October and November 1949.

52. NBC broadcast quoted in *WTH*, 19 June 1949.

53. *LEJ*, 2 November 1949.

54. *BDN*, 10 October 1949.

55. Ibid., 15 November 1949; *NYT*, 12 November 1949.

56. *WES*, 14 September 1949.

57. *PST*, 10 April 1949.

58. *DKJ*, 7 October 1949; *WES*, 19 April 1950; " The Lady from Maine," *Newsweek,* 12 June 1950, 24–26.

59. Washington Trends, *Newsweek*, 20 June 1949, 14.

60. Smith interview in Statements & Speeches, vol. 6, 18 September 1949; AP story, 19 September 1949, Scrapbook 74.

61. Statements & Speeches, vol. 7, 25 February 1950.

62. *Lincoln (Nebraska) Journal*, 26 May 1949, clipping Scrapbook 73; Statements & Speeches, vol. 9, 27 February 1952.

63. Statements & Speeches, vol. 6, 30 January 1949.

64. Bernard Baruch file, MCSL; Harry Shapiro, *WP*, 20 March 1949.

65. MCSI, 2 May 1989.

66. *WN*, 19 August 1949; *The Five Percenter Investigation,* 81st Cong., 2d Sess., January 1950, Interim Report in Government Operations Committee file, MCSL.

67. Picture of Hunt's office wall, including her photo, in "Friendship Racket," *Life*, 1 August 1949, 21; see also *WTH*, 29 August, 1949; Lewis Summary: *Marion Martin*, MCSL.

68. Richard M. Rovere, *Senator Joe McCarthy* (New York: Harper & Row, Publishers, 1959), 105–106; David M. Oshinsky, *A Conspiracy So Immense: The World of Joe McCarthy* (New York: The Free Press, 1983), 63.

69. Smith, *Declaration*, 6.

70. Letter to Theta Sigma Phi, 7 February 1950, Joseph R. McCarthy file, MCSL.

71. Statements & Speeches, vol. 7, 1 January 1950.

72. Ibid., 14 January 1950.

73. Ibid., 10 February 1950. Also in *CR*, 81st Cong., 2d Sess., 3 March 1950, A1,591–1,592.

74. The only differences between the Smith version and the official "digest" was the latter dropped her last point, "smashing the filibuster on civil rights," in favor of a less precise "preserving the rights of veterans and minorities," and added a promise of fair market prices for farm products. Digest, 3 April 1950, copy in Scrapbook 84; see also *PPH*, 31 March 1950.

75. *PPH*, 4 January 1950.

76. For discussions of Republican frustration, see Robert Griffith, *The Politics of Fear: Joseph R. McCarthy and the Senate*, 2d ed. (Amherst: The University of Massachusetts Press, 1987), 48; Richard M. Fried, *Men Against McCarthy* (New York: Columbia University Press, 1976), 15–19.

CHAPTER EIGHT: A DECLARATION OF CONSCIENCE

1. Oshinsky discusses the origins of McCarthy's information and numbers in *Conspiracy*, 107–111.
2. Wire, McCarthy to Harry S Truman, 11 February 1950, in *CR*, 81st Cong., 2d Sess., 20 February 1950, 1953.
3. This rhetoric was fairly common in Republican circles. For example, Smith used the phrase "the iron curtain of the Democratic administration" in an earlier speech to denounce administration secrecy about foreign policy objectives; *BDN*, 15 April 1948.
4. Rovere, *Senator Joe*, 131–133.
5. S.Res.231, introduced by Scott Lucas (D-IL) authorizing the Tydings investigation in *CR*, 81st Cong., 2d Sess., 21 February 1950, 2,062; passed 22 February 1950, 2,150.
6. Smith, *Declaration,* 7; MCSI, 2 May 1989.
7. The *Amerasia* case was not prosecuted for a number of valid reasons, among them that the great bulk of the documents found were not in any real sense secret and did not imperil national defense, and that the evidence was obtained in violation of the Fourth Amendment and hence could not be used by the government. See U.S. Senate, Subcommittee of the Committee on Foreign Relations, A Resolution to Investigate Whether There Are Employees in the State Department Disloyal to the United States. Hearings Pursuant to S.Res. 231 (hereinafter cited as *Tydings Subcommittee Hearings*), 81st Cong., 2d Sess., 26 January 1950. *Amerasia* summary in McCarthy file.
8. Oshinsky, *Conspiracy*, 98.
9. Griffith, *Politics of Fear*, 32.
10. Heale, *American Anticommunism*, 136.
11. *Official Report of the Proceedings*, 197.
12. Motto and Statement of Principles in *Republican State* Convention 1950 file, MCSL; *CSM*, 7 February 1950.
13. Michael Schaller et al., *Present Tense: The United States Since 1945* (Boston: Houghton Mifflin Co., 1992), 65.
14. *NYT*, 6 August 1948.
15. Griffith, *Politics of Fear*, 44.
16. Stephen E. Ambrose, *Nixon*, vol. 1: *The Education of a Politician, 1913–1962* (New York: Simon & Schuster, 1987), 211.
17. Oshinsky, *Conspiracy*, 158–59.
18. *CSM*, 24 March 1950, 4 April 1950; Tyler Abell, ed. *Drew Pearson Diaries 1949–1959* (New York: Holt, Rinehart & Winston, 1974), 112–115; James T. Patterson, *Mr. Republican: A Biography of Robert Taft* (Boston: Houghton Mifflin Co., 1972), 455.
19. *CR*, 81st Cong., 2d Sess., 20 February 1950, 1969; *NYT*, 23 March 1950.
20. 1948 platform, CQ, *Guide to U.S. Elections*, 101.
21. *CR*, 81st Cong., 2d Sess., 9 May 1950, A3,426–3,428.
22. Ibid., 6,696.
23. Smith, *Declaration*, 7.
24. *CR*, 81st Cong., 2d Sess., 21 April 1950, A2,863–2,864.
25. Case against Kenyon in *Tydings Subcommittee Hearings*, 16–32.
26. MCSI, 2 May 1989; Smith comments on Kenyon in *USA Confidential* file, MCSL.

27. Oshinsky, *Conspiracy,* 125, 137.

28. Smith vote against establishment of a permanent HUAC, 3 January 1945, and against appropriations of $75,000 for HUAC, 17 May 1946 in *Voting Record,* MCSL; FBI comment in Frank Graham, Frank, *Margaret Chase Smith: Woman of Courage* (New York: The John Day Co.), 1964, 53.

29. S.R.2, 81st Cong., 1st Sess., June 1949; never adopted. "Washington and You," 23 July 1947.

30. MCSI, 2 December 1988, 2 May 1989.

31. Smith, *Declaration,* 8–10.

32. MCSI, 2 May 1989; Smith, *Declaration,* 10.

33. MCSI, 2 May 1989, 15 June 1993.

34. Smith, *Declaration,* 11.

35. They had only agreed to endorse the statement itself. Gregory Gallant, *Margaret Chase Smith, McCarthyism and the Drive for Political Purification* (Ph.D. diss. University of Maine, 1992), 72–75.

36. Her speech was later called her Declaration of Conscience, but that title was initially used to describe only the statement signed by the seven Republican senators; she used the ungainly title "The Growing Confusion—Need for Patriotic Thinking" when recording it on her list of speeches. Complete text of speech and statement in Smith, *Declaration,* 12–18; *CR,* 81st Cong., 2d Sess., 1 June 1950, 7,894–7,895.

37. Smith, *Declaration,* 18.

38. Appointment letter in Scrapbook 86; materials in Labor Organizations, MCSL.

39. *PPH,* 12 June 1950.

40. *BC,* 23 June 1950.

41. *NYDN,* 7 June 1950.

42. Letters in *Declaration of Conscience* file, MCSL.

43. The message was relayed by Doris Fleeson; Front Office Memo, 2 June 1950, copy in Scrapbook 89.

44. From a list of press responses (undated) in *Declaration of Conscience* file, MCSL.

45. "Lady from Maine," 24.

46. Harold L. Ickes, "And a Woman Shall Lead Them," *The New Republic,* 19 June 1950, 16.

47. Pegler, 3 June 1950, clipping in Scrapbook 89.

48. "Smearing is Evil, But Whitewashing of Reds is Worse," *Saturday Evening Post,* 15 July 1950, 10.

49. *NYDN,* 7 June 1950; *WTH,* 11 June 1950; letter to editor of *New Bedford Times* in *CR,* 81st Cong., 2d Sess., 26 June 1950, A4,671.

50. *WP,* 2 June 1950.

51. Rule 19 discussed in "Washington and You," 27 September 1950; Tacheron and Udall, *The Job,* 224.

52. Clippings in Scrapbook 88, June 1950.

53. *PPH,* 3 February 1951.

54. Griffith, *Politics of Fear,* 105.

55. *NYT,* 2 June 1950.

56. See, for example, Rovere, *Senator Joe,* 180; Oshinsky, *Conspiracy,* 165; Gallant, *Political Purification,* 82–84.

57. This apt phrase from Austine, *WTH*, 2 July 1950.

58. Excerpt from Elmer Davis, CBS, 6 June 1950, *USA Confidential* file, MCSL.

59. Ibid., *CR*, 81st Cong., 2d Sess., 6 June 1950, 8,121.

60. *BC*, 11 June 1950, 23 June 1950.

61. Oshinsky, *Conspiracy*, 165.

62. Smith, *Declaration*, 10–11, 26, 29; MCSI, 15 June 1993, 3 August 1993. Morse was always considered too liberal to be taken seriously by the Republican leadership; he later changed parties to run as a Democrat. Correspondence regarding McCarthy in Box 136, Series A, WMP.

63. Oshinsky, *Conspiracy*, 168–169.

64. *NYT*, 18 July 1950.

65. Oshinsky, *Conspiracy*, 169–171.

66. Statements & Speeches, vol. 7, 26 June 1950.

67. Goulden, *Korea*, 62–69.

68. "Washington and You," 16 June 1949.

69. Statements & Speeches, vol. 7, 10 August 1950; "Washington and You," 16 June 1949, 29 September 1950; Statements & Speeches, vol. 7, basic speeches, October 1950.

70. *Maryland Senatorial Election of 1950*, Report No. 647, U.S. Senate, 82d Cong., 1st Sess., Report of the Committee on Rules and Administration pursuant to S.Res.250, 20 August 1951 (hereinafter, *Maryland Election Report*).

71. Scobie, *Center Stage*, 253–281.

72. "Washington and You," 20 October 1950.

73. Ibid., 20 March 1951; Statements & Speeches, vol. 8, 4 January 1951.

74. Truman address to Congress, 19 July 1950, discussed by James Matray, "Truman's Plan for Victory," *The Journal of American History*, September 1979, 314–317.

75. Statements & Speeches, vol. 7, 10 August 1950.

76. Ibid., vol. 8, 4 January 1951.

77. "Washington and You," 9 January 1951.

78. *WP*, 3 December 1950.

79. To Hugh Butler (R-NE), 18 November 1950, Nebraska Congressional Delegation file, MCSL.

80. Steven S. Smith and Christopher J. Deering, *Committees in Congress* (Washington DC: Congressional Quarterly, Inc., 1984), 76–78.

81. 27 November 1950, Owen Brewster file, MCSL.

82. McCarthy to Smith, 25 January 1951, Government Operations Committee file, MCSL. Executive Expenditures became Government Operations in 1953.

83. Smith, *Declaration*, 23.

84. *Maryland Election Report*, MCSL, 8–9.

85. Benton to Smith, 4 August 1951, Signature file, MCSL.

86. S.Res.187, 6 August 1951, copy in McCarthy file, MCSl.

87. Smith, *Declaration*, 29.

88. Quoted in "Benton Tries to Throw Him Out," *Life*, 15 October 1951, 58.

89. *CR*, 82d Cong., 1st Sess., 20 August 1951, 10,332–10,334.

90. Ibid.

91. Ibid., 10,336–10,337.

92. Statements & Speeches, vol. 9, 6 February 1952.

93. *Investigations of Senators Joseph R. McCarthy and William Benton pursuant*

to *S.Res.187 and S.Res.304*, Report of the Subcommittee on Privileges and Elections to the Committee on Rules and Administration, 61.

94. Ibid., 59–102; quotation on 62.

95. P&E Minutes, 7 March 1952, Rules and Administration file, MCSL; letter, 21 March 1952, *Investigations of Senators McCarthy and Benton*, 67–68.

96. S.Res. 300, 82d Cong., 2d Sess., 8 April 1952; *Investigations of Senators McCarthy and Benton*, 68–69.

97. Robert L. Strout, *CSM*, 20 April 1952.

98. *CR*, 82d Cong., 2d Sess., 10 April 1952, 3,942–3,943.

99. *Investigations of Senators McCarthy and Benton*, 1–11.

100. Ibid., 45.

101. Lait and Mortimer, *USA Confidential*, book jacket.

102. Ibid., 128, 88.

103. Wels first demanded a retraction, then filed *Civil Action No. 75–246*, "U.S. District Court, Southern District of New York; Margaret Chase Smith, Plaintiff vs Crown Publishers, Inc., Jack Lait and Lee Mortimer, Defendants," 7 May 1952, in *USA Confidential* file, MCSL.

104. *NYP*, 18 June 1952; "The Sued Sue," *Time*, 26 May 1952, 47.

105. Letter, Wels to Lewis, 9 March 1952, and discussion of libel law as pertaining to public officials from Legislative Reference Service, *USA Confidential* file, MCSL.

106. *Civil Action No.75–246*, deposition of Lee Mortimer, 21 July 1955, 22–29, *USA Confidential file*, MCSL.

107. *CR*, 82d Cong., 2d Sess., 26 May 1952, 5,963.

108. Brunauer's husband, Stephen, had been suspended from the Navy for refusing to testify before the Loyalty Board. Mrs. Brunauer, though exonerated on loyalty grounds, was deemed a security risk because of her marriage and dismissed in 1952. Depositions in *USA Confidential* file. MCSL.

109. Ibid., Interrogatories.

110. Ibid., Exhibit B.

111. Ibid., Smith deposition, 6 February 1954, 234.

112. Ibid., Mortimer deposition, 21 September 1956, 20.

113. *NYHT*, 18 October 1956.

114. *USA Confidential* file, MCSL, *Declaration*, 40–41.

115. *USA Confidential* file, MCSL.

116. MCSI, 3 August 1993.

117. Staple speech of 1950–1952; for examples see Statements & Speeches, vol. 8, 16 June 51 and 2 October 1951.

118. Talberth, *PST*, 22 July 1951.

119. *PPH*, 27 September 1951.

120. *PPH*, 23 September 1951; Tris Coffin, "The Drive to Stop Eisenhower," *The New Republic*, 1 October 1951, 9.

121. *PPH*, 18 September 1951; letter, Smith to Judge Conant, 25 September 1951, Correspondence files, MCSL.

122. *PEE*, 17 September 1951; Statements & Speeches, vol. 9, 16 March 1952.

123. *PST*, 30 March 1952; *BC*, 30 March 1952.

124. George Gallup, "What the GOP Needs to Win in '52," *Look*, 25 September 1951, 37–39; *CSM*, 21 May 1952.

125. "Their Hats Were in the Ring," *Independent Woman*, August 1952, 226.
126. Ibid.
127. Sherman Adams, *Firsthand Report: The Story of the Eisenhower Administration* (New York: Harper & Brothers, 1961), 15–17; MCSI, 2 May 1989, 2 November 1989.
128. Her usual response to such talk was to claim, accurately, that her Declaration of Conscience, "removed even the remotest possibility of that happening." Statements & Speeches, vol. 7, 6 July 1950.
129. Luce to Smith, 13 August 1952, Signature file, MCSL.
130. Smith's handwritten memo, Eisenhower Administration file, MCSL.
131. Letter, 12 September 1952, Papers as President, Name Series, Box 31, DDEL.
132. Although Eisenhower was disturbed by the reference to her being an American first, he decided to let it stand. As received, her letter omitted that concern. Eisenhower draft, 23 August 1952, in Ibid. Letter, 25 August 1952, Signature file.
133. Smith letter to William Peters, 20 August 1952, Papers as President, Box 31, DDEL.
134. *WP*, 21 August 1952.
135. Smith, "Why Vote for Eisenhower?" *Woman's Home Companion*, November 1952, 38–39; full text as submitted in Smith, *Declaration*, 125–134.
136. Memos, Eisenhower Administration file, MCSL.
137. Adams, *Firsthand Report*, 31; Griffith, *Politics of Fear*, 193.
138. Memo, Eisenhower Administration files, MCSL.
139. Margaret Smith for Vice President file, MCSL.
140. Eisenhower to Smith, 25 November 1952, Signature file, MCSL; letter, Smith to Eisenhower, 19 December 1952, Eisenhower Administration file, MCSL.

CHAPTER NINE: SMITH VERSUS JONES

1. Tris Coffin and Douglass Cater, "About–Face! The Story of Senator Brewster," *The Reporter*, 10 June 1952, 12–16. Series in *BC*, 18 May to 15 June 1952; *WP*, 1 August 1954; *WN*, 4 August 1954.
2. Payne was exonerated after a four-month probe by the state attorney general but not before he was challenged to demonstrate his fitness to take his seat in the Senate. *BDN*, 3 January 1953; *PPH*, 30 July 1953; Maine Liquor Commission Investigation file, MCSL.
3. Quoted in *NYT*, 18 June 1952.
4. MCSI, 18 January 1989, 2 May 1989.
5. *Congressional Directory*, 83d Cong., 1st Sess., MCSL.
6. *WES*, 30 February 1954.
7. Letters in Brewster file, MCSL.
8. Abell, *Pearson Diaries*, 33; Pearson, *WP*, 18 August 1954.
9. Brewster file, MCSL.
10. *BG*, 12 April 1953; *BC*, 19 April 1953; "Gen. Van Fleet: Enough Ammunition for What? Not to Win the War, and That Was What He Wanted," *U.S. News and World Report*, 20 March 1953, 76–80; Smith audiotapes with Fred Rhodes, 27 June 1985, MCSL.
11. *Ammunition Shortages in the Armed Services*, Hearings before Preparedness Subcommittee No. 2 of the Committee on Armed Services, U.S. Senate,

83d Congress, 1st Session, 1, 8, 9, 10, 13, 15, 16, 17 and 20 April 1953, 1–709; Van Fleet testimony, 5–23.

12. Ibid., Interim report, 12.

13. Ibid., Hearings, 589–655.

14. MacArthur to Harry F. Byrd, 19 April 1953; copy in ASC file, MCSL.

15. Ibid., Interim report, 8.

16. Statements & Speeches, vol. 10, 24 May 1953.

17. *Ammunition Shortages,* Interim report, 15–18; *WN,* 18 April 1953.

18. Statements & Speeches, vol. 11, 30 August 1954; like many of her speeches, parts of this one were used many times for other occasions.

19. Statements & Speeches, vol. 10, 20 May 1953. She did not get the answers she sought and complained about it on the floor. *CR,* 83d Cong., 1st Sess., 22 July 1953, 9,472–9,474.

20. WHCF, Official Files, Box 652, Folder OF133, DDEL.

21. MCSI, 24 June 1993.

22. Bouchard, interview; Joe Gonzales, interview by author, Showhegan, ME, 2 September 1992.

23. S.200 and S.1409 (later renumbered S.1824), 7 January 1953, 83d Cmng., 1st Sess.; copies in Communism file, MCSL.

24. Statements & Speeches, vol. 10, 30 May 1952.

25. Legislative Reference Service, "Bills to Outlaw the Communist Party and Related Bills 77th Through 82d Congresses (First Session)," 15 January 1952, Communism file, MCSL.

26. *Vermont Courier* editorial, n.d.; other clippings in Scrapbook 135.

27. Communism file, MCSL.

28. S.Res 211; Statements & Speeches, vol. 11, 4 July 1954.

29. Ibid., 22 May 1954.

30. Stephen Schlesinger and Stephen Kinzer, *Bitter Fruit: The Untold Story of the American Coup in Guatemala* (New York: Anchor Press, 1983); Kermit Roosevelt, *Countercoup: The Struggle for the Control of Iran* (New York: McGraw-Hill Publishing Co., 1979).

31. Texas and Pennsylvania outlawed the Communist Party; Delaware and Michigan required Communists to register, and thirteen states had statutes barring the Communist Party from election ballots. *WP,* 2 May 1954.

32. *CR,* 83d Cong., 2d Sess., 12 August 1954, 14,208–14,234; 17 August 1954, 14,721–14,727.

33. *WP,* 13 August 1954.

34. *CR,* 83d Cong., 2d Sess., 17 August 1954, 14,725.

35. Public Law 637, *CR,* 83d Cong., 2d Sess., 24 August 1954, 15,837.

36. "Washington and You," 13 August 1953; portions reprinted in "Bomb for Barbarians," *Time,* 24 August 1953, 12.

37. *CR,* 83d Cong., 1st Sess., 3 August 1953, 11,073; Marquis Childs, *NYP,* 23 August 1963; letters, Smith to *NYT,* August and September 1953, Press Relationships file, MCSL.

38. "McCarthyism—First Test," *Newsweek,* 5 April 1954, 23.

39. *WES,* 19 August 1954; Elizabeth Donahue, "Maine: Can Jones Beat Smith?" *The New Republic,* 17 May 1954, 10–11.

40. Oshinsky, *Conspiracy,* 374–377.

41. *CSM,* 17 June 1954.

42. *NYT*, 23 February 1954; Charles E. Potter, *Days of Shame* (New York: Coward-McCann, 1965), 85.

43. *Newsweek,* 5 April 1954, 23.

44. Craig, *PPH*, 30 May 1954.

45. *Newsweek*, 5 April 1954, 23.

46. Memo, Charles F. Willis, Jr. to RNC Chair Leonard Hall, 13 April 1954, WHCF, Official File, Box 692, Maine, DDEL.

47. Geoffrey Elan, "Smith versus Jones," *Yankee*, June 1954, 34.

48. *PPE*, 23 February 1954; Elan, "Smith versus Jones," 33.

49. The Army McCarthy hearings consumed 35 sessions and 187 hours of live television over a period of 57 days. Oshinsky, *Conspiracy*, 416–471.

50. Quoted in Thomas C. Reeves, *Life and Times of Joe McCarthy* (New York: Stein & Day), 547.

51. Oshinsky, *Conspiracy*, 464.

52. Smith, *Declaration*, 53.

53. *PPH*, 23 February 1954; *CSM*, 27 February 1954.

54. *FFR*, 28 April 1954. Contributions verified by Tris Coffin, *PST*, 19 February 1956; Coffin Affidavit, 14 June 1961, in Election 1954 file, MCSL.

55. Front Office Notes, Vol.3, MCSL.

56. Abrahamson Correspondence file, MCSL; *PPH*, 30 May 1953.

57. *RFT*, 4 June 1954.

58. *See It Now* broadcast, 9 March 1954, MCSL; discussion of broadcast and reactions to it in Oshinsky, *Conspiracy*, 399.

59. Edward R. Murrow, *See It Now*, 8 June 1954, videotape, MCSL.

60. Smith: 96,457; Jones: 19,336. Data from MCSL.

61. *NYHT*, 23 June 1954.

62. *NYT,* 23 June 1954.

63. "Senator McCarthy's Political Power," *The Christian Century*, 7 July 1954, 811–812.

64. Smith, *Declaration*, 58–59.

65. Oshinsky, *Conspiracy*, 396–397.

66. *CR*, 83d Cong., 2d Sess., 1 June 1954, 7,389–7,390.

67. Ibid., 30 July 1954, 1,2729–1,2742.

68. Henry interview, 10 July 1991; Garland, *Pine Tree Politics*, 82; David Clayton Smith, "Maine Politics 1950–1956" (M.A. thesis, University of Maine, 1958), 91–95.

69. *DKJ*, 5 April 1954; Nicoll interview, 17 February 1994; Garland, *Pine Tree Politics*, 166–168.

70. *LDS*, 6 August 1954.

71. Staple campaign speech, Statements & Speeches, vol. 11, 8 May 1954, 30 August 1954.

72. Quoted in Smith, *Declaration*, 151.

73. Statements & Speeches, vol. 11, 12 September 1954; text also in Smith, *Declaration*.

74. The practice was "common in Maine . . . liberal Democrats would enroll as Republicans so they could vote in the primary." Donald E. Nicoll, interview by author, Portland, ME, 17 February 1994.

75. Smith, *Declaration,* 163. Less than a year later, Fullam died of a heart ailment.

76. Smith, *Maine Politics*, 106–110.

77. 1954 had been expected to be a "building year" in preparation for a big push in 1956. Nicoll interview.

78. Theo Lippman, Jr., and Donald C. Hansen, *Muskie* (New York: W.W. Norton & Co., 1971), 75.

79. AP clipping in Callaghan Collection, College Files, CC1–2, ESMA.

CHAPTER TEN: AMAZON WARMONGER

1. MCSI, 7 May 1989, 6 June 1989.

2. She visited twenty-three countries—Great Britain, France, Germany, Switzerland, Czechoslovakia, Russia, Finland, Denmark, Spain, Ireland, Japan, Formosa, Philippines, Vietnam, Hong Kong, Thailand, Burma, India, Pakistan, Egypt, Turkey, Greece, and Italy—and interviewed nearly every major world leader, including British Prime Minister Winston Churchill, French General Charles De Gaulle, German Chancellor Konrad Adenauer, USSR Deputy Premier and Foreign Minister Vyacheslav Molotov, Generalissimo and Madame Chiang Kai–Shek, Vietnam President Ngo Dinh Diem, Burmese Prime Minister U Nu, India's Prime Minister Jawaharlal Nehru, Prime Minister Gamel Abdel Nasser of Egypt, and Generalissimo Francisco Franco of Spain. World Trip, 1954–1955 file, MCSL.

3. Statements & Speeches, vol. 11, 21 September 1954. Complete set of CBS videotapes, edited televised programs, and raw footage, in MCSL.

4. World Trip file, MCSL.

5. *See It Now* videos and transcripts, MCSL.

6. *DKJ*, 30 March 1955.

7. Reports, Parts I through VI, in World Trip file, MCSL.

8. "World Trip, Part II," World Trip file, MCSL.

9. "Russian Embassy," World Trip file, MCSL.

10. Smith describes the incident on *See It Now* videotape, *East Berlin Visit, October 20, 1954*; see also German newspaper clipping with English translation in World Trip file, MCSL; MCSI, 7 May 1989.

11. Quotes from *LEJ*, 10 December 1954; *PPH*, 11 December 1954.

12. The camera crew was not allowed in Russia. Summary prepared by Frank G. Siscoe, First Secretary of the American Embassy, from notes taken of Smith's and Lewis's oral recollections of the interview shortly after its completion, and memo of Charles A. Bohlen, American Ambassador to the Soviet Union, in World Trip.

13. *PPH*, 31 October 1954; Rose McKee, *WP*, 13 November 1954; "World Trip, Part III."

14. Statements & Speeches, vol. 12, 18 April 1955.

15. U.S. Senate, 83d Cong., 2d Sess., *Report of the Select Subcommittee to Study Censure Charges*, Report #2508, pursuant to the order on S.Res.301, "A Resolution to Censure the Senator from Wisconsin, Mr. McCarthy," copy in McCarthy file, MCSL.

16. Price Daniel (D-TX) and Barry Goldwater also urged apology to head off censure. Merle Miller, *Lyndon: An Oral Biography.* (New York: G. P. Putnam's Sons, 1980), 172–173.

17. Copy in Working Papers, F1790, EMDP; Oshinsky, *Conspiracy*, 488.

18. Brunelle, *MST*, 28 November 1971. Payne voted with the majority for censure.

19. *CR*, 83d Cong., 2d Sess., 10 November 1954, 15,953.

20. Ibid., 2 December 1954, 16,392; *BP,* 3 December 1954; clippings in File 128, Folder 32, CHP.

21. Official cause of death was "acute hepatitis," but his biographer says simply, "he drank himself to death." Oshinsky, *Conspiracy,* 505.

22. Resolution and letter in McCarthy file.

23. Letters concerning move to expunge the record and JFK's discomfort with the issue of censure in Pre-Presidential Papers; Senate Files; Legislation Files 1953–1960; Box 674, Senator McCarthy, JFKL; Working Papers, F1790, EMDP. Criticism of Smith in McCarthy file; *WP,* 14 June 1957; David Lawrence, "Justice to the Memory of Senator McCarthy," *U.S. News and World Report,* 7 June 1957, 139–144.

24. Dwight D. Eisenhower, *The White House Years: Mandate for Change, 1953–1956* (Garden City, N.Y.: Doubleday & Co., 1963), 470.

25. Ibid., 476–477.

26. *CR*, 84th Cong., 1st Sess., 26 January 1955, 764–765.

27. Eisenhower, *Mandate,* 459–475; Bundy, McGeorge, *Danger and Survival: Choices About the Bomb in the First Fifty Years* (New York: Random House, 1988), 273–279.

28. "World Trip Part IV," *See It Now,* #26, videotape, MCSL.

29. Stephen E. Ambrose, *Eisenhower: The President* (New York: Simon & Schuster, 1984), 47, 235–244.

30. *See It Now,* #26, broadcast 15 March 1955, MCSL.

31. Bundy, *Danger and Survival,* 279; Ambrose, *The President,* 244.

32. *Red Star,* 4 March 1955, in *PPH,* 5 March 1955. *PPH* editorial, 7 March 1955, called the designation an honor and noted such an attack should silence those who taunt Smith about her softness towards the Reds.

33. *CR*, 84th Cong., 1st Sess., 2 June 1955, 7,598–7,600. Myriad other examples especially during the 1950s in Statements & Speeches.

34. "World Trip, Part VI," World Trip files, MCSL.

35. *BDN,* 14 March 1955; *PPH,* 28 March 1955; *DKJ,* 30 March 1955.

36. Statements & Speeches, vol. 12, 24 March 1955.

37. "World Trip Report" to the Senate, World Trip file, MCSL.

38. Statements & Speeches, vol. 12, 26 May 1955.

39. Smith's overall support for Eisenhower was 86%, 100% on foreign policy. Congressional Quarterly file, MCSL.

40. The House failed to authorize the funds for the survey. Smith to Sherman Adams, 12 January 1955, Eisenhower Administration file; WHCF; Box 838; Folder 155–E–G "Passamaquoddy Dam," DDEL; chronology in Passamaquoddy Tidal Power Project file, MCSL.

41. *BDN,* 11 February 1955.

42. Ibid; *PST,* 27 February 1955; *BP,* 6 March 1955.

43. *BG,* 28 June 1955; Rose McKee, *WP,* n.d., clip in Scrapbook 163; *PEE,* 28 June 1955.

44. Richard Nixon, *RN: The Memoirs of Richard Nixon* (New York: Grosset & Dunlap, 1978), 167–170. Letters and petitions to oust Nixon in WHCF, General File, Box 96, File 109–A–16, DDEL. Those specific to Smith in Box 574, File 109–A–16 and Box 563, File 109–A–10, DDEL. Robert J. Dinkin, *Campaigning in America: A History of Election Practices* (Westport, CT: Greenwood Press, 1989),183.

45. *WP*, 17 June 1955; *CSM*, 28 April 1955; Fletcher Knebel, "Did Ike Really Want Nixon?" *Look*, 30 October 1956, 25–27.
46. *PPH*, 24 March 1956; *PPH*, 20 August 1956.
47. *BSA*, 19 August 1956.
48. "An Interview with Frank M. Coffin, Democratic State Chairman, *U.S. News and World Report*, 21 September 1956, 39–40.
49. Lippman and Hansen, *Muskie*, 84–86.
50. *FFR*, 29 August 1956; *WMS*, 12 September 1956.
51. *IR*, 11 September 1956.
52. Lippman and Hansen, *Muskie*, 87.
53. Smith, *Maine Politics*, 122.
54. Smith, *Declaration*, 203–211.
55. Cease-fire in Egypt ordered by Great Britain and France on November 6; it was early December before they agreed, under U.S. pressure, to withdraw from the territory. Eight Soviet divisions moved into Hungary November 4 (the very day of the broadcast) while most of the world was distracted by events in the Middle East.
56. Ambrose, *The President*, 329–338.
57. *CR*, 84th Cong., 2d Sess., 27 June 1956, 11,111; 28 June 1956, 11,253.
58. Statements & Speeches, vol. 13, 18 August 1956.
59. Ambrose, *The President*, 358–31.
60. Ibid., 367.
61. *Face the Nation*, 4 November 1956, videotape, MCSL.
62. MCSI, 2 November 1989.
63. Statements & Speeches, vol. 16, 26 September 1958.
64. Average wages at Boston were $2.50; average at Kittery, $2.21 per hour.
65. *CR*, 85th Cong., 2d Sess., 12 August 1958, 17,022–17,026; MCSI, 2 December 1988, 31 July 1989.
66. Congressional Quarterly, *Congress and the Nation 1945–1964*. vol. 1. (Washington, D.C.: Congressional Quarterly, 1964), 645.
67. Eve Moertl Bither, interview by author, Augusta, ME, 10 September 1990; Bither Correspondence file, MCSL.
68. Smith, "The Nation's Progress in Education, Social Security, Health and the General Welfare Under Republican Administration," *CR*, 86th Cong., 2d Sess., 1 July 1960, 15,447–15,449.
69. Lyndon Baines Johnson, *The Vantage Point: Perspectives of the Presidency, 1963–1969* (New York: Holt, Rinehart & Winston, 1971), 272–277.
70. Bill Deachman, interview by Margaret Chase Smith (about the Aeronautical and Space Science Committee), audiotape, MCSL; MCSI, 5 September 1990.
71. Statements & Speeches, vol. 16, 12 January 1958; Statements & Speeches, vol. 15, 1 December 1957.
72. *Congress and the Nation*, 1:1,582.
73. Lewis served with Director of Legislation and Liaison, USAF, 1955–1959 and Deputy Assistant to the Secretary of Defense for Legislative Affairs, 1959–1972. Lewis's service record in WHCF; Exec National Security–Defense; Box 168, Folder ND 9–8–1/FG130 12/18/65–1/17/66, LBJL. See also letters between Lewis and Defense Secretary Melvin Laird, 21 December 1972, in WCL file, MCSL.

74. Among 40 reserve officers in Congress, 6 of them were generals: 2 Representatives and 4 Senators, including Goldwater, Thurmond and Howard Cannon (D-NV), who served on the Armed Services Committee; Rep. Robert Sikes (D-FL) served on the Defense Appropriations Subcommittee. *Congress and the Nation*, 1:1582.

75. *CR*, 85th Cong., 1st Sess., 30 August 1957, 16,708–16,719; Smith, *Declaration*, 225.

76. *CR*, 85th Cong., 1st Sess., 23 August 1957, 15,729–15,730.

77. *WES*, 17 July 1959; Smith, *Declaration*, 232.

78. Smith to Russell, 19 May 1959, ASC file, MCSL.

79. *NYHT*, 19 June 1959.

80. *Promotion of Reserve Officers to General and Flag Ranks*, Report of the Preparedness Investigating Subcommittee of the Committee on Armed Services, U.S. Senate, 86th Cong., 1st Sess., 1959, in Scrapbook 210.

81. *LDS*, 18 March 1959; *PPH*, 23 July 1959.

82. *NYT*, 18 June 1953.

83. Clinton P. Anderson, *Outsider in the Senate: Senator Clinton Anderson's Memoirs* (New York: World Publishing Co., 1970), 188–189.

84. MCSI, 2 December 1988, 1 August 1989; Smith, *Declaration*, 139–140.

85. Anderson, *Outsider*, 192–197.

86. Richard Pfau, *No Sacrifice Too Great: The Life of Lewis L. Strauss* (Charlottesville: University Press of Virginia, 1984), 222–223.

87. Ibid., 228.

88. The 1958 elections changed the Senate from 49 Democrats, 47 Republicans to 64 Democrats, 34 Republicans.

89. Anderson, *Outsider*, 185–221; Ambrose, *The President*, 345.

90. Quoted in Miller, *Lyndon*, 221.

91. Pfau, *No Sacrifice*, 241.

92. *Nomination of Lewis L. Strauss . . .*, Report of the Committee on Interstate and Foreign Commerce, Executive Report No.4, in Lewis L. Strauss file, MCSL; *WP*, 2 June 1959.

93. *LDS*, 1 June 1959.

94. Smith's Front Office Notes, 22 May 1959, mention Strauss visit, "did not ask for com [*sic*]—I did not make one." Copy in Strauss file, MCSL.

95. *WP*, 4 June 1959; MCSI, 1 August 1989.

96. Anderson, *Outsider*, 219.

97. *WP*, 24 June 1959; *Newsweek*, 29 June 1959, clipping with Goldwater disclaimer in Election 1960 file, MCSL; Shaffer, *On and Off the Floor*, 198. Acknowledging Strauss as "a very close personal friend of mine," Goldwater later disclaimed any threats against Smith, saying he just banged his hand on the desk; Senator Barry Goldwater, interview by author, Phoenix, AZ, 7 March 1994. MCSI, 6 June 1989, 27 July 1989.

98. Pfau, *No Sacrifice*, 240.

99. Anderson, *Outsider*, 218; "The Congress: 'This Sad Episode,'" *Time*, 29 June 1959, 8–10; John L. Steele, "Passions and Stratagems in the Fall of Strauss," *Life*, 29 June 1959, 28; Jack Anderson, *Confessions of a Muckraker* (New York: Random House, 1979), 321–323; Tyler Abell, ed., *Pearson Diaries*, 524; Pfau, *No Sacrifice*, 240; Samuel Shaffer, *On and Off the Floor*,198.

100. Smith's copy of *Nomination* report with underlinings in Strauss file, MCSL.

101. *PPH*, 25 June 1959; editorials and letters of support in Scrapbook 207, June 1959.

102. Eisenhower, *Waging Peace*, 395–396.

103. Ambrose, *Eisenhower,* 530.

104. Smith, *Declaration*, 141.

105. Statements & Speeches, vol. 17, 29 August 1958; MCSI, 14 February 1989, 2 May 1989.

106. *BDN*, 15 June 1958; *WES*, 18 August 1958; Lippman and Hansen, *Muskie*, 92–93.

107. *CR*, 85th Cong., 2d Sess., 14 March 1958, 4,397–4,398. Later, charges of bribery and influence peddling by some oil company lobbyists led to an investigation of corrupt practices by a Special Senate Committee. *Congress and the Nation*, 1:1,736.

108. *LEJ*, 20 February 1958.

109. Letter, 14 February 1958, Republican Party Senatorial Committee file, MCSL.

110. *WP*, 26 February 1958; *WES*, 22 February 1958; *PPH*, 24 February 1958; "National Affairs: The Lady Said No." *Newsweek,* 3 March 1958, 24.

111. Governor Clinton Clauson, Senator Muskie, Frank Coffin was reelected in the Second District, and James Oliver won over the incumbent, Robert Hale, in the First District.

112. *Congress and the Nation,* 1:78.

113. *LDJ*, 6 January 1959.

114. Smith went through her whole campaign without any money from the Senatorial Campaign Committee. A check for her customary $5000 arrived November 14, dated November 10, two days after the election on November 8, in Election 1960, MCSL.

115. See, for example, their exchange of letters regarding National Guard training criteria, which rapidly deteriorates into accusations of deliberate misunderstandings and unwarranted criticism, 30 January 1957 through 4 March 1957; many others in Muskie Correspondence file, MCSL.

116. *BDN*, 13 July 1960, 30 August 1958; *WP*, 2 September 1958.

117. *PPH*, 8 January 1959; *WP*, 11 January 1959.

118. *BDN*, 23 January 1960; *PST*, 31 January 1960; Nicoll, interview, 17 February 1994.

119. Smith, *Declaration*, 242; Cormier interview with May Craig, audiotape, MCSL.

120. Election 1960 file, MCSL; MCSI, 14 February 1989, 16 April 1992.

121. *WP*, 6 November 1960.

122. *PST*, 5 June 1960; *PEE*, 9 August 1960; *WMS*, 15 September 1960.

123. *NYHT*, 18 September 1960.

124. Statements & Speeches, vol. 15, 22 September 1957 and 8 October 1957. *WP*, 1 March 1960; *CSM*, 7 March 1960.

125. Statements & Speeches, vol. 19, 19 November 1959; Statements & Speeches, vol. 20, 30 April 1960.

126. *WES*, 19 January 1964; Judge Donald Nichols, interview by author, Waterville, ME, 23 March 1994.

127. *PST*, 16 October 1960; *WP*, 6 November 1960.

128. *PPH*, 31 October 1960; *WP*, 6 July 1961; *FFR*, 9 October 1963.

129. Most of the letters are by Lewis, often indicated by an "L" on the dictation

line; hers were usually rough drafts or notes to friends typed on what appeared to be an ancient typewriter. For abundant examples, see Press Relationships files, MCSL.

130. WCL Summaries, MCSL.
131. *BDN*, 2 August 1960; raw footage of receiving lines in MCSL.
132. *NYT*, 1 October 1960.
133. Ambrose, *The President*, 569–579.
134. *WP*, 19 May 1960; *NYT*, 19 May 1960.
135. *CR*, 86th Cong., 2d Sess., 23 May 1960, 10,794–10,796; 24 May 1960, 10,926; 14 June 1960, 12,536, 12,544–12,545.
136. Eisenhower Administration file, MCSL.
137. "Women: As Maine Goes. . . . ", *Time*, 5 September 1960, 13–16.
138. *PEE*, 14 June 1960; Anne Hannan, *Newsday*, 18 October 1960, 43; similar remarks in Statements & Speeches, vol. 21, 28 October 1960; MCSI, 29 October 1993.
139. *PPH*, 7 November 1960; *WP*, 6 November 1960.
140. *BH*, 3 July 1960.
141. *PPH*, 31 October 1960; *PPH*, 7 November 1960.
142. Election 1960 file, MCSL.
143. Cormier reported $11,250 from AFL-CIO's COPE and $1,000 from the Textile Workers Union. Smith reported no labor contributions, although she did have a number of endorsements from labor groups. For some of the confusion this caused, see *PST*, 22 November 1959. Official disclosure forms in Elections 1960 file, MCSL.
144. *WES*, 30 October 1960.
145. CQ, *Guide to U.S. Elections*, 619.
146. *PPH*, 9 November 1960.

CHAPTER ELEVEN: DREAM TICKET

1. Statements & Speeches, vol. 22, 4 January 1961.
2. Correspondence in Neuberger file, MCSL; Senator Maurine Neuberger, telephone interview by author, 29 January 1989.
3. Clippings, Scrapbook 228, January 1961.
4. Statements & Speeches, vol. 22, 3 January 1961; *WP*, 4 January 1961; Allen Hoffard, n.a., 5 January 1961, Box 36, MNP.
5. Neuberger interview.
6. *PPH*, 16 June 1958; "The Crusader's Widow," *Newsweek*, 21 March 1960, 42–43.
7. MCSI, 3 September 1989.
8. "Gentlewoman from Maine: Margaret Chase Smith," *Ladies' Home Journal*, January 1961, 65–66, 111; Statements & Speeches, vol. 14, 23 May 1957.
9. *MST*, 11 January 1959.
10. Clipping, n.a., 17 February 1962, Scrapbook 241; also see *WES*, 8 February 1962.
11. *CR*, 87th Cong., 1st Sess., 16 June 1961, 10,629; UPI ticker, 18 November 1963, Box 7, MNP.
12. Neuberger, interview.
13. *CR*, 87th Cong., 1st Sess., 13 January 1961, 697–698.
14. After many years of effort, the plan finally died about 1970, mostly due to

resistance by the Canadians and Central Maine Power Company. For a time, Dickey-Lincoln, another public power project to dam the upper St. John River supplanted Quoddy as more cost effective, but it too was ultimately abandoned due, in no small measure, to intense opposition from private power. *Passamaquoddy Tidal Power Project* and Dickey-Lincoln Project files, MCSL; Senate Office; Box 10, Folder 10–9 730, ESMA; WH Subject Files; Box 650, P, JFKL; *PPH*, 22 September 1970.

15. Statements & Speeches, vol. 23, 7 September 1961; WH Name File, Box 2619, JFKL; ASC file, MCSL.

16. McGiffert letter, 30 August 1962; O'Brien letter 12 September 1962, ASC file, MCSL.

17. Memo, Manatos to O'Brien, 3 April 1961, WH Staff Files, Papers of Mike Manatos, Box 1, Memoranda, JFKL; *PPH*, 14 August 1962.

18. *WSJ*, 14 October 1963.

19. Robert S. McNamara, *In Retrospect: The Tragedy and Lessons of Vietnam* (New York: Random House, 1995), 77–79.

20. Smith to McNamara, 14 October 1963, ASC file, MCSL.

21. Memo, Claude Desautels to O'Brien, 15 October 1963, in WH Staff Files; Lawrence F. O'Brien; Box 21, JFKL.

22. ASC file, MCSL.

23. *PPH*, 21 December 1962; *CR*, 88th Cong., 1st Sess., 16 January 1963, 418–419; "Maggie vs. May," *Newsweek*, 8 April 1963, 23–24.

24. Statements & Speeches, vol. 25, 16 September 1962; also in *CR*, 87th Cong., 2d Sess., 18 September 1962, 19,788–19,789. She continued her complaints six months later. Statements & Speeches, vol. 26, 10 March 1963; *CR*, 88th Cong., 1st Sess., 19 March 1963, 4,531–4,532.

25. *PPH*, 21 September 1962.

26. *PPH*, 23 May 1965; MCSI, 2 May 1989.

27. Craig clippings, including a series of columns she wrote defending McCarthy against his colleagues who censured him, in McCarthy file, MCSL.

28. Press Relationships file, MCSL; Donald R. Larrabee, interview by author, Bethesda, MD, 10 April 1994.

29. *PPH*, 3 December 1960.

30. Goldwater, *With No Apologies*, 94–96.

31. Ibid.

32. Mary C. Brennan, *Turning Right in the Sixties: The Conservative Capture of the GOP* (Chapel Hill: University of North Carolina Press, 1995), 35; Nixon, *RN*, 215; Theodore H. White, *The Making of the President 1960* (New York: Atheneum House, 1961), 467.

33. Brennan, 36.

34. Barry M. Goldwater, *With No Apologies* (New York: William Murrow & Co., 1979), 114–117.

35. *PPH*, 26 July 1960; Goldwater telegram, Scrapbook 219, 26 July 1960.

36. Brewster to Frank Hanighen, 4 September 1961, Brewster file, MCSL.

37. Only two other women had previously run for president, neither of them for a major party: Victoria Claflin Woodhull, 1872, National Radical Reformer Party and Belva Bennett Lockwood, 1884 and 1888, Equal Rights Party.

38. Arthur M. Schlesinger, Jr., *A Thousand Days: John F. Kennedy in the White House* (Boston: Houghton Mifflin Co., 1965), 68.

39. Theodore C. Sorensen, *Kennedy* (New York: Harper & Row, Publishers, 1965), 511.

40. Peter Wyden, *Bay of Pigs: The Untold Story* (New York: Simon & Schuster, 1979), 65.

41. Some of the same CIA operatives were involved in the planning of both actions: Richard Bissell, E. Howard Hunt, David Atlee Phillips, Frank Wisner and Tracy Barnes among them. Ibid., 20–22.

42. Ibid., passim.

43. Schlesinger, *A Thousand Days*, 390–400.

44. Herbert S. Parmet, *JFK: The Presidency of John F. Kennedy* (New York: Penguin Books, 1983), 148–152.

45. George C. Herring, *America's Longest War: The United States and Vietnam 1950–1975* (New York: John Wiley & Sons, 1979), 77.

46. *CR*, 87th Cong., 1st Sess., 21 September 1961, 20,623–20,626.

47. Thomas G. Paterson, *Meeting the Communist Threat*, (New York: Oxford University Press, 1988), 191–210.

48. Statements & Speeches, vol. 24, 4 October 1961.

49. *CR*, 87th Cong., 1st Sess., 23 September 1961, 20,986–20,989.

50. William W. Kaufmann, *The McNamara Strategy* (New York: Harper & Row, Publishers, 1964), 68–69.

51. *NYT*, 25 September 1961.

52. *CR*, 87th Cong., 1st Sess., 23 September 1961, 21,003.

53. Smith, *Declaration*, 273.

54. Schlesinger, *A Thousand Days,* 485.

55. Statements & Speeches, vol. 23, October 1961.

56. Smith, *Declaration*, 290–292; MCSI, 13 March 1989.

57. Kennedy considered Smith one of his two Senate "enemies." The other was Joe McCarthy. Sorenson, *Kennedy*, 45.

58. *NYP*, 25 September 1961.

59. Memo of Nixon call in Scrapbook 235; Goldwater's remarks in *CR*, 87th Cong., 1st Sess., 25 September 1961, 21,162, 26 September 1961, 21,378.

60. "Credibility and Incredibility," *Commonweal*, 13 October 1961, 60–61; *NYP*, 25 September 1961; clippings in Scrapbook 236.

61. Moscow TASS transcripts of I. Orlov and Ryzhikov commentaries, 23 September 1961, and 24 September 1961, in Scrapbook 235.

62. Khrushchev reply to 58 Labor Party members (Kennedy received a similar letter), TASS translation, Scrapbook 236, 13 October 1961.

63. *WES*, 14 November 1961; *WP*, 15 November 1961.

64. *CR*, 87th Cong., 1st Sess., 26 September 1961, 21,378.

65. Statements & Speeches, vol. 23, 13 October 1961 and 16 November 1961.

66. This was staple rhetoric for this period; see for example, Statements & Speeches, vol. 23, 29 October 1961.

67. Statements & Speeches, vol. 24, 12 February 1962.

68. *BDN*, 17 February 1962.

69. F. Clifton White, with William J. Gill, *Suite 3505: The Story of the Draft Goldwater Movement* (New Rochelle, NY: Arlington House, 1967),106–107; *PST*, 9 December 1962.

70. *PST*, 25 February 1962.

71. Statements & Speeches, vol. 24, 12 March 1962.

72. Ibid., vol. 24, 8 May 1962. The MCSL files contain no such letters.

73. *CR*, 87th Cong., 2d Sess., 24 March 1962, 4,955–4,959.

74. Gibson, *NYDN*, 19 May 1962.

75. Kennedy Administration file, MCSL; Smith, *Declaration*, 293–306.

76. Wyden, *Bay of Pigs*, 310.

77. Divine, *Cuban Missile Crisis*, 335; Parmet, *JFK*, 282.

78. Divine, 16.

79. Barry M. Goldwater, *Why Not Victory? A Fresh Look at American Foreign Policy* (New York: Macfadden-Bartell, 1962), 104–111.

80. *CR*, 87th Cong., 2d Sess., 21 September 1962, 20,344–20,346.

81. Ibid., 10 October 1962, 22,957.

82. *Congress and the Nation*, 1:133.

83. Ernest R. May and Philip D. Zelikow, *The Kennedy Tapes* (Cambridge: Harvard University Press, 1997), 278.

84. Ibid., 485–91, 505–508, 630–635.

85. Statements & Speeches, vol. 25, 2 December 1962.

86. *CR*, 88th Cong., 1st Sess., 9 May 1963, 8,251–8,254.

87. *BDN*, 28 February 1963.

88. Smith, *Declaration*, 313.

89. *CR*, 88th Cong., 1st Sess., 9 September 1963, 16,519–16,520.

90. Ibid., 24 September 1963, 17,830–17,832.

91. Smith, *Declaration*, 327.

92. *WP*, 28 September 1963.

93. *WP*, 12 November 1963; *CR*, 88th Cong., 1st Sess., 12 November 1963, 21590.

94. Letter originally labeled "V.P." currently in Arizona Congressional Delegation file, MCSL.

95. *WTH*, 7 October 1963.

96. Arizona file (labeled in Smith's handwriting "save V.P."), MCSL.

97. *PPH*, 30 October 1963.

98. Independent Editorial Services Ltd., *Newsletter*, Scrapbook 249, 7 October 1962.

99. Bill Hart, "It May Interest You," clipping, Scrapbook 241.

100. *PST*, 29 September 1963.

101. *WP*, 7 November 1963; *PPH*, 8 November 1963.

102. *WP*, 15 November 1963.

103. Ibid.

104. Clipping, n.a., Scrapbook 287, 21 November 1963.

105. *NYT*, 15 November 1963.

106. Ibid., 26 November 1963; Smith gave credit for suggesting the gesture to Mansfield. *CR*, 88th Cong., 1st Sess., 10 December 1963, 24,088.

CHAPTER TWELVE: *LEAVE IT TO THE GIRLS*

1. *CR*, 88th Cong., 2d Sess., 28 January 1964, 1,246–1,248; *CSM*, 31 January 1964.

2. *WES*, 28 January 1964.

3. MCSI, 16 March 1987, 8 December 1989.

4. *NYDN*, 28 January 1964.

5. "Madame Candidate," *Time*, 7 February 1964, 23.

6. Richard Starnes, n.a., clipping in Scrapbook 263.

7. McGrory, "The New Hampshire Primary," *America*, 22 February 1964, 246; "Madame Candidate," *Time*, 7 February 1964, 23.

8. *PPH*, 12 February 1964; *WP*, 16 February 1964.

9. *WES*, 10 February 1964; *WP*, 16 February 1964.

10. Ibid.

11. Statements & Speeches, vol. 28, 23 February 1964.

12. *WES*, 12 February 1964; other clippings in Presidential Campaign file.

13. *WES*, 19 January 1964.

14. Statements & Speeches, vol. 28, February 1964.

15. Margaret Viens, "New Hampshire Express" in *Never Underestimate . . .* (Waterville, ME: Northwood University Margaret Chase Smith Library, 1993), 122.

16. *Face the Nation*, 2 February 1964, videotape, MCSL.

17. *WN*, 4 February 1964.

18. *WES*, 12 February 1964.

19. *BG*, 16 February 1964.

20. *WES*, 19 December 1963; *CSM*, 31 January 1964; "The Lady from Maine: Her Record, Her Views," *U.S. News & World Report*, 3 February 1964, 16; *NYHT*, 24 November 1963; Herbert Klein in Smith, *Declaration*, 362.

21. Cleveland Amory, "A Woman for President? Nay!" n.a., Scrapbook 304; Jim Bishop, "A Woman President? NO!" n.a., Scrapbook 294, 10 March 1964; *LEJ*, 28 January 1964; Richard Wilson, *LAT*, Scrapbook 291, February 1964.

22. Andrew Tully, n.a., Scrapbook 287; Wayne Lubenow, n.a., Scrapbook 289.

23. "Tees, Tigers, Titmice—& a President Too?" *Time*, 6 March 1964, 22.

24. *BG*, 18 November 1963.

25. *BDN*, 15 February 1964.

26. *Face the Nation*, 2 February 1964, videotape, MCSL.

27. See letters, February 1964, in Presidential Campaign file, MCSL.

28. *WES*, 16 February 1964; Statements & Speeches, vol. 28, 23 February 1964; "Republicans: With an Eye on July," *Newsweek*, 24 February 1964, 19–20.

29. Harold, Faber, ed., *The Road to the White House* (New York: McGraw-Hill Publishing Co., 1965), 82.

30. Ibid., 19–31.

31. Stephen Shadegg, *What Happened to Goldwater? The Inside Story of the 1964 Republican Campaign* (New York: Holt, Rinehart & Winston, 1965), 100.

32. Faber, *Road to the White House,* 12.

33. Ibid., 28; *PEE*, 11 March 1964; *PPH*, 19 April 1964.

34. Statements & Speeches, vol. 28, 10 March 1964; MCSI, 1 August 1989.

35. 12 March 1964, in Arizona file, MCSL.

36. Ron Nessen, NBC News, 10 March 1964, transcript in Scrapbook 296.

37. Judge Lewis V. Morgan, Jr., interview by author, Wheaton, IL, 3 November 1991; Craig, *PPH*, 24 December 1963; clippings in Presidential Campaign; MCSI, 1 August 1989, 8 December 1989.

38. *Rockford (IL) Morning Star*, 12 April 1964.

39. Angell, interview; Morgan interview; MCSI, 1 August 1989, 8 December 1989.

40. Presidential Campaign files, MCSL.

41. Ibid.

42. Angell, interview; Morgan, interview.

43. Invitation and her regrets in Alpha file: 1964–Smith, EMDP.

44. Smith, *Declaration*, 378.

45. *CA*, 15 April 1964; *WES*, 15 April 1964; other clippings in Scrapbook 297.

46. Press release, 15 April 1964, Presidential Campaign file, MCSL.

47. By the end of the primary season, she had picked up 231,688 popular votes in twelve states. David A. Nichols, *Maine Political Yearbook, 1964–1965*, 37–43, in Presidential Campaign file, MCSL.

48. Oregon clippings in Scrapbook 293, 294, 297 and 299; *Newsweek*, 25 May 1964, 18. Broadcasting from the convention, David Brinkley talked about the trading stamps, 1964 Convention videotape, MCSL.

49. Lyrics by Gladys Shelley, recorded by Hildegarde on the Spiral Record label. Reprinted by permission of Gladys Shelley. *PPH*, 30 January 1964; *WP*, 6 May 1964.

50. S.478 through S.484; *CR*, 87th Cong., 1st Sess., 17 January 1961, 855–856.

51. Charles Whalen and Barbara Whalen, *The Longest Debate: A Legislative History of the 1964 Civil Rights Act* (New York: New American Library, 1985), xxi.

52. *CR*, 88th Cong., 2d Sess., 8 February 1964, 2,577–2,592.

53. Harrison, *On Account of Sex*, 177; Carl M. Brauer, "Women Activists, Southern Conservatives, and the Prohibition of Sex Discrimination in Title VII of the 1964 Civil Rights Act" *The Journal of Southern History*, February 1983, 37–56; Jo Freeman, "How 'Sex' Got Into Title VII: Persistent Opportunism as a Maker of Public Policy," *Law and Inequality*, March 1991, 168–184.

54. Whalen, *The Longest Debate*, 143–156.

55. Dirksen notes, Congressional Leadership file, Folder 50, EMDP.

56. Working Papers file, Folder 256, EMDP.

57. *PPH*, 10 April 1964; Betty Bryden, interview by author, Showhegan, ME, 25 June 1993; MCSI, 30 August 1989.

58. Robert Mann, *The Walls of Jericho*, (New York: Harcourt Brace & Co., 1996), 409–411.

59. Presidential Campaign file, MCSL.

60. Otsea Report, Ibid.

61. Faber, *Road to the White House*, 42.

62. *CR*, 88th Cong., 2d Sess., 17 February 1964–19 June 1964, 2,642–14,506.

63. Ibid., 18 June 1964, 14,318–14,319.

64. Mann, *Walls of Jericho*, 401–403.

65. Miller, *Lyndon,* 371.

66. *NYHT*, 15 June 1964; *NYT*, 16 June 1964.

67. Theodore H. White, *Making of the President 1964* (New York: Signet Books, 1965), 189–90.

68. Shadegg, *What Happened*, 140.

69. *BDN*, 14 July 1964.

70. MCSI, 8 December 1989.

71. *CSM*, 15 July 1964.

72. Shaddeg, *What Happened*, 136–160; White, *Suite 3505*, 381–382.

73. White, *Making of the President 1964*, 238.

74. Shadegg, *What Happened*, 152–154; Goldwater, *With No Apologies*, 183–185.

75. "National Affairs: The GOP," *Newsweek*, 27 July 1964, 21–22.

76. *LDS*, 6 July 1964.

77. *BDN*, 14 July 1964.

78. White, *Suite 3505*, 401; Official Proceedings, 301–305, MCSL.

79. Presidential Campaign file, MCSL.

80. Ibid.

81. White, *Suite 3505*, 402.

82. Smith, *Declaration*, 388; *WES*, 21 July 1964; Horne's speech in Scrapbook 303.

83. Smith's delegate votes came from Maine (14), Vermont (5), North Dakota (3), Alaska (2), Ohio (1), Washington (1), Massachusetts (1).

84. A form letter, mailed August 1964 from her office, asserted that she was "particularly proud of the way the Smith delegates remained loyal to the end . . . in the final tally I finished second and ahead of even Scranton and Rockefeller;" Presidential Campaign file, MCSL; *BDN*, 17 July 1964; *PEE*, 17 July 1964.

85. Barry M. Goldwater, with Jack Casserly, *Goldwater* (New York: St. Martin's Press, 1988), 235.

86. These lines were underlined on Goldwater's own speech notes, presumably so that he would emphasize them all the more. White, *Making of the President 1964*, 261.

87. White, *Suite 3505*, 14; Stephen E. Ambrose, *Nixon*, Vol. 2: *The Triumph of a Politician, 1962–1972* (New York: Simon & Schuster, 1989), 54; Nixon, *RN*, 260. *Newsweek*, 27 July 1964, 20–22.

88. Shadegg, *What Happened*, 165.

89. Letter, Goldwater to author, 2 March 1990, author's possession.

90. 22 July 1964, in Arizona file, MCSL.

91. MCSI, 1 August 1989, 8 December 1989.

92. Statements & Speeches, vol. 27, 1 March 1964.

93. Phyllis Battelle, "OK, Sen. Smith, but Run Like a Man," n.a., 30 January 1964, Scrapbook 291; also William Wallace, "The Sixties," n.a., 19 February 1964, Scrapbook 294.

94. *PPH*, 16 July 1965.

95. These same assumptions about women's "essential nature" and her "inherent" unfitness for leadership still have salience in American culture. See, for example, Carroll, *Women as Candidates*; Linda Witt et al., *Running as a Woman: Gender and Power in American Politics* (New York: The Free Press, 1994).

96. Smith estimated total expenditures for the campaign "by everyone" at about $7,000. Statements & Speeches, vol. 29, 13 September 1964.

97. *PPH*, 16 July 1965.

CHAPTER THIRTEEN: THE GRAND OLD LADY

1. Arizona file, MCSL.

2. John H. Kessel, *The Goldwater Coalition: Republican Strategies in 1964* (Indianapolis: The Bobbs-Merrill Co., Inc., 1968),199–207.

3. Shadegg, *What Happened*, 243; ibid., 197.

4. Goldwater's positions best expressed in his precampaign book, *Why Not Victory?*

5. *NYT*, 11 September 1964.

6. *NYT*, 5 August 1964.

7. H.J. Res.1145, Southeast Asia Resolution, 88th Cong., 2d Sess., 7 August 1964; copy in ASC file.

8. Statement, 6 August 1964, Vietnam War file, MCSL.

9. U.S. Senate Committee on Foreign Relations, *Hearings on the Gulf of Tonkin, The 1964 Incidents*, 90th Cong., 2d Sess., February 1968; Robert D. Schulzinger, *A Time for War: The United States and Vietnam, 1941–1975* (New York: Oxford University Press, 1997), 145–152.

10. *PPH*, 24 September 1964.

11. H.P. 1154, 24 May 1965, *Legislative Record of the One Hundred and Second Legislature of the State of Maine*, vol. 2, May 17–June 4, 1965, 2,498–2,499.

12. Ibid., 2574.

13. H.P. 1158; ibid., 2,799, 2,837.

14. *PPH*, 30 May 1965; Elections 1966 file, MCSL.

15. *PPH*, 14 October 1965; *PST*, 2 January 1966.

16. Elections 1966 file, MCSL; *BDN*, 14 October 1966.

17. *BTR*, 3 November 1966.

18. Statements & Speeches, vol. 31, 21 October 1965.

19. *CR*, 89th Cong., 1st Sess., 5 May 1965, 9,466.

20. Operation Rolling Thunder began in February and the first combat troops arrived in Da Nang in March, 1965. *PPH*, 8 April 1965; letters in Vietnam War file, MCSL.

21. *WES*, 18 October 1966.

22. Lady Bird Johnson, *A White House Diary* (New York: Holt, Rinehart & Winston, 1970), 414.

23. *BDN*, 3 February 1964; Johnson Administration file, MCSL.

24. White House Central Files, Box 356, PR 18, LBJL.

25. Ibid., Box 359.

26. Smith, *Declaration*, 259.

27. *PPH*, 8 April 1965.

28. Statements & Speeches, vol. 34, 11 August 1967.

29. 11 August 1967, Signature file, MCSL.

30. 14 August 1967, ASC file, MCSL.

31. Letters in ASC file, MCSL; MCSI 6 June 1989, 31 March 1992.

32. Herring, *America's Longest War*, 142.

33. Leslie H. Gelb, with Richard K. Betts, *The Irony of Vietnam: The System Worked* (Washington, D.C.: The Brookings Institution, 1979), 137–139.

34. *NYT*, 17 May 1967, cited in McNamara, *In Retrospect*, 284.

35. David Halberstam, *The Best and the Brightest* (New York: Random House, 1972), 641–645.

36. Senate ASC hearings, 23 January 1967, cited in McNamara, *In Retrospect*, 246–247.

37. McNamara, *In Retrospect*, 289.

38. Summary Report of Preparedness Investigating Subcommittee of the Committee on Armed Services, *Air War Against North Vietnam*, 31 August 1967, in ASC file, MCSL.

39. Neil Sheehan, *A Bright Shining Lie: John Paul Vann and America in Vietnam* (New York: Random House, 1988), 692.

40. "Why I Worry About the Vietnam War," *PST*, 16 April 1967; "Vietnam Crucible," *PST*, 24 March 1968.

41. Letters in Vietnam War file, MCSL; *MST*, 17 March 1968; Statements & Speeches, vol. 36, 6 August 1969.

42. W. Bradford Greeley, Vietnam War file, MCSL.

43. *BTR*, 5 September 1967.

44. Sheehan, *Bright Shining Lie*, 698.

45. *CR*, 90th Cong., 2d Sess., 18 April 1968, 9,929.

46. Statements & Speeches, vol. 34, 8 September 1967.

47. *MST*, 16 November 1969.

48. Smith, *Declaration*, 197–198.

49. 13 November 1968, Diary, Surgery file, MCSL.

50. Shaffer, *On and Off the Floor*, 90–91; Norris Cotton statement, 25 July 1968, Fortas file, MCSL.

51. CR, 91st Cong., 1st Sess., 8 October 1969, 29,040–29,041; Statements & Speeches, vol. 36, 8 October 1969.

52. *WES*, 21 November 1969.

53. H. R. Haldeman, *The Haldeman Diaries: Inside the Nixon White House* (New York: G. P. Putnam's Sons, 1994), 113.

54. Congressional Quarterly, *Congress and the Nation 1969–1972*, vol. 3 (Washington, DC: Congressional Quarterly, 1973).

55. *Congress and the Nation*, 3:296.

56. She later forced a public apology from Harlow published in *The New Yorker*, 1 March 1971, clipping and letters in Carswell file, MCSL; *CR*, 91st Cong., 1st Sess., 10 April 1970, 11,227–11,231 and 13 April 1970, 11,472–11,473.

57. "A Nixon Crisis: Advice But No Consent," *Newsweek*, 20 April 1970, 35.

58. Rowland Evans, Jr. and Robert D. Novak, *Nixon in the White House: The Frustration of Power* (New York: Random House, 1971), 111–114.

59. "Congress Calls It a Sonic Bust," *Newsweek*, 5 April 1971, 19. *Congress and the Nation*, 3:197.

60. SST funding defeated 217 to 204 in House, 51 to 46 in Senate. *NYT*, 28 March 1971; Statements & Speeches, vol. 39, 29 March 1971.

61. Statements & Speeches, vol. 39, 15 September 1971.

62. *MST*, 15 March 1970.

63. Smith, *Declaration*, 428.

64. Ibid., 429.

65. John Cole, editorial, *MT*, 15 May 1970; *LEJ*, 12 May 1970.

66. *NYP*, 6 March 1970; letter, 12 June 1970, Vietnam War file, MCSL.

67. CR, 91st Cong., 2d Sess., 1 June 1970, 17,683–17,685; Smith, *Declaration*, 431–435.

68. *WP*, 2 June 1970.

69. Letters to Edward W. Brooke, 9 June 1970, Hubert H. Humphrey, 12 June 1970, Second Declaration file, MCSL.

70. "Voice of Reason: Call to the Center," *Time*, 15 June 1970, 18; *NYT*, 3 June 1970.

71. *NYT*, 2 June 1970; *WES*, 3 June 1970; *NYP*, 6 June 1970.

72. Surgery diary, Anecdotes.

73. Elections 1972 file, MCSL.

74. *MST*, 6 June 1971.

75. Donald R. Larrabee, *It's News to Me: A Maine Yankee Reports from Washington* (Washington, DC: Trades Unionist Printing Co., 1989), 83.

76. *MST*, 19 December 1971.

77. Larrabee, *It's News to Me*, 84.

78. MCSI, 18 July 1992; Henry, interview, 10 July 1991; Statements & Speeches, vol. 39, 7 February 1972.

79. Berkeley Rice, "Is the Great Lady from Maine Out of Touch?" *NYT* Magazine, 11 June 1972, 50.

80. Ibid.; Statements & Speeches, vol. 39, 18 March 1972; *WSJ*, 9 October 1972.

81. *WSJ*, 9 October 1972.

82. 76,964 to 38,345; data from MCSL.

83. *WSJ*, 9 October 1972; Bernard Asbell, *The Senate Nobody Knows* (Baltimore: The Johns Hopkins University Press, 1978), 55.

84. *PPH*, 19 October 1972.

85. Ibid.

86. *PH*, 13 October 1972.

87. Letter to Editor, *MST*, 24 September 1972, in Press Relationships file, MCSL.

88. *MST*, 1 October 1972, 8 October 1972; *BDN*, 4 October 1972.

89. Hathaway, who apparently had been more accommodating, received glowing praise for his folksy liberalism and his "consistent cooperation and responsiveness to the Congress Project." Copies of both reports in Election 1972 file, MCSL.

90. Quoted by Maxwell Wiesenthal, *WP*, 9 November 1972.

91. "Moonlighters," *Commonweal*, 10 March 1972, 4; clippings in Roll Call Resolution file, MCSL.

92. Editorial, *PPH*, 22 December 1971.

93. *NYT*, 11 June 1972, 50.

94. Stanley Tupper quoted by Larrabee, *MST*, 4 April 1972.

95. *PPH*, 12 July 1972.

96. Smith remarks to Republican state convention and national convention, Statements & Speeches, vol. 39, 28 April 1972, 23 August 1972. Jack Aley, *PPH*, 28 June 1972; Ramona Barth, conversation with the author, Alna, ME, 26 September 1989.

97. *PEE*, 20 March 1972.

98. Barth remained a self-described radical in the late 1980s, calling herself Ramona X, revising the Bible, and performing "feminist exorcisms" by burning misogynist tracts. Smith's appeal to mainstream women indicated by 1972 American Women's Opinion Survey ranking her fourth in list of most respected women. *PPH*, 28 June 1972; conversation with Barth, 26 September 1989.

99. MCSI, 3 September 1989.

100. Hathaway: 224,270; Smith: 197,040. In Skowhegan, she lost 1,130 to 1993. Data from MCSL.

101. Larrabee reports an election-night phone call from Charles Colson asking how Smith was doing, reporting that Nixon was "very much interested" in the outcome. Nixon did almost no campaigning for others; on election night, RNC Chair Robert Dole called his victory "a personal triumph for Mr. Nixon

but not a party triumph." Democrats retained control of both Houses. Larrabee, *It's News to Me*, 91; Henry, interview, 11 July 1991; *WP*, 18 November 1972; William S. White, *WP*, 25 November 1972.

102. MCSI, 1 May 1989, 30 August 1989.
103. Smith's "liberal quotient," as determined by Americans for Democratic Action, reached its high point in the early 1960s, topping out at 84% in 1964; by 1971, it had slipped to 19%. Sharp, *Congressional Voting*, 944.
104. MCSI, 8 November 1989.
105. Henry, interview; Nichols, interview.
106. Statements & Speeches, vol. 40, 8 November 1972.
107. *MST*, 3 December 1972.

CHAPTER FOURTEEN: SENATOR EMERITUS

1. *MST*, 3 December 1972.
2. *NYT*, 6 February 1973.
3. *MST*, 11 February 1973.
4. See Statements & Speeches, vol. 41, November 1973.
5. The group also included Mrs. Claire Giannini Hoffman, director of the Bank of America and daughter of its founder; Robert T. Stevens, former Secretary of the Army and CEO of J.P. Stevens Textile Company; and former Congresswomen Clare Boothe Luce and Frances Bolton. MCSL genesis in Biography file, MCSL.
6. Ibid.; Gosselin interview, 27 August 1991.
7. *BTR*, 5 August 1977.
8. *WMS*, 14 July 1987.
9. Smith's niece, Anne Herrin, noted, "Politics was her family—that's all she had and she lived on it." Herrin interview, 22 June 1994.
10. MCSI, 11 August 1989, 16 April 1992.
11. *WMS*, 14 December 1993; *MST*, 28 January 1990.
12. Author's notes, 14 December 1987, in author's possession; *DKJ*, 15 December 1987.
13. *WMS*, 2 April 1992.
14. MCSI, 18 July 1992.
15. Quoted in *Margaret Chase Smith: A Centennial Remembrance*, 14, MCSL.
16. Ibid., 24.
17. Memorial Service, 16 June 1995.

Bibliography

MANUSCRIPT COLLECTIONS

The Arthur and Elizabeth Schlesinger Library on the History of Women in America, Radcliffe College. Cambridge, MA.

Carl Hayden Papers, Arizona State University. Tempe, AZ.

Dwight David Eisenhower Presidential Library. Abilene, KS.

Everett McKinley Dirksen Congressional Research Center. Pekin, IL.

Edmund S. Muskie Archives. Lewiston, ME.

Franklin Delano Roosevelt Presidential Library. Hyde Park, NY.

Harry S. Truman Presidential Library. Independence, MO.

John Fitzgerald Kennedy Presidential Library. Boston, MA.

Lyndon Baines Johnson Presidential Library. Austin, TX.

Margaret Chase Smith Library. Skowhegan, ME.

Mary T. Norton Papers, Rutgers University. New Brunswick, NJ.

Maurine Neuberger Papers, University of Oregon. Eugene, OR.

Wayne Morse Papers, University of Oregon. Eugene, OR.

INTERVIEWS

Senator Margaret Chase Smith, Skowhegan, Maine.
- 1986: 17 October
- 1987: 8, 9, 10 January; 16 March
- 1988: 2 December
- 1989: 18, 28, 29, 30 January; 14 February; 9, 13 March; 1, 2, 7 May; 6 June; 12, 26, 27, 31 July; 1, 11, 30 August; 3, 7 September; 2, 8, 29 November; 8, 10 December
- 1990: 5 September
- 1991: 2, 9 July; 7, 28 August
- 1992: 10, 18, 31 March; 1, 16, 22 April; 5, 6, 28 May; 15, 26 June; 18, 24 July; 22 September; 24 October; 9 November
- 1993: 15, 24 June; 8 July; 3 August; 16 September; 29 October

Angell, Gwendolyn and Patricia Angell. 4 November 1991. Chicago, IL.

Anton, Jane, Dorinda Putnam, and Louise Marsh. 20 July 1990. Scarborough, ME.

Bernier, John M. and Charlotte Bernier. 9 October 1992. Carrabassett, ME.

Bither, Eve Moertl. 10 September 1990. Augusta, ME.

Bouchard, Sam. 11 June 1993. Skowhegan, ME.

Bryden, Betty. 25 June 1993, Skowhegan, ME.

Goldwater, Senator Barry. 7 March 1994. Phoenix, AZ.

Gonzales, Joe. 2 September 1992. Skowhegan, ME.

Gosselin, Hal L. 27 August 1991. Skowhegan, ME.

Henry, Merton G. 10 July 1991 and 11 July 1991. Skowhegan, ME.

Herrin, Anne. 22 June 1994. Canaan, ME.

Larrabee, Donald R. 10 April 1994. telephone from Bethesda, MD.

Morgan, Jr., Judge Lewis V. 3 November 1991. Wheaton, IL.

Nichols, Judge Donald. 23 March 1994. Waterville, ME.

Nicoll, Donald E. 17 February 1994. Portland, ME.

NEWSPAPERS

Maine

Bangor Commercial, 1948–1949, 1950, 1952–1953

Bangor Daily News, 1929, 1934, 1936–1937, 1938, 1948

Brunswick Times-Record, 1966–1967, 1977

Camden Herald, 1942

Daily Kennebec Journal 1927, 1930, 1934, 1939, 1940–1941, 1947–1949, 1954–1955, 1987

Fort Fairfield Review, 1954, 1956, 1963

Independent-Reporter, 1909–1911, 1914–1917, 1922, 1925–1926, 1929, 1930–1934, 1936–1948, 1956

Lewiston Daily Sun, 1940, 1948, 1959, 1964

Lewiston Evening Journal, 1927, 1930, 1934–1935, 1939, 1940–1941, 1946–1949, 1954, 1958, 1964, 1970

Lincoln County News, 1942, 1947–1948

Lisbon Enterprise, 1948

Portland Sunday Telegram, 1930, 1935, 1940, 1947–1949, 1951–1952, 1955–1956, 1959–1960, 1962–1963, 1966–1968; [after 1968] *Maine Sunday Telegram*, 1968–1973, 1990

Maine Times, 1970

Pittsfield Advertiser, 1903

Portland Evening Express, 1930, 1947–1948, 1951, 1955, 1960, 1964, 1972

Portland Press Herald, 1924, 1936, 1938, 1940–1941, 1943, 1947–1951, 1953–1956, 1958–1960, 1962–1965, 1970–1972

Rockland Courier-Gazette, 1940, 1942, 1946

Rumford Falls Times, 1954

Somerset Reporter, 1905, 1907–1909

Waterville Morning Sentinel, 1930, 1940, 1944, 1946, 1949, 1956, 1960, 1987, 1992, 1993

National

Boston Globe, 1947–1948, 1953, 1955, 1963–1964, 1972

Boston Herald, 1950, 1960

Boston Post, 1954–1955

Boston Sunday Advertiser, 1936, 1956

Chicago American, 1964

Christian Science Monitor, 1948, 1950, 1952, 1954–1955, 1960, 1964

Los Angeles Times, 1964

New York Herald-Tribune, 1934, 1954, 1956, 1959–1960, 1963–1964

New York Mirror, 49

New York Post, 1952, 1961, 1963, 1970

New York Times, 1943–1945, 1948–1950, 1952, 1954, 1960–1961, 1963–1964, 1967, 1970–1973

New York World-Telegram, 1945

Wall Street Journal, 1963, 1972

Washington Evening Star, 1943, 1945, 1947–1950, 1954, 1958, 1958, 1960–1964, 1966, 1969, 1970

Washington News, 1937, 1943, 1949, 1953–1954, 1964

Washington Post, 1940, 1943–1944, 1949–1950, 1952, 1954–1955, 1957–1961, 1963–1964, 1970, 1972

Washington Times-Herald, 1947–1950, 1963

Secondary Sources

Abell, Tyler, ed. *Drew Pearson Diaries 1949–1959*. New York: Holt, Rinehart & Winston, 1974.

Adams, Sherman. *Firsthand Report: The Story of the Eisenhower Administration.* New York: Harper & Brothers, 1961.

Ambrose, Stephen E. *Eisenhower: The President.* New York: Simon & Schuster, 1984.

———. *Nixon*, Vol. 1: *The Education of a Politician, 1913–1962.* New York: Simon & Schuster, 1987.

———. *Nixon*, Vol. 2: *The Triumph of a Politician, 1962–1972.* New York: Simon & Schuster, 1989.

Ammunition Shortages in the Armed Services. Hearings before Preparedness Subcommittee No. 2 of the Committee on Armed Services, U.S. Senate, 83rd Cong., 1st Sess., 1, 8, 9, 10, 13, 15, 16, 17 and 20 April 1953, 1–709.

Anderson, Clinton P. *Outsider in the Senate: Senator Clinton Anderson's Memoirs.* New York: World Publishing Co., 1970.

Anderson, Jack. *Confessions of a Muckraker.* New York: Random House, 1979.

Anderson, Karen. *Wartime Women: Sex Roles, Family Relations, and the Status of Women During World War II.* Westport, CT: Greenwood Press, 1981.

"Army Cracks Down on Vice That Still Preys on Soldiers." *Newsweek*, 31 August 1942, 27–31.

Asbell, Bernard. *The Senate Nobody Knows.* Baltimore: The Johns Hopkins University Press, 1978.

Baker, Ross. *Friend and Foe in the U.S. Senate.* New York: The Free Press, 1980.

"Benton Tries to Throw Him Out," *Life*, 15 October 1951, 58.

Blair, Karen J. *The Clubwoman as Feminist: True Womanhood Refined, 1868–1914.* New York: Holmes & Meier, 1980.

"Bomb for Barbarians," *Time*, 24 August 1953, 12.

Bowman, Geline MacDonald, and Earlene White. *A History of the National Federation of Business and Professional Women's Clubs, Inc., 1919–1944.* Washington, DC: NFBPWC, 1979.

Brandt, Allan M. *No Magic Bullet: A Social History of Venereal Disease in the United States Since 1880.* New York: Oxford University Press, 1985.

Brauer, Carl M. "Women Activists, Southern Conservatives, and the Prohibition of Sex Discrimination in Title VII of the 1964 Civil Rights Act." *The Journal of Southern History*, February 1983, 37–56.

Brault, Gerald J. "The Franco-Americans of Maine." In *A History Through Selected Readings*, edited by David C. Smith and Edward O. Schriver. Dubuque, IA: Kendall Hunt Publishing Co., 1985.

Breckinridge, Sophonisba P. *Women in the Twentieth Century: A Study of Their Political, Social and Economic Activities.* New York: McGraw-Hill Publishing Co., 1933.

Brennan, Mary C. *Turning Right in the Sixties: The Conservative Capture of the GOP.* Chapel Hill: University of North Carolina Press, 1995.

Breton, Rita Mae. "Red Scare: A Study in Maine Nativism, 1919–1925." M.A. thesis, University of Maine, 1972.

Brinkley, Alan. *Voices of Protest: Huey Long, Father Coughlin and the Great Depression.* New York: Vantage Books, 1982.

Brinkley, David. *Washington Goes to War.* New York: Alfred A. Knopf, 1988.

Brown, Dorothy M. *Setting a Course: American Women in the 1920s.* Boston: Twayne Publishers, 1987.

Brunelle, Jim. *The Maine Almanac.* Portland: Guy Gannett Publishing Co., 1978.

Bundy, McGeorge. *Danger and Survival: Choices About the Bomb in the First Fifty Years.* New York: Random House, 1988.

Butler, Joyce. *Wildfire Loose: The Week Maine Burned.* Camden, Me.: Down East Books, 1987.

Campbell, D'Ann. *Women at War with America: Private Lives in a Patriotic Era.* Cambridge, MA: Harvard University Press, 1984.

Carroll, Susan J. *Women as Candidates in American Politics.* Bloomington: Indiana University Press, 1985.

Cater, Douglass. *Power in Washington.* New York: Random House, 1964.

Chafe, William H. *The American Woman: Her Changing Social, Economic and Political Roles, 1920–1970.* New York: Oxford University Press, 1972.

Chalmers, David M. *Hooded Americanism: The First Century of the Ku Klux Klan, 1856–1956.* Garden City, N.Y.: Doubleday & Co., 1965.

Clapp, Charles L. *The Congressman: His Work as He Sees It.* Garden City, N.Y.: Doubleday & Co., 1963.

Clark, Charles E. *Maine: A History.* Hanover, NH: University Press of New England, 1990.

Clark, Joseph S. *Congress: The Sapless Branch.* New York: Harper & Row, Publishers, 1965.

Coburn, Louise Helen. *Skowhegan on the Kennebec.* 2 vols. Skowhegan, ME: Independent-Reporter Press, 1941.

Coffin, Robert P. Tristan. *Kennebec, Cradle of Americans.* New York: Farrar and Rinehart, 1937.

Coffin, Tris, "The Drive to Stop Eisenhower." *The New Republic*, 1 October 1951, 9.

Coffin, Tris, and Douglass Cater. "About-Face! The Story of Senator Brewster." *The Reporter*, 10 June 1952, 12–16.

"The Coming Wage-Hour Struggle," *United States News*, 29 May 1940, 30–31.

"Congress Calls It a Sonic Bust," *Newsweek*, 5 April 1971, 19.

"The Congress: 'This Sad Episode.'" *Time*, 29 June 1959, 8–10.

Congressional Quarterly. *Congress and the Nation 1945–1964*. Vol. 1. Washington, DC: Congressional Quarterly, 1964.

———. *Congress and the Nation 1969–1972*. Vol. 3. Washington, DC: Congressional Quarterly, 1973.

———. *Guide to U.S. Elections*. 2nd ed. Washington, DC: Congressional Quarterly, 1985.

Cott, Nancy. *The Grounding of Modern Feminism*. New Haven: Yale University Press, 1987.

"Credibility and Incredibility," *Commonweal*, 13 October 1961, 60–61.

"The Crusader's Widow," *Newsweek*, 21 March 1960, 42–43.

Curtis, Wayne. "Maine's Golden Decade." *Down East*, 1992, annual issue, 25.

Dallek, Robert. *Franklin D. Roosevelt and American Foreign Policy, 1932–1945*. New York: Oxford University Press, 1979.

Daniels, Johnathan. "Soldiers' Saturday Nights." *The Nation*, 17 May 1941, 586.

Davies, Margery W. *Woman's Place is at the Typewriter: Office Work and Office Workers 1870–1930*. Philadelphia: Temple University Press, 1982.

Diggins, John Patrick. *The Proud Decades: America in War and Peace, 1941–1960*. New York: W.W. Norton & Co., 1988.

Dinkin, Robert J. *Campaigning in America: A History of Election Practices*. Westport, CT: Greenwood Press, 1989.

Divine, Robert A., ed. *The Cuban Missile Crisis*, 2nd ed. New York: Markus Wiener Publishing, 1988.

———. *The Reluctant Belligerent: American Entry into World War II*. New York: Wiley Publishers, 1965.

Donahue, Elizabeth. "Maine: Can Jones Beat Smith?" *The New Republic*, 17 May 1954, 10–11.

Duverger, Maurice. *The Political Role of Women*. New York: United Nations Press, 1955.

Edel, Leon. "The Figure Under the Carpet." In *Biography as High Adventure: Life-Writers Speak on Their Art*, edited by Stephen B. Oates. Amherst: University of Massachusetts Press, 1986.

Eisenhower, Dwight D. *The White House Years: Mandate for Change, 1953–1956*. Garden City, N.Y.: Doubleday & Co., 1963.

———. *The White House Years: Waging Peace, 1956–1961*. Garden City, N.Y.: Doubleday & Co., 1965.

Elan, Geoffrey. "Smith versus Jones." *Yankee*, June 1954, 33–35, 87–88.

Evans, Rowland Jr., and Robert D. Novak. *Nixon in the White House: The Frustration of Power*. New York: Random House, 1971.

Faber, Harold, ed. *The Road to the White House*. New York: McGraw-Hill Publishing Co., 1965.

Fleeson, Doris. "They Wear No Man's Collar." *Nation's Business*, September 1946, 72.

Fox, Harrison W. Jr., and Susan Webb Hammond. *Congressional Staffs: The Invisible Force in American Lawmaking*. New York: The Free Press, 1977.

Freeman, Jo. "How 'Sex' Got Into Title VII: Persistent Opportunism as a Maker of Public Policy." *Law and Inequality*, March 1991, 168–184.

Fried, Richard M. *Men Against McCarthy*. New York: Columbia University Press, 1976.

"Friendship Racket," *Life*, 1 August 1949.

Gaffney, Thomas L. "A Study of Maine Elections, 1930–1936." M.A. thesis, University of Maine, 1968.

Gallant, Gregory. "Margaret Chase Smith, McCarthyism and the Drive for Political Purification." Ph.D. dissertation, University of Maine, 1992.

Gallup, George H. *The Gallup Poll: Public Opinion, 1935–1971.* Wilmington, DE: Scholarly Resources, 1972.

———. "What the GOP Needs to Win in '52," *Look*, 25 September 1951, 37–39.

Garland, Whitmore Barron. "Pine Tree Politics: Maine Political Party Battles, 1820–1972." Ph.D. dissertation, University of Massachusetts, 1979.

Garraty, John A. *The Great Depression.* Garden City, N.Y.: Doubleday & Co., 1987.

Gelb, Leslie H., with Richard K. Betts. *The Irony of Vietnam: The System Worked.* Washington, DC: The Brookings Institution, 1979.

"Gentlewoman from Maine, The." *Ladies' Home Journal*, January 1961, 111.

"Gen. Van Fleet: Enough Ammunition for What? Not to Win the War, and That Was What He Wanted." *U.S. News and World Report*, 20 March 1953, 76–80.

Gertzog, Irwin N. *Congressional Women: Their Recruitment, Treatment and Behavior.* Westport, Ct: Praeger Publishers, 1984.

Goldwater, Barry M. *With No Apologies.* New York: William Morrow & Co., 1979.

———. *Why Not Victory? A Fresh Look at American Foreign Policy.* New York: Macfadden-Bartell, 1962.

———, with Jack Casserly. *Goldwater.* New York: St. Martin's Press, 1988.

Goulden, Joseph C. *Korea: The Untold Story of the War.* New York: McGraw-Hill Publishing Co., 1982.

Graham, Frank. *Margaret Chase Smith: Woman of Courage.* New York: The John Day Co., 1964.

Griffith, Robert. *The Politics of Fear: Joseph R. McCarthy and the Senate.* 2d ed. Amherst: The University of Massachusetts Press, 1987.

Halberstam, David. *The Best and the Brightest.* New York: Random House, 1972.

Haldeman, H. R. *The Haldeman Diaries: Inside the Nixon White House.* New York: G. P. Putnam's Sons, 1994.

Harrison, Cynthia. *On Account of Sex: The Politics of Women's Issues, 1945–1968.* Berkeley: University of California Press, 1988.

Hartmann, Susan M. *The Home Front and Beyond: American Women in the 1940s.* Boston: Twayne Publishers, 1982.

———. *Truman and the Eightieth Congress.* Columbia: University of Missouri Press, 1971.

Haskell, Molly. *From Reverence to Rape.* Chicago: University of Chicago Press, 1987.

Heale, M. J. *American Anticommunism: Combating the Enemy Within, 1830–1970.* Baltimore: The Johns Hopkins University Press, 1990.

Heilbrun, Carolyn G. *Writing a Woman's Life.* New York: W.W. Norton & Co., 1988.

Herring, George C. *America's Longest War: The United States and Vietnam 1950–1975.* New York: John Wiley & Sons, 1979.

Holtzman, Abraham. *The Townsend Movement: A Political Study.* New York: Bookman Associates, 1963.

Honey, Maureen. *Creating Rosie the Riveter: Class, Gender, and Propaganda During World War II.* Amherst: University of Massachusetts Press, 1984.

Horan, James F., John C. Quinn, Allen G. Pease, Kenneth T. Palmer, and Eugene A. Mawhinney. *Downeast Politics: The Government of the State of Maine.* Dubuque, IA: Kendall Hunt Publishing Co., 1975.

Hummer, Patricia M. *Decade of Illusive Promise: Professional Women in the United States, 1920–1930*. Ann Arbor: University of Michigan Research Press, 1979.

Ickes, Harold L. "And a Woman Shall Lead Them." *The New Republic*, 19 June 1950, 16.

——. *The Secret Diary of Harold Ickes,* Vol. 1, *The First Thousand Days, 1933–1936*. New York: Simon & Schuster, 1953.

Important Data on the History of Skowhegan. Skowhegan, ME: Independent-Reporter, 1926.

"An Interview with Frank M. Coffin, Democratic State Chairman." *U.S. News and World Report*, 21 September 1956, 39–40.

Investigations of Senators Joseph R. McCarthy and William Benton pursuant to S.Res.187 and S.Res.304. Report of the Subcommittee on Privileges and Elections to the Committee on Rules and Administration.

Janeway, Eliot. "The Man Who Owns the Navy." *Saturday Evening Post*, 15 December 1945, 17.

Johnson, Bascom. "The Vice Problem and Defense." *Survey Midmonthly*, May 1941, 142.

Johnson, Lady Bird. *A White House Diary*. New York: Holt, Rinehart & Winston, 1970.

Johnson, Lyndon Baines. *The Vantage Point: Perspectives of the Presidency, 1963–1969*. New York: Holt, Rinehart & Winston, 1971.

Jones, James H. *Bad Blood: The Tuskegee Syphilis Experiment*. New York: The Free Press, 1981.

Kaufmann, William W. *The McNamara Strategy*. New York: Harper & Row, Publishers, 1964.

Kessel, John H. *The Goldwater Coalition: Republican Strategies in 1964*. Indianapolis: The Bobbs-Merrill Co., Inc., 1968.

Kessler-Harris, Alice. *Out to Work: A History of Wage Earning Women in the United States*. New York: Oxford University Press, 1982.

Kincaid, Diane D. "Over His Dead Body: A Positive Perspective on Widows in the U.S. Congress." *Western Political Quarterly* (fall 1978): 96–104.

Kirkpatrick, Jeane J. *Political Women*. New York: Basic Books, 1974.

Knebel, Fletcher. "Did Ike Really Want Nixon?" *Look*, 30 October 1956, 25–27.

Kohmehl, Kenneth. *Professional Staffs of Congress*. West Lafayette, IN: Purdue University Studies, 1962.

Labonte, Youville. *Marriages of Our Lady of Lourdes, Skowhegan, Maine (1881–1980) and St. Peter, Bingham, Maine*. Augusta: Maine State Library, 1981.

"The Lady from Maine," *Newsweek*, 12 June 1950, 24–26.

"The Lady from Maine: Her Record, Her Views," *U.S. News & World Report*, 3 February 1964, 16.

LaFeber, Walter. *America, Russia, and the Cold War, 1945–1984*. New York: Alfred A. Knopf, 1985.

Lait, Jack, and Lee Mortimer, *USA Confidential*. New York: Crown Publishers, Inc., 1952.

Larrabee, Donald R. *It's News to Me: A Maine Yankee Reports from Washington*. Washington, DC: Trades Unionist Printing Co., 1989.

Lawrence, David. "Justice to the Memory of Senator McCarthy." *U.S. News and World Report*, 7 June 1957, 139–144.

Lemke, William. *The Wild, Wild East: Unusual Tales of Maine History*. Camden, ME.: Yankee Books, 1990.

Leuchtenburg, William. *FDR and the New Deal*. New York: Harper & Row, Publishers, 1963.

Lippman, Theo, Jr., and Donald C. Hansen. *Muskie*. New York: W. W. Norton & Co., 1971.

Lo Gerfo, Marianne. "Three Ways of Reminiscence." In *Oral History*, edited by David K. Dunaway and Willa K. Baum. Nashville: American Association for State and Local History, 1984.

"'McCarthyism'—First Test." *Newsweek*, 5 April 1954, 23.

McCullough, David. *Truman*. New York: Simon & Schuster, 1992.

McGrory, Mary. "The New Hampshire Primary." *America*, 22 February 1964, 246.

McNamara, Robert S. *In Retrospect: The Tragedy and Lessons of Vietnam*. New York: Random House, 1995.

"Madame Candidate." *Time*, 7 February 1964, 23.

"Maggie vs. May." *Newsweek*, 8 April 1963, 23–24.

Mandel, Ruth B. *In the Running: The New Woman Candidate*. Boston: Beacon Press, 1981.

Mann, Robert. *The Walls of Jericho*. New York: Harcourt, Brace & Co., 1996.

Markel, Helen. "Twenty-four Hours in the Life of Margaret Chase Smith." *McCall's*, May 1964, 161.

Matray, James. "Truman's Plan for Victory." *The Journal of American History*, September 1979, 314–317.

Matthews, Donald R. *U.S. Senators and Their World*. Chapel Hill: University of North Carolina Press, 1960.

May, Ernest R., and Philip D. Zelikow. *The Kennedy Tapes*. Cambridge: Harvard University Press, 1997.

Milkman, Ruth. *Gender at Work: The Dynamics of Job Segregation by Sex During World War II*. Urbana: University of Illinois Press, 1987.

Miller, Alan Robert. *The History of Current Maine Newspapers*. Lisbon Falls, ME: Eastland Press, 1978.

Miller, Merle. *Lyndon: An Oral Biography*. New York: G. P. Putnam's Sons, 1980.

Mills, Walter, and E. S. Duffield, eds. *The Forrestal Diaries*. New York: Viking Press, 1951.

Mitchell, H. E. and Paul Davis. *Skowhegan Register*. Brunswick, ME: H. E. Mitchell Co., 1905.

"Moonlighters." *Commonweal*, 10 March 1972, 4.

Morse, David A. "Truman's Assistant Secretary of Labor." In *Economics of the Truman Administration*," edited by Frances H. Heller. Lawrence: Regents Press of Kansas, 1981.

"National Affairs: The Lady Said No." *Newsweek*, 3 March 1958, 24.

Neuenschwander, John A. "Oral Historians and Long-Term Memory." In *Oral History*, edited by David K. Dunaway and Willa K. Baum. Nashville: American Association for State and Local History, 1984.

Nixon, Richard. *RN: The Memoirs of Richard Nixon*. New York: Grosset & Dunlap, 1978.

"A Nixon Crisis: Advice But No Consent." *Newsweek*, 20 April 1970, 35–38.

Oleszek, Walter J. *Congressional Procedures and the Policy Process*. 2nd ed. Washington, DC: Congressional Quarterly, 1984.

Oshinsky, David M. *A Conspiracy So Immense: The World of Joe McCarthy*. New York: The Free Press, 1983.

"Our Senator." *Independent Woman*, November 1949, 335.

Parmet, Herbert S. *JFK: The Presidency of John F. Kennedy*. New York:Penguin Books, 1983.

Parren, Thomas, and R. A. Vonderlehr. *No. 1 Saboteur of Our Defense: Plain Words About Venereal Disease*. New York: Reynal & Hitchcock, 1941.

Paterson, Thomas G. *Meeting the Communist Threat*. New York: Oxford University Press, 1988.

———. *On Every Front: The Making of the Cold War*. New York: W.W. Norton & Co., 1979.

Patterson, James T. *Mr. Republican: A Biography of Robert Taft*. Boston: Houghton Mifflin Co., 1972.

Perkins, Frances. *The Roosevelt I Knew*. New York: Viking Press, 1946.

Pfau, Richard. *No Sacrifice Too Great: The Life of Lewis L. Strauss*. Charlottesville: University Press of Virginia, 1984.

Potter, Charles E. *Days of Shame*. New York: Coward-McCann, 1965.

Rawalt, Marguerite. *History of the National Federation of Business and Professional Women's Clubs, Inc.* Vol.II. Washington, DC: NFBPWC, 1979.

Reeves, Thomas C. *The Life and Times of Joe McCarthy*. New York: Stein & Day, 1982.

Republican National Committee. *Official Report of the Proceedings of the Twenty-fourth Republican National Convention*. Washington, D.C., 1948.

"Republicans: With an Eye on July." *Newsweek*, 24 February 1964, 19–20.

Rice, Berkeley. "Is the Great Lady from Maine Out of Touch?" *NYT Magazine*, 11 June 1972, 38–54.

Rixey, Lillian. "Mrs. Smith Really Goes to Town." *Colliers*, 29 July 1950, 42.

Roosevelt, Kermit. *Countercoup: The Struggle for the Control of Iran*. New York: McGraw-Hill Publishing Co., 1979.

Rosen, Marjorie. *Popcorn Venus: Women, Movies and the American Dream*. New York: Avon Books, 1974.

Ross, Irwin. "Sex in the Army." *American Mercury*, December 1941, 661–669.

———. "Sex in the Boom Towns." *American Mercury*, November 1942, 606–613.

Rovere, Richard H. *Senator Joe McCarthy*. New York: Harper & Row, Publishers, 1959.

Rupp, Leila J. *Mobilizing Women for War: German and American Propaganda, 1939–1945*. Princeton: Princeton University Press, 1978.

Sargent, Ruth. *Gail Laughlin: ERA's Advocate*. Portland, ME: House of Falmouth Publishers, 1979.

Schaller, Michael, Virginia Scharff, and Robert D. Schulzinger. *Present Tense: The United States Since 1945*. Boston: Houghton Mifflin Co., 1992.

Schlesinger, Arthur M. Jr. *A Thousand Days: John F. Kennedy in the White House*. Boston: Houghton Mifflin Co., 1965.

Schlesinger, Stephen, and Stephen Kinzer. *Bitter Fruit: The Untold Story of the American Coup in Guatemala*. New York: Anchor Press, 1983.

Schmidt, Patricia L. *Margaret Chase Smith: Beyond Convention*. Orono: University of Maine Press, 1996.

Schulzinger, Robert D. *A Time for War: The United States and Vietnam, 1941–1975*. New York: Oxford University Press, 1997.

Scobie, Ingrid Winther. *Center Stage: Helen Gahagan Douglas, A Life*. New York: Oxford University Press, 1992.

"Senator McCarthy's Political Power." *The Christian Century*, 7 July 1954, 811–812.

Sergio, Lisa. *A Measure Filled: The Life of Lena Madesin Philips*. New York: Robert B. Luce, 1972.

Shadegg, Stephen. *What Happened to Goldwater? The Inside Story of the 1964 Republican Campaign*. New York: Holt, Rinehart & Winston, 1965.

Shaffer, Samuel. *On and Off the Floor: Thirty Years as a Correspondent on Capitol Hill*. New York: Newsweek Books, 1980.

Sharp, J. Michael. *The Directory of Congressional Voting Scores and Interest Group Ratings*. New York: Facts on File Publications, 1988.

Sheehan, Neil. *A Bright Shining Lie: John Paul Vann and America in Vietnam*. New York: Random House, 1988.

Sherman, Janann. "Margaret Chase Smith: The Making of a Senator" Ph.D. dissertation, Rutgers University, 1993.

"Significance of Maine Election." *U.S. News and World Report*, 24 September 1948, 14–15.

"Smearing is Evil, But Whitewashing of Reds is Worse." *Saturday Evening Post*, 15 July 1950, 10.

Smith, Beverly. "Senator from the Five-and-Ten." *Saturday Evening Post*, 11 September 1948, 36.

Smith, David Clayton. "Maine Politics 1950–1956." M.A. thesis, University of Maine, 1958.

Smith, Margaret Chase. *Declaration of Conscience*. Edited by William Chesley Lewis, Jr. Garden City, NY: Doubleday & Co., 1972.

Smith, Steven S., and Christopher J. Deering. *Committees in Congress*. Washington DC: Congressional Quarterly, Inc., 1984.

Sorensen, Theodore C. *Kennedy*. New York: Harper & Row, Publishers, 1965.

Spacks, Patricia Meyers. "Selves in Hiding." In *Women's Autobiography: Essays in Criticism*, edited by Estelle C. Jelinek. Bloomington: Indiana University Press, 1980.

Steele, John L. "Passions and Stratagems in the Fall of Strauss." *Life*, 29 June 1959, 28.

Sturtevant, Lawrence M. *Chronicles of the Good Will Home, 1889–1989*. Hinckley, ME: The Good Will Home Association, 1989.

"The Sued Sue." *Time*, 26 May 1952, 47.

Tacheron, Donald G., and Morris K. Udall. *The Job of the Congressman*. 2d ed. Indianapolis: Bobbs-Merrill Co., 1970.

"Tees, Tigers, Titmice—& A President Too?" *Time*, 6 March 1964, 22.

"Their Hats Were in the Ring." *Independent Woman*, August 1952, 226.

Thompson, Paul. *The Voice of the Past*. New York: Oxford University Press, 1978.

U.S. Senate Committee on Foreign Relations. *Hearings on the Gulf of Tonkin, The 1964 Incidents*, 90th Cong., 2nd Sess., February 1968.

Van Urk, J. Blan. "Norfolk—Our Worst War Town." *American Mercury*, February 1943, 144–151.

Viens, Margaret. *Never Underestimate . . .* Waterville, ME: Northwood University Margaret Chase Smith Library, 1993.

"Voice of Reason: Call to the Center." *Time*, 15 June 1970, 18.

Wallace, Patricia Ward. *Politics of Conscience: A Biography of Margaret Chase Smith*. Westport, CT: Praeger Publishers, 1995.

Ward, Ellen MacDonald. "Notables of the Nineties." *Down East*, 1992, annual issue, 46.

Ware, Susan. *Beyond Suffrage: Women in the New Deal*. Cambridge: Harvard University Press, 1981.

Warford, Pamela Neal. *Margaret Chase Smith: In Her Own Words*. Oral history project, University of Maine, 1989.

"Washington Trends." *Newsweek*, 20 June 1949, 14.

Whalen, Charles, and Barbara Whalen. *The Longest Debate: A Legislative History of the 1964 Civil Rights Act*. New York: New American Library, 1985.

White, F. Clifton, with William J. Gill. *Suite 3505: The Story of the Draft Goldwater Movement*. New Rochelle, NY: Arlington House, 1967.

White, Theodore H. *The Making of the President 1960*. New York: Atheneum House, 1961.

———. *The Making of the President 1964*. New York: Signet Books, 1965.

White, William S. *Citadel: The Story of the U.S. Senate*. Boston: Houghton Mifflin Co., 1968.

Wickware, Francis Still. "National Defense vs. Venereal Disease." *Life*, 13 October 1941, 128.

Willard, Lawrence F. "The Lady from Maine." *Yankee*, November 1977, 148.

Williams, Clare B. *History of the Founding and Development of the National Federation of Republican Women*. Washington, D.C.: Republican National Committee, 1962.

Witt, Linda, Karen M. Paget, and Glenna Matthews. *Running as a Woman: Gender and Power in American Politics*. New York: The Free Press, 1994.

Witte, Edwin E. *The Development of the Social Security Act*. Madison: University of Wisconsin Press, 1962.

"Women: As Maine Goes. . . . " *Time*, 5 September 1960, 13–16.

Wyden, Peter. *Bay of Pigs: The Untold Story*. New York: Simon & Schuster, 1979.

Zieger, Robert H. *American Workers, American Unions, 1920–1985*. Baltimore: The Johns Hopkins University Press, 1989.

Index

About the Author

Dr. Janann Sherman is an assistant professor of history at the University of Memphis.